Development control:

Law, policy and practice

Second edition

Peter Morgan BA (Leics), PhD (Wales)

Professor and Director of the School of the Built Environment, Liverpool John Moores University

Susan Nott LLB (Wales), BCL (Durham)

Senior Lecturer, Faculty of Law, Liverpool University

Butterworth
London, Dub
1995

United Kingdom	Butterworths a Division of Reed Elsevier (UK) Ltd, Halsbury House, 35 Chancery Lane, LONDON WC2A 1EL and 4 Hill Street, EDINBURGH EH2 3JZ
Australia	Butterworths, SYDNEY, MELBOURNE, BRISBANE, ADELAIDE, PERTH, CANBERRA and HOBART
Canada	Butterworths Canada Ltd, TORONTO and VANCOUVER
Ireland	Butterworth (Ireland) Ltd, DUBLIN
Malaysia	Malayan Law Journal Sdn Bhd, KUALA LUMPUR
New Zealand	Butterworths of New Zealand Ltd, WELLINGTON and AUCKLAND
Puerto Rico	Butterworth of Puerto Rico, Inc, SAN JUAN
Singapore	Reed Elsevier (Singapore) Pte Ltd, SINGAPORE
South Africa	Butterworths Publishers (Pty) Ltd, DURBAN
USA	Michie, Charlottesville, VIRGINIA

A CIP Catalogue record for this book is available from the British Library.

ISBN 0 406 05003 1

Printed and bound in Great Britain by Clays Ltd, St Ives plc

Preface

The original idea for this work emerged from the continuing attempts of one of the authors to explain to disparate groups of students, studying in various environmental disciplines, what was actually meant by the development control system. Clearly, it is a system that depends on the law for its structure, but equally clearly, it cannot be understood by a study of the law alone. Policy from a wide range of sources has to be taken into account and an appreciation gained of its place within the system. Only then is it possible to begin to comprehend the forces at work in the development control process that, to most people, is represented by the making of an application for planning permission.

This work attempts to analyse that process by presenting an examination of the development control system that includes references to planning theory, philosophy, policy and practice, as well as planning law. Given the legal content of the work and the fact that one of the authors is a lecturer in law, it is perhaps worth stressing that this work is in no way an attempt to add to the books on planning law. As has already been said, the development control system is inextricably linked to the legal system, but this work is very much an attempt to examine the former with reference to the latter.

Much has changed in the details of the development control system since the first edition was written eight years ago, but even with the new legislation and General Development Orders the essential principles of the process remain intact. Nevertheless, re-editing proved to be extensive and demanding and the authors would like to thank each other for the patience that each normally displayed, as well as the usual criticisms that each made on the other's work, in which nothing was spared, as may possibly be common between husbands and wives who choose to write together. Finally, thanks are once again due to our publishers who believed with us that a second edition was worthwhile, while especial thanks go to our editor whose understanding and patience, particularly in relation to deadlines, was very much appreciated.

P.H.M
S.M.N
September 1995

In memoriam
H.W.M.

Contents

Table of statutes

References in this Table to *Statutes* are to Halsbury's Statutes of England (Fourth Edition) showing the volume and page number at which the annotated text of the Act will be found.

Table of cases

PAGE

T

W

Y

Chapter 1

Introduction to development control

> Quick they were whirled over long, straight, hopeless streets of regularly-built houses, all small and of brick. Here and there a great oblong many-windowed factory stood up, like a hen among her chickens, puffing out black 'unparliamentary' smoke, and sufficiently accounting for the cloud which Margaret had taken to foretell rain. As they drove through the larger and wider streets, from the station to the hotel, they had to stop constantly; great loaded lurries blocked up the not over-wide thoroughfares.[1]

Town and country planning has been defined as the:

> art and science of ordering the use of land and the character and siting of buildings and communication routes so as to secure the maximum practicable degree of economy, convenience and beauty.[2]

Judged on these criteria, the Victorian city, realistically rather than romantically or dramatically described by a contemporary novelist, was clearly unplanned. Free market forces dictated the form and location of all development, creating the bewildering mixture of functions and qualities of environment that typified the Victorian city. The result was an environment, which, at the turn of the century, was unacceptable on several grounds. First, it was disorganised in layout which had the effect of producing inefficiencies in communication. Second, its buildings were of variable quality and age. Third, it contained levels of social and economic deprivation that were totally unacceptable, not only for those that had to suffer them, but also for those whose task it was to administer the environment. Finally, it was evident that the free market was possibly unwilling and probably unable to redevelop

1 Gaskell E *North and South* (first published 1854-55, republished 1970, Penguin) p 96.
2 Keeble L *Principles and Practice of Town and Country Planning* (4th edn, 1969) p 1.

the environment in either the manner or on the scale that was required. Naturally, this state of affairs stimulated debate[3] on what constituted the ideal environment, how it could be achieved and who should be responsible for instigating the change.

Gradually there emerged the concept of a planned and ordered environment with the emphasis on the importance of pleasant housing conditions. Strategies were evolved for the ordering and controlling of land uses, transport networks and the wholesale redevelopment of the then existing urban areas. Implementation of this vision was seen to depend on legislation, as only by utilising the force of the law did it seem possible to control and direct free market forces. The scheme was to be orchestrated by the local authorities, since they already had limited practical experience in urban development.[4] The first piece of legislation – the Housing, Town Planning, etc, Act 1909 – gave local authorities additional powers to prepare schemes to control the development of new housing areas.

From these modest beginnings the planning system slowly started to develop, and this development has been well documented elsewhere.[5] It only needs to be said that by 1947 the modern system of town and country planning had emerged. The means by which its philosophy would be put into practice was provided by the Town and Country Planning Act 1947. Subsequent legislation, the Town and Country Planning Act 1990, for example, has changed the details of the system, but its underlying characteristics remain undisturbed. It is that system which forms the focus of this book.

Development control

Until this point, reference has been made to the emergence of town and country planning as a discipline charged with securing

3 For example: Geddes P *Cities in Evolution* (1949); Howard E *Garden Cities of Tomorrow* (Reprint 1985).

4 For example, the Public Health Act 1875 gave local authorities not only the power to ensure the provision of public health facilities, such as sewers, but also to control building densities and the width of streets. The Artisans and Labourers Dwellings Improvement Acts 1875 and 1879 allowed local authorities to undertake slum clearance, while the Housing of the Working Classes Act 1890 allowed them to build housing.

5 For example: Cherry G E *The Evolution of British Town Planning* (1974); Cullingworth J B *Peacetime History of Environmental Planning* (1978-80); Ashworth W *The Genesis of Modern British Town Planning* (1954).

an orderly and pleasant environment. This book, however, is concerned not with town and country planning in general, but with one specific aspect of that discipline, namely, an analysis of the development control system in England and Wales. Scotland and Northern Ireland are excluded from that analysis as the arrangements for town and country planning, and consequently development control in those countries, are somewhat different from those experienced in England and Wales. To have attempted to take account of these differences would, it was felt, have made the analysis unnecessarily complex, whilst at the same time, obscuring the principles of development control that it is the intention of this work to explore.

As the first step in this analysis, therefore, the relationship which exists between town and country planning and development control in England and Wales will be explained. Town and country planning consists, according to those commentators who have ventured an opinion on the matter, of a philosophy on the use of land which seeks to attain an environment which is most pleasing to the community as a whole. Ideas and opinions on the practical changes which are necessary to achieve this utopia vary with the times. Densely packed terraced housing set in a gridiron pattern of streets constituted the standard form of housing up to the 1939-45 war. In post-war Britain this form of housing was no longer considered appropriate, and the concrete high-rise tower blocks of the 1960s were believed to be the ideal replacement. Within a decade, however, these were seen as unacceptable and the low-rise, high density blocks were produced as an alternative. Today these are also thought of as inadequate in terms of the housing environment they provide, and the trend is towards more traditional housing at a low density, preferably with gardens. If town and country planning can, therefore, be taken to represent the search for the unattainable ideal environment in the form in which it is currently perceived as most obtainable, what is the process of development control?

The Department of the Environment,[6] which at present is responsible for administering the planning system, frequently employs the term 'development control' but never adequately defines it. This may be because the term is self-explanatory, simply denoting the process of controlling development. If this

6 The Department of the Environment was established in 1970 (SI 1970/1681). Prior to that planning had been the responsibility of the Ministry of Housing and Local Government, established in 1951. Its predecessor, the Ministry of Town and Country Planning, was established in 1943.

is true, then the key issue is those principles on the basis of which control is exercised. At this stage in the argument it is essential to appreciate the derivation of the goals of town and country planning, since development control represents a means of realising schemes which are judged to advance these goals at any particular time, whilst restricting those that do not. The problem is that there may be considerable disagreement on what those goals are and how they can best be achieved.[7] In addition, the price that has to be paid for attaining the ideal environment through the process of development control is seen in some quarters as a heavy one. The view has been expressed that controlling development can stifle enterprise and the creation of jobs.[8]

In the past, books have been devoted to individual aspects of what is undoubtedly the multi-faceted process of town and country planning. There are, therefore, books to be found on the law of town and country planning,[9] the philosophy of planning[10] and the practice of planning.[11] Yet each of these does not tell the whole story. Take, for example, section 70(2) of the Town and Country Planning Act 1990 (the 1990 Act). This provides that where an application is made to a local planning authority for planning permission:

> In dealing with such an application the authority shall have regard to the provisions of the development plan, so far as material to the application, and to any other material considerations.

To understand fully the terms of this particular subsection it is not enough to know what constitutes a development plan or its purpose, or simply to appreciate the legal meaning of 'other

7 Disagreement seems to focus on the prioritisation of the goals; that is, should the main goal be to improve society or to improve the environment and hope that society will consequently also improve? One means of prioritising the goals is by weighting them according to their ability to be achieved. This then produces the argument that only the easiest goals will be aimed for, rather than the most important. For two discussions of this view of planning, see Chadwick G *A Systems View of Planning* (1971); McLoughlin J B *Urban and Regional Planning: A Systems Approach* (1969).

8 Lifting the Burden (Cmnd 9571).

9 For example: Grant M *Urban Planning Law* (1982, updated 1986); Telling A E and Duxbury RMC *Planning Law and Procedure* (9th edn, 1993); Heap D *An Outline of Planning Law* (10th edn, 1991).

10 For example: MacAuslan P *Land, Law and Planning* (1975) and *The Ideologies of Planning Law* (1980); Faludi A *A Reader in Planning Theory* (1984); Harvey D *Social Justice and the City* (1988).

11 For example: Cullingworth J B *Town and Country Planning in Britain* (1972); Burke G *Town Planning and the Surveyor* (2nd edn, 1990).

material considerations'. To understand these aspects of development control more completely it is also necessary to have some insight into the philosophy of town and country planning. What the succeeding chapters of this work will seek to illustrate, therefore, is this integrated approach, an approach which is, moreover, focused on this particular facet of the system – development control. The purpose of the work is to demonstrate how these integrated ideas and subsequent policies of town and country planning are transformed, through the process of development control, into an environmental reality. Not that this transfer from concept to practice has always been successfully achieved. Witness, for example, the transformation of Le Corbusier's[12] cities in the sky, surrounded by acres of unspoilt countryside, into high-rise tower blocks set amid a sea of urban decay. The purpose of this book, however, is not to pass judgment on such individual policies; instead, it aims to demonstrate exactly how the development control system takes such policies and makes them into a reality.

The development control system at work

The development control system effectively works on two levels. An indication is given by the local planning authority of what it considers to be the ideal environment for a particular area in a document called a development plan. It is a legal requirement that local planning authorities prepare such a plan.[13] In addition, a local planning authority is given the power, by virtue of the 1990 Act, to control development in its area by making sure that any development proposed will be in accordance with the development plan and other material circumstances.[14] What constitutes development is defined in section 55(1) of the 1990 Act as:

> the carrying out of building, engineering, mining or other operations in, on, over or under land, or the making of any material change in the use of any buildings or other land.

12 Le Corbusier *Concerning Town Planning* (1947).

13 The term 'development plan' covers a range of plans that can date from the Town and Country Planning Act 1947. At present it is a requirement by virtue of s 12(1) of the Town and Country Planning Act 1990 that local planning authorities in Greater London or a metropolitan county in England and Wales prepare unitary plans. Additionally, by virtue of 1990 Act, s 32 which relates to structure plans and 1990 Act, s 36 which deals with local plans, local planning authorities in the non-metropolitan counties must either revise or prepare as appropriate structure and local plans.

14 1990 Act, s 70(2).

The correct legal interpretation of this definition is an extensive topic for consideration in its own right, and has formed the basis for much comment.[15] Indeed, the importance of understanding what development is thought to mean in law will be considered in Chapter 3, but initially it is sufficient to realise that the local planning authority considers, in the first instance, whether or not a particular activity does constitute development. If development is thought to be involved, the individual contemplating such activity requires planning permission.[16]

Even at this early stage the complexity of the development control system should be apparent, as should be the various forces which are at work. On the one hand, there is the local planning authority's plan for an ideal environment in its administrative area. On the other, there is the individual who wishes to undertake an activity which might have an impact on the environment. The proposed activity and the plan are thus compared, and their compatibility assessed, provided the activity in question constitutes development, for if it does not, no matter how considerable its impact may be on the environment, it cannot be controlled through the system of development control. Perhaps this situation is best illustrated by an example.

The owner of a fine old Victorian pier at a popular seaside resort wishes to attract more visitors onto his pier. Consequently, he purchases an inflatable pink elephant, thirty feet high and forty feet long, which he attaches to the roof of the pier's concert hall. The local authority immediately indicates to the pier owner that planning permission is necessary before the elephant can be displayed, as its erection constitutes development. In these circumstances the likelihood is that planning permission will be refused, since such a device is hardly in keeping with the architectural character of the Victorian pier. Probably, therefore, there will be a direct conflict of interest between the local planning authority's view of an appropriate environment, the pier owner's need to make a profit, and the legal question of whether such a device constitutes development. Does the erection of an inflatable and thus intrinsically non-permanent pink elephant constitute a 'building, engineering, mining or other operation in, on, over or under land'? If it does not, then the pier owner can display the elephant, however out of keeping with the environment the device may be.

15 See, for example, Grant, ch 4; Telling, ch 5.
16 1990 Act, s 57(1).

It is the application for planning permission that is the deceptively simple process which lies at the heart of the development control system. It marks the start of the attempt to turn policy into practice. What follows, therefore, is a general description of that process in order that its salient points may be appreciated and the chief actors emerge. Before proceeding, however, a word needs to be said about this choice of starting point. As will become evident as the system is analysed in more detail, one of the major problems in attempting to explain the development control system is its essentially circular nature. Consequently, it is difficult to decide where to break into that circle at the point that will be most appropriate in introducing the whole system. Names and labels have already been used that mean a great deal to the reader who understands something of the organisation of planning, and the legal system within this country, but which, to the total novice, may mean little or nothing at present. In this introduction, therefore, the intention is to present the whole system in outline, while the details will be expanded upon in the rest of the work. This still leaves the problem of the chosen starting point – the application for planning permission. This is chosen as the most obvious starting place since, in reality, it represents the point from which many would-be developers start in their own attempts to comprehend, and, indeed, comply with the planning system. Having established this pragmatic justification, therefore, it is possible to return to the consideration of an application for planning permission.

Essentially anyone, either an individual or a corporate body,[17] who intends to undertake some activity that constitutes development, must apply to the local planning authority for planning permission. An application is made in writing on the appropriate form supplied by the local planning authority. This requires either a broad description of the proposed development or detailed drawings of what is proposed, depending on whether the application is for 'outline' or 'full' planning permission.[18]

17 An individual member of the public, a group of people forming some type of organisation, a company either public or private, a local authority or any form of local or central government organisation – all can apply for planning permission.

18 An outline application may be made in respect of a development involving a building operation only. It effectively establishes the principle of the right to develop, if it is allowed. The application consists only of the site plan and a brief description of the proposed development. A full application involves providing far more detail regarding the proposed development, including plans and drawings. See the Town and Country Planning (Applications) Regulations 1988, SI 1988/1812, and the Town and Country Planning (General Development Procedure) Order 1995, SI 1995/419.

When the authority receives the application it is considered first by the planning officers, whose job it is to examine the proposals in the light of how they may affect the building or buildings, if any are involved, the surrounding area, and any planning policy, particularly in the form of development plans. This analysis is undertaken, not only by taking into account physical and land use factors, but also by considering less tangible factors that relate to the social and economic criteria of the location and its containing area. The planning officers do not usually take the final decision on the planning application, however, as this is a matter for the local planning authority in the form of the elected representatives[19] on the planning committee who are guided by the planning officers, but are, nevertheless, free to reach their own decision.

At this stage, the parties involved in the planning system possibly need some introduction. Effectively, two principal parties have been introduced, in the form of the developer, who is seeking planning permission, and the local planning authority, which is considering the application with a view to approving or rejecting it. These parties in no way represent all the actors involved in the development control process, as will be fully explained in Chapter 2. Furthermore, the developer and the local planning authority do not represent structurally simple entities. To show them as such, even at this stage, would be a gross over-simplification, as the developer and the local planning authority are both potentially rather more complex.

A local planning authority has certain specified legal duties to undertake in its area of administration. Amongst these duties there is the requirement to control development, but on the basis of what criteria is not very clear. Theoretically, the present planning system was created as a means of ensuring that central government policy concerning land use and development was translated down to a local level, with local planning authorities acting as the main control mechanism. In reality, however, it can justifiably be argued that central government land use policy has never materialised in a cohesive form and that, as a consequence, local planning authorities have had to establish their own criteria for judging what constitutes appropriate development. Elements of central policy undoubtedly do exist to control, to a certain extent, the actions of local planning authorities. These include the various forms

19 The councillors elected to sit on the council also comprise the planning committee which makes the decisions regarding the planning applications.

of development plan[20] and Department of the Environment circulars and planning policy guidance notes (PPGs),[1] but effectively the majority of development control decisions are made by the local planning authority in whose area the development is proposed. What criteria do local planning authorities, therefore, employ in reaching their decisions?

In order to answer this question fully it must first be understood that the term 'local planning authority' is potentially a misleading term. Within any local planning authority, two groups of individuals have a contribution to make whenever a development control decision is taken. On the one hand, there is the chief planning officer and his professional planning team, on the other, there are the local councillors. A planning officer is apolitical, giving his opinion as a professional planner on the positive or negative effects on the local community of a proposed development. The councillors, on the other hand, who are unlikely to be professional planners, may take account of the political implications of a particular application. Where, for example, an application involves industrial development, the planning officers might recommend that the application should be refused for some perfectly valid planning reasons – the road network is unsuitable for the increased flow of heavy goods traffic that the development would produce; the proposal is too large and unsightly in an area designated for inclusion in a green belt. The councillors may accept the truth of these criticisms, but may still decide to give their approval to the development as it will bring new jobs and investment to the area at a time of recession. It is difficult to say in these circumstances who has made the right decision, as each party has a perfectly valid point of view.

This increasingly intricate pattern of decision-making is further complicated when that other major actor, the developer, is included. It should not be imagined that the local planning authority is the most significant element within the planning system, simply because the discussion so far has concentrated on that body. Arguably, the role of the developer is the more important, as without his desire to undertake what constitutes development, there would be no role for the local planning authority to perform. Developers effectively fall into two groups – the public and the private developer – and the motivations of

20 Development plans appear in a variety of forms – unitary, structure and local – and are considered fully in chapter 4.

1 Department of the Environment circulars and planning policy guidance notes are particular forms of central government policy advice and are considered fully in chapter 6.

each group tend to be distinctive. The public developer, that is, a local authority or some branch of central government, is normally motivated by the public need for a particular development, without undue concern for the eventual profitability of the investment. This is, of course, not to suggest that public bodies undertake development with a total disregard to costs, which is very far from the truth, but rather, that the motivation for the development is more related to public need, or possibly a perceived public need, than an eventual profit. In contrast, the private developer, whilst also being concerned with public needs in the form of market demands, is normally concerned with the potential profitability of a proposed development.

At this point it becomes necessary to reconsider more fully the role of the planning committee, and its relationship with the planning officers, as it is the committee, rather than the officers, that usually takes the decisions on planning applications. The planning committee comprises a number of local councillors placed on the committee as the nominees of the different political parties they represent. Political representation on the committee is in proportion to a party's political strength on the council as a whole, with the chairman usually being a member of the majority party. As with all forms of local authority work, the councillors are advised by a permanent professional staff of local government officers, whose additional duty it is to carry out the instructions of the duly elected council.

With the exception of certain minor planning applications, all planning applications are brought before the planning committee, usually on a monthly basis. Among the documents which accompany each application will be the recommendation of the chief planning officer, who is responsible for presenting the applications to the committee. The committee may call upon the chief planning officer or some other member of his team, to explain any recommendation more fully, as well as hearing the comments of the applicant. Any member of the public also has the right to make representations[2] regarding the application, but usually they have to be content with submitting any such comments in writing. Having taken account of all these opinions, the committee then normally reaches one of four possible decisions. Firstly, they may consider that the

2 The operation of development control is undertaken in public, for the public good, so it follows that members of the public may make their opinions known.

application is important enough, or indeed is contentious enough, to be brought before the full council of the local authority and a decision will be deferred. Secondly, they may choose to reject the application outright. Thirdly, they may accept the application as it stands. Finally, they may approve the application subject to certain conditions.[3] The important point to realise at this stage is that the planning committee can reach any of these decisions regardless of any advice offered, or recommendation made, by the planning officers. This simple fact obviously raises many questions that lie at the very foundation, not only of the planning system, but of the system of local government in England and Wales, and aspects of this complex question will be considered in subsequent chapters.

At this point, however, the general outline of the procedures involved in an application for planning permission may usefully be illustrated by way of two examples. In these, an attempt will be made to illustrate in some detail the range of issues that have to be taken into account before the local planning authority reaches its decision. These issues are very broadly defined in section 70 of the 1990 Act as comprising the provisions of the development plan and any other material considerations. As will now become apparent, however, the phrase 'other material considerations' is a catch-all concept that is of fundamental importance to the effective working of the development control system. It enables the planning officers, in the first instance, to take into account any factors that are thought to be relevant to the application and its potential effect on the neighbourhood.

Two examples of development control

THE FIRST EXAMPLE

The intention is to consider an application for planning permission to convert a large Victorian villa into six separate flats. Such a villa would probably be located in the inner residential suburbs of a substantial town or city, in an area that contains buildings that are similar in both size and age. Faced with such an application, therefore, what factors are taken into account by the local planning officers before they recommend to the planning committee whether planning permission should be granted or refused?

3 Planning permission may be subject to various conditions attached by the local planning authority as it thinks fit (s 70(1)). These conditions must fulfil certain specific criteria, however, which are examined fully in chapter 8.

Local planning policy All factual development control issues would be considered against a background of both local and national planning policies, and the forms these policies take can now be considered. At the local level, the planning officers would have to consult two basic policy sources – the development plan and any additional policy documentation. The development plan is not usually a simple document. In fact, the term 'development plan' can refer to a collection of plans that are likely to have been prepared by different local authorities.[4] First, there would be a structure plan if the site is in a non-metropolitan county,[5] which will have been prepared by the county planning authority. This deals in broad outline with planning issues that concern the whole county and will have been considered by the Secretary of State as part of its review procedures. In the example under consideration, the structure plan may be consulted for information on the county-wide projections of housing need, or possibly some general policy relating to the redevelopment of old inner-city housing. The structure plan will not be site specific however, that is, it will not mention any specific location beyond the area or district. Alternatively, if the site is in a metropolitan county, the development plan to be considered would be the unitary plan,[6] Part I of which also deals with the broad strategic planning issues. For a level of detail that may include specific planning policies and guidelines for the actual area within which the proposed development is situated, the planning officers will have to consult either a local plan,[7] Part II of the unitary plan or what is termed the 'old style' development plan.[8]

The local plan will be a planning document prepared and approved by either the county or district planning authority. It sets out in considerable detail local planning policies that are drawn from the broad policies of the structure plan. These local policies will offer some specific advice, both about the area as a whole and the actual site of the proposed development. The land use of the site will be indicated, for example, together with the suggested housing density for that area. Policies will also be found concerning multiple occupation, social mix and public transport, and all can be referred to by the planning officers when considering the proposal. Part II of the unitary plan would

4 PPG 12, Development Plans and Regional Planning Guidance, para 1.4, gives the full definition of what may comprise the development plan.

5 1990 Act, ss 31-35.

6 Ibid, ss 12-16.

7 Ibid, ss 36-45.

8 Plans prepared under the Town and Country Planning Act 1947.

also be identical in terms of coverage and detail. If a local plan or Part II of the unitary plan have not yet been approved, however, it should be possible to consult the 'old style' development plan, which will contain far less information but will indicate the acceptable land use for the specific site, and may indicate what were considered to be the acceptable housing densities at the time the plan was approved.[9] Finally, attention must be paid to any revisions which are in hand to the content of all forms of development plans, since these revisions might affect the proposed development.

All these plans comprise what is known as statutory planning policy and have to undergo legally prescribed procedures before they become official planning documents.[10] Their significance is such that, once they are in place, decisions are in principle to be made in accordance with the policies they contain.[11] These plans are, therefore of fundamental importance in the development control system and are therefore considered in detail in chapter 4, where their practical impact on the planning system is assessed.

Apart from statutory planning policy, other forms of local planning policy might exist and furnish additional guidance on whether or not to allow the villa to be converted into flats. Some of this policy may be in the form of informal policy. Informal planning policy means that the policy in question, although it has been produced by the local planning officers, has not gone through all the legal procedures that are used to create development plans. As a consequence, documents containing such policy are used only as an indication of, rather than an actual specific guide to, local planning policy. In some instances, however, this informal policy elaborates upon some of the information in a local plan, indicating, for example, what are regarded as appropriate window or door designs when refurbishing old houses in particular districts. Although these documents would therefore be consulted by the local planning officers, they would not be given as much weight as the proposals in the local plan.

9 Plans prepared under the Town and Country Planning Act 1947 were to be regularly revised but in many instances this did not occur. After the Town and Country Planning Act 1971 came into operation any such plans could not be revised, only superseded, and this did not happen in many parts of the country. Consequently, the old plan may still remain as a valid planning document.

10 The procedures for approval of development plans are to be found in the 1990 Act, Pt II and the Town and Country Planning (Development Plans) Regulations 1991, SI 1991/2794.

11 1990 Act, s 54A.

The range and form of this type of policy is enormous and whilst lacking the importance of the development plan, it still plays a vital part in the development control process, especially when it is realised that all forms of current development plans will not necessarily exist for, or, indeed, cover the site of the planning application.

This local policy will be examined in detail in chapter 5 where its different forms with their varying impact upon the system will become apparent.

National planning policy Having consulted these local policy documents and related their contents to the particular application, the planning officers would then consider any policy guidance available from the Department of the Environment. This comes in two forms, either as planning policy guidance notes[12] and circulars, or as Acts of Parliament and their related statutory instruments.

Taking these legal materials first, the local planning officers may, for example, consult sections 1 and 2 of the Planning (Listed Buildings and Conservation Areas) Act 1990 which deal with listed buildings, since, given the age of the building in the example, it may have been given this special protection.[13] In order to understand more fully the consequences of a proposal to alter a listed building, the planning officers might then consult the Planning (Listed Buildings and Conservation Areas) Regulations 1990[14] which stipulate what procedures must be followed when dealing with these specially protected buildings. These legal sources of reference, however, usually deal with the procedures rather than give any guidance on matters of policy or interpretation. They are however important as they, among other things, supply the framework within which the planning system operates.

Of far more help probably to the planning officers at this stage are those other forms of Department of the Environment guidance – the planning policy guidance note and circular. If

12 Planning policy guidance notes (PPG) are a form of central government advice on general planning issues. They replaced the old development control policy notes, first issued in 1969, and have been published quite regularly since 1988. They now represent the main source of practical policy guidance and circulars, in contrast, are now used primarily to give guidance on the impact of planning legislation.

13 The Planning (Listed Buildings and Conservation Areas) Act 1990, s 1 gives the Secretary of State for National Heritage the power to protect buildings. The implications of this are fully explained in PPG 15, Planning and the Historic Environment.

14 SI 1990/1519.

indeed the building is listed, the planning officers could turn to the advice to be found in PPG 15, Planning and the Historic Environment which, together with Circular 8/87,[15] gives comprehensive general guidance. The importance, for example, of discovering a suitable use for a listed building is emphasised, and residential uses are especially mentioned.[16] The significance of the setting of the building is examined and it is even suggested that local authorities should seek expert advice on the quality and potential of the building from bodies such as the Historic Buildings and Monuments Commission for England.[17] All this general advice would be taken into account when considering the specific proposals for the particular building used in this example if it were listed, and it would be interpreted in relation to all the local factors.

Clearly the Department of the Environment's input into the planning system is significant. What is now problematic is assessing how significant that input is, particularly its guidance on planning policy, when decisions are now expected to be made in accordance with the policies set out in the development plan.

Chapter 6 of this book will, consequently, assess Department of the Environment policy, taking into account its use by all parties concerned with development control, as well as considering the forms this policy can take.

Other factors The local planning officers' search for information is not yet complete, however, as other sources of published data still remain. Of major importance would be the planning history, if any, of the site in question. This is the record of any previous planning applications and their outcome. If permission had been given in the past for a similar development on the site this would have to be taken into account by the planning officers, even if, as would obviously be the case, the old permission had expired.[18] Details of similar applications in the area would also be of interest, but it should be realised that the legal concept of precedent[19] does not apply to a planning

15 Historic Buildings and Conservation Areas – Policy and Procedures. Now cancelled except for the directions.

16 Circular 8/87, paras 19-24; PPG 15, paras 3.8-3.11.

17 Circular 8/87, paras 12-18; PPG 15, annex A.

18 Full planning permission normally lasts for five years from the date of the approval – 1990 Act, s 91. Outline planning permission lasts for three years – 1990 Act, s 92.

19 Precedent in a judicial context means that inferior courts are bound to follow a decision of a superior court on a legal issue such as the interpretation of a statute. In the context of development control there is no such concept, though if an inspector chooses to disregard the decisions of other inspectors brought to his attention, it is important that he give his reasons for so doing.

application. In other words, if approval has recently been given for a similar development only a few yards away in the same road, this does not mean that approval will also be given for this application. The reasons for this are obvious, since the planning officers have to take into account whether there is a need for such a development, or whether there are already too many developments of this kind in the area. In addition, the unique location of every site produces different problems relating, for example, to traffic and access.

This argument usefully introduces the other all-important task that has to be undertaken by the planning officers in taking into account material considerations. This involves a detailed examination of the proposals in the light of how they might affect both the building, the site and the immediate locality. The significance of these factors is considered in chapter 7 where a sequence of possible sites and forms of development are examined.

In the context of the example being considered, the most obvious factors are probably those that relate to the effect of the proposals on the building itself. The existing condition of the building would be likely to be taken into account. If, for example, the building is in a run down or even a semi-derelict condition, then the planning officers may be inclined to favour the proposals, as this would result in the elimination of an 'eyesore' from the area. If, on the other hand, the building is still being used as a single family dwelling and is in good condition, then this might militate against the proposals. The planning officers would also assess what physical effects, if any, the proposals would have on the fabric of the building. Would the new flats require a new entrance, or even entrances, to be formed, possibly at first and second floor levels? Such additions would clearly have a marked effect on the building's outward appearance, so attention would have to be paid to their proposed position, whether or not they could be seen from adjacent properties or roads, their design and the materials to be employed in their construction. Having considered the effect of the proposals on the fabric of the building, the planning officers would then turn their attention to the immediate site. Would the proposals necessitate either the removal of existing out-buildings, or possibly the building of new ones, such as garages? If buildings were removed, would this affect the privacy of the site or surrounding sites, and if new buildings were constructed how might this affect the visual appearance of the site? The interest of planning officers extends beyond buildings to the protection of mature trees,[20] especially if any trees would have to be felled, as well as to any minor man-made features, such as old garden walls or stone gateposts.

Besides taking the physical effects of the proposals into account, the planning officers would also turn their attention to the wider implications of the proposed development. Since, for example, it is proposed to intensify the use of the building, this will produce more vehicular and pedestrian traffic. Consequently, an examination should be undertaken of how these increases might affect existing local traffic. What level of traffic already uses the road onto which the 'new' traffic will exit? What is the exact position of this exit in relation to other existing exits and road junctions? Is there any possibility that the exit point is likely to be dangerous, or will the increase in traffic produce levels of noise that are unacceptable? Again, there are likely to be local and national planning policies on these matters which would have to be considered in conjunction with the local factors.

Another issue might be the demand for the accommodation proposed and the likely effect its provision might have on local facilities, such as shops and schools. The conversion of the house into flats might be seen as a benefit if, as was mentioned, the house was in a poor structural condition, and there was a local need for accommodation of this nature. There may be many reasons, however, why such accommodation is not suitable for all types of family – too small, no garden, no play area for children, too many stairs and no lift – and so local need would have to be judged on detailed information indicating the types of household seeking accommodation. Account would also be taken of whether the flats were for sale or for rent, not because of the financial implications of the two forms of tenure, but rather in order to assess the likely effect on the locality. If the house was in a poor condition, while all other houses were in a good condition and were owner-occupied, then the conversion of the property into flats for sale would probably be the planners' first choice, flats for rent being slightly less acceptable as this could alter the social mix of the area. On the other hand, if this was the first such conversion proposed, the alteration in the social mix[1] would be so slight as to be unimportant, but if many

20 Specified trees can be protected by the making of a tree preservation order under the 1990 Act, s 198.

1 A sociological term that refers to the mixture of social classes within an area, for example, the number of manual workers to the number of clerical workers to the number of professionals.

of the older houses in the area have already undergone such alteration, then the planning officers have to decide if the social mix of the area should continue to change.

Then there is the related issue of the possible impact of the development on facilities in the area, which would depend, in turn, on whether or not the proposals are the first of their kind, or the latest of many. Concern will focus on the local shops, primary school, public facilities and public transport, and whether they can cope with the increased demand. Naturally, the form of demand is related to the type of occupier likely to be attracted to the proposed development, and this fact would be taken into account. Clearly, one of the concerns could be the age of the likely occupiers, as different age groups place different demands on different local services – young families with children need schools, older people may need a wide range of medical services. Another factor might be the social class of the inhabitants, and whether they are private car users, as this could have an effect on the demand for public transport facilities.

Finally, two remaining sources of information need to be considered. First, colleagues within the department may be consulted on a formal or informal basis, as may colleagues from departments representing other aspects of the local authority's duties, such as the architects' department or the estates and valuers' department. Indeed, in some cases it may be a statutory duty to consult adjacent local authorities or even civil servants representing other forms of administrative or policy body.[2] Second, the planning officer, or rather his planning authority, is under a duty to consult the public. Exactly how this is done varies depending on the nature and location of the proposed development,[3] but at the very least, a notice of the application for planning permission is usually published in the local newspapers, which gives any member of the public an opportunity to contact the local planning authority with comments on the scheme.

The planning officers then take all the information they have accumulated and reach a conclusion, accompanied by their reasons, whether or not, in their opinion, planning permission should be granted. This conclusion is then presented, as has already been outlined, in the form of a recommendation to the local councillors who sit on the planning committee of the local

2 Consultations are normally prescribed by the Town and Country Planning (General Development Procedure) Order 1995, SI 1995/419, art 10.

3 For example, as prescribed by the 1990 Act, s 65; or alternatively, for development in conservation areas – Planning (Listed Buildings and Conservation Areas) Act 1990, s 73.

council, and it is these elected representatives who actually make the decision in each instance.

Before returning to a consideration of the next stage in the possible progress of a planning application, it is undoubtedly useful to illustrate the many factors which have to be taken into account, by way of another contrasting example. This will not only ensure that the procedure is clearly understood in outline, but will also allow the introduction of other aspects of the planning system that would have been inappropriate in the first example.

THE SECOND EXAMPLE

By way of contrast, it will now be assumed that a planning application has been received with a proposal to develop a new factory on the outskirts of a large town. The proposed development will cover twenty-five acres of land which at present is being used as arable pasture. The plan is to build fifteen one-storey industrial units together with related delivery and parking spaces.

As in the previous example, the planning officers will have to consider a wide range of information and they can assess this in any order they think fit. Arguably, the procedure adopted in the first example is the most logical, that is, the working 'inwards' from the broad policy issues that are invariably documented, concluding with a site analysis. Naturally, the specific site of the proposed development will have to be borne in mind at all times, as the broader policy issues have to be related to the particular application, but it is often easier to consider the wider implications of the application first, because if these are totally unacceptable, there is little point in considering the site in any detail.

Local planning policy In considering this second example, the planning officers can start their assessment by referring to the development plan. Immediately several broad issues may be raised by policies to be found within whatever forms of development plan apply to the area. The structure plan or Part I of the unitary plan, for example, will almost invariably contain policy proposals relating to industrial development and employment, and both of these will probably be encouraged in general terms. It is also likely, however, that the plans will contain proposals concerning the need to prevent the incursion of urban areas into the countryside, with the resulting loss of high grade agricultural land. When applied to the proposed development, therefore, it may well be that these policies appear contradictory and in the circumstances it is only the planning officers 'on the spot' who can begin to unravel the problem. Obviously, the next step would be to consult the local plan or Part II of the unitary plan, if either have been approved, as these will show any planning proposals for the site in considerably greater detail. The relevant plan may indicate that the area is part of a green belt,[4] in which case the proposed industrial development is likely to be regarded as inappropriate, unless, of course, other planning policies exist, demonstrating that there is a very specific local need for employment. Alternatively, the planning officers may discover that no land has been allocated within the plan as appropriate for industrial development of the type proposed, as part of a deliberate policy to relocate such development in another part of the county. On the other hand, there may be clear statements within the plans emphasising the need to keep existing industry within the area. If this is so and the application has been made by a local industrialist who wishes to expand his business, but is unable to do so on his existing site, the situation may not be as clear-cut as it first appeared. Effectively, therefore, the planning officers have to weigh up all the relevant policies within the statutory development plans in order to form at least a broad impression of the general policy as it affects the application.

The planning officers could then turn to a consideration of any other policy documentation that may exist locally and that relates in any way to the application. There may, for example, be no informal statements regarding industry, but advice notes may well exist on the form of landscaping which is desirable when industrial developments of this nature are proposed. The planning officers may also look to organisations, other than central and local government, for relevant information, such as annual reports from local Chambers of Commerce and Industry. Such information is obviously less important than formally established planning policy, but would form part of the total information package that the planning officers are seeking to create in relation to the application.

National planning policy In the case of this type of development, however, there may be other important policies apart from development plans, which may be of crucial

4 A particular form of planning policy designed to prevent the undue outward spread of an urban area into the countryside. See PPG 2, Green Belts.

importance in the deliberations of the planning officers. Industrial development plays a key role in the national land policy of the present government, as indeed it has done with previous governments. As a result of some quite specific legislation,[5] the government has sought to encourage industry by creating enterprise zones.[6] If the proposals under discussion were to relate to land within one of these designated zones, almost thirty of which are scattered over England and Wales, then planning permission for the industrial proposals would be virtually certain, as the prime policy objective in establishing these zones is to encourage just such development. Other special areas of various kinds also exist (a product of national land use policy) and whilst some of these are designed to encourage industry, others, such as the National Parks,[7] are founded on policies that would actively discourage industrial development, except in very specific locations. In practice, therefore, various 'official' policy statements may have to be taken into account in relation to the proposed development.

Recourse will then be had to the advice proffered in the policy notes and circulars from the Department of the Environment. As in the previous example, there may well be specific notes and circulars that relate directly to the proposed development, for example, PPG 4, Industrial and Commercial Development and Small Firms. In addition, there may be PPGs and circulars which contain advice on a wider topic, such as Circular 2/93, Public Rights of Way, or PPG 7, The Countryside and the Rural Economy, which also relate to the proposals. In every instance, however, it is important to stress that such documentation is nothing more than advisory and must be interpreted in the light of local policy and in particular the development plan.

Other factors The next stage would involve a consideration of the planning history, if any, of the site, as well as an examination of any similar developments that may have been undertaken in the local authority area in the immediate past. Again, it must be appreciated that the planning officers are not

5 Local Government, Planning and Land Act 1980, s 179, Sch 32. Various aspects of the legislation are now incorporated into the 1990 Act.

6 An enterprise zone is a designated area within which various benefits, such as exemption from certain taxes and planning controls, are allowed with the aim of encouraging commercial development.

7 The National Parks and Access to the Countryside Act 1949 established National Parks with a view to protecting the natural beauty of the area for the enjoyment of the public.

looking for any binding precedents, but are simply trying to establish a background of information against which to consider the particular application that is before them.

Ultimately, therefore, their examination will concentrate on the area within which the development is proposed, and on a detailed consideration of its possible effects. As with the first example, there are two levels to such an investigation: the possible effects on the area in the immediate vicinity of the site as well as the possible effects on the site itself. In this example, an obvious concern would be the volume of traffic that such a development could conceivably generate, which would be on a very much greater scale than the traffic generated by the small residential development considered in the first example. In this instance, not only the quantity but also the nature of the traffic would be relevant, as industrial developments are likely to generate heavy goods traffic as well as cars and vans. Calculations of the likely numbers and type of vehicles, as well as the rate of vehicles per hour would therefore be attempted, probably with the help of the local authority's own transport planning section and traffic engineers. Substantial increases in traffic would have an impact, not merely in the vicinity of the proposed development, but over a much wider area, especially at junctions and at any accident black spots. In reality, however, it would be surprising if the developer who had proposed such a scheme, had not already taken these important factors into account and ensured that the site was well situated, with a connection to either a main trunk road, or preferably a motorway. This might not be attributable to the developer's concern over the environmental implications of his proposal, but is more likely to be linked to commercial considerations which demand good transport links for industrial developments.

Apart from its impact upon the existing road network, the proposed development might have implications for other services, such as housing. On the question of housing provision, the type of industrial development intended would be crucial, as different groups within the workforce might require different forms of housing. Clearly, many related factors are involved. For example, if it is assumed that the proposed development intends to concentrate on high technology industry, then it can also be assumed that the workforce will consist of either highly technically skilled, or highly qualified individuals. If this development will represent a move into the area by an existing company, then a proportion of its present workforce may wish to move with it, and will require housing. If the workers belong to a relatively high socio-economic class,[8] it may be assumed that they will enter the private housing market, so that the planning officers will have to take account of the availability of such housing within this area. In addition, given the workers' socio-economic class, the planning officers would also be aware that they probably have a high level of car ownership and could consequently journey to work over a considerable distance, thus distributing the likely housing demand. If, on the other hand, it is assumed that the proposed development will be made up of mixed, small-scale industrial enterprises, with a workforce consisting mainly of semi-skilled or unskilled workers, then the need would be for public sector rented accommodation, situated in the near vicinity and enjoying good public transport links with the site.

Once the implications which the proposal may have for the wider area have been evaluated, attention can be focused on the site. Many factors will have to be considered, including the density of buildings covering the site, the internal road layout, the proposed access points and the design of the development. On the question of design, the planning officers are likely to be concerned, not only with the appearance of the industrial units, their size, height, colour and the materials to be used in their construction, but also with the visual impact of the development as a whole. In these circumstances the inclusion of proposals to landscape the perimeter of the site, or their omission, may be crucial, given that the location is in the countryside immediately adjacent to an urban area.

Finally, public reaction to the proposals will be sought, and any views expressed should be taken into account by the planning officers in drafting their recommendation on the application. At this juncture, the planning committee will reach a decision on the planning application for the proposed industrial development. This is the same stage at which the first example was concluded. In using these two distinct examples, it has been possible to illustrate some of the diverse forms of policy and information that have to be considered in resolving any application for planning permission. In the subsequent stages of this introductory examination of the development control process, however, it is no longer necessary to refer in any detail to either example. This is because the procedures

8 Socio-economic classes are a means of classifying the population according to their income and the status of their job. Class 1 would be a professional with an above average income, Class 5 would be a manual labourer with a minimum wage.

involved are either administrative, and thus take no account of the particular facts of an application, or are likely to cover the same information about policy and site detail already considered in the examples.

The decision

When the planning committee takes a decision on a planning application, it has a number of options open to it. The major options are either to refuse a grant of planning permission, or to grant planning permission with or without conditions. It is also possible for a planning committee to approve a proposed development in principle, leaving detailed matters to be resolved at a later date. This is the effect of granting outline planning permission. It is not necessary at the introductory stage to consider these different forms of decision in any greater detail, as they will be fully examined in Chapter 8, except to note that where the planning committee approves an application, that approval is subject to time limits within which a start must have been made on the development. A refusal of planning permission can, however, set in motion another aspect of the development control system that needs to be outlined in this introduction.

If planning permission is refused or if the applicant is unhappy with any of the conditions attached to a grant of planning permission, he can appeal against the decision of the local planning authority, by using an appeals procedure that is a fundamental and important part of the whole system of planning and development control. The applicant initiates the procedure with a written notice of appeal to the Secretary of State for the Environment. Only the applicant may make such an appeal. No right of appeal exists against the grant of planning permission. Consequently, the appeals procedure is a means whereby only the disgruntled applicant can have his application for planning permission reassessed. The disgruntled member of the public, worried by the noise, traffic or loss of amenity that an approved development may represent, has no second chance to seek reappraisal of the local planning authority's decision.

Planning appeals

Once an appeal is launched, the Secretary of State usually appoints an inspector to determine the case or, in certain circumstances, determines it himself. Planning inspectors are used by the Department of the Environment to adjudicate on planning appeals. Their suitability for this task rests on the fact that they have an extensive knowledge of the planning system, often holding one or more professional qualifications. Their task is to assess the merits of the case put before them by the applicant and by the local planning authority, a procedure which involves exploring the workings of the development control system.

An appeal is conducted either in the form of a public inquiry, or if both parties agree, by written representations. At present, the majority of appeals are resolved with an exchange of written representations, since this procedure saves both time and money. Public inquiries are normally reserved for the more significant planning applications, though the choice of procedure is entirely a matter for the parties. A planning appeal allows both parties to set out their arguments aimed at persuading the inspector to either allow the appeal, or uphold the original decision. The information likely to be presented in the course of such arguments is the same as would have been taken into account when the original application for planning permission was determined. All aspects of the proposals would, therefore, be examined, both in relation to any policy and the standing of that policy, and in relation to the possible effects of the development on the whole environment.

The procedures adopted at a public inquiry are partially at the discretion of the inspector but usually follow an established pattern[9] that allows both parties to argue their case, as well as question each other on their suggested interpretation of relevant policy and the possible effects that the proposed development may have. Expert witnesses may be called by either side in order to make a specific point, especially in a technically complex area involving, for example, transport. At the same time other interested parties, such as amenity societies,[10] other public bodies and, indeed, ordinary members of the public, are usually given an opportunity to express their views. In contrast to a court of law, the atmosphere at a public inquiry is as informal as possible, the sole purpose of the inquiry being an attempt by each party to convince the inspector that their case is right.

9 Town and Country Planning (Inquiries Procedure) Rules 1992, SI 1992/2038.

10 These come in various forms, but all consist of organised groups that have an informed interest in some aspect of development and the environment. They are more fully explained in chapter 2.

Finally having heard all the arguments, and after seeking clarification on any points, the inspector visits the site in question accompanied by both parties.

In making a decision, the inspector treats the application as if he were determining it afresh. Effectively this means that he can reach any conclusion that he thinks fit. For example, it has been mentioned that transport issues can play a significant part in any planning application. This could mean that in the case of the example given of an industrial development, planning permission was refused partly because the local authority were of the opinion that the proposed development would have an adverse effect on traffic flows as a result of introducing more heavy traffic on surrounding roads. In the inquiry the applicant for planning permission might produce reasons as to why the local authority were wrong in this assumption while the local authority would reiterate their reasons for reaching that conclusion. In making his decision, however, the inspector could decide that he favoured the arguments presented by the applicant and grant planning permission with or without conditions. Alternatively, he could support the local planning authority by preferring their analysis of the likely traffic implications and recommend that planning permission not be granted. In short, he can do whatever he thinks appropriate.

In determining an appeal, the Secretary of State or the inspector must give reasons for their decision. Usually, therefore, a decision letter will summarise the arguments presented during the course of the appeal, together with the decision-maker's findings and conclusions, as well as the reasoning which supports them. It should be made clear, however, that only a very small percentage of planning applications are the subject of an appeal, because the majority are either approved, or the developer, refused planning permission, decides to take no further action. The appeals procedure is, nevertheless, an important aspect of the planning system and as such is examined fully in chapter 9.

Judicial challenge

Under the terms of section 288 of the 1990 Act the decisions of the inspector and the Secretary of State are open to challenge in the High Court. This process will be considered in detail in chapter 10 where the impact of the courts on the development control process will be assessed. At this stage it is sufficient to make two important points about the task performed by the courts. Firstly, section 288 sets out very clearly the grounds on which decisions may be challenged. These include the failure to observe the correct procedure when processing an appeal, and exceeding the powers conferred in the 1990 Act, by omitting, for example, to give reasons for a decision, or breaching the rules of natural justice.[11] What needs to be emphasised at this stage, however, is that it is not the court's business to re-examine the various development control issues which were relevant to the case. This was the task of the inspector or the Secretary of State at the appeal stage, and should not be repeated by the court. The court's only role is to determine whether or not the law has been observed. What, however, in theory seems a straightforward distinction is in reality much harder to draw, as will become apparent in chapter 10.

The second point which needs to be appreciated, is that, compared to the number of planning applications and planning appeals, very few cases reach the courts.[12] There may be many explanations for this, including the cost of litigation and the limited objectives which a litigant can achieve by adopting this course of action. If a developer has been refused planning permission, has appealed to the Secretary of State and lost, has challenged that decision in the High Court and won on the grounds that, for example, the rules of natural justice have been breached, he does not then end up with planning permission. The individual responsible for the legal error can simply correct it and still arrive at the same conclusion.

Two further processes within the planning system remain to be outlined in order to complete this introductory examination. They are enforcement and compensation.

Enforcement

Enforcement procedures are the powers possessed by a local planning authority to control unauthorised development. These

11 There are two rules of natural justice. The first requires impartiality of a decision-maker. The second requires that before a decision is taken an individual should be given a chance to put his point of view. Failure to comply with the rules of natural justice can result in a decision being set aside by the court.

12 Basically this is because the powers of the courts in relation to development control decisions are very specific. The court usually acts as a review body determining whether a local planning authority, an inspector or the Secretary of State has acted in accordance with the powers given to them by statute.

powers are used when a development has been carried out either without planning permission, or in breach of a condition attached to the grant of planning permission. It should be noted, however, that they are not resorted to lightly. In many cases the local planning authority will content itself with informing the developer that planning permission should have been obtained, whilst agreeing to consider a retrospective application, or, in the case of a breach of a condition, draw the developer's attention to the fact, and suggest that the condition should be observed. If these warnings do not achieve the desired result, an alternative option would be to issue a planning contravention notice. If neither of these 'warnings' have the desired effect then the enforcement procedures can be brought into use. Effectively, these require that the development or breach of planning permission cease, and that specified steps be taken to restore the property to the condition it was in prior to the breach, all of which are to be undertaken within a specified period.

At this stage it is possible for the developer to appeal to the Secretary of State against the enforcement notice. The procedures adopted for hearing an enforcement appeal resemble those used in a planning appeal. An inspector is appointed to hold a public inquiry or assess, in the form of written representations, the arguments put forward by the appellant and the local planning authority. Section 174 of the 1990 Act specifies the grounds for appealing against an enforcement notice, and these will be considered in greater detail in Chapter 9. It is worth noting at this stage that one of those grounds is that planning permission should have been granted. Where this is relied on, all the usual development control factors will be considered, with the result that the enforcement appeal will be almost identical to a planning appeal. Other grounds for appeal rely very heavily on issues of fact, such as the assertion that copies of the enforcement notice were not served in the legally specified manner.[13]

When the enforcement appeal is in progress the enforcement notice itself is suspended, and, depending on the outcome of the appeal, the notice can be quashed as being invalid, planning permission can be given, or the appeal can be dismissed and the enforcement notice upheld. Whilst the appeal is in progress, however, the local planning authority can issue a stop notice[14] to prevent the continuation of the alleged breach of development control. This action highlights exactly what this very complex

13 1990 Act, s 172.
14 Ibid, ss 183–187.

procedure seeks to achieve, namely, to allow the local planning authority to act in its role as development controller, seeking to protect the whole community from any inappropriate developments.

If the enforcement notice is upheld, then it will be acted upon by the local planning authority with the result that a failure to comply can lead to a criminal prosecution. It is also possible for the developer to institute an appeal on a point of law to the courts, during which time enforcement proceedings would again be suspended, but the development could continue to be restrained by the stop notice.

Compensation

It should be stressed that the development control process does not normally take account of financial matters. In other words, the cost of a proposed development is not normally a planning issue, nor is the cost to the developer of a refused planning permission, nor, indeed, the cost of implementing a planning condition. Development control is, therefore, purely a question of whether or not the proposed development is suitable for its specific location at that particular time, and the question of the profits or losses that may or may not be made in relation to the development are not usually considered relevant. It must be mentioned, however, that in certain contexts the economic implications of a proposed development can be significant, such as the extra employment it would bring to the area, but in normal circumstances the question of direct costs will not be considered.

Distinct from the financial implications of a proposed development is the issue of compensation. This is a complex and extremely specialised aspect of the planning system[15] which has only indirect relevance for the development control process. There are various situations where a developer may attempt to claim compensation from a local authority. While it would take more than a few paragraphs to list all those situations, as well as to explain the manner in which the amount of compensation is calculated, it is possible to give some examples which will illustrate why compensation is available and its relevance for the development control process.

15 For example: *Encyclopedia of Compulsory Purchase and Compensation*, Sweet & Maxwell; Rowan-Robinson J, Brand C *Compulsory Purchase and Compensation* (1994); Circular 15/91, Planning and Compensation Act 1991 – Land Compensation and Compulsory Purchase.

Consider the situation described in the second example where a local planning authority is faced with a planning application to develop industrial units. It was mentioned that the proposed site was presently being used as agricultural land – obviously the value of the site as an industrial development would be far greater than its agricultural value. If the application for planning permission were to be refused, would the local planning authority then be liable to a claim for compensation for the loss of development value of the land? This question would depend on a whole host of factors, all of which are now covered in the Planning and Compensation Act 1991. If the local planning authority were to seek advice on its liability for compensation, it would probably be advised that in circumstances such as the ones described, compensation would not be payable, as the land was still capable of its original use and thus retained its original value as farm land, so nothing had been lost.

If this were the case, therefore, the question of compensation would be unlikely to affect the local planning authority's decision regarding planning permission. If, on the other hand, the land had been acquired by the developer as land designated for industrial development in a development plan, and then there was a change of planning policy which had the effect of including the land in a green belt, then there would be a much greater probability that compensation would be available in these circumstances. The question the local planning authority would have to ask itself, would be whether a refusal of planning permission in order to preserve the green belt was sufficiently in the public interest to risk the possibility of a compensation claim. The decision would obviously involve wide issues, such as local politics and finance, as well as the planning aspects. If the decision was to award planning permission, despite good planning reasons to the contrary, then it is obvious that the question of compensation has indeed affected the development control process. It should be stressed, however, that circumstances such as the ones described arise only infrequently.

Far more common is the serving of the local planning authority with a purchase notice as a consequence of an adverse planning decision or action. These activities are still contained within the 1990 Act or its companion, the Planning (Listed Buildings and Conservation Areas) Act 1990. In the various circumstances covered within this legislation, the compensation usually takes the form of the local planning authority being compelled to purchase the property in question. In similar vein is the blight notice, which is served on the local planning authority by the land owner whose property has been adversely affected by a planning decision. Here financial compensation is sought as recompense for the adverse effects of the planning decision. From these examples it is possible to determine that the award of compensation depends on there being a fall in the value, or potential value, of property. For any form of compensation to be gained the cause of such a fall must be directly attributable to a planning decision reached by the local planning authority. The important question is, therefore, whether the possibility of being served with such notices will, in any way, affect the development control decisions made by the local planning authority. Limited research suggests that this does sometimes occur,[16] but normally the local planning authority seems unaffected. For example, when roads are under construction, circumstances can arise which often lead to purchase or blight notices being served, but most local authorities seem to take them in their stride. This suggests that when a planning decision can clearly be shown to be in the public interest, the possibility of financial claims against the authority interferes little, if at all, with the normal processes of a development control decision. Since, therefore, the availability of compensation is not a factor normally taken into account when development control decisions are reached, no attempt has been made in this book to consider the subject in any detail. This is not to deny its importance. Its omission simply serves to emphasise the theme of this book, namely an examination of the process whereby development control policy is put into practice. Only when this has been achieved does compensation become an issue.

Exceptions

To conclude this introductory chapter, passing reference will be made to those aspects of the planning system that may be considered as being exceptions to the development control process described so far. Despite the impression which might have been given, it should be mentioned that it is not always obligatory to obtain planning permission for development in the

16 The personal experience of one of the authors, who has been involved in several local amenity societies, suggests that this may have occurred very occasionally in relation to some local planning decisions with which he is familiar.

manner and form described in these pages. Planning permission is not needed for developments on Crown land, for example, where a process of 'consultation' is sufficient.[17] What constitutes Crown land is more comprehensive than land held by the Crown and the Duchies of Lancaster and Cornwall, since it includes land held by government departments. What is all-important is that the land must be owned by the department, and not simply controlled by it. So, for example, the British Broadcasting Corporation, although a public corporation and thereby funded by the government, is not regarded as a government department and thus is not exempt from the need to apply for planning permission. In contrast, any land which is directly vested in any government department, is Crown land. The effect that this and similar exceptions have on the development control system is usually slight for several reasons, not least of which is the fact that, in the case of disagreement between the local planning authority and the government department over a proposed development, the matter may be referred to the Secretary of State. This can result in a public inquiry being held as for any other planning dispute. Such public airings of differences of opinion between what are, in effect, public servants, supposedly acting for the public good, are not occurrences that either party welcomes. Consequently, the consultation which is required when developments on Crown land are proposed, will in most circumstances serve as an adequate alternative to the normal development control procedures.

Other exceptions are made in the case of local authorities and statutory undertakers[18] carrying out development on their own land, but again there are mandatory procedures that effectively substitute for development control when needed. Indeed, the number of special instances when the normal planning controls are in some way modified, or even dispensed with altogether, are increasing, as there has been a trend since 1980 for the government to introduce a variety of special areas in which development is controlled by unique systems. The Local Government, Planning and Land Act 1980 was responsible for creating urban development corporations[19] and enterprise zones. In each of these areas, the system of development control employed differs in some respect, be it large or small, from what has already been described. With all of these areas two

17 In March 1994 the Secretary of State announced that legislation would be introduced to remove this crown exemption. This leislation is currently awaited.

18 See definition in 1990 Act, s 262.

19 Part XVI, ss 134-171, Schs 26-31.

important points must be appreciated in order to understand their impact on the development control system in general. One is that the areas have quite specific boundaries, so that there should be no debate over the system of development control in operation in any specific location. More important still are the implications that their existence may have for the area in which they are located, an aspect that will be considered further in later chapters.

The list of anomalies can be added to by mentioning the fact that in certain cases specific forms of development will require not only planning permission but additional authorisation from a government department. A good example of extra departmental control is provided by the additional safeguards that relate to any form of mineral development, while another example is found in relation to highways, both of which will be considered fully in chapter 5. Other forms of anomaly within the development control system can be found in relation to some special local planning authority powers which can have a very marked effect on the development of an area. For example, it is possible for a local authority to compulsorily acquire property[20] in order to undertake development that it considers necessary. It is also possible for that same authority to enter into an agreement[1] with a private developer regarding the actual construction and management of the development.

Conclusion

In concluding this introductory chapter, the hope is to have succeeded in giving a simple and straightforward account of the development control system. What should have become apparent is that, in order to understand the system, certain points need to be appreciated. They are why the development control system exists and what it seeks to achieve, as well as how it goes about achieving it. The brief answer is that the development control system exists for the benefit of the community at large to protect it from development which is a response solely to market forces, rather than to the well-being of that community. The system's goal is an environment which offers the greatest good to the greatest number of people. How that is achieved, if it ever can be, is the subject matter of this

20 See pp 29-31.
1 Planning agreements can take several forms and they are examined in chapter 8.

book. The remaining chapters will be devoted to a detailed analysis of many of the issues briefly mentioned in the course of this chapter. The question will always be to what extent the procedures of the development control system can help transform the dream into reality, the policy into practice.

Chapter 2

The personnel of planning

It seems a relatively straightforward task to describe the personnel of planning. Nothing seems simpler than to list those individuals and organisations whose task it is to administer the planning system in England and Wales. Yet the simplicity of the task is deceptive for reasons which are implicit in the planning system itself. At the heart of that system is the notion of development control which insists that the use to which a particular piece of land or a building is put must be regulated. The nature of that regulation varies. It can take the form of plans which, in varying degrees of detail, offer a blueprint for future development in a particular area. It can take the form of a grant or refusal of planning permission for a specific development. It can take the form of designating buildings as of particular historic or architectural interest in order to preserve them. In all these ways, as was intimated in the introductory chapter, development can be controlled.

It is the fact that development control is a comprehensive term involving many separate processes which makes the task of describing the personnel of planning harder than it might otherwise be. The role, not to mention the importance, of the individuals and organisations discussed in this chapter can vary depending on the particular process being described. An example may illustrate this point. The Department of the Environment is the central government department responsible for formulating current central government policy on development control and publicising it to those who might be affected. Powers are given to the same Department to review and amend local planning authority policy on development control. The Department of the Environment also has responsibility for resolving planning appeals. In this role it can, for example, overturn local authority decisions to refuse planning permission. Indeed, should the issue be of sufficient importance, the initial application for planning permission can be dealt with directly by the Department of the Environment. Therefore, far from having a fixed role in the development control process, the Department of the Environment has several, very distinct, roles to play.

With this in mind, the next problem is how to determine exactly who is involved in the making of development control decisions. The simple answer is to consult the relevant legislation. The Town and Country Planning Act 1990, for example, provides that an application for planning permission is to be made to the local planning authority.[1] Yet the matter does not rest here. The 1990 Act and its associated legislation[2] make it plain that there are individuals and organisations who have a right to be consulted so that they may, if they wish, express their views on an application for planning permission. Sometimes the legislation names the specific individuals and organisations,[3] while on other occasions it simply provides for the application to be given publicity.[4] Much depends on the exact terms of the application. In contrast to those individuals who must be given an opportunity to participate in the decision-making process, there are others who are invited to have their say, merely because it is thought desirable. Some local planning authorities make it their practice to consult many more individuals than they are legally required to when they receive an application for planning permission.[5] Consequently, the legislation alone is not always able to provide a sure indication of who will be involved in a development control decision. Additional information may be found in sources such as Department of the Environment circulars or what is termed 'usual practice'.[6]

Apart from those directly involved in making development control decisions, there are certain individuals included among the personnel of planning whose task is to contribute only when something has gone amiss with the way in which the process has been administered. Such individuals are not, therefore, a part of the decision-making process. Instead, theirs is a supervisory role which has its limits determined by statute. In short,

1 Town and Country Planning Act 1990, s 62.
2 Town and Country Planning (General Development Procedure) Order 1995, SI 1995/419.
3 Ibid, art 10.
4 Ibid, art 12B.
5 The necessary consultations are prescribed in the Town and Country Planning (General Development Procedure) Order 1995, SI 1995/419, arts 10 and 11. See also Harrison J 'Who is my Neighbour' Journal of Planning and Environment Law, 1994, p 219.
6 Circular 15/92, Publicity for Planning Applications.

that role is to intervene when a decision-maker has not acted fairly and, if possible, set the decision aside. There are two bodies entrusted with this supervisory role, the courts and the ombudsman system.[7] They represent the community's guarantee that those individuals entrusted with decision-making powers do not abuse them, and, as such, those bodies will be discussed in this chapter.

What these opening paragraphs are attempting to emphasise, therefore, is that 'development control' is a comprehensive term which, when analysed, can consist of many processes. The performance of those processes will involve, to a greater or lesser degree, the individuals and organisations described in the remainder of this chapter.

The Department of the Environment

The Department of the Environment is the central government department responsible for administering the planning system in England. Separate arrangements are made for Wales. The Department was created in 1970 when the Ministries of Housing and Local Government, Public Building and Works, and Transport were amalgamated.[8] The merger was considered desirable because of the links which existed between these Ministries and the functions each performed. Broadly stated, the Ministry of Housing and Local Government was responsible for land use planning and the protection of the environment, while the other Ministries, including the Ministry of Housing, were responsible for initiating major public sector developments, such as the building of roads. The creation of the Department of the Environment was seen as essential in order to provide administrative and policy co-ordination of what were often conflicting functions. This point was clearly made in the White Paper which suggested that the Department of the Environment be established.

7 While it is possible for the courts to set aside a decision, an ombudsman has more limited powers. On some occasions it may be feasible for a decision to be reconsidered. If not, the ombudsman may be able to secure an apology or an *ex gratia* payment. It is also possible for a body to refuse to act on an ombudsman's findings – see chapter 10.

8 All the functions of the Minister of Public Buildings and Works, the Minister of Housing and Local Government and the Minister of Transport were transferred to the Secretary of State for the Environment by the Secretary of State for the Environment Order 1970, SI 1970/1681.

> It is increasingly accepted that maintaining a decent environment, improving people's living conditions and providing for adequate transport facilities all come together in the planning of development. These are among the main functions of local authorities and are having an ever-increasing impact on ordinary people, in town and country and especially in and around the larger urban areas. Because these functions interact, and because they give rise to acute and conflicting requirements, a new form of organisation is needed at the centre of the administrative system...the new department will be responsible for the whole range of functions which affect people's living environment. It will cover the planning of land – where people live, work, move and enjoy themselves. It will be responsible for the construction industries, including the housing programme, and for the transport industries, including public programmes of support and development for the means of transport. There is a need to associate with these functions responsibility for other major environmental matters: the preservation of amenity, the protection of the coast and countryside, the preservation of historic towns and monuments, and the control of air, water and noise pollution, all of which must be pursued locally, regionally, nationally and in some cases internationally. And it will have the leading responsibility for regional policy; ...It will also have the particular responsibility of ensuring that people's rights are adequately protected wherever they are affected by the proposals of their neighbours or of public authorities. Local authorities are profoundly involved in these fields and the new department will, therefore, carry responsibility at the centre for the structure and functioning of local government as well as for regional affairs.[9]

The Department of the Environment is still performing the role outlined for it in the White Paper. Its task may not have been made any easier by the creation in 1976 of a separate Department of Transport.[10] Hence, although of necessity close ties exist between the two, they operate once more as separate Ministries. More recently the Department of the Environment lost some of its functions in relation to conservation policy to the newly created Department of National Heritage. The new Department has assumed responsibility for such matters as the listing of historic buildings and the designation of conservation areas. Hearing appeals against the refusal of listed building consent and enforcement action remains the function of the Department of the Environment.[11]

9 The Reorganisation of Central Government (Cmnd 4506) paras 30-31.
10 Secretary of State for Transport Order 1976, SI 1976/1775.
11 Circular 20/92, Responsibilities for Conservation Policy and Casework.

To describe the functions performed by the Department of the Environment is, as the extract from the White Paper makes clear, no easy task. Although the major interest of this book is planning in general, and development control in particular, the Department of the Environment is by no means a Ministry of Town and Country Planning under another name. The Department has overall responsibility for many matters. They include local government, environmental protection, and housing as well as town and country planning. For example, the Department of the Environment initiated the legislation which secured the abolition of the metropolitan counties.[12] The same Department distributes finance, via the rate support grant, among local authorities. Housing too is within this Department's remit, and the legislation giving council tenants the right to buy council housing originated in the Department of the Environment.[13]

Given the range of responsibilities entrusted to the Department of the Environment, the logic of including town and country planning among them might appear open to question. It is possible, however, to advance a simple justification. Town and country planning is a function of both central and local government. Therefore, it is sensible that the government department which has the responsibility for local government should have this additional responsibility. Consequently, when changes are made in the system of local government, necessary changes can be made in the planning system. More important still, such an arrangement allows central government to initiate policy in relation to land use planning which it can then communicate to local planning authorities for implementation in their areas.

If the reason for including planning within the remit of the Department of the Environment is the opportunity it offers for policy co-ordination, then practical evidence might be expected of this process at work, with the Secretary of State as the key figure in the Department of the Environment, having a leading role to play. Indeed, it is interesting to note that predecessors of the Secretary of State were charged with a particular statutory responsibility which is now apparently defunct. This was to secure 'consistency and continuity in the framing and execution of a national policy with respect to the use and development of land throughout England and Wales'.[14] Reference to the planning system in its current form shows that devices exist which can make such 'consistency and continuity' a reality. The

12 Local Government Act 1985.
13 Housing Act 1985.
14 Minister of Town and Country Planning Act 1943, s 1, repealed by the Secretary of State for the Environment Order 1970, SI 1970/1681.

first of these is the development plan.

The evolution of the development plan will be described in detail in chapter 4. At present it is sufficient to state that development plans, which may assume several forms, are documents prepared by local planning authorities which set out an individual local planning authority's policy for the future use of land in its area. Included in the development plan may be a local planning authority's strategy for encouraging industry in its area, its policy on the conservation of buildings of architectural interest, as well as the designation of land for specific purposes, such as residential development. The Secretary of State has the power to intervene at various stages in the development plan process,[15] and can exercise this power with regard to all forms of development plan.[16] At his direction, therefore, specific policies may be removed or modified within any development plan. By entrusting this task to the Secretary of State, the Department of the Environment can, if it wishes, ensure that development plans are consistent with each other and that nothing in them impedes the implementation of central government land use policy.

Apart from scrutinising development plans, the Secretary of State is also responsible for resolving planning appeals. The 1990 Act permits an individual refused planning permission by a local planning authority, or unhappy with the terms upon which he has been granted planning permission, to appeal to the Secretary of State.[17] The process of determining such appeals gives the Department of the Environment yet another opportunity to monitor the performance of local planning authorities. Consistency with the development plan as well as central government policy can thus be assessed, and a decision can be reversed on appeal if this is felt to be warranted.

In short, there appears to be the potential within the Department of the Environment to allow it to direct generally land use planning in England. This is confirmed by the fact that other legislative provisions exist which give significant positive powers to the Secretary of State to further such a process. These include the power to 'call in' certain decisions.[18] For example, if

15 For a description of the Secretary of State's role, see chapter 4 and PPG 12, Development Plans and Regional Planning Guidance, para 4.16 and annex A, paras 71-76.

16 For an explanation of each type of plan see PPG 12, section 3.

17 1990 Act, ss 78 and 79.

18 The Secretary of State has the power under the terms of the 1990 Act to call in planning applications (s 77) and planning appeals (ss 78 and 79) for his determination.

a development is proposed which will have far-reaching consequences both at a local and at a national level, then the Secretary of State, by calling in the application for planning permission, can make the decision rather than leaving it to the relevant local planning authority. Last, but by no means least, is the power of the Secretary of State to introduce primary and secondary legislation which can radically alter the face of land use planning, providing such legislation is approved by Parliament. It is such legislation which defines permitted development, that is, development which can proceed without the need to secure planning permission.[19]

Having briefly outlined the various powers possessed by the Department of the Environment, it only remains to assess the effectiveness with which the department performs its role. Before forming an opinion, some appreciation is necessary of the administrative organisation within the Department of the Environment. In overall charge is the Secretary of State. In addition, there are three Ministers, for Local Government, for Environment and Countryside and for Construction and Planning respectively. These four leading figures within the depart-ment are, of course, politicians and therefore their stay in the department is unlikely to be lengthy. As should already be apparent, the Secretary of State is responsible for taking many key decisions. Yet to say this is to risk misunderstanding the way in which the Department of the Environment functions. The day-to-day business of the Department is obviously conducted by civil servants employed in the Department's London and regional offices. The bulk of the decision-making will be delegated to them. In this respect, the Department of the Environment is no different from any other government department. It is clear that no Secretary of State would have the time to give every decision his personal attention. All he can hope to do is to make sure that any possibly contentious item is brought to his attention. That said, the Secretary of State is, of course, answerable in Parliament for any of his Department's shortcomings whether or not he personally took the decision.[20]

Given the emphasis on delegation within the Department, it is possible that it may have adverse effects on its ability to monitor and co-ordinate land use planning. The dangers involved are possibly best illustrated by considering the Secretary of State's responsibility to decide planning appeals and how this

19 Town and Country Planning (General Permitted Development) Order 1995, SI 1995/418.

20 This is the doctrine of Ministerial responsibility.

task has been gradually delegated to a body of individuals known as the Planning Inspectorate who function as an executive agency within the Department of the Environment. The Planning Inspectorate is made up of planning inspectors. They perform a variety of functions on the Secretary of State's behalf, including hearing the majority of appeals against the refusal of planning permission or objections to planning conditions.

Indeed, the majority of planning appeals are now determined by inspectors without any recourse to the Secretary of State.[1] The consequences of this change, which was designed to speed up the planning process, are many. It was argued in the preceding paragraphs that one of the reasons for setting up the Department of the Environment was to secure a co-ordinated land use policy with the department at its centre, disseminating central government policy and, in various ways, ensuring that policy was observed. The centralisation of the planning appeal system within the Department of the Environment was one of those ways. Whether this is a satisfactory method is open to doubt, since an individual refused planning permission may choose not to appeal, though the chances are that any sizeable and, therefore, significant development which is refused planning permission will be the subject of an appeal.

If there is an appeal this would seem to give a golden opportunity to ensure departmental policy is observed. Arguably, however, the greater delegation to inspectors of the power to make decisions is undermining the Department's policy co-ordination in a variety of ways. There may be inconsistency between inspectors, with certain inspectors acquiring a reputation for favouring or opposing certain developments. Since they are not the originators of the policy they may have to apply, inspectors may not appreciate its true significance, nor be able to create the necessary exceptions to a policy, as the Secretary of State would theoretically be able to do. In addition, there is the possibility that inspectors may be applying policies which are totally at variance with departmental policy. That these dangers are inherent in the process of delegation cannot be denied. To what extent the decisions show this is happening remains a matter for speculation, particularly since inspectors' decisions can hardly be described as freely available.[2] A further

1 Town and Country Planning Appeals (Determination by Inspectors) (Inquiries Procedure) Rules 1992, SI 1992/2039; Circular 24/92, Town and Country Planning (Inquiries Procedure) Rules 1992.

2 Selected decisions are reported in the Journal of Planning and Environment Law. Copies of individual decisions may be obtained from the Department of the Environment.

anomaly is introduced by the fact that a grant of planning permission, as opposed to the conditions attached to it, cannot be appealed.[3] This presents local planning authorities with the opportunity to ignore or reinterpret central government policy on a particular issue, and grant planning permission to a development totally at odds with Department of the Environment development control policy. In these circumstances, there is little chance for central government to reinstate its policy.

Other government departments

Although the Department of the Environment is the central government department responsible for the administration of the land use planning system in England, it is necessary to mention briefly the involvement of other Ministries in the process. That involvement varies in character. The Department of the Environment has little or no responsibility for land use planning in either Scotland or Wales. In those areas, the Scottish Office and the Welsh Office respectively, handle planning and environment matters. In reality, policies applied by the Department of the Environment in England tend also to be applied by the Welsh Office in Wales. This is borne out by the fact that legislation, such as the Town and Country Planning Act 1990, is as relevant in Wales as it is in England. In addition, circulars offering guidance to those engaged in the planning process tend to be issued jointly by the Department of the Environment and the Welsh Office.[4] That said, it is the Welsh Office which administers the planning system in Wales. Therefore, functions performed by the Secretary of State at the Department of the Environment in England, are normally performed in Wales by the Secretary of State in the Welsh Office. With this division of labour, therefore, comes the possibility that policies jointly agreed upon will not be applied with the same degree of consistency as they would be if one Minister were responsible.

In contrast, Scotland and the Scottish Office enjoy greater autonomy. Legislation is often passed which applies only to

3 The remedy open to those who unsuccessfully oppose a grant of planning permission is the application for judicial review.

4 Whether a circular applies equally in England and Wales is apparent from the heading to the circular. One example of separate circulars is Department of the Environment Circular 1/94, Gypsy Sites and Planning and Welsh Office Circular 2/94 of the same title.

Scotland.[5] Therefore, the planning system is distinct from that in England and Wales, though the policies underpinning it may be similar. As has been pointed out in chapter 1, the Scottish system is outside the scope of this book. The responsibilities of the Scottish Office are noted merely to make it plain that the Department of the Environment has no administrative responsibilities in Scotland.

The creation of the Department of National Heritage has also had an impact on the Department of the Environment's land use planning functions. Responsibility for the conservation of the built environment and archaeological sites now rests with the National Heritage Department. It does not however deal with operational activities such as development in a conservation area, appeals regarding listed buildings or the decision to 'call in' a planning application. These are still the responsibility of the Department of the Environment.[6] Whether dividing auth-ority in this manner allows a more objective view of conservation issues or simply creates the potential for greater bureaucracy and possible confusion remains to be seen.

The relationship between other Ministries and the development control process is a twofold one. On the one hand, Ministries such as the Department of Transport will engage directly in development. There is no denying the impact that the Department of Transport's road building programme has on the environment and on individuals living in the vicinity. That said, there is an apparent anomaly in the fact that government departments are outside the system of development control. In contrast with the private developer, government departments are free to proceed with whatever development they choose, without the need to secure the permission of the relevant local authority.[7] The justification for this freedom arguably lies in the desire to prevent individual local authorities from blocking schemes of national importance and benefit. In addition, government departments are seen as representing the Crown, and it is a matter of tradition that the Crown is not subject to the systems which it is itself responsible for creating, unless specific provision is made for this.[8]

5 See, for example, the Town and Country Planning (Scotland) Act 1972. For an account of planning law in Scotland see Collar N *Planning* (1994).

6 Circular 20/94, Responsibilities for Conservation Policy and Casework.

7 Government departments must, however, consult with local planning authorities before undertaking development.

8 So far as the 1990 Act is concerned some of its provisions can affect Crown land. For example, a policy in a development plan can relate to Crown land and buildings on Crown land can be listed. See 1990 Act, s 296 and Planning (Listed Buildings and Conservation Areas) Act 1990, s 83.

However, since government departments cannot be left totally free to ignore the development control system, the duty to consult is placed on such departments.

> Development by the Crown does not require planning permission. But Government Departments will consult local planning authorities before proceeding with development ... which would otherwise require planning permission.[9]

As well as consulting local planning authorities, government departments must publicise their proposals so that members of the public may object.[10] If as a consequence objections are received, it is the Department of the Environment which determines the dispute.

Secondly, apart from initiating development, development proposals from private citizens can have a considerable impact on the activities of certain Ministries. Provision has been made, therefore, to keep such Ministries informed. The Ministry of Agriculture, Fisheries and Food, for example, must be alerted to non-agricultural developments which are not in accordance with the development plan and will involve the loss of not less than twenty hectares of agricultural land.[11] Its views will then be taken into account when the local planning authority decides whether or not to let the proposed development go ahead. Bearing in mind that development and agriculture may be competitors for land,[12] local planning authorities are advised to involve the Ministry of Agriculture in other aspects of the development control process. Most particularly, when local planning authorities are drawing up plans for the future use of land in their area, discussions should be held with the Ministry over the impact their proposals will have on the supply of agricultural land.[13]

This involvement of the Ministry of Agriculture in the development control process is hardly exceptional. The Department of Transport also has the right to be consulted, since proposed developments, especially residential or retail developments, can greatly increase the flow of traffic on a particular road. Consequently, the Department of Transport must be

9 Circular 18/84, Crown Land and Crown Development, Pt IV, para 4.
10 Publicity will usually be given to the proposal by the local planning authority acting on their behalf. See Circular 15/92, para 30.
11 Town and Country Planning (General Development Procedure) Order 1995, SI 1995/419, art 10 (1), table (w).
12 The government's current policy on development and agriculture is to be found in PPG 7, The Countryside and the Rural Economy.
13 PPG 12, Development Plans and Regional Planning Guidance, annex E.

informed by a local planning authority of any proposed development which, for example, involves new or altered access to a motorway or trunk road on which speeds of more than 40 mph are permitted.[14]

It should be apparent, therefore, that government departments, apart from the Department of the Environment, can have an impact on the development control system in very distinct ways. Local planning authorities may canvass their opinions on proposed private developments. Alternatively, government departments may canvass the opinions of local planning authorities on developments which those departments propose to undertake. There is, however, yet another way in which the process of development control assumes a significance beyond the confines of any particular government department.

For many years much attention has been focused on the high levels of unemployment in the United Kingdom. The solution to this problem may seem far removed from the planning responsibilities of the Department of the Environment. In practice, the desire to create more jobs and, in particular, jobs in certain parts of the United Kingdom may have an impact on planning policies. In the past, attempts were made to disperse offices and industry into particular parts of the country with policies involving the allocation of office development permits and industrial development certificates.[15] The former scheme was administered through the Department of the Environment and has now been abolished for almost a decade.[16] The latter scheme was the responsibility of the Department of Industry and has also been abolished for many years.[17] Over the past few years, the desire to create jobs has led to suggestions for simplifying planning controls in certain areas in an attempt to create development and its related employment.[18] This serves as an example of how the policies related to land use planning can be significant in addressing the economic issues which face the United Kingdom. As a consequence, therefore, the thinking of the Department of the Environment can clearly have an effect on and equally be affected by the thinking of many other central

14 Town and Country Planning (General Development Procedure) Order 1995, SI 1995/419, art 15.
15 1971 Act, ss 66-86.
16 Housing and Planning Act 1986, s 48.
17 Control of Office Development (Cessation) Order 1979, SI 1979/908.
18 For government thinking over the last decade see, for example, the White Paper, Lifting the Burden (Cmnd 9571), aspects of which are implemented in the Housing and Planning Act 1986 and are now consolidated into the 1990 Act.

government departments. Direct legal or policy relationships are thus not always needed, as will be illustrated in later chapters.

The European Union

Development control policy might be regarded as an essentially national issue and one where government should be given a free hand in determining policy. The world's increasing preoccupation with environmental issues such as global warming and the conservation of endangered species and habitats is, however, having an increasing impact on development control policy within the United Kingdom. For example, the development control decision to allow the construction of a major new road or the construction of an oil terminal on a previously undeveloped coastal site, has obvious implications for the environment, and thus generates interest at a local, national and international level.

One international body that is becoming increasingly preoccupied with the environment is the European Union of which the United Kingdom is a member. The Union's original aims and objectives as set out in the Treaty of Rome[19] made no mention of the environment. This did not, however, prevent environmental issues from figuring in the Union's legislative programme, for example, the Environmental Assessment Directive.[20] Later amendments to the Treaty of Rome, such as those in the Maastricht Treaty, have led to environmental protection being included as a Union objective. In addition Article 130 now specifically authorises the adoption of:

> measures concerning town and country planning, land use with the exception of waste management and measures of a general nature, and management of water resources.

As a member of the European Union the United Kingdom's freedom to adopt whatever development control measures it sees fit would appear to have been curtailed. Environmental protection measures already agreed by the Union, such as the Habitats Directive[1] and the Birds Directive[2] have the potential to make a considerable impact on the process of development

19 Treaty of Rome 1957, arts 2, 3.
20 Environmental Assessment Directive 85/337.
1 Habitats Directive 92/43.
2 Birds Directive 79/409.

control. Both Directives call for the designation of special sites. Once such sites are designated, proposed development which may have a significant effect on these areas has to be assessed for its probable impact. Projects which are likely to have an adverse impact are to proceed only if they need to be carried out 'for imperative reasons of overriding public interest'.[3] Where the site in question is particularly important then dev-elopment can go ahead only in very limited circumstances, such as the need to protect public safety.

As with all European legislation the United Kingdom was involved in the preparation of these Directives. Indeed, any future legislation on town and country planning and land use requires unanimous voting in the Council and thus allows a member state to block proposed legislation.[4] Once agreed, failure to implement European legislation can result either in action being taken against the defaulting state or the direct application of the legislation by national courts.

With the European Union set to produce fresh environmental measures[5] its influence on the development control process is undoubtedly growing but it remains at present an indirect influence. Whether the time will come when much of the United Kingdom's development control agenda will be set by Europe is unclear. Although the Maastricht Treaty refers directly to town and country planning any future proposals for European legislation is subject to the concept of subsidiarity. This means that the Union will take action only if it, rather than member states, is better suited to achieving a particular objective. This raises the question of how practical it would be to set development control policy at an international rather than national level. What is not yet clear, therefore, is whether the notion of subsidiarity will work against the development of a European Union system of planning law. If it does then the ability of the United Kingdom to arrive at independent development control decisions will be limited only marginally. If, however, subsidiarity has little practical effect on the desire of the Union to intervene, then the competence of the United Kingdom to create its own independent development control policies might be severely curtailed.

3 Habitats Directive, art 6.
4 This indicates the importance of these measures as qualified majority voting is used in other environmental contexts.
5 To make environmental assessment part of the development plan process.

Local government

ORGANISATION

In order to appreciate the role played by local government in the development control process, attention has initially to be focused on the way in which local government in England and Wales is organised. The logical starting point would appear to be the Local Government Act 1972 which reorganised local government on a two-tier basis, that of counties and districts. It is, however, necessary to mention briefly the situation which existed prior to the passage of the 1972 Act, since reference will be made, on occasions, to the planning functions performed by local authorities prior to local government reorganisation.

Before 1 April 1974 when the 1972 Act took effect, the pattern of local government in England and Wales varied. Leaving aside Greater London, there were some areas where there was a single tier of local government. These were the county boroughs whose councils exercised all the relevant local government functions.[6] In contrast, other areas had two tiers of local government. These were the administrative counties which were further subdivided into county districts – that is municipal boroughs, urban districts and rural districts.[7] Functions were divided between the tiers.

Given these complications, it might be thought that the objective of any local government reform would be uniformity. To a certain extent this was achieved in the 1972 Act when England and Wales were divided into counties and those counties subdivided into districts. Those new counties did not necessarily correspond with the old counties. Wales, for example, was divided into eight counties for the purposes of the 1972 Act, as opposed to the traditional thirteen. The functions allocated to the counties included responsibility for such matters as education, personal social services and libraries. As for the districts, responsibility was allocated to them for items such as housing and environmental health. It has to be said that this allocation of functions was perhaps not as clear-cut as might first have appeared. The management of services such as parks, playing fields and car parking provision was left to local negotiation

6 In order to qualify as a county borough a certain level of population was required. In the Local Government Act 1894, which established county boroughs, this was 50,000, but it increased over the years.

7 This arrangement originated in the Local Government Act 1894.

between district and county councils;[8] while on issues such as housing, which was in the remit of district councils, county councils were given reserve powers.[9]

This scheme of county and district councils was not, however, uniformly applied across England and Wales. Six areas in England were given the title of metropolitan counties.[10] These were large conurbations, such as Merseyside, and the responsibilities of metropolitan county councils were more limited than those of non-metropolitan county councils.[11] In contrast, the functions of metropolitan districts were more extensive than those of their non-metropolitan counterparts. These six areas apart, Greater London was also the subject of special arrangements. The Greater London Council was created in 1965 when the London Government Act 1963 came into operation. Also created in that Act were thirty-two London borough councils, with only the City of London remaining unaffected by these changes. This arrangement was left in place by the 1972 Act.[12]

To add to an already complex picture, reference must also be made to a third tier of local government. The 1972 Act made provision for parish councils in England, where they were confined to rural areas,[13] and community councils in Wales.[14] Their powers and functions were strictly limited, however, being mainly consultative, with few positive activities to perform such as the provision of recreational space.[15]

The picture which has emerged so far of local government reorganisation is of an essentially two-tier system with the tiers being in no sense hierarchical. Functions are divided between those tiers with adjustments in the division being made in the metropolitan and Greater London areas. This situation changed with the passage of legislation to abolish the Greater London Council and the six metropolitan county councils. On 1 April

8 See the Local Government Act 1972, Sch 19, for the complex arrangements made in relation to car parking.
9 Ibid, s 194.
10 Greater Manchester, Merseyside, West Midlands, West Yorkshire, South Yorkshire and Tyne and Wear.
11 Education and social services were the responsibility of county councils in non-metropolitan areas, but of the district councils in metropolitan areas.
12 Local Government Act 1972, s 1(1).
13 Ibid, s 1. Rural parishes already in existence when the Act came into force remained. Additional parishes were added to their number by the Local Government (Successor Parishes) Orders 1973 and 1974, SI 1973/1110, and SI 1974/569.
14 Local Government Act 1972, s 20(4).
15 Ibid, Sch 14, para 27. Parish councils also have the power to acquire land for the purpose of their functions under ss 124 and 125.

1986 these councils disappeared. The justification advanced for this step was that since these councils were responsible for so few services – as compared with non-metropolitan counties – yet consumed much in the way of resources, abolition was the only sensible solution. The functions previously exercised by the metropolitan counties have, where possible, been taken over by the districts. Alternatively, special non-elected boards have been created to cope with matters which cannot conveniently be handled at the district level, for example, the fire service.

The situation in the non-metropolitan areas has not, however, remained static. Changes have been instituted and continue to take place. The end result of this process will be a system of local government that, in England at least, will not be uniform. This is because in England, instead of reviewing local government as a whole and recommending wholesale change, a Local Government Commission for England was constituted. This independent Commission was given the task of looking at particular areas of England, such as Cleveland and Durham and Derbyshire and then making recommendations to central government regarding the future organisation of local government in those areas. The Local Government Commission began this process in 1992 and has now considered and made recommendations in respect of the whole of England. In some but not every instance it has recommended a change from the two-tier system of counties and districts to a system of unitary authorities. The government is, however, not obliged to act on these recommendations and has on various occasions referred recommendations back to the Local Government Commission for further consideration.

The end result of this procedure will be a series of orders issued by the Secretary of State for the Environment which will reorganise local government in a specific area. In the case of Cleveland County Council, for example, an order has been made for its abolition from 1 April 1996. Its functions will then be transferred to the existing district councils – Middlesborough, Hartlepool, Stockton-on-Tees and Langbourgh, which will be renamed Redcar and Cleveland – which will become unitary councils. The same is true of Avon County Council which is to be replaced by four new unitary councils. In some areas, however, only part of the county council will be replaced by a unitary authority. In Bedfordshire, for example only Luton will become a unitary authority. By 1 April 1996, which is the date set for the implementation of these changes throughout England, what is currently a predominantly two-tier system of local government will have become a largely unitary system. Whatever views there may be about the advantages of unitary authorities over the current system there is no doubt that these changes will have an impact on the land use planning system and, in particular, the preparation of development plans.

In comparison to what is occurring in England the situation in Wales is much more straightforward. The Local Government (Wales) Act 1994 provides for a total abolition of the two-tier system of local government in the Principality. In place of existing arrangements twenty-one unitary councils will be created. Although these new authorities will provide local government services for their area, community councils will remain in being. Whilst the powers of the community councils will not be enhanced, they are given the right in the legislation to be consulted on certain issues and have their views taken into account before a decision is reached by the relevant unitary authority.

PLANNING

The business of land use planning is an important function of local government. It is at this level that policies can be adapted to suit the realities of a particular situation. From the description in the previous section it should be apparent that the present norm is for two tiers of local government. Functions are assigned between the tiers according to opinion on the best and most efficient way to deliver a particular service. Prior to reorganisation under the Local Government Act 1972, planning was a function of the counties in those areas where two tiers of local government existed. They were responsible for producing the development plan in the form then required. County councils could, and did, delegate some of their authority for carrying out planning functions to the district councils.

After reorganisation in 1972, planning still remained a function for which responsibility is shared. The task of preparing the new style development plans is divided between the counties and districts.[16] This was the situation even in the metropolitan counties and Greater London.[17] In addition, two categories of application for planning permission are created. Where the application involves 'county matters' – for example the mining of minerals – then the county council is responsible for de-

16 Structure plans are prepared by the county planning authorities and local plans are normally drawn up by district planning authorities.

17 In the case of Greater London, the system was adapted somewhat in the Town and Country Planning Act 1990, s 19, Sch 4.

termining the application.[18] The remaining applications for planning permission, and by far the greater number, are handled by the district councils.

As matters stand at present, county councils are responsible for formulating the general strategy for land use in their area, normally in the form of a structure plan. In contrast, detailed matters such as applications for planning permission, the enforcement of the planning system and the preparation of detailed development proposals for a particular area – local plans – are the responsibility of district councils although in certain circumstances they are under a duty to consult with county planning authorities before reaching a decision.[19] Parish and community councils have no specific role to play in this planning system. All aspects of decision-making are undertaken by the county and district councils, leaving the third tier simply to comment upon any proposals which might affect their area.[20] In this respect these councils have little more impact on the planning system than members of the public.

There remain, of course, those areas where two tiers of local government no longer exist, the metropolitan counties and Greater London. Since it was the metropolitan county councils which were abolished and the metropolitan district councils which survived, the responsibility for development control is largely undisturbed. It is only in respect of the preparation of development plans that some adjustments have had to be made. A new style of development plan, called a unitary plan, was devised.[1] The metropolitan district councils and the London borough councils are each responsible for preparing a unitary plan. If it seems sensible, a number of metropolitan district councils or London borough councils can join forces to prepare a joint unitary plan,[2] and this process is examined in Chapter 4.

The reorganisation of local government which is currently taking place in England and Wales is set to have an impact on the allocation of primary functions. Where county councils are abolished and are replaced by unitary district authorities these

18 What constituted county matters was set out in the Local Government Act 1972, Sch 16, para 32. The current distribution of planning functions between county and district authorities is dealt with in the Town and Country Planning Act 1990, Sch 1. This provides a definition of what constitutes a 'county matter'.

19 1990 Act, Sch 1, para 7.

20 Town and Country Planning (General Development Procedure) Order 1995, SI 1995/419, art 13.

1 Introduced by the Local Government Act 1985, Sch 1, they are now incorporated into the 1990 Act, ss 10-28.

2 1990 Act, s 23.

new authorities will be responsible for all existing planning functions. Since virtually all planning applications are currently determined by district planning authorities this may produce little in the way of change. So called 'county matters', for example applications involving the mining of minerals, will be determined by the new authorities and they may be required to amend existing local plans or mineral local plans where applicable to insert their new or revised policies on such issues.

In the case of development plans the situation is more complex. Responsibility for revising and updating structure plans will be taken over by the newly created unitary authorities. So, for example, on the abolition of Cleveland County Council in 1996 the Cleveland Structure Plan will be treated as if it had been prepared by the newly formed unitary authorities. What is not clear, however, is whether each of the unitary authorities will simply be responsible for revising that part of the structure plan that affects their area or whether they will have to combine to revise it jointly. The Secretary of State for the Environment has the power[3] to impose this obligation to act jointly upon such authorities, and the Local Government Commission certainly believed that there were advantages to retaining the old two-tier arrangements with the new unitary authorities becoming joint structure planning authorities for the whole of their combined areas.[4]

To what extent the Secretary of State will act on this advice appears uncertain. In the case of the Isle of Wight, for example, the new unitary authority established there has been authorised by the Secretary of State to prepare a unitary development plan 'on the basis that this would be quicker, more efficient and simpler'.[5] It therefore appears that in future there will be diversity in the arrangements in England for revising structure plans. Whilst there is no intrinsic objection to diversity the possibility exists that it will undermine the strategic objectives that structure plans are meant to achieve. In particular the breadth of vision that structure plans are supposed to contain may be sacrificed in return for administrative simplicity. In Wales however all twenty-one new authorities will be responsible for producing a unitary development plan for their area.[6]

3 Local Government Act 1992, s 21.

4 Local Government Commission for England, Renewing Local Government in the English Shires: A Progress Report, para 60.

5 Ibid, para 66.

6 Local Government (Wales) Act 1994, s 20, Sch 4, 5.

From what has been said on the subject of local government, certain points should be clear. Central government decides how local government is organised, and the hope is that any decisions are arrived at with an eye to efficiency, rather than political advantage. Central government also allocates responsibility for development control. Arguably, this too should be done on the basis of which body is best able to perform a particular development control function. Most functions, at present, are concentrated in the hands of the district councils. Development plans are partly the exception since the feeling is that general policies for the future land use are best devised at county rather than district level. It remains to be seen whether the reformed system of local government in England and Wales represents an improvement, at least in planning terms, on current arrangements. There are undoubtedly dangers associated with that new system. General strategic planning may suffer because of lack of co-ordination between authorities and its application within areas that are too small. Detailed development control planning may also suffer because policies have to be formulated for an area that is too large and diverse in its demands.

Whatever the future may hold, it is vital to understand that development control is not a single process, but, as this book will demonstrate, a number of procedures. The important question is what particular expertise is called for in the performance of these procedures and which tier of local government possesses that expertise.

THE ROLE OF LOCAL GOVERNMENT IN DEVELOPMENT CONTROL

While it is obvious from what has been said so far that local authorities have a role to play in the process of development control, attention now needs to be focused on what exactly that role is. Central government, in the shape of the Department of the Environment, is responsible for formulating policies on how land should be used, which are in turn communicated to local authorities. In addition, central government has at its disposal ways of monitoring how closely those policies are adhered to, not to mention the means of completely transforming the role local authorities play in the process of development control. What needs to be examined, therefore, is the relationship between central and local government.

It must be appreciated that local authorities are not agents for central government, in the sense that they do exactly what central government wants. A local authority consists of elected representatives, the local councillors. This may appear a rather obvious statement but it gives a clue to some of the dilemmas facing local government. In 1965, the Maud Committee, in a survey of local authorities, found that 50% were controlled by a political party or coalition of parties.[7] More recently a report on the conduct of local authority business found that the proportion of councils in political control had risen to 84%.[8] This was attributed, in part, to local government reorganisation reducing the total number of councils. Another contributing factor was the decline of councils dominated by independent councillors who owe allegiance to none of the major political parties. In short, the likelihood is that local councillors will belong to one of the major political parties and their decisions will reflect the policies of that party.

From this development flow several significant consequences. When a local authority is discharging whatever development control functions have been assigned to it, the practice is not for the whole council to take every decision.[9] This would be impossible and not in the interests of good administration. Instead, the power to take such decisions is quite legitimately delegated to a committee, the planning committee.[10] It is this committee which will take decisions, such as whether or not to grant planning permission. There is no legislation governing the composition of these committees. In theory, therefore, the majority political party on a particular council, if there is one, could, if it chose, allot all the seats to members of its party. In reality, seats are allocated according to the political parties' strength on the council. This means that the political views and tensions in the council as a whole may be reflected on a committee such as the planning committee.

Much of the business transacted by the planning committee will not be politically contentious. The decision whether or not to grant planning permission for a kitchen extension is hardly the stuff of high political drama. Faced with plans for large scale developments, however, political views can, and do surface. Certain political parties may see particular forms of development as more in line with their political aspirations than others.

7 Quoted in The Conduct of Local Authority Business (Cmnd 9797) para 2.39. The 50% is an average. For example, at that time 100% of London boroughs were politically controlled but only 20%-40% of counties.

8 The Conduct of Local Authority Business (Cmnd 9797) para 2.40.

9 The power of a local authority to delegate the exercise of specific functions to a committee is to be found in the Local Government Act 1972, s 101.

10 This does not prevent particularly controversial or complex planning applications being referred to the full council for a decision with simply a recommendation from the planning committee.

Each of the major political parties has a policy on the environment. When that policy is put into practice at local government level, it may result in certain forms of development being favoured at the expense of others. This mix of politics and planning can be a dangerous one. On the one hand, it may mean that the development control policy being favoured by a particular local authority is totally at odds with central government policy. Consequently, appeals may proliferate as applicants attempt to have decisions reversed and central government policy reinstated. In addition, development control decisions must be taken for good planning reasons, not good political reasons. If they are not, then the courts may have grounds for saying that a decision has not been lawfully reached.

In relation to development control, a local authority will have a planning department which will administer the planning system for that particular area. It will be this department which receives applications for planning permission and processes them. The personnel within a planning department will vary depending on the administrative structure, but a considerable number will be professional planners holding professional qualifications from either the Royal Town Planning Institute, the Royal Institute of British Architects, or the Royal Institution of Chartered Surveyors. This signifies that these individuals have received a professional training, usually at least to first degree level, in some aspect of planning or design. Persons such as these will be employed as planning officers, and their role within the department is a difficult one to describe. Besides administering the planning system, these individuals will obviously have an expertise in land use planning. Therefore, the senior members of the department will offer advice and guidance on the consequences of their actions to members of the council.

It is difficult to articulate how influential individual planning officers are in determining the actions of their particular local authority. A great deal will depend on the personalities of the individuals involved. Research in the past has indicated that councillors felt that council officials had too much influence over decision-making.[11] This feeling was particularly strong among councillors in parties in the minority on the council. That view may reflect the fact that where there are majority and minority parties on a council, contact between councillors representing the majority party and council officials is going to prove more frequent, thereby possibly exaggerating the amount of influence

11 Cmnd 9797, para 2.52.

such officials possess. It is interesting to note that in a research study conducted some years ago in a London borough, planning officers did not feel that their influence was particularly strong.[12]

Therefore, rather than engage in speculation it is perhaps sensible to consider what positive statements can be made regarding the relationships between councillors and their officials. The most important of these is the fact that although planning officers can and do offer advice and although that advice may frequently be taken, ultimately the decision-making power rests with the council and its committees. In short local councillors can arrive at whatever land use policies they choose. The fact that these may not meet with the approval of their planning officers is immaterial.

Quite clearly a planning committee whose decisions ignore central government policy or the relevant development plan might find these decisions are the subject of appeal or judicial challenge or complaint to the local ombudsman. In spite of this there is evidence of local planning committees behaving in just this fashion. In North Cornwall, for example, an inquiry revealed evidence of planning permission being given for development in open countryside contrary to national and local planning policy. This arose out of a desire on the part of local representatives to improve the job prospects of local people but illustrates how a planning committee can, if it wishes, ignore the policy framework within which it should make its decisions.[13]

Another point which needs to be emphasised is that although councillors are responsible for taking decisions they can, if they choose, delegate certain planning functions to a planning officer but not to a member of the planning committee. This might be useful in dealing with minor or routine planning questions since it will save time and prove more efficient. Where it is not acceptable is when this occurs to such an extent that major decisions are being taken by unelected officials and public confidence in the planning process and the accountability of local government is undermined.

The role which local authorities have to play in the development control process is therefore a complex one. It involves making specific decisions on how most appropriately to utilise land and property within their area. In reaching those decisions

12 Underwood J *Town Planners in Search of a Role* (1980).

13 'Enquiry into the Planning System in North Cornwall District' Journal of Planning and Environment Law, 1994, p 101.

various forces may be at work. These include the views of central government on appropriate development control policy, not to mention the opinions of the local authority's own planning officers on such matters. Nor will local councillors be without their own views, influenced by their party politics or the opinions of their constituents. It is in this context that local authorities take their development control decisions. While those decisions undoubtedly have an impact on the environment, it is an impact which is limited by one particular factor. A local authority can suggest in the development plan how it wishes land and property to be developed. It can grant and refuse planning permission in accordance with those aspirations. Yet a local authority has no positive way to ensure that its suggestions are followed, apart, that is, from engaging in development itself.

On occasions, local authorities do act as developers.[14] They build houses, schools and sports centres. Nor has it been uncommon for a local authority to enter into partnership with a private developer to redevelop a shopping centre,[15] for example. Yet, this is the exception rather than the rule. The development control system exists to regulate development. Unfortunately the ideas of the developer on what is appropriate development may be totally at odds with those of the local authority. A national supermarket chain may want to build a store and create jobs. The problem is that the site which the company considers ideal may not be the one designated by the local authority for such a development. In such a situation, the local authority cannot force the company to build on the site it considers appropriate. The aspirations of potential developers may therefore act as powerful constraints on the development control policy of a local authority.

The developer

The term 'developer' normally conjures up images of large companies with grandiose schemes to build shopping centres or office blocks. In reality, developers come in many shapes and forms. Literally, a developer is any individual or organisation

14 As is more fully discussed in chapter 4, one of the basic concepts of the Town and Country Planning Act 1947, and of every subsequent Town and Country Planning Act, is that local planning authorities shall act as developers. Powers, such as powers of compulsory purchase, are proof of this fact.

15 See, for example, *Jones v Secretary of State for Wales* (1974) 28 P & CR 280.

which wishes to undertake development as defined in the 1990 Act.[16] As has already been mentioned, development may be undertaken by central government departments and local authorities. The development undertaken by public bodies is, however, in certain ways distinguishable from that undertaken by private developers. When a local authority builds a school or the Department of Transport constructs a road, that development is seen as for the greater good of the community. Even the decision of a government department, such as the Inland Revenue, to build office accommodation, may be an attempt to bring jobs to a region where there is high unemployment. In deciding whether to undertake development, public developers may place less emphasis on the financial implications of their decisions than private developers. Local authorities, for example, may build housing to high standards on land that is available to them. A private developer will want to build houses in an area where people wish to live and at standards which are acceptable. Most of all, the private developer will wish to make a profit.

Motives apart, development by public bodies may not appear to be the subject of the same rigorous scrutiny as that undertaken by private developers. It has already been mentioned that central government departments do not have to apply for planning permission, though they consult with local authorities. As for local authorities, they apply to themselves for planning permission.[17] Industries which supply a public service, such as a gas supply or a postal service, whether or not they are in public ownership, have the power to undertake certain developments, described as permitted development, without securing planning permission.[18] In comparison, the private developer may find his plans subject to considerably greater levels of scrutiny. In addition, even if those plans are approved, conditions may accompany the approval which can severely limit the developer's freedom of action. Conditions may, for example, be imposed in an attempt to restrict the companies who can occupy industrial units to local companies.[19]

As a group, private developers are not alike. They can range from the individual householder who wishes to improve his

16 1990 Act, s 55.

17 For the procedure see the Town and Country Planning General Regulations 1992, SI 1992/1492, regs 2-11.

18 Town and Country Planning (General Permitted Development) Order 1995, SI 1995/418, Sch 2, Pt 17 (development by statutory undertakers).

19 See Williams M, 'The Validity of Occupancy Conditions – A Review', Journal of Planning and Environment Law, 1991, p 319; See also *Slough Industrial Estates Ltd v Secretary of State for the Environment* [1987] JPL 353.

house by extending it or to run a business from it, via the small builder, to international property developers. Development is undertaken by the private sector for a purpose, and more often than not that purpose will be to make a profit. At the level of the individual householder the profit motive may be at its weakest and may be accompanied by other motives, such as the desire to improve the neighbourhood or make changes which are in keeping with the character of the area. Yet even individual householders may think ahead to the day when they sell their property and recoup the cost of the improvement. Given the importance which profit may assume, the need to apply for planning permission and the conditions which may accompany a grant of planning permission seem no bad thing. They can be used to prevent the worst excesses of the developer, such as building houses at a density which is totally unsuited to a site or destroying trees so as to build an extra house.

The profit motive of the private developer should not assume distorted proportions, however, but rather should be viewed in the context of any normal business organisation seeking to make a reasonable profit. Consequently, property development is also guided by common business standards, such as the quality of the product, which the better developer will continually seek to improve in order to uphold his reputation, and thus ensure a future share of the market. A distinction must also be made between those who fund property developments and those who organise and undertake the development. In some instances this may be the same organisation, but more usually the development is undertaken on behalf of a funding organisation, a pension fund for example, by professional developers. These individuals are often drawn from the ranks of the same professional institutions as those that furnished the planning officers mentioned above. In this instance, however, the Royal Institution of Chartered Surveyors is likely to be the major source, while other professionals, such as accountants, lawyers and engineers may also be involved in the complex development process. These individuals may be considered as forming a distinct sub-group, as they constitute what can be termed as the professional advisers to the private developer. As such, their services are available throughout the whole range of private developments, from the simple house extension to the major office development, and consequently, they play an important role in the development control system.

Whatever sort of private developer is applying for planning permission, his is a vital role, as without him there would be little development to control. The development control system exists to prevent his worst excesses, for example, to prevent factories being built too close to residential development, or farmland being indiscriminately developed with housing. Yet, the system also responds to the developer's needs and demands. Policies are formulated on out-of-town shopping developments and the density of residential development because these are matters which concern the developer. Nor is the developer simply concerned with that aspect of the development control system which grants or refuses planning permission. Indeed, it is interesting to note that of the judicial challenges which have been made to development plans, many have involved private developers.[20] This shows that developers have a contribution to make when policy for future land use is being formulated, since such policies can seriously restrict their plans for future development.

Members of the public

It might be tempting to dismiss in a few sentences the role which members of the public play in the planning process as being simply the ability to comment on proposals for development. Once an application for planning permission is made, members of the public may be able to give their views on it.[1] Should there be an appeal, either because the application for planning permission is refused, or exception is taken to a condition, members of the public may make representations during the appeal proceedings.[2] When proposals are made regarding the shape of future development in an area, comment is sought from members of the public before including those policies in the development plan.[3] This right of members of the public to comment is sometimes provided for in the relevant legislation, sometimes encouraged by a local planning authority.

Elsewhere in this book where specific features of the development control process are considered, it will be made clear

20 *Westminster City Council v Great Portland Estates* [1985] AC 661, [1984] 3 All ER 744; *Buckinghamshire County Council v Hall Aggregates (Thames Valley) Ltd* [1985] JPL 634.

1 This is by virtue of the fact that all planning applications are available for public inspection. New applications are normally listed in local newspapers.

2 The appeals procedure is discussed in chapter 9. The Town and Country Planning (Determination by Inspectors)(Inquiries Procedure) Rules 1992, SI 1992/2039, r 11(2) leaves it to the discretion of the inspector whether members of the public can appear at a public inquiry.

3 1990 Act, ss 13, 33 and 40.

if members of the public have to be consulted. What follows is an attempt to assess how influential members of the public can be within the planning process. The right of individuals to comment upon proposed developments would, at first sight, appear to be an important right. Yet, members of the public, although they might express general disquiet over developments in their community, are unlikely to make specific comments on particular developments within that community. There may be many reasons for this apparent apathy. They include the need to know when a particular development is proposed, the ability to gain access to[4] and understand exactly what the suggested development entails, as well as sufficient confidence to express an opinion on the scheme if this is felt necessary. Although an individual may be prepared to do this if particularly affected by a development, such as a proposal to build a public house in the vicinity of his home, an interest in the community as a whole is harder for the individual to maintain.

It is, therefore, as a member of an organisation that an individual is better able to influence the planning process. The logic underlying this statement is that, as a member of a group, an individual will have access to the resources of that group, whether financial or in the shape of specialist knowledge. In addition, local government is more likely to take notice of an organisation which represents hundreds of individuals than a lone member of the public. Indeed, in certain circumstances a local planning authority is bound to ask community groups for comments concerning proposed developments. Where the local planning authority creates a conservation area for example, it will be expected to encourage the formation of an amenity society, and ask for their comments on proposed developments in the area as well as their assistance in the formulation of suitable policies.[5] An amenity or civic society will be locally based and has as its objective the protection of the environment in that locality. On the positive side, it can be seen as a vehicle to encourage individuals to take an interest in their environment. The criticism has sometimes been made, however, that membership of such groups is confined to middle class professionals who resist change, not for the sake of the community

4 See comments in Journal of Planning and Environment Law, Current Topics, 1994, p 198 regarding the ease of public access to planning documents.

5 Circular 8/87, Historic Buildings and Conservation Areas – Policy and Procedures, para 68; PPG 15, Planning and the Historic Environment, para 4.13.

as a whole, but to protect the residential environment which caused them to live in that locality.[6]

Apart from groups formed to take an interest in a specific locality, there are national groups whose business it is to protect and conserve the environment. This emphasis on protection is important, since these bodies will, in the main, comment upon development which threatens the well-being of the item they aim to protect. The National Trust, for example, is concerned with the preservation and management of important historic buildings and their grounds, as well as areas of the countryside and coast. The National Trust owns the buildings and the land which it administers and will, therefore, for the most part, be able to resist development on its property which it considers undesirable. In contrast, other groups with an interest in the preservation of buildings, such as the Georgian Group, which is dedicated to preserving Georgian architecture, will not normally own property, but simply act as pressure groups whenever property of the kind in which they have an interest is threatened, either by unsympathetic renovation or by demolition.

There are many national and international groups of this nature dedicated to preserving a particular aspect of the environment. They range from the Victorian Society to Greenpeace. Their membership varies in size and for a great many of those members, membership signifies not an active wish to participate but a general concern with the environment and what may adversely affect it. Obviously proposed development may appear damaging, depending on the perspective the particular organisation adopts. A plan to build a nuclear power station might be unacceptable to members of Greenpeace because of their objections to nuclear energy, to members of the Council for the Protection of Rural England because of the countryside which will disappear and to members of the general public because they will be unhappy living near a nuclear power station. That opposition, for whatever reasons, may make its mark through the opportunity given in the development control system for members of the public to make their views known.

In addition to their ability to mobilise opposition to what are seen as damaging developments, national groups can use their resources to press for legislation. This can be either legislation designed better to protect that group's particular interests, such as the Wildlife and Countryside Act 1981, or legislation simply

6 Lowe P and Goyder J *Environmental Groups in Politics* (1983). This work contains a study of a local amenity group, the Henley Society.

to aid the management of the group, such as improvements in the tax position of charities. In addition, national groups have the ability to attract the attention of the media to a particular cause and this may again make it easier to resist development. A study on environmental groups concluded:

> There are nearly a hundred national environmental groups and several thousand local ones. Some are quite old, dating from the 19th century, but many others have emerged during the past two decades. Their concerns range from global issues to do with the future of industrial society, the extinction of species and even human survival, down to local issues such as preserving neighbourhood amenities. These concerns have been taken into the political arena; since the 1960s, environmental groups have emerged as a significant force, enjoying contacts with local government, Parliament and the civil service, and using the media to mount campaigns. Not only have they influenced legislation and official policy, but they have also gained considerable public sympathy.[7]

What can be added to this is that their impact on land use, whether direct or indirect, is undeniable, since they represent not downright resistance to change, but the desire not to wantonly destroy the environment.

Other groups

The organisations considered in this section are bodies whose impact on the development control process is spasmodic, yet none the less significant for that. Such bodies are brought into being by central government in order to perform a specific task. In fulfilling their objective they can have an impact on the development control process in two ways. Organisations of this nature may either undertake development or else protect certain aspects of the environment from the encroachment of developers. In addition, central government funds may be allocated to these bodies, which they then distribute at their discretion. The organisations which could feature in this section are distinct from central government departments, local authorities, pressure groups and members of the public. Some specific examples have been selected, therefore, in the hope of illustrating the range of organisations which can sometimes be involved in the development control process.

7 Lowe and Goyder, p 1.

DEVELOPMENT CORPORATIONS

These are bodies created by legislation to direct development in certain parts of the country.[8] They take two forms – new town development corporations and urban development corporations. New town development corporations have now effectively been disbanded and their functions transferred to local authorities as their task of creating the new towns has been completed.[9] The task of the urban development corporations, that of regenerating existing urban areas, is, however, now reaching maturity. The Merseyside Development Corporation, for example, was created to promote development and regeneration in Merseyside's declining dock areas. Urban development corporations are directly financed by central government. They engage directly in development, either alone or in partnership with private developers. On Merseyside, part of Liverpool's historic south docks have been refurbished by the Merseyside Development Corporation, then developed by a private developer as shops, offices and private accommodation. The point to note about urban development corporations is that they possess all the planning powers which would, in normal circumstances, be exercised by the local planning authority. Prospective developers within their area will apply to the development corporation for planning permission and not to the relevant local planning authority.[10] The procedures used and the rights of appeal will be exactly the same as with a local planning authority.[11] Where the development corporation intends to undertake development, it will apply to itself for planning permission, taking care to consult with interested parties, including the neighbouring local authority, with regard to its proposals.[12] The body responsible for taking the decisions to grant or refuse planning permission is comprised of the non-elected members of the development corporation's board. The members of the

8 The New Towns Act 1946 authorised the setting up of new town development corporations in those areas selected for new town development. The Local Government, Planning and Land Act 1980, Pt XVI established urban development corporations.

9 New Towns and Urban Development Corporations Act 1985 – this legislation provides for the winding up of the new town programme.

10 1990 Act, s 7.

11 The only distinction is that there is no equivalent of the local planning authority's planning committee. The applications for planning permission are discussed by the officers and the members of the corporation. All other procedures involving publicity and consultation with the public and interested parties are the same.

12 Local Government, Planning and Land Act 1980, s 140.

corporation are appointed by central government. Therefore, the political pressures discernible in the case of local government are not apparent here.

STATUTORY UNDERTAKERS

Statutory undertakers are in a unique position as they are permitted to embark on certain forms of development without securing planning permission. They are not totally outside the scope of the development control system, however, unlike central government departments. Nor are they subject to the full rigours of the system as a private developer would be. Their special status is emphasised by the fact that the term statutory undertaker is specifically defined. According to the 1990 Act a statutory undertaker means:

> persons authorised by any enactment, to carry on any railway, light railway, tramway, road transport, water transport, canal, inland navigation, dock, harbour, pier or lighthouse undertaking, or any undertaking for the supply of hydraulic power and a relevant airport operator.[13]

The list used to be longer including, for example, electricity boards and water boards but since privatisation the list deals almost exclusively with transport related activities. Those public utilities that were formerly statutory undertakers by virtue of being public bodies supplying a public service, but have now been privatised, are accorded a hybrid status in the 1990 Act. For some planning purposes they are specifically accorded the title 'statutory undertaker'. For example, section 55 of the 1990 Act excludes from the definition of development work carried out by a statutory undertaker for the purposes of inspecting, repairing or renewing any sewers, mains pipes, cables or other apparatus. In this context privatised gas suppliers as well as the water companies are deemed to be statutory undertakers.

BODIES CHARGED WITH PROTECTING THE ENVIRONMENT

The organisations discussed to date represent peculiarities in the development control system, since development undertaken by them may not be subject to the usual planning procedures. In contrast, bodies, such as English Heritage or the Nature

13 1990 Act, s 262(1).

Conservancy Councils exist to protect a particular aspect of the environment. In the case of the Nature Conservancy Council for England it is areas of countryside which are of special interest. The Council has a range of powers including the designation of such areas and the power to protect them from adverse developments.[14] English Heritage, on the other hand, was constituted in order to manage sites of historic interest[15] such as Stonehenge, which were formerly the responsibility of the Department of the Environment.

Bodies of this kind need to be mentioned because they have an undoubted impact on development control. Their task is to keep a watching brief on certain important features of the environment and safeguard them from unsympathetic development. Described in this way, the task they perform may seem similar to that undertaken by a body such as the National Trust. There are distinctions, however, since the Nature Conservancy Council and bodies like it are quangos, that is quasi non-governmental organisations. They have a statutory status and their membership is appointed by government. In contrast, the National Trust draws its membership from the general public and its governing body is elected from that membership. The National Trust's major sources of revenue, therefore, are its membership subscriptions, entrance fees to its properties, bequests and investment income. Bodies such as English Heritage, however, receive funds from central government, some of which are available for distribution to voluntary organisations.

Whether the different constitutions of organisations such as English Heritage and the National Trust, lead to different attitudes on such matters as proposed development is a matter for speculation. What is important is that the reader is familiar with organisations of this nature, representing, as they do, a particular interest, whose views will have to be taken into account by potential developers as well as central and local government.

The courts

Until this point it might have appeared obvious what role the various individuals and organisations mentioned have to play

14 Environmental Protection Act 1990, ss 132, 133.
15 National Heritage Act 1983.

in the development control process. This may not be the case with the courts, yet for all that, their role is one worth mentioning. Briefly stated, it is the business of the courts to ensure that those most closely concerned with the development control process, that is the decision-makers, behave lawfully. By virtue of specific statutory provisions,[16] the courts have the power to decide whether the Secretary of State, a planning inspector or the local planning authority have exceeded the powers given to them by law or ignored a procedure set out in the relevant legislation. If, for example, a local planning authority fails to give the necessary publicity to its proposed development plan or refuses an individual planning permission, not on planning grounds, but because it disapproves of his political views, these will be grounds for applying to the courts to set aside the decisions in question. While, therefore, it is the business of the courts to make legal as opposed to planning judgments, there is no denying that such judgments can and do have an impact on the planning process.[17] Failure to comply with the relevant procedure to constitute a valid development plan can result in parts or indeed the whole of the development plan being rendered inoperative.[18] Refusal of planning permission on irrelevant grounds can force the local planning authority to consider the application afresh.

Consequently, the courts have a significant role to play and it will be dealt with in Chapter 10 in much greater detail, since it raises many important questions, including whether the courts can and do refrain from commenting on the planning merits of the issue before them. All that needs to be appreciated at present is the power of the courts to upset what appears to be a perfectly valid decision on the grounds that it has been improperly made.

Apart from this power to review decisions, the courts have another role to play. They are the body with responsibility for ensuring that the development control system is respected and observed by professionals and public alike. If, therefore, an individual demolishes a building designated to be of particular historic or architectural significance without consent,[19] or turns

16 1990 Act, ss 287 and 288.

17 That impact is usually not a direct impact but an indirect one, in the sense that the courts will indicate the parameters within which development control decisions are made.

18 1990 Act, s 287(2).

19 Consent known as listed building consent is needed by virtue of the Planning (Listed Buildings and Conservation Areas) Act 1990, ss 7, 8.

his land into a caravan site without planning permission, it is to the courts that the local planning authority charged with administering the planning system may ultimately look. Under various statutory provisions it is a criminal offence to flout the planning system, and the courts have the job of deciding whether an offence has been committed and what punishment to impose.[20]

The ombudsmen

The ombudsmen are another group of individuals whose role within the development control system is not immediately apparent. They act in a supervisory capacity, ensuring that satisfactory standards of administration are observed. In this respect, ombudsmen differ from the courts, since it is not their task to determine whether a particular action is lawful. There are two categories of ombudsmen. Local commissioners are ombudsmen responsible for ensuring good administration in local government.[1] The Parliamentary Commissioner for Administration oversees the administrative activity of central government.[2] If an ombudsman finds that either central or local government departments have been guilty of maladministration resulting in injustice, then he will seek a remedy for the individual affected. The term 'maladministration'[3] is an open-ended concept and covers such failings as delay, ineptitude and carelessness on the part of the administration. The significance of the ombudsman system for the development control process lies in the fact that both central and local government have a role to play in the administration of the planning system. If, therefore, they perform that role badly and, for example, fail to inform an individual of an application for planning permission which may affect him then the ombudsman may decide that this amounts to maladministration causing injustice to the indi-

20 It is an offence, for example, to fell a tree which is the object of a tree preservation order by virtue of the 1990 Act, s 210. Normally, however, a breach of the development control system does not automatically render the offender liable to prosecution.

1 The powers of the local commissioners are set out in the Local Government Act 1974, Pt III.

2 Parliamentary Commissioner Act 1967.

3 The term is not defined in either of the relevant Acts. The best description of what amounts to maladministration was given in a Parliamentary debate. It was said to consist of '...bias, neglect, arbitrariness and so on'.

vidual.[4] While the ombudsman has no power to set a decision aside as the courts can do, an ex gratia payment may be secured from the local authority to compensate for its carelessness.[5]

The ombudsman appears to have little direct impact on the development control system.[6] Yet, by ensuring that both central and local government observe high standards of administration, this has the indirect effect of ensuring that the planning system is administered as efficiently as possible. In addition, if something does go wrong, the ombudsman system may offer the opportunity of securing a remedy where none previously existed, since the shortcomings the ombudsman investigates are not normally of the sort which would attract a remedy from the courts.[7]

4 According to the relevant Acts, maladministration, if it has occurred, must have caused injustice. Sometimes, therefore, an ombudsman will feel that no remedy is necessary since no injustice has been caused.

5 Local authorities are empowered to make such payments by the Local Government Act 1978.

6 This may not always be so. See Hammersley R 'Plans, Policies and the Local Ombudsman: the *Chellaston* Case' Journal of Planning and Environment Law, 1987, p 101.

7 For an assessment of the overlap between the courts and the ombudsman, see Macpherson M 'Local Ombudsman or the Courts?' Journal of Planning and Environment Law, 1987, p 92.

Chapter 3

Planning permission – the application

The purpose of this chapter is to examine the notion of planning permission. Yet, before the chapter involves itself with the minutiae of the subject, it is as well to concentrate on two very basic questions – essentially, why and when does an individual have to apply for planning permission? If a start is made with the 'why', then it appears that the need to obtain planning permission rests on the notion of restricting what the individual may do with either land or buildings. The desirability of such controls is a comparatively recent phenomenon. In the past, few cities and towns have been planned. Instead, market forces and other forces of change have been allowed to take command, producing what has been termed the 'organic town'. Therefore, in the descriptions which exist of seventeenth and eighteenth century town life, a picture is presented of mixed uses, including residential and industrial uses, existing side by side or even within the same building. In addition, there were irregular narrow streets and no uniformity of building height or style, the crescents of Bath and squares of London being an exception rather than the rule. In short, the picture that emerges is of haphazard development which, rather than being planned, simply responded to the various forces at work within developing cities and towns.

When controls were finally introduced in the nineteenth century their primary aim was to improve public health rather than the built environment, and any effect that such legislation had on the environment was indirect. Gradually, however, theories began to emerge which canvassed the possibility of planning cities and towns in order to provide a better, as well as a more healthy, environment. As has been explained in chapter 1, the concept of the ideal or utopian town was developed, and a body of town planning theory and practice grew up from the turn of this century. This growth in town planning together with its related statutory developments has been extensively analysed in other works[1] and as it does not form the main theme of this work, that analysis need not be reiterated.

It is expedient, therefore, to move on to the Town and Country Planning Act 1947 in order to observe the concepts and practices of town planning being presented in a fully mature form for the first time. The legislation itself can be viewed as a socialist measure, in that its basic aim was to provide the greatest good for the greatest number of people. In future, communities would be planned with incompatible uses separated from one another, with a co-ordinated transport system designed to meet the needs of the inhabitants, and with the integrated provision of community facilities, such as schools and open spaces. Moreover, the period immediately after the 1939-45 war appeared an ideal time to contemplate such a venture, due to the pressing need to restore devastated city centres and provide homes fit for heroes. In order to achieve this ideal environment the 1947 Act and all subsequent Acts up to the present day, are based on a simple premise; in order to undertake development it is necessary to secure planning permission. As currently defined in section 55 of the Town and Country Planning Act 1990, development constitutes 'the carrying out of building, engineering, mining or other operations in, on, over or under land, or the making of any material change in the use of any buildings or other land'.

Having briefly dealt with why planning permission may be needed, it is now possible to consider when it is needed. Since the need to obtain planning permission depends on there being development, it is obviously important to understand exactly what is meant by the term. In order to do this there are a number of factors which have to be considered and any notion that there is a single easy answer should immediately be abandoned. Yet, this is not to suggest that the issue of whether or not a particular activity constitutes development is constantly open to debate. In most instances it is obvious right from the outset that the particular activity does or does not constitute development. For example, the intention to build a house, or a superstore, or an office block, or to mine for coal or gravel are obvious instances of the 'carrying out of building, engineering, mining or other operations in, on, over or under land'. Alternatively, a plan to turn a dwelling-house into a fish and chip shop, or a warehouse into a hotel would appear to qualify as a 'material change in the use of any buildings or other land'.

1 Cherry G E *The Evolution of British Town Planning* (1974); Cullingworth J B *Peacetime History of Environmental Planning* (1978-80); Ashworth W *The Genesis of Modern British Town Planning* (1954).

The statutory meaning of development

Apart from defining development as 'the carrying out of building, engineering, mining or other operations in, on, over or under land, or the making of any material change in the use of any buildings or other land', section 55 of the 1990 Act indicates various activities which are included and excluded from that general definition. In the first place it provides guidance on what constitutes either building or mining operations. Building operations are said to include the demolition of buildings as well as rebuilding, structural alterations and other operations normally performed by a builder.[2] Mining operations include specific activities such as the removal of material from a mineral working deposit or a deposit of iron, steel or other metallic slags thus clearly indicating that mining is taken to include activities above as well as below ground.[3]

As well as singling out these examples of operational development in order to stress that they do constitute development, the 1990 Act indicates that certain activities which might fall within the definition of development can go ahead without the need for planning permission. Briefly, the following activities fall into this category.

(a) Internal or external improvements or maintenance works none of which materially affects the external appearance of the building so treated.[4]

The purpose of this exception is to make clear that routine maintenance, such as painting and decorating or installing a new kitchen, will not require planning permission. Maintenance, however, means just that and cannot be of such proportions that it constitutes re-building. If, of course, the purpose of the alterations is to change the use of a building, then the answer is very different. In addition, there are certain buildings called listed buildings, or buildings within a conservation area, which may not be treated in this manner. Alteration to them may require special permission, not planning permission but listed building consent, before the alteration is undertaken.[5] Obviously, the question as to what materially

2 1990 Act, s 55(1A).
3 Ibid, s 55(4).
4 Ibid, s 55(2)(a).
5 Planning (Listed Buildings and Conservation Areas) Act 1990, ss 7, 8, 9 (listed buildings), ss 74, 75 (conservation areas). See chapter 5 for details. According to the decision in *Windsor and Maidenhead Royal Borough*

affects the external appearance of a building and, therefore, may require planning permission by virtue of falling within the definition of development, is open to argument. It could include the fitting of replacement windows or stone cladding, or even painting the building in a particular distinctive colour.[6] A final point to note about this first exception is its application to works for the alteration of a building by providing additional space in the building below ground level. This can constitute development though it may not alter the external appearance of a building.[7]

(b) Maintenance or improvement works carried out by a local highway authority to, and within the boundaries of, a road.[8]
(c) The breaking open of streets for the inspection, repair or renewal of sewers, mains, pipes, cables by a local authority or statutory undertaker.[9]

Exceptions (b) and (c) make it clear that maintenance work on the highway or a statutory service will not require planning permission. Exception (c) appears a sensible provision given that many holes in the road have to be dug in an emergency, and that their impact on the environment is limited, since they are only temporary. More contentious, perhaps, is the exception in relation to the local highway authority. In an environmentally sensitive area, a conservation area for example, the repairing of a York stone pavement with concrete flags may cause considerable resentment because of what is perceived as its adverse effect on the environment. Despite this, such actions would appear to fall under the heading of maintenance and not require planning permission.

(d) The use of any buildings or other land within the curtilage of a dwelling-house for any purpose incidental to the enjoyment of the dwelling-house as a dwelling-house.[10]

Exception (d) allows buildings and land to be used for purposes that are incidental to the use of a dwelling-house provided certain conditions are satisfied. In the first place the buildings and land in question must be within the curtilage

Council v Secretary of State for the Environment [1988] JPL 410 the repainting of a listed building can constitute such an alteration.

6 See, for example, *City of Bradford Metropolitan District Council v Secretary of State for the Environment* (1977) 35 P & CR 387.

7 1990 Act, s 55(2)(a).

8 Ibid, s 55(2)(b).

9 Ibid, s 55(2)(c).

10 Ibid, s 55(2)(d).

of the dwelling-house. The meaning of 'curtilage' has been analysed on various occasions.[11] It refers to an area of land that is closely associated with a dwelling-house. The simplest example would be the garden attached to a house. Problems can arise where a house is surrounded by a considerable area of land, some of which is formal garden and the remainder simply a grassed or overgrown area. It then becomes a matter of fact and degree what can be considered as within that property's curtilage.

Once it is established that land or buildings are within the curtilage, the second issue is whether they can be used for any activity. The answer would appear to be no. Whatever the activity it must not become the dominant purpose for which the property is used since the legislation refers to a use incidental to the enjoyment of the property as a dwelling. In addition, if the activity in question is commercial in nature, as opposed to a hobby or interest, it may well fall outside this exception. Indeed, even a hobby may be pursued to such lengths that the activity is no longer incidental to the enjoyment of a dwelling. In one particular case the keeping of forty-four dogs was said to be outside the scope of this exception, even though the activity was a hobby.[12] The inference that can be drawn from this decision is that this exception is subject to a test of reasonableness or normality based on the nature and size of the house. In other words an objective approach may well be taken regarding what is incidental to the enjoyment of a dwelling-house. For example, a person's wish to be buried in their back garden may not fall within this dispensation and therefore require planning permission.[13]

(e) The use of land for agriculture or forestry and the use for such purposes of any building occupied with land so used.[14]

Exception (e) appears to sanction the use of any land for agricultural purposes or forestry without the need for planning permission. At first sight this seems acceptable, since the

11 As for what constitutes the curtilage of a dwelling-house, see *Sinclair-Lockhart's Trustees v Central Land Board* (1950) 1 P & CR 195; *Dyer v Dorset County Council* [1989] QB 346; *A-G (ex rel Sutcliffe) v Calderdale Borough Council* (1982) 46 P & CR 399, CA; *James v Secretary of State for the Environment* [1991] JPL 550; *McAlpine v Secretary of State for the Environment* [1994] EGCS 189.

12 *Wallington v Secretary of State for Wales* [1991] JPL 942, CA.

13 Journal of Planning and Environment Law, 1994, p 397.

14 1990 Act, s 55(2)(e).

production of food and timber are admirable objectives. On further consideration, it would appear worthwhile to examine the impact each undertaking may have on the landscape. In order to make land viable for farming it may be necessary to drain marshlands, clear trees and remove hedges, all of which can have a considerable effect on the visual qualities of an area, besides destroying the habitat of animals and birds. The same is true of using land for forestry, particularly if the trees to be grown are all of one type which may not be a native species of the area. Indeed, the scope of this particular provision has been limited by other legislation, such as that concerned with tree preservation orders and sites of special scientific interest.[15] While this legislation does not reimpose the need to apply for planning permission, it does impose other duties on the owner.[16]

(f) In the case of buildings or other land used for a purpose of any class specified in an Order made by the Secretary of State, the use thereof for any purpose in the same class.[17]

Exception (f) is probably the most important exception of those listed. From time to time, and most recently in 1987, a revised Use Classes Order[18] is produced by the Secretary of State for the Environment. Briefly, since the Use Classes Order will be considered in greater detail at a later stage, the Order lists various classes of use, for example, Shops (Class A1), Business (Class B1) and Assembly and Leisure (Class D2). The idea is that if buildings or land are functioning within a particular class of use, then their use for some different purpose within the same class is not to be deemed as involving development, and planning permission will not be required. The logic behind this exception is, that if premises are being used as a shop, for example a newsagent's, then the individual should be free to change the shop to, say, a chemist's, without being put to the time and expense of applying for planning permission. In this way the planning system will not be clogged with unobjectionable proposals, while it is usually to the overall benefit of the economy that premises should be left vacant for as short a time as possible.

(g) The demolition of any description of building specified in a direction given by the Secretary of State.

15 Wildlife and Countryside Act 1981, s 28.
16 Ibid, ss 28-33.
17 1990 Act, s 55(2)(f).
18 SI 1987/764.

Previous planning legislation contained no unambiguous statement that demolition required planning permission. There were exceptions in the case of specially and specifically protected structures, for example, listed buildings. However, in an attempt to end legal debate on whether demolition constituted development, such as occurred in the *Cambridge* case,[19] section 55 of the 1990 Act was amended.[20] Demolition now specifically constitutes a 'building operation' and thus would normally require planing permission. However, under a direction[1] issued by the Secretary of State, the demolition of listed buildings, buildings in conservation areas, scheduled monuments, any building (other than a dwelling-house or building adjoining a dwelling-house), a building whose cubic content does not exceed 50 cubic metres, gates, fences and walls are excluded from constituting development. Additionally, the demolition of other specified buildings is allowed by Schedule 2 to the General Permitted Development Order.[2]

The logic of including demolition within the general definition of development and then specifically excluding most acts of demolition from the controls associated with development appears suspect. The justification is that the demolition of listed building, buildings in conservation areas and scheduled monuments is already controlled under separate legislation. Buildings of less than 50 cubic metres, gates, fences and walls are presumably of little consequence and so their demolition can be tolerated. On the other hand there might appear less justification in permitting the demolition of factories, shops and office blocks without some attempt at control. What seems to be at issue, therefore, is why demolition needs controlling in the first place. If there was no control whatsoever important buildings could be demolished and the character of an area could be transformed. Total regulation, on the other hand, could clog the development control machinery with applications for planning permission. Presumably the direction attempts to strike a balance, excluding activity that is already controlled by other legislation as well as any which can be safely allowed to continue without adverse consequences for the environment. Whether the balance is right remains an issue.

19 *Cambridge City Council v Secretary of State for the Environment* [1991] JPL 428: revsd [1992] JPL 644, CA.
20 Planning and Compensation Act 1991, s 13.
1 Town and Country Planning (Demolition–Description of Buildings) Direction 1995.
2 Town and Country Planning (General Permitted Development) Order 1995, SI 1995/418, Sch 2, Pt 31.

Besides listing those activities which do not constitute development, section 55 of the 1990 Act provides that the following activities do constitute development.

(i) The use of a single dwelling-house for the purpose of two or more separate dwellings.[3]

(ii) The deposit of refuse or waste materials on an existing dump if either (a) the superficial area of the dump is extended or (b) the height of the dump is extended and exceeds the level of the land adjoining the dump.[4]

(iii) The creation of any tank or cage in inland waters for the purpose of fish farming.[5]

(iv) The display of advertisements on the external part of a building not normally used for such a display.[6]

It is not to be imagined, however, that section 55 is the only section with guidance to give on what constitutes development. Many of the terms referred to in the course of that section are defined elsewhere in the 1990 Act, and most particularly in section 336, the interpretation section. Words such as 'agriculture', 'building', 'advertisement' and 'local highway authority' have particular meanings assigned to them. The interpretation section, in giving very precise definitions of certain terms, adds to the overall picture of what does or does not constitute development.

The term development is clearly a key concept so far as the 1990 Act is concerned, since the fact that an operation or change of use constitutes development makes it necessary to apply for planning permission. Equally obviously, the description of development given in the 1990 Act is a general description. It would be foolish to expect anything else, as a more precise definition would undoubtedly exclude activities which the legislators would wish to include. Yet the 1990 Act has itself gone some way to expanding that definition, by dealing with specific activities as well as defining, in their turn, some of the key terms. In addition, supplementary rules, called delegated legislation have been issued, whose purpose is to exclude additional activities from the definition of development where they would otherwise be included. The two main bodies of such rules

3 1990 Act, s 55(3)(a).
4 Ibid, s 55(3)(b).
5 Ibid, s 55(4A).
6 Ibid, s 55(5).

are known as the General Permitted Development Order[7] and the Use Classes Order.[8]

Yet, for all the guidance given in primary and delegated legislation, difficulties are bound to arise. An individual may, for example, contemplate using a half-acre of land he owns, and which is presently not used for any purpose but is simply waste land, as a place to breed Alsatian dogs. There may be outbuildings on the land where the dogs will be locked at night and where puppies can be kept. The question is, therefore, whether the landowner will need planning permission before he goes ahead with his scheme. In these circumstances the landowner may seek advice, either informally from the staff of the planning department, or from a private planning consultant. Alternatively, the machinery exists under section 192 of the 1990 Act for him to request a formal determination from the local planning authority that the activity contemplated would be lawful and not require planning permission. If this is the case he would be issued with a certificate stating the fact.[9] In giving advice, either on a formal or an informal basis, the local planning authority will take account of the general definition of development, as well as any exceptions to it. In the example given, it might be argued that there has been a change of use, but is the land, as a consequence, being used for agriculture? The extended definition of agriculture given in section 336 includes the keeping and breeding of livestock. The local planning authority is therefore left with the task of deciding whether dog breeding fits this description. If it does, then planning permission is not necessary. In reaching a decision the local planning authority may be aware of other instances where this or a similar problem has arisen and take account of them.

Eventually, the would-be dog-breeder will be given a decision indicating whether or not planning permission is required. What it is important to note about this decision is that it constitutes a piece of statutory interpretation on the part of the local planning authority. Its task is to take the general terms of the Act and decide whether they apply to the specific situation before it. The development control issue of whether or not it favours having a dog-breeder on that piece of land is irrelevant for these purposes, and only becomes relevant if and when an application for planning permission is made.

7 Town and Country Planning (General Permitted Development) Order 1995, SI 1995/418.

8 Town and Country Planning (Use Classes) Order 1987, SI 1987/764.

9 A certificate of lawfulness of proposed use or development.

Once the local planning authority has reached a conclusion it will be passed on to the person making the inquiry. If the local planning authority has been consulted on an informal basis, the individual concerned can choose to follow its advice or ignore it. If, however, the local planning authority does believe that the activity in question constitutes development, it may be tempted to take action against an individual who ignores its advice.[10] Where a local planning authority has been asked to give a formal ruling on the matter under the terms of section 192, then the situation is somewhat different. Its decision must be in the form prescribed and be given within eight weeks of being requested unless there is some agreement to the contrary.[11] If this decision is to the effect that the action contemplated would be lawful without the need for planning permission then a certificate to that effect is issued. Alternatively, the planning authority can refuse to issue such a certificate or fail to give a decision within the stipulated period. In these circumstances an applicant can appeal to the Secretary of State by virtue of section 195 of the 1990 Act. The decision of the Secretary of State can, in its turn, be subject to review by the courts under the terms of section 288 of the 1990 Act.

The introduction of the courts into the picture at this stage is timely, since statutory interpretation is looked upon as their particular task. Yet, strangely, the opportunities which the courts have for interpreting the terms of the 1990 Act are limited. Because going to law costs time and money and remedies are available only in certain situations, there may be a marked reluctance on the part of the individual to turn to the courts for relief. This is not to deny that there have been numerous occasions when the courts have interpreted a particular section of the 1990 Act. So far as the definition of development is concerned its application has frequently been considered by the courts, with the result that considerable attention is paid to these decisions in those texts which are devoted to an analysis of planning law.[12]

10 A local planning authority has various powers under Pt VII of the 1990 Act to enforce compliance with the requirements of planning control. These powers are discussed in chapter 9.

11 Town and Country Planning (General Development Procedure) Order 1995, SI 1995/419, art 24.

12 For example: Telling A E and Duxbury R M C *Planning Law and Procedure* (9th edn, 1993) ch 5.

Development as interpreted by the courts

As is pointed out in the majority of planning law texts, there are two aspects to the definition of development set out in section 55; the undertaking of an operation or the making of a material change of use. Reference is normally made to the comment of Lord Denning in *Parkes v Secretary of State for the Environment*[13] where he compared the two activities:

> the first half, 'operations', comprises activities which result in some physical alteration to the land, which has some degree of permanence to the land itself, whereas the second half, 'use', comprises activities which are done in, alongside or on the land but do not interfere with the actual physical characteristics of the land.[14]

This observation raises a number of questions. The first of these is whether the distinction matters in practice. In the case of an individual applying for planning permission it is unnecessary to specify whether the activity in question constitutes an operation or change of use. Instead, the emphasis focuses on full disclosure of what exactly that individual proposes to do. The local planning authority has the power to require further particulars in order that, when the development control decision is taken, it is an informed decision where everything possible has been taken into account.[15] It is also the case that many activities for which planning permission is sought will involve both a change of use and operations. A proposal to turn a warehouse into a superstore might involve building operations, such as the construction of a customer car park, as well as the change of use.

Where both aspects of the definition are involved it is conceivable that problems might arise. If the example just mentioned is considered, then it is possible that an application for planning permission might concentrate on the change of use from warehouse to superstore and not mention any related operations that would have to be undertaken. It is probable that such an oversight or omission would be revealed when the planning implications of the change of use were considered by the local planning authority. If this were not so, can it be assumed that planning permission for the change of use, by

13 [1979] 1 All ER 211.
14 Ibid, at 213.
15 Town and Country Planning (Applications) Regulations 1988, SI 1988/1812, reg 4.

implication, includes any related development? This point was considered by the courts in *Wivenhoe Port Ltd v Colchester Borough Council.*[16] Here, planning permission was granted for a change of use to warehousing in a manner described as a less than satisfactory example of clear and accurate draftsmanship. On the question of whether this permitted the construction of warehouses, the Court of Appeal held that it did not. Given the fact that the definition of development distinguishes between a use and an operation, and that the application for planning permission when considered by the court showed no evidence that permission to construct warehouses had been sought, the planning permission was no more than an agreement to allow land to be used for warehousing. If this decision does nothing more, it highlights the need for an applicant for planning permission to make clear what he wishes to do and for a local planning authority to be precise in what it is willing to permit.

OPERATIONS

Apart from acknowledging the distinction drawn in section 55 of the 1990 Act between operations and change of use, the courts have also concentrated on interpreting the essential qualities of each contrasting activity. In interpreting the term 'building operations', the approach of the courts appears to be to inquire whether the end product of the enterprise under scrutiny is a building. If it is, then, by implication, the activities involved will in the normal course of events, constitute building operations. There appears to be an inevitable logic to this, since the purpose of building operations would seem to be the production of buildings. As for the term 'building', that is defined in section 336 which states that it includes 'any structure or erection, and any part of a building, as so defined, but does not include plant or machinery comprised in a building'.

Using this framework, the courts have given further indications of what may be considered a building. Normally they have done this when asked whether a particular structure constitutes a building for the purposes of the planning legislation, and its erection, building operations. Bearing in mind that each case turns on its own particular facts, such cases can still prove important for the specific and general guidance which they provide. The factors which appear crucial in distinguishing

16 [1985] JPL 396. In contrast the granting of planning permission for building operations might, by implication, sanction a particular use of that building. See 1990 Act, s 75(3).

a building are size, permanence and physical attachment. The smaller an item is, and the fact that it is brought on site complete, the less likely it is to be considered a building. As most commentators point out, a model village was considered a building in *Buckingham County Council v Callingham*,[17] whereas in *James v Brecon County Council*[18] a set of fairground swingboats was not. A conclusive factor in the latter case was not so much their size, and their lack of resemblance to what may conventionally be thought of as a building, but their lack of permanence, since they could simply be carried away when the need arose. Lack of permanence also relates to the final characteristic of a building highlighted by the courts, namely physical attachment to the land. This may have influenced the court in the swingboats case, though it may not always be decisive, as shown by a contrasting pair of cases, *Cheshire County Council v Woodward*[19] and *Barvis Ltd v Secretary of State for the Environment.*[20] In the former, the installation of a wheeled coal hopper with a conveyor sixteen to twenty feet high did not constitute development, while in the latter case a tower crane eighty-nine feet high running on rails did constitute a building and hence development. The decisive issue is perhaps the overall impact of any installation, movable or otherwise, on the land.

While buildings and building operations have been the subject of considerable judicial comment, the same is not true of engineering operations. In section 336 of the 1990 Act, engineering operations are said to include 'the formation or laying out of means of access to highways'.[1] Means of access include 'any means of access, whether private or public, for vehicles or for foot passengers, and includes a street'. In normal usage the term engineering tends to be associated with the construction of roads, bridges, canals and railways, and this sort of activity is implied by the definition given in section 336. When the courts have had occasion to consider the term, the emphasis has been on the connection between engineers and engineering operations. That connection does not necessarily mean that engineering operations have to be supervised by a qualified

17 [1952] 2 QB 515, [1952] 1 All ER 1166, CA.
18 (1963) 15 P & CR 20.
19 [1962] 2 QB 126, [1962] 1 All ER 517.
20 (1971) 22 P & CR 710.
1 This should be considered in conjunction with the classes of permitted development sanctioned by the General Permitted Development Order 1995.

engineer according to plans drawn up by him. This point was made in *Fayrewood Fish Farms Ltd v Secretary of State for the Environment*[2] where engineering operations were said to be 'of the kind usually undertaken by engineers, ie, operations calling for the skill of an engineer'.[3] The court emphasised, however, that this 'did not mean that an engineer must actually be engaged on the project'.[4] Though the engineering operations being considered in this case were those mentioned in the then current General Development Order,[5] the likelihood is that the courts would take the same approach to the term when it is used in section 55. Besides the more obvious road and bridge building, engineering operations may therefore involve large-scale earth-moving and excavations, the latter possibly as part of a mining or building operation, but not automatically.

Mining operations are normally associated with the winning of minerals from the land though section 55(4) makes it plain that the extraction of minerals from waste tips, such as slag heaps, is also included. For development control purposes there is a contrast between mining operations and building and engineering operations. The latter take place over a specified period, which can be long or short depending on the complexity of the project involved. Although mining operations will also be concluded when supplies of the mineral in question have been exhausted, or can no longer be economically extracted, this can take decades if not hundreds of years. Consequently, the impact of mining operations on the environment is much more long-term. Added to this is the fact that building and engineering operations normally involve construction resulting in an end product capable of use. Whilst there is also an end product of mining, the nature of the extraction process is likely to produce little that is of positive benefit and a great deal that may be environmentally detrimental.

The final type of operation mentioned in section 55 is 'other operations'. What exactly is included in this expression was considered by the House of Lords in *Coleshill and District Investment Co Ltd v Minister of Housing and Local Government*.[6] When the courts are called upon to interpret an expression used in a statute, certain rules are said to exist

2 [1984] JPL 267.
3 Ibid, at 268.
4 Ibid.
5 Town and Country Planning General Development Order 1977, SI 1977/289, Sch 1, Class VI.
6 [1969] 2 All ER 525.

indicating how they should go about this task. One of these rules is termed the *eiusdem generis* rule. Essentially this means that where a series of specific terms are used – building, mining, engineering – followed by a general phrase – or other operations – then that general phrase should be interpreted in such a way that it reflects the specific activities. When this argument was put to the House of Lords in the *Coleshill* case it was rejected on the basis that it was impossible to discover a common denominator between the various activities. The expression 'other operations' could therefore be given an exceedingly wide meaning in order to bring the maximum number of activities under control, provided, that is, that they do not amount to permitted development. In practice,[7] this does not seem to have occurred, perhaps because the accompanying expressions are so broad that little which would seem to merit the attention of the development control process will not be covered by them.

MATERIAL CHANGE OF USE

Apart from operations, the other limb to the definition of development is a material change of use. Section 336 of the 1990 Act says of the term 'use' that 'in relation to land, it does not include the use of land for the carrying out of any building or other operations on it'. From this it can be deduced that a use of land involves activity on the land which is not of a type that would be covered by the operational limb of the definition of development. Section 55 makes it clear that in order to constitute development there must be not merely a change of use, but a material change of use. It does not take a great deal of insight to appreciate that the term 'material' is important and likely to give rise to difficulties. Consequently, it is hardly surprising that there has been a considerable amount of litigation regarding this particular aspect of the definition of development.

In order to determine whether or not a particular change of use can be said to be a material change of use, a comparison is required between the activities which are or were being carried out and any proposed or new use. In making this comparison the court in *London Residuary Body v Secretary of State for the*

7 Very few decisions, either planning appeal decisions, or judicial decisions refer to an activity as constituting 'or other operations'. On this point see [1983] JPL 618 (planning appeal decision) and *Bedfordshire County Council v Central Electricity Generating Board* [1985] JPL 43, CA.

Environment[8] indicated that certain factors were irrelevant except insofar as they were able to throw light on the character of the use. These were:

> (a) the identity of the occupier or person who carried on the activities; (b) the particular purpose why he carried on those activities; (c) the ownership of source of supply of any materials employed in those activities; (d) the destination elsewhere of the products of those activities; and (e) activities elsewhere even if related to activities on the land in question.[9]

Here the use of County Hall, the former headquarters of the Greater London Council, was said to be for the exercise of local government statutory functions rather than a general office use and hence any proposed future use as offices would require planning permission. The character of that use was identified by considering the physical construction of the building and the range of activities performed there, and perhaps indirectly its owner. This does not mean, however, that whenever property is used by a local authority, its use falls into this particular category.[10]

Once past and future use have been established it still remains to be seen whether the change is material. The fact that the two uses which are being compared can be described in the same general fashion, for example, residential, does not mean there is never a material change of use. In support of this, reference may be made to the Use Classes Order. The purpose of this Order is to establish certain classes of use and then state that, as a general rule, a change that remains within a class is permitted development, subject, of course, to any other legislative provisions. The use of the term 'permitted development' implies that a change of use within a general class, such as shops, can be a material change of use in certain circumstances. This approach has been judicially approved. In *Forest of Dean District Council v Secretary of State for the Environment*[11] for example, the court held that a change of use from a holiday caravan park to one where caravans were occupied as permanent residential accommodation could constitute a material change of use since there were planning consequences that resulted from the change.

If changes of this nature can constitute a material change of use it seems logical to suggest that a change from one use to

8 [1988] JPL 637.
9 Ibid, at 639.
10 *Inner London Education Authority v Secretary of State for the Environment* [1990] JPL 200, CA.
11 [1994] EGCS 138.

another completely different use within the Use Classes Order would be a material change of use. In many cases this may be so but it is not automatically so. In *Rann v Secretary of State for the Environment*[12] the court stressed that the purpose of the Order was to indicate what was permitted. It follows, therefore, that it should not be used as incontrovertible evidence that a material change of use has occurred.[13] Indeed, the Use Classes Order does not cover every conceivable use that may exist. Some uses are very specific and it will be hard to accommodate them in the Order. So it is important to consider the circumstances as they exist and then conclude whether there has been a material change of use.

In order, therefore, to be considered a material change of use, some important, as opposed to trivial, alteration in the use to which a building or land is put, must have occurred. A change in the ownership of the property is normally irrelevant provided the use remains constant. Whether a material change of use has occurred will be answered, in the first instance, by the local planning authority and, if there is an appeal, by an inspector or the Secretary of State for the Environment. Only in a minority of cases will the issue come before the courts, enabling them to give general advice on how the term 'material change of use' should be interpreted. Yet that advice can only be general since, as has been pointed out on numerous occasions,[14] whether there has been a material change of use is 'a question of fact and degree'.[15]

Until this point, the material changes of use under discussion have been those where a building or land ceases to be used for one purpose, and is put to some different use. Obviously this frequently occurs in practice, yet if this were all that was meant by a material change of use, then many activities with a considerable impact on the environment could take place without being subject to development control. The 1990 Act itself gives due consideration to this aspect in section 55. Here, the use of what was previously a single dwelling-house as two or more

12 (1979) 40 P & CR 113.

13 In *London Residuary Body v Secretary of State for the Environment* [1988] JPL 637 at 642, the court appeared to do just that.

14 In reality, in almost every one of the decisions mentioned in this section.

15 What is implied by this is that the courts acknowledge the right of the Secretary of State to make appropriate development control decisions on the facts as they appear to him. They will intervene only if there is no evidence, or his decision is totally outrageous or based on facts which are immaterial. The courts' tolerance is illustrated by a case such as *Bendles Motors v Bristol Corpn* [1963] 1 All ER 578.

separate dwelling units is specifically said to constitute a material change of use.[16] This would seem to be on the basis that, although the use remains residential, the character of that use has materially altered by virtue of its intensification.

At what stage the intensification of a use is so considerable as to amount to a material change of use, is a difficult issue. That it does occur is borne out by decisions in cases such as *Brooks and Burton Ltd v Secretary of State for the Environment*.[17] Here a shed was used for the manufacture of concrete blocks which were then dried in the open air. The site was acquired by a firm who increased the number of concrete blocks being manufactured by installing specialist machinery, 25 feet high, in the open air. The local planning authority issued an enforcement notice which was upheld on appeal. One of the Secretary of State's findings was that there had been an intensification of use resulting in a material change of use. The Court of Appeal said on this point:

> We have no doubt that intensification of use can be a material change of use. Whether it is or not depends on the degree of intensification. Matters of degree are for the Secretary of State to decide. He did so in this case. There was ample evidence to support his decision on this point.[18]

The steps taken to increase production in *Brooks and Burton Ltd* did bring about a material change of use. It cannot be assumed, however, that 'more of the same' will always amount to material change. This was the conclusion reached by the court in *Royal London Borough of Kensington and Chelsea v Secretary of State for the Environment*.[19] Here, the use of a garden adjoining a restaurant for dining was not an intensification of use. Of that expression the court said:

> In ordinary language, intensification meant more of the same thing or possibly a denser composition of the same thing. In planning language, intensification meant a change to something different. It was much too late no doubt to suggest that the word 'intensification' should be deleted from the language of planners, but it had to be used with very considerable circumspection, and it had to be clearly understood by all concerned that intensification which did not amount to a material change of use was merely intensification and not a breach of planning control.[20]

16 1990 Act, s 55(3)(a).
17 [1978] 1 All ER 733.
18 Ibid, at 744.
19 [1981] JPL 50.
20 Ibid, at 51.

There may be good reason for the court to criticise the use made of the expression intensification of use. In particular, it impedes an appreciation of those situations where changes in emphasis are occurring which could result in a material change of use.

This often occurs where premises or land may have primary, as well as ancillary, uses. Normally, such ancillary uses are tolerated, and need not be the subject of an application for planning permission as long as they are linked to the primary purpose.[1] Circumstances can occur, however, when an ancillary use grows to such a degree that it becomes the primary use. When this happens, what was previously tolerated as incidental may have assumed such importance as to constitute a material change of use. The owner of a smallholding may be able to sell crops that are surplus to his requirements at the farm gate or in a farm shop. Where, however, the smallholder begins to buy in produce from neighbouring smallholders and sells items, such as washing powder or tinned food, as well as fresh produce, it can be argued that a material change of use has occurred. In *Hilliard v Secretary of State for the Environment*,[2] produce was sold on a farm which had been grown there and elsewhere. A building was erected with planning permission supposedly for the storage of farm implements. In reality it was used to store fruit and vegetables which were then sold wholesale to hospitals and schools in the area. The local planning authority served an enforcement notice which was confirmed on appeal by the Secretary of State. This was on the basis that the sale of fruit and vegetables had so intensified as to represent a material change of use. The Court of Appeal rejected the Secretary of State's finding. In their judgment, since no evidence had been produced on the amount of fruit and vegetables bought in and distributed from the farm, there was no material on which this conclusion could be reached. The only evidence was that of a building not being put to the use intended. Arguably, here the expression intensification is misleading as it obscures the real issue – was this no longer a farm but a fruit and vegetable wholesale business?

In this discussion no mention has been made to date of the planning unit. According to one source:

1 See, for example, *Hussain v Secretary of State for the Environment* (1971) 23 P & CR 330.

2 (1978) 37 P & CR 129.

> The planning unit is a concept which has evolved as a means of determining the most appropriate physical area against which to assess the materiality of change, to ensure consistency in applying the formula of material change of use.[3]

In other words, when asking whether one primary use has succeeded another, or whether an ancillary use has become a primary use, the question must be answered, not in the abstract, but with full knowledge of the extent of the physical surroundings where the activities occur. In *Burdle v Secretary of State for the Environment*,[4] it was indicated that a useful working rule in determining what was the appropriate planning unit was to assume that it was the whole unit of occupation, unless some smaller unit could be recognised as the site of activities which amounted, in substance, to a separate use both physically and functionally. Therefore, in this case and in *Hilliard*'s case, considerable emphasis was placed on choosing the correct planning unit before concluding whether or not there was a material change of use.

When dealing with the question of material change of use, the first step is to isolate the unit of occupation, which will be a building or piece of land. It is usual, but not essential, for the planning unit to be owned or occupied by a single individual or organisation.[5] Once the unit has been identified, its primary and ancillary uses can be assessed and any subsequent changes in use, or between the balance of uses, can be monitored. It is however, a fundamental characteristic of a planning unit that it must have a primary use, which may or may not be combined with a number of appropriate ancillary uses. A planning unit can not have an ancillary use alone. In *Essex Water Co v Secretary of State for the Environment*[6] a discrete planning unit which was used for storage was treated as if that use was ancillary to activities outside the unit – namely, water treatment. It was held that this was a misapplication of the notion of a planning unit.

Clearly the larger the planning unit, then the more difficult it will be to show a material change of use. If planning permission is granted to use a warehouse for the sale of carpets to the public, for example, the primary use of the planning unit would appear to be a retail use. If, in the years to come, a portion

3 *Encyclopedia of Planning Law and Practice*, Vol 2, 55.23.

4 [1972] 3 All ER 240.

5 In *Rawlins v Secretary of State for the Environment* [1989] JPL 439 for example, the planning unit was made up of a series of plots owned by a number of individuals.

6 [1989] JPL 914.

of the warehouse becomes an office for handling customers' accounts, and another part, a staff rest room, it would seem difficult to argue that the primary use has changed, as these additional uses would appear to be ancillary uses related to the primary use of a large unit.

According to the judgment in *Burdle v Secretary of State for the Environment*, the way in which a unit of occupation can be regarded, not as a single planning unit, but as several planning units, is for there to be physical and functional separation. If, therefore, the carpet warehouse of the above example were partitioned, with two-thirds being used for retail purposes and the other third as a staff canteen and rest room, would there be a material change of use? In reality, each case will depend on its own particular facts, and especially, whether two separate planning units have been created.[7] In *Winton v Secretary of State for the Environment*,[8] a building used originally for the manufacture of concrete blocks was divided into two. It was agreed that this had the effect of creating two planning units, one used for metalworking and the other to convert motor cars to right-hand drive. The local planning authority served an enforcement notice which was confirmed on appeal by the Secretary of State. In this case the court held that a division of a building does not automatically constitute development. This occurs only if the division has planning consequences, amounting to a material change of use. That is a question of fact and degree for the Secretary of State and here he had held that it was a material change of use.

Interpretation of development in planning appeals

As the heading to this section indicates, the term development is interpreted not only in the courts, but also in the course of planning appeals. Local planning authorities, as a prelude to taking enforcement action or a related activity,[9] or to granting or refusing planning permission, may have to decide whether

7 Some light has been thrown on this issue by the Town and Country Planning (Use Classes) Order 1987, SI 1987/764, para 4; Circular 13/87, Changes of Use of Buildings and Other Land, para 9.

8 (1982) 46 P & CR 205.

9 Enforcement and its related activities are described in chapter 9. If an individual undertakes development without planning permission, the local

the activity in question constitutes development. The point may still be in contention on appeal to a Department of the Environment inspector whose decision will settle the matter.[10] These decisions are important, since they may be considered to represent the working definition of development as used by one of those parties who operate within the development control system on a daily basis. To appreciate the true content of that working definition would, however, require a great deal of research. In the case of a local planning authority, it would require the analysis of its planning decisions over the years in order to build up a picture of what, in its opinion, did or did not constitute development. Nor would an analysis of one local planning authority's working definition of development necessarily be the same as that of another local planning authority. A considerable degree of consistency could be expected but not complete uniformity.

The task of analysing the interpretation put on the term 'development' in planning appeals would be less onerous in certain respects. Written copies of inspectors' decisions are available from the Department of the Environment. In addition, selected decisions are published in specialist journals.[11] Should a situation arise where there is doubt over whether the activity in question constitutes development, such decisions may represent a source of guidance. If, for example, the owner of a public house decides to erect items in the garden adjoining the public house for children to play on, will this amount to development? Given that there is no direct judicial authority on the point, an inspector's decision on this very issue might appear relevant. Such a decision exists[12] and in it, the distinction was made between objects anchored to the ground, which did constitute development, and free-standing items which did not.

The question is, therefore, if this decision were drawn to the attention of another inspector or a local planning authority, what would be its standing? There is no rule that local planning authorities must follow such decisions, nor, indeed, need other

planning authority has the right to try to remedy that breach of the development control system by instigating a range of enforcement proceedings.

10 It is, of course, possible, as has already been made clear, that the issue will then be referred to the courts. Yet, the majority of disputes over the term 'development' will be settled by an inspector or the Secretary of State for the Environment.

11 Selected decisions are to be found in the Journal of Planning and Environment Law.

12 *Thanet District Council v Host Group Ltd* (1986) 1 PAD 364.

planning inspectors.[13] This, of course, gives scope for diverging practices among local planning authorities and inspectors, and, in the case of a planning appeal, the decision may consequently depend on the opinions of the inspector allocated to the case.

Whilst the judicial system itself can, on occasions, be equally prone to inconsistency, this is normally eliminated once the High Court is reached. In the same way, one might expect such inconsistency to be eliminated at the planning appeal stage. While in theory this could be achieved if every planning appeal decision were to be scrutinised by officials of the Department of the Environment, in reality, this does not occur. Apart from the more important planning appeals,[14] inspectors are authorised to take planning appeal decisions on the Secretary of State's behalf and without his having the opportunity to review them. Consequently, there can be inconsistency between planning inspectors. In a paper analysing the difficulties arising from the delegation of the Secretary of State's powers to the Planning Inspectorate, this problem was referred to, though there is little published research on the extent of the problem.[15]

As the purpose of this section is to consider the interpretation given to the term 'development' in planning appeals, what has been said may seem to suggest that the task is not worth pursuing. Indeed, in the majority of planning appeals the question of what constitutes development will not be an issue but attention will be focused on whether, on planning grounds, planning permission should be granted or refused. The decision by one planning inspector to allow a building society to open an office in one town's prime shopping location, will offer little guidance if the same situation were to arise in a town hundreds of miles away. On the other hand, a finding that a particular activity does amount to development, may fruitfully be followed if similar circumstances arise elsewhere.

Therefore, subject to these qualifications, it might be thought appropriate to summarise the findings of either inspectors or the Secretary of State on what, in their view, does or does not constitute development. Attempts have been made to do this in the past by analysing the views expressed, either in planning

13 There is likely to be a great deal more consistency on what does or does not amount to development than on pure development control issues, such as whether or not to grant planning permission.

14 These are likely to be determined by the Secretary of State for the Environment on appeal.

15 Sullivan J M 'The Implementation of Ministerial/Departmental Policy Objectives' Journal of Planning and Environment Law Occasional Papers *Contemporary Planning Policies*.

appeals, or in appeals against an enforcement notice.[16] Such decisions, whilst they lack the depth of analysis which is normally to be found in a judicial decision, are of interest, since they reflect how a key term, such as 'development', is interpreted in practice. That said, the effort required to undertake such an analysis is beyond the scope of this book. All that can be done is to highlight the significance of these decisions and provide a single example by way of illustration.

It will be recalled that what exactly constitutes a building has already been considered, together with the judicial opinion expressed on the matter. From this it emerged that a building was normally constructed on site rather than transported there ready-made. It had a degree of permanence, though the fact that the object in question was not attached to the site, and could be moved around, did not automatically mean that the item could not be considered a building. Over the years, therefore, the courts have declined to interfere with the Secretary of State's findings that, for example, the installation of a coal hopper and conveyor did not constitute development while the erection of a mobile tower crane did.[17]

By studying the planning decisions on this single point – what does or does not constitute a building for the purpose of the definition of development – the hope is to isolate those features which inspectors and the Secretary of State see as significant. This is allowing for the fact that a particular structure may not be considered a building and its introduction onto the land may not represent building operations, but that development will have taken place as a consequence of a material change of use. This was the situation in *Bendles Motors Ltd v Bristol Corpn*[18] where the court declined to interfere with the Minister's finding that the installation on a garage forecourt of a free-standing egg-vending machine was a material change of use, since it introduced a shop use where planning permission existed for a garage and petrol filling station.

From a review of reported planning and enforcement appeals, it appears that the ministerial approach to what constitutes a building is substantially the same as that of the courts. On

16 Brown H J 'Operations within the Definition of Development' Journal of Planning and Environment Law, 1973, p 642; 'Material Change of Use within the Definition of Development' Journal of Planning and Environment Law, 1974, p 180.

17 *Cheshire County Council v Woodward* [1962] 2 QB 126, [1962] 1 All ER 517; *Barvis Ltd v Secretary of State for the Environment* (1971) 22 P & CR 710.

18 [1963] 1 All ER 578.

various occasions, the introduction of the following items onto land has been held to amount to building operations. Those items are a slide, portable cabins, polythene tunnels used for growing plants, an incinerator used for disposing of the remains of dead pet animals, a model railway track built outdoors and a hut erected on scaffolding. By way of contrast, neither a lorry body used as a workshop, a playhouse in the shape of a boot, metal pegs interlaced with two strands of nylon rope nor an inflatable whale constituted buildings, nor did their installation constitute a building operation. The reasoning underlying such findings seems to be based on the following principles. An item fixed to the land is likely to be considered a building and covered by the definition of building given in section 336 of the 1990 Act. Therefore, it was said of a slide erected on Felixstowe Pier '...it took ten days to erect and would take three days to dismantle and is secured to the pier decking by sixty-four bolts'.[19]

In a separate instance,[20] involving an appeal against an enforcement notice, the owners of a hotel had installed play equipment in a pub garden. Whilst it was conceded that a slide, climbing frame and swings, which were set in concrete, required planning permission, the same was not true of a plastic playhouse in the shape of a boot. The latter was distinguished on the basis that it was secured to the ground by four metal pegs and could be removed by one man in a matter of minutes. Therefore, in the opinion of the inspector '...the installation of the boot did not itself constitute operational development requiring planning permission'.[1]

The fact that an item is not securely fixed to the land and can be moved is not, however, decisive. An incinerator, installed in the garden of a veterinary surgery, measured 4 feet by 2 feet by 4 feet high and was made from sheet metal. It stood on four legs on concrete, and was connected to some nearby gas cylinders. In an appeal against an enforcement notice,[2] it was argued that the incinerator was portable and, therefore, planning permission was not required. In rejecting this argument, the point was made that:

> the fact that a structure is physically capable of being moved and is not affixed to the ground does not of itself determine whether development is involved: account must be taken of the degree of permanency of the structure on the land which is affected by that

19 [1979] JPL 547 at 548.
20 (1986) 1 PAD 364.
1 Ibid, at 366, 5.1.
2 [1978] JPL 487.

structure and indeed of all the circumstances concerning the matter.[3]

On this basis the incinerator was found to constitute a building as defined in the Act, since it had not been moved from the time when it had been constructed, nor was there any indication that it would be moved in the future. In addition, the incinerator was not thought to be easily portable and would have to be dismantled before it could be moved.

The same reasoning was adopted in relation to a portakabin being used as an office. In what was a complex appeal against an enforcement notice,[4] the inspector concluded that, since the portakabin was not fixed to its concrete base, its installation was not a building operation. In commenting on the inspector's conclusion, the Secretary of State felt that the fact that the structure was not fixed to the ground was not decisive. It was important that the portable office had not been moved in the past nor were there plans to move it. Indeed, since telephone wires and electricity cables were attached to the portakabin, moving it was no easy task. The Secretary of State concluded, therefore, that the installation of the portakabin was a building operation, which required planning permission.

Apart from the issue of ease of movement, it might be thought that size is a factor in determining whether an item constitutes a building. The items considered so far have been substantial objects. The same description does not appear true of polythene tunnels or ropes and metal pegs. In the case of the tunnels[5] they were 20 feet by 40 feet and consisted of polythene sheeting over metal hoops. In finding that the siting of such tunnels on land constituted building operations, the Secretary of State drew attention to their substantial size and the manner of fixing them to the ground. Although it was conceded that they could be moved, it was felt that a considerable amount of work would be involved in their repositioning. In contrast, the marking out of plots with metal pegs and nylon rope did not amount to development.[6] It was stated that 'the works involved in driving into the ground these twelve small pegs...and the stringing between them of two strands of thin nylon rope'[7] did not constitute a building within the terms of the Act nor an operation of the type

3 Ibid, at p 488.

4 [1978] JPL 571. See also [1994] JPL 474 where a hut containing office equipment and standing on scaffolding in the garden of a house required planning permission.

5 1986, 1 PAD 237.

6 [1977] JPL 122.

7 Ibid, at 123.

amounting to development. They were so insubstantial that they could be disregarded.

In view of the decisions just mentioned, there might appear to be a correlation between size and what may or may not constitute a building. It would seem, however, that matters are more complex than this. Reference has already been made to the playhouse in the shape of a boot. On another occasion,[8] a lorry body used as a garden shed was described as 'a chattel and not a structure' though no further explanation was given for this description. Perhaps the most vivid illustration that size is not the only consideration involved an inflatable whale.[9] The whale was 80 feet long, 15 feet wide and 15 feet high. It was stationed on Felixstowe Pier where it was secured by ropes. When inflated, on most days from April to October, it served as a children's playroom. Deflated, it was stored on the pier. The question which had to be resolved in this case was whether the inflatable whale could be considered a building within the terms of the section 336 definition. The conclusion reached on this point was that it could not. The following extract from the inspector's report shows how this conclusion was reached.

> By virtue of section 290 of the 1971 Act,[10] 'building' is defined as including 'any structure or erection'. The fact that a structure may be physically capable of being moved or is not permanently fixed to the ground does not of itself determine whether its installation involves the carrying out of operations constituting a development for the purposes of the Planning Acts. However, in this particular case, the whale is only inflated for relatively short periods for use as a type of enclosed trampoline for children and the view is taken that, when inflated, it is more in the nature of a piece of equipment.[11]

From the series of decisions discussed in the preceding paragraphs, certain generalisations are possible about the nature of a building for the purposes of development control. The list of decisions is by no means comprehensive, yet certain points are constantly stressed. These include whether or not the item in question is fixed to the ground. If it is not, this is not conclusive, since questions will then be raised concerning the ease with which the item can, and indeed has in the past, been moved. Size appears immaterial except where the item in question is so small that it can safely be ignored. A combination,

8 [1982] JPL 202.
9 [1979] JPL 547.
10 Now 1990 Act, s 336.
11 [1979] JPL 547 at 548.

therefore, of considerable size with ease of removal, may convince an inspector that the item in question is outside the scope of the definition of development. The inflatable whale is a case in point. In this context, the purpose for which an item is used and the duration of its impact on the neighbourhood may be important factors. In contrast, a marquee with a floor area of 1,000 square feet which was erected in the grounds of an inn and used for functions was said to require planning permission.[12]

Circulars and PPGs: their interpretation of development

The significance of circulars and planning policy guidance notes (PPG) in the planning process has already been men-tioned in an earlier chapter. The intention here is merely to consider what guidance is given in these documents on the question of planning permission in general, and development in particular. What has constantly to be borne in mind is that once it has been established that development is involved, a whole new set of considerations then arise on the issue of whether or not to grant planning permission. These development control considerations, which form the core of this work, have yet to be discussed. Circulars and PPGs, however, as opposed to judicial decisions, have a great deal to say on development control. This is in the nature of these documents, since they are essentially vehicles for the dissemination of central government policy. Judicial decisions, on the other hand, can only ever be indirectly concerned with planning policy, in theory at least. The court's task is to interpret legislation and decide whether the powers and procedures laid out in the legislation have been observed.

Given this analysis of the situation, it might be expected that circulars and PPGs would have little to say on the appropriate definition of development, since this is not their task, nor would any opinion expressed on this matter appear to carry much authority. In the case of circulars, however, many do refer to current legislation and are intended to focus on legislative and procedural matters. Their purpose is normally to alert those who might have an interest in planning legislation to its existence and what it seeks to achieve. In Circular 26/92, Planning

12 [1993] JPL 391.

Controls over Demolition, for example, reference is frequently made to the term 'development' and the meaning to be attached to it. This is because the main object of the Circular is to make it plain that demolition in certain circumstances now constitutes dev-elopment and thus may require planning permission. In contrast PPGs are seen principally as a source of guidance on planning policy. Little reference is made to legislation and the interpretation of development. More typically, as in the case of PPG 20, Coastal Planning, advice is offered concerning planning policies for coastal areas, whilst specific activities requiring a coastal location, such as ports, are considered.

What needs to be borne in mind, however, is that despite the interpretation of development that may be specifically or incidently offered by any circular or PPG, such interpretation is irrelevant, if the words of the relevant Act cannot bear that particular meaning.[13] The court's analysis of legislation is the only authoritative interpretation, and whatever a circular or PPG says must be read with this fact in mind. In the majority of cases these documents will be accurate in their assessment of legislation, but the possibility remains that they can be the source of disinformation.

Bearing this in mind, it appears that what reference there is, more especially in circulars, to the term 'development', is concerned, for the most part, with reiterating what is said in relevant legislation. There is little, if any, attempt in either circulars or PPGs to amplify the terms used in the legislation. There may be various explanations for this. They include the fact that the language used in the 1990 Act is deliberately left open-ended, so that as and when cases arise, decisions can be made as to whether or not development is involved. The whole object of this would be defeated if circulars and PPGs were to try to anticipate such decisions. In addition, on those very rare occasions when these documents have attempted to do just this, the advice they contained has not always met with the approval of the court.[14] The contribution, therefore, that these documents make to the analysis of the term development is exceedingly limited. The reason for this is rooted in the nature of circulars and PPGs and the role which they play in the development control process.

13 Circulars and PPGs are not binding in the sense that primary and delegated legislation are binding. They merely offer advice.

14 *Coleshill and District Investment Co Ltd v Minister of Housing and Local Government* [1969] 2 All ER 525, HL.

General Permitted Development Order and Use Classes Order

Although this chapter is entitled 'Planning permission', so far it has mainly been devoted to analysing the notion of development. This is unavoidable, however, as the concepts of development and planning permission are inextricably linked. As can now be appreciated, the concepts of 'building, engineering, mining or other operations' and 'material change of use', which are the cornerstones of the definition of development, cover a whole range of activity from the comparatively trivial domestic development to major undertakings, such as the redevelopment of city centres.

This fact that certain types of development will have the minimum of impact on the environment has led to the creation of the General Permitted Development Order and the Use Classes Order, both of which have already been referred to in passing. These Orders work on the basis that certain developments may be permitted without the need to obtain planning permission beforehand. In this fashion, the administrative machinery of the development control process does not become overloaded with what are relatively trivial matters. Instead, time can be devoted by officials to those developments which will have a substantial impact on the environment and the community at large.

If the logic of this concept is sound, therefore, those categories of development permitted without the need to secure planning permission should be selected using planning policy criteria. The aim should be to ensure that the activities specified in either the General Permitted Development Order, or the Use Classes Order, will be those which have the minimum impact on the environment in terms of traffic generated, noise produced or buildings erected. It is equally logical that there may be areas, perhaps of outstanding natural beauty or architectural interest, where even the smallest amount of development may have a disproportionate impact. It may be necessary, therefore, to exclude such areas from the scope of the General Permitted Development Order or Use Classes Order.

In the analysis of the General Permitted Development Order which follows, these opening remarks should be borne in mind in order to detect whether there is such a logic underlying the terms of the Order. The impact of the permitted development on the environment should be assessed in the hope of determining whether the General Permitted Development Order successfully balances administrative convenience with a proper regard for the environment, and the normal issues of development control.

GENERAL PERMITTED DEVELOPMENT ORDER

The General Permitted Development Order 1995 provides that:

> 3 (1) Subject to the provisions of this Order ..., planning permission is hereby granted for the classes of development described as permitted development in Schedule 2.
>
> (2) Any permission granted by paragraph (1) is subject to any relevant exception, limitation or condition specified in Schedule 2.

From this it is clear that there is a very specific purpose to the Order which is to indicate a list of permitted developments and to detail the particular restrictions on these forms of development activity. Schedule 2 to the General Permitted Development Order, which sets out what amounts to permitted development, is arranged in a particular fashion. It consists of thirty-three parts each of which describes a general form of development. Each part is then subdivided into classes of permitted develop-ment. For example, Part 1, Development within the curtilage of a dwelling-house, is divided into eight classes which are lettered A to H. On the other hand Part 14, Development by Drainage Bodies, consists of a single class A. Each class, besides describing permitted development and any conditions asso-ciated with its execution, may also indicate development which is not permitted within that class as well as an interpretation of the class. Key terms used in Schedule 2 are in many instances defined in Article 1(2) of the Order. What follows, therefore, is a summary of Schedule 2 to the Order which is intended to provide a general picture of what it includes and excludes.

Part 1 Development within the curtilage of a dwelling-house This permits quite considerable 'improvements' to be made to a dwelling-house or to land associated with that property.[15] A house may be extended provided certain restrictions relating to cubic content, ground area, height, distance from the highway or property boundary are not exceeded. Also authorised are the erection of a porch, the provision of buildings, including a swimming pool, for purposes incidental to the enjoyment of the

15 For a definition of the term 'curtilage' see n11, p 76 supra.

house, and the installation of satellite receiver dishes and oil tanks. This work is also subject to restrictions on matters such as the size of the satellite dish.

Part 2 Minor operations Certain minor operations can be undertaken. These include the construction of fences, walls, access to certain highways and the exterior painting of buildings. Restrictions are imposed on matters such as the height of any wall or fence.

Part 3 Changes of use Obviously this has to be read in conjunction with the Use Classes Order. According to the terms of the Use Classes Order a change of use within a class – for example from an insurance office to a solicitors' office – is not deemed to involve development. The change permitted in Part 3 of the General Permitted Development Order is from one class of use to another entirely separate class which might, in normal circumstances, amount to development. The criterion used is that the permitted change is to a use that is likely to be less environmentally damaging, thus creating fewer development control problems. For example, premises being used for the sale of food and drink (Class A3) or for the sale or display of motor vehicles can be used as shops (Class A1). Other changes from general industrial (Class B2) to storage and distribution (Class B8) are permitted subject to restrictions on floor area.

Part 4 Temporary buildings and uses This permits temporary buildings to be erected in order to facilitate the performance of building or engineering operations for which planning permission has been granted. Mining operations are specifically excluded. Once the operation has come to an end, the buildings must be removed. In addition, land, excluding buildings and the land within the curtilage of a building, can be put to a particular use without planning permission for not more than 28 days of a calendar year, subject to various restrictions.

Part 5 Caravan sites The control of caravan sites is complex and is considered in more detail in Chapter 5. Part 5 allows the stationing of caravans on land in circumstances where a caravan site licence is not required. For example, where caravans are used to house agricultural or forestry workers or those employed on building and engineering sites. Where a caravan site is licensed Part 5 permits development required under the terms of the site licence.

Part 6 Agricultural buildings and operations This permits building and engineering operations to be carried out on agricultural land with an area of five or more hectares. Where less than five hectares of land is involved a more restricted range of activities is permitted. In both instances there are restrictions, different in each case, on the height, size and siting of buildings. The operations in question must be related to the agricultural purposes to which the land is put. The extraction of minerals is also permitted, provided they are to be used for agricultural purposes on the property from which they were extracted. The permitted development authorised by Part 6 does not include the construction of dwelling-houses. It may also be necessary in certain circumstances to notify the local planning authority of the proposed development.

Part 7 Forestry buildings and operations Where land is being used for the purposes of forestry, building and other operations are permitted, provided they are relevant to the forestry industry. The erection of buildings, not including dwelling-houses, is subject to compliance with various conditions including notifying the local planning authority of the proposed work.

Part 8 Industrial and warehouse development A broad range of development is permitted in relation to industrial buildings or warehouses, industrial land or industrial processes – terms which are defined in Part 8. Subject to various restrictions, a warehouse or industrial building may be extended or altered, items such as machinery may be installed on industrial land and waste from an industrial process may be deposited. Restrictions include limits on the height of machinery, the increase in floor space and provisions designed to ensure that the external appearance of buildings is not materially altered.

Part 9 Repairs to unadopted streets and private ways Repairs of this nature can be undertaken provided the works are carried out on land within the boundaries of the street or way.

Part 10 Repairs to services This permits the inspection and repair of services such as sewers and electricity cables by others apart from local authorities and statutory undertakers who have statutory authority to undertake such work.[16]

16 1990 Act, s 55(2)(c).

Part 11 Development under local or private Acts or Orders Development authorised in this fashion is permitted provided, if it includes the construction of certain items such as a building or means of access to the highway, the approval of the appropriate authority is obtained. This can be refused only in certain specified circumstances.

Part 12 Development by local authorities This permits local authorities and urban development corporations to provide items such as bus shelters and refuse bins, as well as allowing them to undertake small-scale construction operations on their property for purposes related to those for which the property is used. In addition, it allows waste to be deposited on an approved site.

Part 13 Development by local highway authorities Works can be undertaken to improve or maintain the highway on land which borders the highway.

Part 14 Development by drainage bodies Works can be undertaken by drainage bodies to improve or maintain water courses or drainage works.

Part 15 Development by the National Rivers Authority The National Rivers Authority can, without planning permission, undertake such works as the laying of pipes or the improvement of drainage systems and water courses. Buildings can be constructed and equipment installed in order to facilitate the conduct of surveys, provided that the land is restored to its original use and appearance at the end of six months. Subject to various restrictions, buildings can also be extended or altered provided they are on land used by the National Rivers Authority for the performance of its functions.

Part 16 Development by or on behalf of sewerage undertakers This allows sewerage undertakers, which are the privatised water companies or those acting on their behalf, to undertake a range of works. These include work to maintain, improve and construct sewers, to erect temporary buildings for the conduct of surveys and to alter or extend buildings on land used to discharge their specific functions.

Part 17 Development by statutory undertakers Part 17 deals with a variety of statutory undertakers and the permitted development that each is allowed to undertake. For example, public gas suppliers can lay pipes underground and build structures for protecting gas supply equipment. The Post Office can install post boxes or self-service machines. There are various restrictions on these rights, including in some instances the proviso that they can be exercised only in relation to operational land, that is land used, or in which an interest is held, by the undertaker for the purpose of the undertaking. When undertaking development authorised by Part 17, statutory undertakers are advised in Circular 15/92[17] to 'inform both local planning authorities and the public of developments likely to have a significant effect on amenity and environment well in advance of work starting'.

Part 18 Aviation development This allows an airport operator to erect or alter within specified limits buildings or equipment in and around an airport provided these activities are related to its operation. It also permits the Civil Aviation Authority to undertake development that is connected with the provision of air traffic control services. Not all airports and airport operators are covered by Part 18 as its provisions relate to those included in the Airports Act 1986.[18]

Part 19 Development ancillary to mining operations The type of development which can be undertaken is related to the erection, extension or installation of buildings, plant or machinery on land used as a mine or, in certain circumstances, adjacent land. Some of the works will require the prior approval of the mineral planning authority as distinct from planning permission.

Part 20 Coal mining development The Coal Authority and its licences are permitted to carry out a range of activities subject to various restrictions. These activities specifically include mining as well as the erection of operational buildings in the vicinity of the pit-head. The approval of the mineral planning authority is required for certain operations.

Part 21 Waste tipping at a mine This enables mining waste to be deposited at the site of the mine from which it was extracted. An exception is made in the case of tips which existed on 1 July 1948 and were used for waste not generated on the site.

17 Circular 15/92, Publicity for Planning Applications, para 33.
18 Airports Act 1986, Pt V and s 57.

Part 22 Mineral exploration This enables the operations associated with such exploration to be undertaken for specified temporary periods but specifically excludes petroleum exploration. Many restrictions are imposed to protect the environment. Trees cannot normally be felled and at the end of the period allotted for exploration all buildings and equipment must be removed and the land restored.

Part 23 Removal of material from mineral-working deposits Part 23 reflects the fact that extraction of minerals from a deposit on the land, for example, a slag heap, is specifically said to constitute development. As a consequence, certain activities of this nature can go ahead without planning permission provided various conditions and restrictions are observed. These include the need to notify the relevant mineral planning authority.

Part 24 Development by telecommunications code system operators Subject to restrictions regarding size, authorisation is given for the installation of communications equipment an individual will need in order to function as a telecommunications code system operator on land controlled by the operator or in accordance with the terms of the operational licence. Such operators must be licensed under the Telecommunications Act 1984.

Part 25 Other telecommunications development Installation of microwave and satellite antennae on buildings, other than dwelling-houses[19] is authorised where such permission is not available under Part 24. There are restrictions on the size of antennas and efforts are made to minimise their effect on the appearance of buildings. Part 25 is not restricted to telecommunications code systems operators.

Part 26 Development by the Historic Buildings and Monuments Commission for England Development, including maintenance or restoration but not extension, can be undertaken to preserve buildings or monuments in the care of the Commission.

Part 27 Use by members of certain recreational organisations This permits the use of land (excluding buildings)

19 See Part 1 of the Order for provisions dealing with satellite antennae and dwelling-houses.

provided it is not within the curtilage of a dwelling-house, for recreational or instructional purposes and includes permission for the erection of tents. The users must belong to an organisation with a certificate of exemption, such as the Girl Guides or the Scouts.[20]

Part 28 Development at amusement parks Where land or a seaside pier is used as an amusement park, certain operations can be undertaken. These include the erection of booths or stalls, which are to be used to provide amusement or entertainment for the public, as well as the extension, alteration or replacement of those stalls. Restrictions are imposed on size.

Part 29 Driver Information Systems This allows equipment for the purpose of driver communications, as in the case of taxis, to be set up, subject to restrictions on size and location.

Part 30 Toll Road Facilities This allows the setting up and maintenance of facilities for the collection of tolls in relation to toll roads.

Part 31 Demolition of Buildings Part 31 allows demolition to be undertaken without planning permission except in the circumstances specified, for example, where a building has been deliberately rendered unsafe. The development permitted relates only to the demolition of those buildings that are not specifically excluded by Ministerial direction[1] from the scope of planning control over demolition.

Part 32 Schools, colleges, universities and hospitals Part 32 enables the institutions mentioned to erect new buildings on their existing sites for purposes related to their current activity. Restrictions are imposed on the size, appearance and position of such new buildings.

Part 33 Closed circuit television cameras This permits the installation of such equipment on a building for the purposes of security. Conditions are imposed regarding the size and positioning of such equipment.

20 That certificate must be granted under the terms of the Public Health Act 1936, s 269.

1 Town and Country Planning (Demolition–Description of Buildings) Direction 1995.

From this brief survey of Schedule 2 to the General Permitted Development Order a picture has now emerged of what constitutes permitted development. Before that picture is complete, however, mention has to be made of certain restrictions set out in the body of the Order. Although a detailed analysis of such restrictions is beyond the scope of this book, an attempt will be made to give an impression of what these restrictions involve. One of the most important allows a local planning authority, sometimes in its own right, or with the approval of the Secretary of State, or the Secretary of State himself,[2] to direct that either all permitted development, or alternatively certain classes of permitted development, cannot take place in a designated area. Instead, planning permission must be obtained in the normal fashion. In certain specific circumstances,[3] the local planning authority may make a direction without the need for the Secretary of State's approval. Alternatively, it can make a direction that becomes operative immediately, but which will expire at the end of six months unless it has been confirmed by the Secretary of State.

Powers to prevent the undertaking of permitted development are also vested in mineral planning authorities.[4] Here, the powers are a great deal more restricted, since they relate only to two very specific forms of permitted development. These are Part 22, Class B – operations and excavations in order to ascertain the presence of minerals– and Part 23, Class B - the removal of materials from a stockpile or mineral-working deposit. A mineral planning authority[5] may make use of this power to require an application for planning permission to be made in the ordinary way, only if what would have been permitted development is seen to pose a threat. That threat must, according to the terms of the General Permitted Development Order, take certain stated forms. The land on which the development is to be carried out must be within a National Park, an area of outstanding natural beauty, a site of archaeological interest or a site of special scientific interest. Alternatively, the development must be seen as posing a serious detriment to the amenity of the area in which it is to be carried out, or to the setting of a Grade 1 listed building, or to the inhabitants of nearby residential buildings, or would endanger aircraft using

2 Town and Country Planning (General Permitted Development) Order 1995, SI 1995/418, arts 4 and 5.
3 Ibid, art 5(3).
4 Ibid, art 7.
5 For a definition of a mineral planning authority, see the 1990 Act, s 1(4).

a nearby aerodrome.[6] Any direction made by a mineral planning authority in pursuance of these powers can be disallowed by the Secretary of State within 28 days.[7]

From the description given of the General Permitted Development Order, together with the restrictions on its operation, certain comments may legitimately be made regarding its effectiveness. It was suggested that the premise behind the General Permitted Development Order was that some activities, whilst undoubtedly constituting development, will have such a limited impact on the environment that they can safely be permitted without the need to apply for planning permission. That this is indeed the logic underpinning the General Permitted Development Order is emphasised by the nature of the restrictions on its operation. As has been demonstrated, where a mineral planning authority issues a direction restricting permitted development it will be because of the sensitive nature of the environment. Local planning authorities have even wider powers to restrict permitted development, and it might be expected that they too will use those powers to protect environmentally sensitive areas. Indeed, even the classes of permitted development take account of discrete environmental areas, such as National Parks and conservation areas, by restricting even more severely in these areas what can be regarded as an acceptable level of permitted development.[8]

On the other hand, if it is true to say that there are areas of such outstanding natural beauty or historical interest in which either all development must be specifically authorised or, at the very least, lower levels of permitted development can be tolerated, it appears to call into question the accuracy of the premise that permitted development can be allowed because it has little impact on the environment. Undoubtedly, it can have a very considerable impact. In some situations that impact may be aesthetic. The proliferation of porches, house extensions, satellite receiving dishes and fences may do little in the opinion of some to improve the visual amenity of a particular area. Visual amenity is therefore sacrificed in order to allow the individual the fullest possible enjoyment of his property. Consequently,

6 Town and Country Planning (General Permitted Development) Order 1995, SI 1995/418, art 7(2).
7 Ibid, art 7(5).
8 See, for example, the Town and Country Planning (General Permitted Development) Order 1995, Sch 2, Pt 1, where the amount by which a house can be enlarged is restricted in such areas as compared to other localities.

only if the visual amenity of the area is outstanding will the individual's freedom to deal with his property be restricted.

Yet, closer examination of the classes of permitted development show that any potential effect may go far beyond the purely visual. Part 12, for example, which deals with development by local authorities, permits them to erect on their land small buildings for the purpose of any function that they perform, as well as allowing them to provide objects, such as refuse bins, that are required in relation to any public service administered by them. Besides their visual impact, such structures may have other effects on neighbouring property, producing noise, fumes or extra traffic. Even something as comparatively trivial as the erection of a bus stop may have a considerable impact on the domestic environment of the surrounding property owners.

Yet another feature of the classes of permitted development is the permission they give to perform routine maintenance work. Part 10, for example, authorises repairs to services, such as sewers, pipes and cables. This seems eminently sensible, since it allows vital services to be maintained, while the impact on the environment will hopefully be minimal and temporary. In contrast, Part 6, which deals with agricultural buildings and operations, allows those who own agricultural land to erect buildings and win minerals from their land. These activities can be engaged in only if certain restrictions are observed, such as where these activities can be carried out, yet there is no denying their impact especially on the amenity of rural areas.

It appears, therefore, that there may be no single explanation for the thirty-three categories of permitted development listed in the General Permitted Development Order. Whilst it may be acceptable that the reasons for the inclusion of classes may vary, the question remains as to what those reasons should be. Should the General Permitted Development Order be used only to permit development where the environmental impact is minimal? Alternatively, should it be used as a much more radical instrument of policy, designed to boost the economic well-being of the community at large by removing the restrictions on planning control, and retaining them only when there is a proven need so to do. As it presently stands, the General Permitted Development Order appears to represent a compromise between those two extremes.

USE CLASSES ORDER

The Town and Country Planning (Use Classes) Order 1987[9] contains provisions which seem at first glance to have little connection with those of the General Permitted Development Order. Article 3(1) of the Order provides as follows:

> ...where a building or other land is used for a purpose of any class specified in the Schedule, the use of that building or that other land for any other purpose of the same class shall not be taken to involve development of the land.

The Schedule lists eleven classes of use in four parts which provide a useful means of summarising the Order.

PART A

Class A1 Shops This gives a list of ten uses, including such examples as post offices and travel agents, which are all to be classed as shops.
Class A2 Financial and professional services This relates to the use of premises for the provision of financial and professional services or any other service which it is appropriate to provide in a shopping area for use by visiting members of the public. The class includes banks, building societies and betting offices. Specifically excluded are premises providing health or medical services.
Class A3 Food and drink This includes fish and chip shops and other shops which provide hot food for consumption off the premises, as well as those premises where food is consumed, such as cafes and restaurants.

PART B

Class B1 Business This is a wide class including offices, other than those found in Class A2, research establishments and industry, provided that the use 'can be carried out in any residential area without detriment to the amenity of that area'. This restriction confines the uses to those that do not cause excessive noise, fumes or smells.
Class B2 General industrial This now includes all industrial activity not included within Class B1 and so the range of uses is very wide.[10]

9 On the operation of the Use Classes Order see Circular 13/87, Changes of Use of Buildings and Other Land.
10 This single industrial class was created by the Town and Country Planning (Use Classes)(Amendment) Order 1995, SI 1995/297.

Class B8 Storage or distribution This includes the use of both buildings and land for these purposes. Where goods are stored and sold to the public from the same premises the use would be classed a shop (A1) rather than a B8 use.

PART C

Class C1 Hotels Specifically excluded from this class are establishments where care is provided, for example, old persons' homes and hostels. Until April 1994 hostels were included in this class but because of the disquiet voiced concerning the use of hotels as hostels for benefit claimants the class was amended to exclude hostels.[11] Planning permission is therefore likely to be required should the owner of a hotel contemplate using it as a hostel.
Class C2 Residential institutions Apart from the obvious examples of hospitals, colleges and boarding schools, this class specifically includes residential homes where care is provided.
Class C3 Dwelling-houses Beside including what might be termed a typical family house, this class also includes a house where up to six residents live together, for example, students, or alternatively old people in a small residential home.

PART D

Class D1 Non-residential institutions Eight uses are listed which include museums, schools and libraries.
Class D2 Assembly and leisure A list of five uses is supplied, ranging from cinemas and dance halls to outdoor sports centres.

The Use Classes Order differs from the General Permitted Development Order in a number of ways. As can be seen from the extract quoted from article 3(1) of the Use Classes Order, the change of use of a building or land to another use in the same class is deemed not to constitute development of the land. This contrasts with the General Permitted Development Order where the activities listed in the various classes are said to constitute development, but development which is permitted, subject, of course, to various restrictions. It appears, therefore, that the underlying purpose of the Orders is different. On the one hand, the General Permitted Development Order permits development for reasons, such as expediency, or the minor

11 Town and Country Planning (Use Classes)(Amendment) Order 1994, SI 1994/724.

nature of the change. In contrast, the Use Classes Order indicates activity which is not to be thought of as development. In addition, it cannot be presumed that a change of use from one class to another does automatically constitute development.[12]

The next distinguishing feature between the two Orders is the language used. The Use Classes Order uses general terms whilst the General Permitted Development Order is much more specific. In one sense the generality of the language of the Use Classes Order is illusory, since definitions are supplied of some of the key terms used in the Schedule such as 'care'.[13] The Use Classes Order is therefore more restricted in its operation than would first appear to be the case. Yet, the underlying purpose of the two Orders is remarkably similar, namely, the liberalising of the development control system. As was remarked earlier, the General Permitted Development Order represents the balancing of two very contradictory forces – the desire to protect the environment and the desire to promote the economic well-being of the community. Since the General Permitted Development Order is a statutory instrument, changes can and have been made to its content with comparative ease, in order to promote one or other of these aims.

The Use Classes Order represents the balancing of the same contradictory forces and can be altered with the same comparative ease. Despite this, many uses of a building or land exist which are seemingly not covered by the Order. Indeed, the very generality of the descriptions used within the Order may make it hard to say whether or not a specific activity is or is not included. Is the use of premises as a bureau de change a Class A1 use (Shops) or a Class A2 use (Financial and professional services) or is it *sui generis* – that is of a unique character not capable of being included in a specific class? The answer to this question may be vital in determining whether or not planning permission is required.[14]

Application for planning permission

Once it has been established that the activity in question does constitute development for which planning permission is re-

12 *Rann v Secretary of State for the Environment* (1979) 40 P & CR 113.

13 Town and Country Planning (Use Classes) Order 1987, SI 1987/764, art 2. Words used in the Order bear the same meaning as they do in the 1990 Act unless a contrary intention is demonstrated.

14 *Palisade Investments Ltd v Secretary of State for the Environment* [1993] 3 PLR 49. It was held to fall within Class A2.

quired, then the procedure examined in the following pages has to be observed. To begin with, an individual or a company seeking planning permission must submit their application to the local planning authority. Details regarding the procedure to be followed are given in the General Development Procedure Order.[15] An application must be made on the form supplied by the local planning authority, and, as well as giving the particulars required by this form, plans and drawings must also be provided so as to enable the land which is the subject of the application to be identified, and to illustrate the nature of the proposed development. All this information is then submitted to the local planning authority, which will then if required consult with certain specified bodies.[16]

Even at this early stage, it is as well to clarify some points. The first of these relates to the identity of the local planning authority. In most instances the local planning authority is the district planning authority.[17] The second point is that the applicant for planning permission does not have to be the owner of the land or building in question. The chances of an individual applying for planning permission when he does not own the property in question, may well seem remote. Yet, on reflection, it is perfectly logical for a prospective purchaser of land to ascertain whether a local planning authority will allow a house to be built on it and, moreover, a house of the type the prospective purchaser desires, before he invests his money. To ensure that this comparative freedom to apply for planning permission is not abused, however, a fee is charged by the local planning authority for processing each application.[18] The scale of fees chargeable varies according to the nature and size of the development and the fee scale that is currently in operation.

It is possible, in certain circumstances, to make an application for outline planning permission, when the application relates to the erection of a building.[19] It is not possible, however, to make an outline application for a change of use. The procedure used to apply for outline planning permission is identical

15 Town and Country Planning (General Development Procedure) Order 1995, SI 1995/419.
16 Ibid, art 10.
17 Ibid, art 5(1). With the reform of local government in England and Wales many areas will cease to have both county and district authorities and instead will have a unitary authority which will be responsible for all planning applications in its area.
18 Town and Country Planning (Fees for Applications and Deemed Applications) (Amendment) Regulations 1993, SI 1993/3170.
19 Town and Country Planning (General Development Procedure) Order 1995, SI 1995/419, art 3.

with that already described. If granted, outline planning permission is usually subject to the condition that certain matters, referred to as reserved matters, have to be approved by the local authority before the development can go ahead. The General Development Procedure Order defines reserved matters as items such as siting, design, external appearance, means of access and landscaping of the site, details of which have not been given in the original application.[20] While an application for outline planning permission allows an individual to judge how his proposals for development will be received without incurring the expense of architect's drawings to show how the building will look, the process has its disadvantages, particularly in areas where the external appearance of a building may be very important, such as in conservation areas. The General Development Procedure Order, therefore, provides that a local planning authority can refuse to entertain an application for outline planning permission, if it believes that information on such matters as external appearance is essential before it can reach a proper development control decision.[1]

Finally, circumstances may arise where a local authority wishes to undertake development on land which it owns. If this is so, a local authority may be in the position of applying to itself for planning permission, since it is the local planning authority. A special procedure has to be observed if, and when, this occurs.[2] Basically this requires the local authority to follow the standard procedures for making a planning application as set out in Part III of the 1990 Act, but subject to certain exceptions and modifications. The amended procedure must be observed exactly, however, or the resulting permission may be challenged.[3] The planning permission obtained in this fashion is referred to as deemed planning permission.

After the application for planning permission has been submitted to the local planning authority, it must reach its decision on whether or not to grant this permission. The General Development Procedure Order states that a local planning authority has eight weeks to arrive at a decision once a valid application has been received.[4] The parties, that is, the local planning

20 Ibid, art 4.
1 Ibid, art 3(2).
2 Town and Country Planning General Regulations 1992, SI 1992/1492, regs 3-11.
3 On the importance of observing these and other procedural requirements, see *Steeples v Derbyshire County Council* [1984] 3 All ER 468.
4 Town and Country Planning (General Development Procedure) Order 1995, SI 1995/419, art 20(2)(a).

authority and the applicant can, however, mutually agree to extend the period.[5] If a planning application fee is payable, but is not sent with the rest of the information required, then this eight-week period does not begin to run until the fee is paid.[6] After eight weeks, if no decision has been reached nor an extension agreed to, the applicant can treat his application as if it has been refused, and appeal to the Secretary of State.[7] From a purely practical point of view, the 1990 Act sets out a deadline, within which a decision must be made in order to ensure that applications for planning permission neither accumulate nor grow stale. That said, the fact that a local planning authority reaches a decision after, say twelve weeks, rather than eight, does not rob the applicant of his right to appeal against a refusal of a planning permission.[8]

Before examining the considerations which a local planning authority has to take into account in reaching its decision, it is worth mentioning that the Secretary of State for the Environment has the power, under the terms of the 1990 Act, to 'call in' an application for planning permission at any stage.[9] If he does so, then he will make the decision on the application, rather than leaving it to the local planning authority. The occasions when the Secretary of State chooses to take advantage of this power are few in number. In a recent parliamentary statement he has indicated the circumstances in which he may use this power. They include cases with effects beyond the immediate locality, cases which give rise to regional or national controversy or which conflict with national policy.[10] When individuals feel that an application for planning permission raises issues of considerable importance, they can alert the Secretary of State to this fact in the hope that he will call in the application. The decision is, however, one for the Secretary of State to make.[11]

5 Ibid, art 20(2)(b).
6 Ibid, art 20(2)(c) and 20(3)(c).
7 1990 Act, s 78.
8 See *James v Minister of Housing and Local Government* [1965] 3 All ER 602, CA, affirmed in *James v Secretary of State for Wales* [1966] 3 All ER 964, HL.
9 1990 Act, s 77. Certain types of planning application, particularly those which, if approved, would conflict with the implementation of the development plan, have to be brought to the attention of the Secretary of State for the Environment to give him an opportunity to call them in. See Circular 19/92, annex 3.
10 Hansard HC Debs, cols 314-315: 26 January 1995.
11 He, in his turn, must act reasonably and not abuse his power. See *Rhys Williams v Secretary of State for Wales* [1985] JPL 29.

PUBLICITY AND CONSULTATION

Whilst the two parties most concerned with an application for planning permission are obviously the person or persons seeking planning permission and the local planning authority considering the application, other individuals may also want to comment on the application. If, for example, planning permission is sought for a change of use from grocery shop to fish and chip shop, a whole range of individuals may wish to air their views. Some persons living in the area may regard the proposed shop as a useful extra amenity. Others may oppose the idea on the ground that it will generate extra traffic, noise and litter. Owners of similar shops in the vicinity may feel that another fish and chip shop will adversely affect their trade.

In order to ensure that the views which an application for planning permission may generate are taken into account, provision is made to publicise applications in addition to seeking comments from interested individuals. So far as publicity is concerned, all applications for planning permission must, within fourteen days of receipt, be entered by the local planning authority on its planning register.[12] The register consists of two parts. One part lists applications, together with relevant plans and drawings. The other part is intended as a permanent record of applications for planning permission and the fashion in which they were decided. The register can be inspected by members of the public during normal office hours.

Although the existence of a planning register ensures a certain level of publicity for planning applications, the onus is on members of the public to keep themselves abreast of develop-ments in their locality. Since this will mean regular trips to wherever the planning register is held, the chances are that not many individuals will choose to avail themselves of this opportunity. Local newspapers can, and do, extract information from the planning register to keep their readers informed of proposed developments in the area, but this information gives a selected rather than comprehensive impression of planning activity.

Given the limitations as to the levels of publicity that the register affords, a new comprehensive code relating to the forms of publicity that should accompany all types of planning

12 A local planning authority is under a duty to keep a register by virtue of the provisions of the 1990 Act, s 69. The Town and Country Planning (General Development Procedure) Order 1995, SI 1995/419, art 25, gives detailed directions on how that register is to be kept.

applications was introduced in 1992.[13] Previously, only certain forms of applications, the so-called 'bad neighbour' developments, required a specific form of publicity. However, it was always accepted that there were other activities not included which might also cause an adverse reaction in near neighbours or members of the general public. A proposal for a large residential property to become a funeral home might not agree with every-one's notion of an ideal neighbour. Since funeral homes were not included in the 'bad neighbour' list, there was no need to give the proposal the publicity which was then required for a cemetery, though the impact of the two would appear similar. The problem was that any list of 'bad neighbour' developments was always going to have omissions. Attempts to make it com-prehensive were doomed to failure and the courts had already ruled that there was no general requirement for publicity that would allow a legitimate expectation of notification.[14] On the other hand many responsible local planning authorities were already ensuring that adequate publicity was given to develop-ments which, in their opinion, were likely to have a particular impact on the neighbourhood in question and the changes introduced in 1992 merely formalised those activities.

All planning applications must now be publicised by the local planning authority either by a site notice or by notifying neighbours in writing. In addition, three categories of application require a notice in a local newspaper.[15] The first category is applications requiring an environmental statement, intending a departure from the development plan or affecting a public right of way. The second category is intended to cover major developments and includes mineral working, waste disposal, residential development providing more than ten houses or covering more than 0.5 hectares, all buildings with a floor space greater than 1,000 square metres and any development on a site greater than 1 hectare. The final 'catch all' category covers all other applications that are likely to create a wider concern and so merit a newspaper notification. Guidance as to what these applications may be is provided in Circular 15/92, Publicity for Planning Applications.

13 As a result of the Planning and Compensation Act 1991, s 71 of the 1990 Act was amended. The required procedure is detailed in the Town and Country Planning (General Development Procedure) Order 1995, SI 1995/419, art 8.

14 *R v Secretary of State for the Environment, ex p Kent* [1988] JPL 706.

15 Town and Country Planning (General Development Procedure) Order 1995, SI 1995/419, art 8.

All this stipulated activity raises a separate but related question about the usefulness of publicising any form of development. While the notion of keeping members of the public in touch with proposed developments in their community appears to have much to recommend it, the usefulness of the opinions gained in this fashion may be questionable. Members of the public, informed that a theatre is about to be built in their neighbourhood, are likely to raise questions over the traffic, parking problems, noise and generally increased activity that such a development is likely to cause. Yet, these are the very planning issues that any prudent local planning authority will consider before reaching a decision on whether or not the proposed development should go ahead. Notices in the newspapers and on the site are hardly likely to alert a local planning authority to any development control issue having a bearing on the proposed development apart, perhaps, from the strength of public opinion. Even this evidence may be illusory, since only a vociferous minority may have chosen to comment. As to the weight which should be accorded public opinion when making a planning decision, there is no simple answer.

Another method of canvassing opinion is to consult certain individuals and organisations for their views on a particular development. While publicity simply invites comment, consultation normally ensures that informed views are sought out, and taken into account once they have been given. Indeed, in certain instances, there is a statutory duty on local planning authorities to consult.[16] The organisations which they have to consult fall into three categories – other local authorities, government organisations and specialist bodies. District planning authorities, for example, should consult county planning authorities where a proposed development is likely to conflict with, or prejudice, a structure plan or local plan proposals or other determinations made by the county planning authority.[17] County councils are also obliged to consult district councils in certain circumstances[18] while even parish and community councils have a right to be consulted in circumstances where a proposed development affects their locality.[19]

The number of governmental organisations which a local planning authority may have to consult is considerable. They range from the Secretary of State for the Environment to the

16 1990 Act, Sch 1, para 7.

17 Town and Country Planning (General Development Procedure) Order 1995, SI 1995/419, art 11.

18 Ibid, art 12.

19 Ibid, art 13.

Minister of Agriculture, Fisheries and Food, and are all specified in a table contained within article 10 of the General Development Procedure Order. Who has to be consulted depends on the nature of the proposed development. The likely loss of agricultural land is a matter for the Minister of Agriculture, while operations in the catchment of, or on the banks of a stream or river, require that the views of the National Rivers Authority be sought. In addition, there are specialised agencies, such as the Nature Conservancy Councils, whose opinions must be sought when the development proposed is in an area of special scientific interest. The whole idea of imposing a duty to consult is to make sure that organisations which possess specialist knowledge, and which may also be responsible for establishing and administering policy at a national or regional level, are informed of current proposals and allowed to express their views on the likely impact of such proposals.

As should now be apparent, during the period between the receipt of an application for planning permission and the determination of that application, a local planning authority is required by law to act in a specific fashion. The aim of those legal requirements is to keep the general public, as well as specific agencies, informed, besides accumulating views on the proposed development. These procedures should not be allowed to obscure the nature of the decision which the local planning authority is taking. The decision is a development control decision taken on sound planning grounds. The whole purpose of consultation and publicity is to have a variety of views expressed on the planning strengths and weaknesses of the proposed development. When the local authority planning committee comes to make its decision, it will have to take account of those views, in addition to any other material considerations, which will help it reach a determination. This is required by section 70 of the 1990 Act. This states that in reaching a decision on a planning application regard must be had to the development plan, if relevant, as well as any other material consideration. It is to this stage of the process that the chapter now turns.

THE DEVELOPMENT PLAN

Specific mention of the development plan is made in section 70 of the 1990 Act in order to stress its importance as a development control policy document. Section 70 emphasises that the development plan cannot lightly be ignored, though the choice of wording 'have regard to' as opposed to 'shall follow' was interpreted as meaning that the plan did not automatically have to be observed. Provided its policies were taken into account, were correctly interpreted and reasons were given for not following them, then other factors, such as central government policy, might prevail. Now, however, section 70 has to be read in conjunction with section 54A of the 1990 Act which provides that where, in making any determination under the planning Acts, regard is to be had to the development plan, the determination shall be made in accordance with the plan unless material considerations indicate otherwise.

The significance of section 54A has been the object of considerable comment. It has been described as signalling 'an important change in Government policy from a market or appeal-led approach to development control to a plan-led approach'.[20] Whether the impact of section 54A is as far-reaching as was first assumed will be fully explored in the next chapter. Clearly, however, given the time and effort that is devoted to preparing development plans, it does not appear appropriate to allow them to be ignored. In general terms, this sentiment is unimpeachable. Reference has already been made to the need for a district planning authority to consult a county planning authority when an application for planning permission is received which conflicts with the structure plan. Indeed local planning authorities are under a general duty to seek to secure the objectives of the relevant structure plan. Provision is also made for a local planning authority that is minded to grant planning permission for development which does not accord with the development plan to refer the application to the Secretary of State in certain circumstances.[1]

Yet, despite the importance of the development plan, it should be possible for the policy which it contains to be set to one side if material considerations indicate that this is appropriate. What is unclear is when a local planning authority would wish to behave in this fashion. Perhaps the answer to this lies in the very nature of the development plan as an instrument of development control policy. The specific circumstances of an application for planning permission may, for example, justify a departure from the general policy statements of a development plan. Even more significant is the fact that development plans

20 Purdue, M, 'The Impact of Section 54A', Journal of Planning Law, 1994, p 399.

1 Circular 19/92, Town and Country Planning General Regulations 1992, annex 3, Town and Country Planning (Development Plans and Consultations) Directions 1992.

grow stale. Although provision is made for these plans to be revised or altered, this can be a lengthy process. A change in policy may, therefore, be decided upon which affects statements in the development plan without being incorporated into the plan itself. This might lead applications for planning permission to be treated differently than if the development plan were the sole consideration.

The other dilemma which may face a local planning authority in its efforts to have regard to the development plan is the fact that such a plan is often either in the course of preparation or revision. At this stage when choices are still being made about the appropriate policy to follow in the plan, an application for planning permission can necessitate choices being made before the consultation period, which precedes the making of a development plan, has occurred. On a purely practical level, the local planning authority must come to a decision or risk being deemed to have refused planning permission. Provided any decision arrived at takes account of all material considerations, which would, therefore, include a development plan in the course of preparation, that decision is unimpeachable.[2] This is the reasoning adopted by the courts and its logic is hard to fault since otherwise, the preparation or revision of a development plan would place an embargo on the consideration of planning applications affected by the embryonic plan.

MATERIAL CONSIDERATIONS

Apart from the specific reference to the development plan, section 70 gives little guidance to the local planning authority on what amounts to a material consideration. Bearing in mind these qualifications, it is possible to compile a list of what may or may not be regarded as a material consideration. That list reflects the contents of this book and many of those matters briefly mentioned here are considered at length in forthcoming chapters.

Local policy It might be expected that a local planning authority's development control policy is, for the most part, to be found in the development plan. Although this is partly true, the statement needs qualifying in order that an accurate picture of the situation is obtained. A county planning authority must, as a matter of law, prepare a structure plan and metropolitan

2 *R v City of London Corpn, ex p Allan* (1980) 79 LGR 223; *Arlington Securities Ltd v Secretary of State* [1989] 1 PLR 14, CA.

authorities must prepare unitary plans. In the past it was a matter of judgment, however, whether local plans were prepared in non-metropolitan areas. If there was no local plan this was not to say that a local planning authority had no policy on future development within its area. Any policy that there was would not have attained the formality of a local plan. Allowing local planning authorities discretion in the matter of whether or not to prepare a local plan resulted in large areas of England and Wales being without such a plan. As a consequence local plans, including district-wide development plans, have now to be prepared by virtue of section 36 of the 1990 Act. In the near future, therefore, local policy will, in the main, be found in the local plan, which is logical given their enhanced status. This will not see the end of informal local policy, however, as it will continue to be produced either to enhance and expand on policy within the local plan, or to introduce new policy in the period prior to the next revision of the plan.

Central government policy The Department of the Environment is the central government Ministry principally concerned with development control policy. That policy can be expressed in many forms; legislation, delegated legislation, circulars and even after-dinner speeches by the Secretary of State. In reaching its decision, a local planning authority should take into account any of this policy which is relevant to the particular circumstances of the application being determined.

Whether or not a local planning authority is forced to adhere to Department of the Environment policy depends on the manner in which that policy is expressed. Legislation, primary or delegated, is binding on any local planning authority to which it applies. The policy which is expressed in legislation tends to be general in character, designed to provide the framework within which actions are taken. Although, for example, a county planning authority is bound by law to prepare a structure plan, the contents of that plan are barely referred to in the relevant legislation.

The detailed strategy of the Department of the Environment's development control policy is normally revealed in circulars and PPGs. As has already been explained, circulars and PPGs are not binding in the sense that legislation is binding. Yet, it is equally true that a local planning authority which chooses to ignore the contents of a particular circular or PPG must have convincing reasons for choosing to do so. Apart from the Department of the Environment's policy input, which is considered in chapter 6, other government Ministries may have policies which have a bearing on development control. The Department of Transport, the Heritage Department and the Ministry of Agriculture, Fisheries and Food are the most obvious examples, and their influence is considered in chapter 5.

The site In resolving an application for planning permission, the site itself is a major factor. The nature of the site and the proposed development will indicate which central government and local planning authority development control policies are relevant. In addition, the past planning history of the site is a material consideration. Factors, such as the site's existing use and past planning permissions, are items which a local planning authority is entitled to take into account in reaching its decision. The weight to be attached to such matters in the process of development control is explored in chapter 7.

Other circumstances It is difficult to be categorical on what may amount to other material considerations. It very much depends on whether an issue is relevant to the development control decision being taken.[3] For example, reference can be made to the personal circumstances of an applicant for planning permission. In reality, it is necessary to qualify this statement, as much depends on which personal circumstances can be taken into account in a development control policy. Two cases need special mention. The first of these is the financial situation of the applicant. In general, it can be a material consideration that the applicant for planning permission is unable to finance the scheme in question.[4] However, the fact that a developer may make a considerable profit, should he be given planning permission, is irrelevant. Second, whether a developer is prepared to offer a planning gain unconnected with a proposed development is also an irrelevant consideration in determining his application for planning per-mission.[5] The concept of planning gain is a vexed one. It refers to the willingness of developers to concede benefits, for example a car park for the use of the public, should their application for planning permission prove successful. Obviously, the availability of planning gain should neither delay the granting of planning permission where this

3 On this point of what amounts to a development control issue or planning policy see *Westminster City Council v Great Portland Estates plc* [1985] AC 661, [1984] 3 All ER 744, HL.

4 *Sosmo Trust v Secretary of State for the Environment* [1983] JPL 806.

5 *Westminster Renslade Ltd v Secretary of State for the Environment* (1983) 48 P & CR 255; *Tesco Stores Ltd v Secretary of State for the Environment* [1995] 2 All ER 636, HL.

is appropriate, nor cause it to be given where it is inappropriate. There is nothing to stop a developer voluntarily offering planning gain, but its availability should not be taken into account. What constitutes planning gain is dealt with in chapter 8.

In listing the items which can amount to material considerations, two factors are seen as important. What is material will vary according to the specific circumstances of the case. A local planning authority then has to balance them against each other, bearing in mind the particular emphasis placed on the development plan, and reach a decision. That decision must indicate the reasoning which lies behind it. If it appears that a material consideration has been ignored or an immaterial one taken into account, the decision can be challenged, either by appealing to the Secretary of State, or by seeking judicial review from the courts, as will be considered in chapters 9 and 10.

Chapter 4

Development plans

As section 70 of the Town and Country Planning Act 1990 states:

> Where an application is made to a local planning authority for planning permission ... In dealing with such an application the authority shall have regard to the provisions of the development plan, so far as material to the application, and to any other material considerations.

The development plan is, therefore, clearly intended to be the first point of reference for the local planning authority when taking its development control decision on any planning application. Indeed the status of the development plan is further enhanced by section 54A of the 1990 Act which states:

> Where, in making any determination under the planning Acts, regard is to be had to the development plan, the determination shall be made in accordance with the plan unless material considerations indicate otherwise.

Consequently, it is crucial to appreciate the form and function of development plans. There is no statutory definition of the term 'development plan'. It is, in fact, a collective term used to cover the various types of plan that have emerged since the passage of the Town and Country Planning Act 1947. PPG 12, Development Plans and Regional Planning Guidance, contains current governmental guidance on these documents. This PPG indicates that the development plan for an area is rarely a single document and that they come in a variety of forms.

In non-metropolitan areas the following plans should either be in existence or in the course of preparation. First, there is the structure plan. In these county planning authorities set out in general terms 'key strategic policies'. Second, there is the local plan which develops the broad policies of the structure plan in relation to a specific locality. The problem with this logical arrangement is that until comparatively recently local planning authorities were under no duty to prepare a local plan or could choose to do so for only part of their area. The preparation of local plans is now obligatory throughout England and Wales under the terms of the Planning and Compensation Act 1991, but it will take time for this objective to be achieved. Until then transitional arrangements are currently in existence.[1] The effect of these is to save any existing local plans until the new local plans are in place. These 'saved' plans may include 'old style' development plans, subject plans and action area plans, all of which will be considered later in the chapter.

The Planning and Compensation Act 1991 also provides for the production of two other forms of plan – the minerals local plan and the waste local plan. The former is expected to set out a local planning authority's policy for the supply of minerals and the related environmental issues associated with such activity. The waste plans are to set out the authority's detailed land use policies for the treatment and disposal of waste using structure plan policy as a framework.[2] In metropolitan areas the situation appears somewhat simpler as the development plan comprises the unitary development plan which is divided into two parts; Part I covering general policies and Part II, the detailed policies needed for development control. However, until the unitary development plan has been approved, any of the pre-1991 Act development plans described in relation to non-metropolitan areas may also be relevant.

Development plans are complex documents of fundamental importance in the development control system. Furthermore, this complexity is increased because the various forms of plan will have been produced at different times. These different forms of plan will also co-exist within a local planning authority area and even overlap in some instances, which does little to aid any attempt to appreciate their function. If the development control process is to be fully understood, therefore, a detailed knowledge of all forms of development plan is required. The plan's main function is as a vehicle of policy in that it contains the approved and formally expressed ideas of the local planning authority regarding the future development of its area. These ideas may be expressed in general or quite specific terms, depending on the type of plan. Regardless of the type of plan, however, it is primarily a policy document and the significance of this will now be considered.

1 Circular 18/91, Planning and Compensation Act 1991: New Development Plans System: Transitional Arrangements (England and Wales).
2 PPG 12, Development Plans and Regional Planning Guidance, para 3.13.

Development plans as policy documents

PPG 12 states that plans need to:

> provide an essential framework for decisions and should convey a clear understanding of the weight to be given to different aspects of the public interest in the use of land and common expectations about the likely broad patterns of development.[3]

At the same time, no indication is provided as to how exactly these policies and proposals are to be produced. In some respects, the sources of such policies may be considered obvious. It is clear to any participant in the development control system that a considerable proportion of such policies will be derived from an analysis of local factors. Indeed, this type of policy is part of what development plans should contain, but related to elements of more general planning policy. What is the source of this general planning policy? If this policy is derived solely from a local analysis, each plan is likely to stand apart from its neighbours, and relate only to its unique locality. This is contrary to the provisions of the 1990 Act, which requires that all such plans should be broadly compatible.[4] To gain a clearer picture of the derivation of this general planning policy, it is necessary to understand the basic concepts of planning philosophy that justify the use of development plans.

THE CONCEPT OF LAND POLICY

It is not the intention of this book to delve deeply into the more esoteric aspects of planning theory, especially when there is more than adequate coverage provided by a host of other sources.[5] Nevertheless, some aspects of the theory must be considered as they are fundamental to a better understanding of the whole planning system. Initially, it must be appreciated that a development plan was regarded as an essential part of those mechanisms created to impose elements of central government land policy at regional and local levels. Land policy is regarded as an element of central government development policy,[6] but opinions differ as to what exactly land policy in-

3 Ibid, para 1.1.
4 1990 Act, s 46.
5 For example: Faludi A *A Reader in Planning Theory* (1973); Friend J K et al *Public Planning: The Intercorporate Diversion* (1974); Bailey J *Social Theory for Planning* (1975); McAuslan P *The Ideologies of Planning Law* (1980).
6 Lichfield N and Darin-Drabkin H *Land Policy in Planning* (1980).

cludes.[7] Clearly, it must be concerned with the ways in which any government interrelates its development policies with those of a social or economic nature. Land policy may, therefore, be better understood if a government's overall purpose in terms of such policy is analysed. In this respect, a government's basic desire is obviously to control the development and use of land. This raises the question of what it may be hoping to achieve, and four suggestions have been made.[8]

First, there is what might be termed the negative purpose of supplying some form of protection for any given area. This has the effect of protecting individual property owners from the actions of their neighbours if these actions could adversely affect their own property interests. As has been suggested elsewhere,[9] such protection exists in the shape of laws governing land and property, for example, the legislation relating to landlord and tenant. Nevertheless, it is a valid purpose for government intervention, and successive planning statutes have added to the existing protection offered by land law in a variety of ways. All such legislation, not only planning statutes, must, therefore, be considered as forming part of the government's development policy.

Second, it is suggested that a government's purpose is to compensate for the failure of free market forces to supply the development needs of the country in terms of land and property. This is an intriguing concept, as it involves the implicit assumption that a government is capable of ascertaining what, and indeed, where, such market shortcomings exist. This concept has provoked speculation,[10] since it not only draws on the assumption of welfare economics regarding a government's ability to ascertain need, but also raises questions of a government's own role. It is, however, apparent that such government attempts to ascertain land use needs, and broadly balance them against actual supply, may produce policy that will form a fundamental element in the preparation of a development plan.

Third, a government's purpose can be seen as intervening to ensure that land is used in the general interest. This is quite distinct from the second suggested purpose, where government is the supplier of what the market fails to provide. In this

7 See the discussions in Lichfield and Darin-Drabkin, and in Dunkerley H B et al *Urban Land Policies and Opportunities* (1978).

8 Healey P *Local Plans in British Land Use Planning* (1983) ch 1.

9 McAuslan P *Land, Law and Planning* (1975).

10 For example: Castells M 'Towards a Political Urban Sociology' in Harloe M (Ed) *Captive Cities* (1977); Hallett G *Urban Land Economics* (1979); Hayward J and Watson M (Eds) *Planning, Politics and Public Policy* (1975).

instance, a government is seen as operating more in the role of the arbitrator between development needs and market responses, although to complicate matters, it may also have participatory and managerial functions. This purpose can best be clarified by referring to some of the roles played by government in the planning system. For example, it can be argued that it acts as a form of arbitrator in planning appeals, where it seeks to discover what is best in the general interest. In its participatory role, however, it is involved in the production of development plans, which themselves may be the subject of its arbitration at a public inquiry. Finally, its managerial role can be seen as extending from the highest official within the Department of the Environment, down to the local planning officer. All three roles can be viewed as combining to play a part in the government's intervention function.

The final purpose involves a government deliberately controlling the land and property market in a direct manner in the interests of the community. This can effectively take two forms. The first is where a government taxes private land development, nationalises land, or indulges in substantial public sector land ownership in order deliberately to structure the land market. The second is where a government actively protects the environment in a variety of ways, so as effectively to constrain the operation of free market forces within the protected areas.

These four suggested purposes may be taken as a summary of the underlying motives of any government in attempting to create an effective land use policy, and elements of each are clearly discernible in the planning system. Consequently, the next stage is to consider how this conceptual land use policy is translated into a form of operational land use planning and the role that development plans play in achieving this. By way of an introduction it is useful to examine the ideas that paved the way for the first truly comprehensive piece of planning legislation – the Town and Country Planning Act 1947.

DEVELOPMENT PLANS AND THE TOWN AND COUNTRY PLANNING ACT 1947

An examination of the 1944 White Paper, The Control of Land Use, reveals that a comprehensive national land use policy, forming part of an overall development policy, was very much in the minds of the authors. It is equally clear that the control of land use was to be a fundamental element in this development policy, and that it would take the appearance of a system of land use planning that would complement the national post-war exercise in social and economic restructuring. This restructuring was to take the form of a considered policy involving new housing, totally new lay-outs for bombed or blighted areas, new schools related to a new Education Bill, the balanced distribution of industry better to maintain active employment, well balanced agricultural production, National Parks and leisure facilities and a modern transport system:

> all these related parts of a single reconstruction programme involve the use of land, and it is essential that their various claims on land should be so harmonized as to ensure for the people of this country the greatest possible measure of individual well being and national prosperity.[11]

The very essence of the government's land policy was that it formed part of a comprehensive scheme for national development. The resulting system of land use planning can only be fully understood in the context of this wider scheme. Support for such a scheme seems to have been almost total from the political, administrative, and economic sectors of post-war Britain, for reasons that are outside the scope of this book.[12] The land use planning system that emerged was, consequently, able to incorporate new and wide-ranging controls over the development of land that, in different circumstances, may well have been unacceptable. At the heart of these controls, as set out in the Town and Country Planning Act 1947, was the need to apply for planning permission when undertaking development. Decisions on individual applications for planning permission were to be made in the light of land use policy, but clearly, such policy needed to be translated from its broad national nature into much more specific local policy for the concept to operate successfully. The main focus for this translation was a single mechanism – the development plan – which was to embody the essence of national land policy in a specific local context.

This concept of a development plan, and what actually emerged from the 1947 Act, is possibly the first instance of the ideas relating to policy and land use planning going fundamentally astray. In Cullingworth's analysis of the events and arguments which led up to the eventual form that development plans were to assume in the 1947 Act, he makes the point that, from the very outset, such plans were seen as natural extensions of the relevant aspects of national policy. Consequently, the vehicle

11 Cullingworth J B *Town and Country Planning in Britain* (1972) p 31.
12 See Hall P et al *The Containment of Urban England* (1973), for commentary on this aspect.

of land use policy, the development plan, as envisaged in the 1944 White Paper, was to be comprised of two levels. The first level was the outline plan. Outline plans were intended to set out the broad land use policy concepts, and were to be prepared by the local authorities for their districts. The plans were then to be submitted to the Minister for Town and Country Planning, who would consider them in relation to his national land use policies. Once these outline plans had been considered and discussed by the Minister and other interested and responsible parties, they would then be approved as policy documents that set out the general land use principles, which, it must again be stressed, were derived from, and compatible with, national land use policy. Using the outline plan as a basis, the second level of plan, the detailed development plan, would then be created, taking into account the various detailed aspects of land use and development that concerned each area. In other words, there would have been a strictly logical policy and decision-making sequence. This would have led from the general principles of national development policy, as decided by the government, through the national land use policy as interpreted by the Minister for Town and Country Planning, to the outline plans prepared by the local authorities. The outline plans would operate as the mechanism for reconciling national and local land use policy, whilst the detailed development plan would translate such policy into development proposals for a specific locality.

Such a logical sequence was not, however, to emerge from the procedures set out within the 1947 Act. Instead, the two levels of plan were merged into a single development plan. Quite why this occurred is open to debate,[13] but what cannot be disputed was that the development plan as represented in the 1947 Act fell far short of the translating mechanism it was originally intended to be. Not only was the plan deficient in this respect, but the problem was exacerbated by the fact that the 1947 Act allowed local authorities, which were to act both as plan producers and as plan enforcers, a considerable element of interpretative discretion regarding the principles embodied in the plan. As has been concluded:

> This discretion was unfettered by any requirement to stick rigidly to these principles. In the interests of a powerful and flexible policy-oriented planning system, no mechanisms other than political representation and central government overview were built in to ensure that these powers were not exercised

13 Cullingworth, p 97.

> arbitrarily. Similarly, no limitation was put on the range of matters which could be brought to bear on making decisions on future development.[14]

At this point, however, it should be realised that although this form of plan seems to be far removed from the specific policy mechanism originally conceived, its metamorphosis did not cause concern, as it was envisaged that the public sector would be the major property developer. In this scenario, therefore, government land use policy would be guaranteed by the fact that government itself would dominate the property market, not only ensuring suitable developments but also, by its very dominance, effecting a control over land values.[15]

Despite, or perhaps because of, these various concepts, the reality of development plans after their introduction in the 1947 Act was not what had been envisaged. Their failure was not due simply to the shortcomings of the plans themselves, but was attributable, in part, to the administrative system within which they had to operate. The problem started at the top with the new Ministry of Town and Country Planning. This was, in theory, the source, not only of the all-important national land use policy, but also of overall development control. In this latter capacity the Ministry was expected to achieve policy consistency by approving plans and monitoring developments by way of planning appeals. As was observed as early as 1950, however, the Minister had in fact:

> only a general mandate for securing consistency and continuity in the planning of land. And this vague direction gives the Minister no real field in which his is the last word, or for which he must bear responsibility.[16]

The problem seemed to be that national development policy, of which land use policy was only one aspect, was being generated by a whole range of Ministries on a far from co-operative basis. The Board of Trade, for example, administered the all-important industrial location policy entirely separately from the land use policy of the Ministry of Town and Country Planning. This contrasted sharply with the function envisaged for the Ministry as the manipulator of a resource and policy base for many other established ministerial areas. The fundamental problem was that these Ministries were unwilling to be so

14 Healey, p 25.
15 Neutze M 'Urban Land Policy in Five Western Countries' Journal of Social Politics, 1975, p 225.
16 Haar C M *Land Planning in a Free Society* (1951) p 30.

manipulated, and there were two main reasons for this. Firstly, they believed it would undermine their own power structure. Secondly, there was reluctance to place a heavy burden of responsibility on the local authorities who, unlike the Ministries, were novices in implementing land use policies.

The second administrative problem centred on the local authorities, which, despite alternative suggestions, were eventually selected to function as local planning authorities under the 1947 Act. This decision produced numerous problems in achieving the implementation of national land use policy through the mechanism of the development plan. As has already been mentioned, the Ministry of Town and Country Planning was producing very little clear land use policy. This obviously left the local planning authorities with only one option when carrying out their duty to prepare development plans. As national policy guidance was not available they would have to use their discretion in preparing the plans. The problem with this exercise in discretion was that there was a shortage of qualified town planners at the local planning authority level who were capable of understanding '...either the thinking behind the legislation or the ideas of the evangelist town planning movement'.[17] Consequently, the development plan was either farmed out to private planning consultants, which was not necessarily a bad step since it would then be prepared by professionals who understood its underlying concepts, or it would be prepared by individuals within the local planning authority, many of whom lacked professional training. This second possibility, which was by far the more common, produced a development plan that tended to be rich in local land use detail, short on local land use proposals, and totally lacking in any concept of national or even neighbouring land use policy.

Despite these shortcomings the planning system lumbered into operation and continued largely unchanged until being reassessed in a major review undertaken by the Planning Advisory Group.[18] In this, the main shortcomings of development plans were summarised as:

(i) a misleading concentration on local detail;
(ii) a largely inflexible form that was difficult to adapt to new issues;
(iii) a general deficiency in the statement of policies, especially those not directly related to land use;

17 Healey, p 26.
18 The Planning Advisory Group *The Future of Development Plans* (1965).

(iv) providing an inadequate guide for development control purposes;
(v) long delays in approval due to an over centralised system.[19]

The Group blamed these failings on a wide range of factors, but undoubtedly the most significant was that the development plan had been sidetracked from its intended purpose, and its function altered as a consequence. This was due to central government losing interest in national and regional land policy, and consequently failing to ensure that the plans reflected national development policy. In addition, the local planning authorities were increasingly being placed under pressure by the unexpected increase in applications for planning permission from the private sector. The development plans that were created, were, therefore, hurried, unco-ordinated attempts to produce some local basis for the development control process, with no reference to the few policy concepts that might exist at regional or national levels. In these circumstances, the development plan became a negative means of controlling land use, rather than a positive policy document establishing general principles that could be used both to control and to promote development.

The Planning Advisory Group recommended changes in the planning system. In particular, the Group recommended that the main objectives of development plans should be:

> providing more positive guidance for developers and development control, by widening the scope of plans in order to deal more fully with policy and also the promotion and quality of development.[20]

The system could, it was suggested, be made more efficient by:

> clarifying levels of responsibility, so that only major policies and objectives are brought before the Minister for approval, while matters of detail and local land use are settled locally.[1]

Their proposals culminated in the suggested reintroduction of a two-level development plan system that was practically identical to that envisaged in the White Paper of 1944. Effectively, there were to be structure plans, which set out the broad policy strategy for an area, whilst taking account of national land use policy, and local plans, that would translate the

19 Ibid, paras 1.2-1.29.
20 Ibid, para 1.22.
1 Ibid.

generality of the structure plans into detailed proposals for the control and development of land in specific parts of that area. Only structure plans, as the policy interpretation documents, would be sent to the Minister for approval.

DEVELOPMENT PLANS AND THE TOWN AND COUNTRY PLANNING ACT 1971

The proposals of the Planning Advisory Group were acted upon in the Town and Country Planning Act 1968, which was later repealed and its contents incorporated into the Town and Country Planning Act 1971. However, it must not be thought that the shortcomings of the development plan system were eliminated, as it has been convincingly argued that the plans still failed to operate in the way originally conceived:

> The identifiable failings of the current planning system ... are a direct result of conceptual deficiencies...These conceptual deficiencies failed to appreciate the purpose and hierarchical nature of strategic planning and failed to appreciate the implications of introducing public participation into planning.[2]

This indicates that the nature of the planning process is essentially hierarchical in which '...each level of planning performs a strategic function for the level below and conversely is constrained by the strategic planning of the level above'.[3] This hierarchy consequently controls the relationships between the policy options produced at different levels, in allowing them to develop within a specific vertical framework. In other words, policy is produced at any given level as a response to the perceived needs at that level, but in a context that respects the policy decisions that have been made by the level above, and in the knowledge that its own policy will effectively define the general context of the policy produced at the level below. Furthermore, these levels will be represented by organisations which:

> may or may not be linked vertically through the different levels of planning activity. However, there is every likelihood that horizontally, at both higher and lower levels of planning, the organisations will be administratively separate and operating

2 Bruton M 'PAG Revisited' in Report on the Policy Symposium on the Future of Development Plans, Town Planning Review, 1980, p 137.

3 Diamond D 'The Uses of Strategic Planning' Town Planning Review, 1979, p 19.

> within a distinctive set of policy guidelines even though they may be concerned with the same problem or issue.[4]

How then did the British planning system relate to this conceptual model with its postulated logical flow of development policy?

At the national level development policy was at its most conspicuous, in the sense that government was constantly voicing a concern for the problems of society, the policies needed to solve them and the resources available to effect such solutions. Most departments, the more obvious being the Department of the Environment, the Department of Employment, the Department of Health and Social Security, the Department of Transport and the Department of Industry, were involved with providing the broad policy framework within which land use planning could take place. As was noted however:

> Although policies are clearly stated at this level, the extent to which co-operation and compatibility between the various sectors of central and local government is ever achieved is far from clear.[5]

At the regional level, a much wider range of agencies were to be found, for example, the Land Authority for Wales, the ten regional Water Boards, the ten regional Health Authorities, the Countryside Commission, and the Manpower Services Commission. Within their fields of expertise, these agencies all performed a variety of co-ordinating and linking functions in relation to both policy and development, but only in a partial way, as each tended to relate only vertically, to the isolated policy of its national body, rather than horizontally, to other agencies. The only real attempt that was made to alter this system was seen in the foundation of the Regional Economic Planning Councils between 1964 and 1965, which were to provide:

> a broadly based source of regional advice for central government and to assist in the commissioning and formulation of plans for regional economic and social development.[6]

A range of such plans was eventually produced whose value varied considerably, but the councils were abolished in 1979, having arguably achieved little of real significance.

At the local level the system was initially formalised in the shape of structure and local plans. Here, the system clearly

4 Ibid.
5 Bruton, p 138.
6 Bruton, p 139.

required that the structure plan should provide a formal statement and explanation of the local policies, indicating both their derivation from policies at the higher levels, and their significance for land use policy at the local plan level. Equally clearly, it was at this point that the system was most likely to break down completely because the local planning authority normally lacked a clear statement of its own planning policy. This was compounded by central government's lack of clarity about its own land use objectives, the absence of a regional economic plan, and further confused by a host of regional agencies' policies, many of which were likely to be incompatible. It is hardly surprising, therefore, that structure plans tended to lack the clear and formal statements of policy that were expected of them. At the level of the local plan, the inadequate structure plan was paid little more than lip-service, when and if the local planning authority decided it needed to prepare a formal local plan.

Further complications were to develop as a result of the Local Government Act 1985, which abolished the Greater London Council and the six metropolitan county councils on 1 April 1986. In a planning context this meant that the whole of the system of structure and local plans as it applied to those areas would eventually cease to exist. In its place would be yet another type of development plan – the unitary development plan. The reasoning behind this abolition is to be found in the White Paper 'Streamlining the Cities'[7] which argued that the planning system in metropolitan areas had become unwieldy as a con-sequence of the actions of the county planning authorities, who had outlived their purpose.[8] However, as Schedule 1 to the Local Government Act 1985 made clear, any 'old style' development plan, structure plan or local plan that was in force on the day of abolition, would continue in force until replaced by a unitary development plan, so once again a transition period was in-evitable.

Unitary plans were prepared either individually, or jointly by the planning authorities of the thirty-three London borough councils and the thirty-six metropolitan district councils in a manner and form detailed in the Local Government Act 1985.[9] There were slightly different arrangements in the Greater

7 Cmnd 9063.

8 As a consequence of a variety of statutory changes the planning responsibilities of the metropolitan county planning authorities had dwindled to almost zero, and their real justification as the preparers of the structure plan was no longer valid.

9 Local Government Act 1985, Sch 1, Pt 1 set out the procedure for the preparation of unitary development plans, and substituted for Pt II of the 1971 Act in those districts where unitary plans were to be prepared.

London area, where a joint planning committee was established to advise the boroughs '...on matters of common interest relating to the planning and development of Greater London'[10] and other related factors.

Consequently, given their number, range and content development plans by the late 1980s were unlikely to be those '..clear and concise statements of policies and proposals for development'[11] but rather a somewhat vague and general collection of what might loosely be termed land use policies for a specific area. Despite this fact, these plans played and still play a formal, and indeed fundamental, role in the development control process, even if their policy basis was less than sound.

DEVELOPMENT PLANS AND THE TOWN AND COUNTRY PLANNING ACT 1990

Various studies[12] were made of the development plan system following the 1971 Act changes and all seemed to agree that it worked tolerably well. The system's major shortcoming was the form and contemporaneity of the policies found in the various plans. Policies crystallise over the period in which any plan is being prepared, and may then be recast during the adoption procedures, all of which inevitably takes time. As a consequence, these policies, when adopted, lag behind the current situation within which they have to operate. This problem is then aggravated if the form that the policy has taken is lacking in flexibility, which inevitably is the case if the policy is map-based as was true of local plans.

Apart from policy issues, another major problem was pinpointed in the Department of the Environment's White Paper, The Future of Development Plans.[13] This was the slowness of the processes involved in both structure and local plan preparation and approval. The reason, it was suggested, was due mainly to the complexity of both documents, and the range of policies they covered, often in too much detail. These problems

10 Local Government Act 1985, s 5(2)(a).
11 Circular 22/84, Memorandum on Structure and Local Plans, introductory para 1.
12 For example: Department of Town Planning, Oxford Polytechnic, The Implementation of Planning Policies and the Role of Development Plans (1986); Healey; Bruton M J 'Local Plans, Local Planning and Development Plan Schemes in England 1974-1982' Town Planning Review, 1983, 54(1), p 18; The Future of Development Plans: PAG Revisited Town Planning Review, 1980, 51(2), p 131.
13 Department of the Environment, 1989 Cmnd 569.

were exacerbated by the fact that policies were often duplicated in both local and structure plans, which led to confusion and a further waste of time. The following proposals were presented for improving the development plan system. The overlap between county and district plans must be removed as it was unnecessary and wasteful; detailed supervision of plan approval by the Secretary of State must be reduced as it wasted time; the content of the plans should be simplified, as this would reduce approval time; preparation procedures should be made more effective by involving the public at an earlier stage.

A modified development plan system was, therefore, proposed. It was contemplated that national land use policy would continue to be stated in Department of Environment circulars and PPGs. At the next level it was suggested that a form of regional policy input be introduced. This should not assume the character of a regional plan, but rather consist of formal policy statements prepared by local planning authorities on major land use issues that were clearly of a regional nature. This activity would be directed by the Secretary of State, who would also be involved in producing the statements. At the next level, the county planning authorities would issue policy statements, rather than produce development plans, on county-wide issues. These issues could also be identified by the Secretary of State. In all instances the regional policy would be taken into account where relevant. Finally, the district planning authorities would produce a district development plan covering their whole area, and taking into account, where appropriate, policies from all these sources. These plans would be mandatory, and would supersede all other forms of plan and any informal policy, thus providing a simple and comprehensive guide to development.

The majority of these proposals have now been acted upon. Regional planning guidance is currently being produced and already covers such areas as the South West. The proposal to abandon development plans at the county level was not, however, carried forward and structure plans remain the vehicle for land use planning policy at this level. The production of local plans, including a district-wide local plan, is now mandatory. Finally, an attempt has been made to simplify the procedures associated with the production and revision of development plans in order to speed up the process. The current system of development plans is thus more integrated. This may not, however, remain the case as the reorganised system of local government, with its mixture of unitary and two-tier authorities, is not consistent in its division of responsibilities for the production of development plans.

Having considered the derivation of the policy contained within development plans, the nature and structure of those plans needs to be explored if their role in the development control process is to be fully appreciated.

Formation and structure

At present four basic types of development plan can still be found covering any particular area in England and Wales.[14] They are: (i) the 'old style' development plans produced under the 1947 Act; (ii) structure plans introduced by the 1971 Act; (iii) local plans that come in a variety of forms but are distinguished by their empowering legislation – either the 1971 Act or the 1990 Act; and (iv) unitary development plans found in Greater London and the six metropolitan areas.

The interrelationships between the various types of plan are indicated in PPG 12,[15] although it is highly unlikely that all four types would be in existence at any one time in any one area since they are mutually exclusive. Structure plans exist for all non-metropolitan areas, normally covering the whole county. County planning authorities are constantly engaged in the process of updating and revising their structure plans, and the resulting amendments, once approved, also form part of the structure plan. After a structure plan has been approved, local plans may be produced by either the county or the district planning authority. Local plans approved under the 1990 Act will cover the whole of the local authority area and will automatically supersede all other local plans. However, in many instances these plans are still in the process of preparation so any existing local plans remain significant. Most relevant are the local plans produced under the 1971 Act but invariably these plans will not cover the whole area of either the district or the county, but only a part. Consequently, for those areas where no local plan has been adopted, the 'old style' development plans introduced by the 1947 Act and perhaps subsequently revised, still apply. In other words, in any non-metropolitan area at the present time it may be possible to have as valid policy documents the following development plans – a structure plan, together with

14 The development plan situation in the Greater London area used to be somewhat different from elsewhere in England and Wales, mainly as a result of the Greater London Plan becoming the structure plan. The Greater London area is now covered by a unitary plan as are the six other metropolitan areas.

15 PPG 12, para 3.2.

revisions; a 1971 Act local plan with some revisions; and an 'old style' development plan in its latest revised form which cannot antedate the approval date of the structure plan and finally 1990 Act local plans in the process of preparation. In any metropolitan area the situation is much simpler as Parts I and II of the unitary development plan will have superseded all other plans.

Given this situation, it is obviously necessary to explain what each of these plans is, and the function it is supposed to perform within the development control process. As has already been made clear, the general intention of all such plans was to translate the principles of national land use planning policy down to the local level, but the various types of plan attempt to achieve this in different ways, largely as a result of chronological changes in planning ideology. Consequently, it seems logical to examine the 'old style' development plan first.

DEVELOPMENT PLANS UNDER THE 1947 ACT – THE OLD STYLE PLAN

As conceived under the 1947 Act:

> Development plans were thus to provide principles for translating...policy into spatial allocations and detailed development, coordinate the public sector development effort, and indicate the basis on which small scale private development would be regulated.[16]

Consequently, these plans were meant to be detailed, indicating precisely the boundaries of present or future land uses as determined by the local interpretation of national land use policy. Such precise interpretation could logically only take one form, so these plans are essentially map-based. The plans were created by taking the appropriate scale of ordnance survey map, which was then colour coded to indicate the various areas of appropriate land use and development opportunity.

A clear indication of the form and content of these plans was to be found in Schedule 5 to the 1971 Act and in the now superseded Development Plan Regulations 1965.[17] The Regulations repeat the original statutory requirement that the plan was to show the manner in which the land was to be used, and the time stages within which the developments shown on the plan were to be undertaken. They then list what topics the plan might be expected to cover, giving a clear indication of the planning policy that the local planning authority was expected

16 Healey, p 45.
17 SI 1965/1453.

to consider. For example, a plan might define the sites of proposed roads, public and other buildings; allocate areas of land for residential, industrial and other purposes; and designate areas of comprehensive development.[18] At a somewhat more mundane but practical level, the Regulations also indicated the scale of the ordnance survey base maps to be used for such an exercise, the most common being 'county maps', on a scale of one inch to one mile, and 'town maps', on a scale of six inches to one mile.[19] Other maps for particular forms of proposal were also specified,[20] while all plans submitted before 1965 had to be accompanied by a programme map indicating the dates within which the proposed developments might be expected to take place.

To constitute a complete development plan, these maps had to be supplemented with a written statement which provided additional information that did not lend itself to being indicated directly on the maps. Information would be provided, for example, indicating the policy on residential densities and the form of development permitted in rural areas. Development plans submitted after 1965 would also contain written information on the phasing of development, information that previously had been indicated on the maps. In addition, if an area had been indicated on the map as a comprehensive development area, the written statement would give some indication of the purpose of such proposals.

The 'old style' development plan, therefore, consists of the maps, of which there are normally many, and the written statement. This is inevitably a concise document that explains little regarding the planning concepts and policies, concentrating instead on details, such as development densities. Despite the fact that these plans are clearly map-based, the written statement is specified as taking precedence if there is a contradiction between it and the maps.[1] This can be explained only on the grounds that the Ministry of Town and Country Planning must have realised that if these plans were to be regarded as the local expression of national land policy, then that policy had to be presented in some form of written statement which indicated some logical reasoning. In reality, however, the plans were seen by both local planning authority and developer as simply a means of controlling land use.

The 1947 Act specified that the plans were to be based on a survey of the local authority area. In addition, the plans were

18 Ibid, reg 4.
19 Ibid, regs 5 and 6.
20 Ibid, regs 7-10.
1 Ibid, reg 15.

to represent a local interpretation of national land use policy, but this policy was not particularly evident in the early 1950s when the plans were first being prepared. Consequently, the plans tended to reflect the findings of the local survey, which usually concentrated on the basic planning elements, such as land use patterns and densities of occupation. Given the belief that the public sector was to undertake the majority of development, and the supposition that the private sector would be making few applications for planning permission, the early plans were little more than graphic indications of existing land use patterns. This was probably recognised as being somewhat less than what a development plan should be, but as the plans were intended to be revised on a regular basis every five years, local planning authorities simply concentrated on getting their first plan approved.

What actually happened is well recorded and is summarised in the Planning Advisory Group Report in 1965. Effectively, the original plans became, in many instances, frozen as the only approved planning control documents for an area. Even when they were revised, that was nothing more than a simple update of the first plan in terms of altered land use zones and new densities. Despite these shortcomings, in some areas these documents still remain the only approved detailed plan and, as such, must be referred to as the approved policy document when a planning application is made. The plans effectively represented negative planning controls and, as such, bore little relationship to the original concept that created them. Although this is no longer the case with modern, post-1971 Act development plans, it is important to understand this usage of the 'old style' development plans, as it may help to place them in their correct perspective if they are encountered in dealing with a current planning application.

Some of these plans were revised, and in this state they may be regarded as having a somewhat greater contribution to make to an understanding of the development of current local planning policy. This is due to the fact that in the 1960s local authority planning departments became more aware of the needs and limitations of the planning system. At the same time more policy guidance became available from central government. This central government policy took several forms but most common were the planning bulletins.[2]

2 For example, Planning Bulletin No 1, Town Centres – Approach to Renewal, included advice and direction on preparing a development plan review relating to the regeneration of town centres.

The plans had to be reviewed every five years, but this did not always occur and the plans, often in only their first revised state, have not been superseded in many areas, and will, there-fore, have to be taken account of as valid planning policy though their relevance is obviously an issue. However, a large number of these 'old style' plans were replaced, in whole or in part by local plans produced under the 1971 Act and their total demise will take place once all authorities have completed their preparation and approval of the 'new' local plans required by the 1990 Act.

DEVELOPMENT PLANS UNDER THE 1971 ACT

Three new forms of development plan were introduced under this Act – structure plans, various forms of local plan, and finally unitary plans. In addition, a whole range of directions regarding plan preparation and approval together with an increasing amount of government advice as to form and content was forthcoming, in contrast to the situation under the earlier legislation. Structure plans and unitary plans were not replaced in the 1990 Act. As a consequence, much of that procedure and advice concerning their production, which was originally offered in the 1971 Act, has been incorporated into the 1990 Act and it will be more appropriate to consider it when that Act is reviewed. The local plan, however, has not been retained in its 1971 form but since it still remains current policy until superseded by the 'new style' local plan, it is important to consider its form and content in some detail here.

The survey Part II of the 1971 Act was concerned with structure and local plans and section 6 deals exclusively with the survey that must precede the creation of both types of plan. Since the work involved in the survey has, in the past, always proved to be a major undertaking, it was generally acknowledged that the one major survey would serve the needs of both structure and local plans and this remains the case under the 1990 Act. The survey was normally undertaken by the county planning authority, since it had always been assumed that the survey was a specific procedure which would precede the formulation of the structure plan. Section 6 was not specific on this point.[3] It simply required that every local planning authority

3 Section 6 of the 1971 Act did not refer to any form of development plan, nor which level of local planning authority was expected to undertake the survey. The situation has not changed as s 30 of the 1990 Act retains virtually the same wording.

must institute a survey of all or part of its area if it had not already done so.

As the requirements for the survey remain largely unaltered it is more appropriate to consider them in detail when the 1990 Act is being examined. All that needs to be noted at this stage is that local plans were required to be based upon a considerable amount of survey information as befitted their role as detailed policy documents.

The local plan Local plans had four main functions:

> (a) to develop the policies and general proposals of the structure plan and relate them to precise areas of land defined on the proposals map; (b) to provide a detailed basis for development control; (c) to provide a detailed basis for co-ordinating and directing development and other use of land – both public and private; and (d) to bring local planning issues before the public.[4]

Clearly, these statements raise issues that need explanation. Some indication is necessary as to who produced such plans and how they have developed within the present planning system; their relationship with structure plans; and the nature of their form and content, as well as the means by which they gained approval.

Function The first of these questions can easily be answered by referring to section 11 of the 1971 Act which dealt with the preparation of local plans. In this section the phrase 'local planning authority' was frequently used in connection with local plan preparation, and no distinction was made between either county planning authority or district planning authority. This implies that either local planning authority could prepare a local plan, the criterion being simply the local planning authority's perceived need for such a plan. What was also made clear in the same section, was that, unlike structure plans, the decision to prepare a local plan was at the discretion of the local planning authority. Although the Secretary of State could direct the matters to be included in such a plan, he had no power to insist that a local plan should be prepared.

Given this fact, it might be concluded that local plans were not expected to play a major role within the planning system, but in reality nothing was further from the truth. The fact that a local planning authority was under no duty to prepare such plans simply reflected the actual situation. This was that many

4 Circular 22/84, para 3.1.

areas were either already fully developed to a level of practical equilibrium, or were areas within which extensive development pressures were unlikely to occur. In these instances, a local plan would be superfluous to the needs of the local planning authority, and, given the lengthy procedures that had to precede its approval, its existence would be an unnecessary luxury.

Local plans were, therefore, usually optional,[5] but a number were prepared and adopted. Available statistics make it possible to gain an accurate indication of the extent of local plan production. From the date of the adoption of the first local plan in the City of Coventry (the Eden Street Action Area Plan) in 1975, production was erratic. In 1976 it was estimated that 3,543 local plans would be adopted in England by 1980, excluding the Greater London Council area.[6] However by that date only 304 had been adopted,[7] whilst some years later in March 1986 this total had risen to 474. Suggestions have been offered on why so few local plans were approved. Local planning authorities were advised by the Department of the Environment[8] that only plans which could be prepared and adopted within one year should be included in their estimations. Local planning authorities also undoubtedly made use of alternative non-statutory policy documents, or simply no longer saw a need for plans proposed in the first flush of enthusiasm. For whatever reason, the fact remains that the number of local plans adopted was far less than originally anticipated.

Form The concept underlying local plans made under the 1971 Act is to be found in the Planning Advisory Group Report of 1965, where they were seen as the vehicles for the local detail that was needed to flesh out the broader planning policies expressed at county level within the structure plans. This idea caused no comment at the time, as it was envisaged that local plans would operate in much the same way as the 'old style' development plan but with one major exception – they would not need central government approval – an aspect which did

5 Any action area local plans indicated in a structure plan approved prior to 13 November 1980 had to be prepared by the relevant local planning authority. This requirement was subsequently removed by the Local Government, Planning and Land Act 1980.

6 Mabey R and Craig L 'Development Plan Schemes' The Planner, 1976, p 70.

7 Bruton M and Nicholson D 'Local Planning in Practice: A Review' The Planner, 1985, December, p 14; Coon A G 'Local Plan Coverage in the UK' The Planner, 1986, January, p 28.

8 Circular 23/81, Local Government, Planning and Land Act 1980 – Town and Country Planning: Development Plans.

indeed generate debate.[9] The Planning Advisory Group, however, seemed unconcerned over this point, possibly because the Group clearly had a view of the plan as performing more of an advisory than a controlling role:

> We would again stress the function of plans not primarily as a control mechanism but as a positive brief for developers, public and private, setting the standards and objectives for future development.[10]

Nevertheless, the local plan was described in their 1965 Report as being a detailed implementation document that not only laid down the basis for the control of all forms of development, both public and private, but also informed the public regarding the planning of their area. In order to enable this form of both positive and public planning to take place, three kinds of local plan were suggested:

(i) *Action area plans.* These were clearly seen as the most important. They were to be created for areas, implicitly urban, in which a total scheme of large-scale comprehensive planning action was to be undertaken within ten years.
(ii) *District plans.* These were intended for urban areas and were effectively to relate the action area plans with each other, while supplying a lower level of development control criteria for the remaining area.
(iii) *Town maps and village plans.* These were for those non-metropolitan areas in the counties, and effectively undertook the same job as a district plan.

The Town and Country Planning Act 1968, however, simply established a procedure for approval and a broad form of content for local plans, but did not go into detail regarding the three types proposed. More advice on the form of local plans was forthcoming in the Development Plan Manual 1970 and related regulations. This advice reiterated the original Planning Advisory Group suggestions, with the exception of the idea for specific town and village plans, which was thought to be unnecessary as these areas could be covered by the district plan. Instead, the idea of a subject plan was introduced. This was seen as a plan designed to concentrate on a single planning issue,

9 For example, see: Heap D 'Exit the Development Plan: or the Shape of Planning Things to Come' Journal of Planning and Property Law, 1965, p 591; Town Planning Institute, 'Council's Observations on the Planning Advisory Group Report' Journal of the Town Planning Institute, 1966, 52(3), p 86.

10 Planning Advisory Group Report (1965) para 5.3.

such as a green belt, that may cross local planning authority boundaries. Stress was also laid upon the fact that local plans '...must conform generally to the approved structure plan; they will develop the policies and proposals in it'.[11]

The Town and Country Planning Act 1968 was, however, repealed and replaced by the Town and Country Planning Act 1971 which established a new statutory basis for local plans. Changes to the system of local government,[12] however, necessitated amendments to the 1971 Act which effectively lengthened the transition period. From 1976 onwards, however, advice from the Department of the Environment concentrated for the first time on the content of local plans.[13] It was made clear that the content of the early plans was far too wide and, in some cases, inappropriate, and that local plans should concentrate on what was seen as their prime role – providing the detail for development control. This has been suggested as contradicting the concept of these plans as envisaged in the Town and Country Planning Acts 1968 and 1971 and their related regulations, where they were seen as much wider policy documents.[14] Their prime role as development control documents was confirmed in a subsequent circular[15] which added to existing advice by clarifying the purpose of the subject plan; emphasising the need for all types of local plan to be site or area specific; and urging that local plans be created as soon as possible to replace non-statutory plans and policies. Further advice then concentrated on the need to make the plans concise, clear and precise documents, while what was considered to be appropriate, as opposed to unacceptable, content was mentioned, using the example of housing. In this context land should be allocated for housing but housing areas should not be allocated to the public or private sectors, that is, 'use' rather than 'user' should be the concern of the local planning authority.

Major changes to the system were then brought about as a consequence of the Conservative administration taking office

11 Development Plan Manual 1970, para 7.4.

12 The Local Government Act 1972 introduced considerable changes to the counties and districts, with wholesale boundary reorganisation resulting in new county and district areas as well as new county names.

13 Circular 55/77, Town and Country Planning Act 1971: Memorandum on Structure and Local Plans, and two advice notes – Local Plans Note 1/76, Development Plan Schemes and Local Plans, and Local Plans Note 1/78, Form and Content of Local Plans.

14 Loughlin M 'Planning Control and the Property Market' Urban Law and Policy, 1980, 3, pp 1-22.

15 Circular 55/77, para 3.28.

in 1979. Immediately, the new Secretary of State initiated work on what was to become the Local Government, Planning and Land Act 1980, which was responsible for the main phase of local plan production under the 1971 Act. Part IX of the 1980 Act, which amends the 1971 Act, was specifically concerned with planning matters involving development plans. The majority of the provisions demonstrated the intention of the government to speed up the planning process by making the preparation of local plans somewhat easier. At the same time, the 1980 Act introduced a considerable devolution of real development control power into the hands of the district planning authorities, with the requirement that county planning authorities now had only to be consulted, rather than acceded to, regarding the likely effects of structure plan policies on local plans. As a consequence, central government control over local plan issues through the indirect medium of structure plan policy was somewhat devalued. Circular 23/81, Development Plans, sought to restore the balance, not only by suggesting that consultation with the regional offices of the Department of the Environment in relation to local plan preparation was advisable, but also by revising slightly the role of local plans. The Circular suggested that local plans were not needed where there was little pressure for development as the structure plan policies would suffice, and also that the absence of a local plan was not a good reason for refusing planning permission.

All this advice was finally summarised in Circular 22/84, Memorandum on Structure and Local Plans, which offers the following comment on the all-important interpretation of the relationship between local plans and structure plans:

> Local plans are likely to be needed where the strategic policies in the structure plan need to be developed in more detail, the structure plan provision for development and other use of land needs to be related to particular sites and local planning issues need to be brought before the public. Where provision for growth is proposed, local plans will be required to identify the locations of land...and to provide a basis for co-ordinating programmes for development, improvement and protecting the environment. Where restraint is necessary, local plans may be required to identify the limits of such growth as is to be permitted.[16]

The point noted in earlier circulars that local plans were not needed for all areas was thus reiterated, and the criteria for needing a local plan remained those of either controlling or encouraging development in specific areas. The question of

16 Circular 22/84, para 3.10.

informal plans was raised, and it was made quite clear that where such documents were to be used primarily for development control, they should be formalised into some kind of local plan as soon as possible.

The three forms of local plan are then described.

(i) A general or district plan could be prepared to cover the whole or any part of the area covered by the structure plan, and contain proposals relating to as many or as few topics as seem appropriate. From this it seems quite clear that the old idea of a development plan covering everything in an area in detail was, at least for the time being, an historic concept. This did not, however, overcome the practical problem that the local planning authority would be faced on a daily basis with development control decisions that were not covered in recent local planning policy.

(ii) The second form of local plan was the subject plan. Its 'purpose is to concentrate on the preparation of proposals for one or two issues across what may be an extensive area'.[17] Many green belt plans were subsequently prepared under the subject plan title, seeming to fit in well with this concept, but Circular 22/84 also suggested that the general or district local plan might be as appropriate a vehicle for such subject plan topics.

(iii) The final form of local plan was also specific, being an action area plan which was intended to indicate priority areas, which, in the opinion of the local planning authority, required extensive development or redevelopment within the immediate future. This form of local plan had a slightly different history from the other two, as prior to the Local Government, Planning and Land Act 1980 these plans were the only local plans mentioned in the structure plan. This meant that they had to be prepared as soon as practicable, a requirement which remained in being for those action areas specified prior to 1980, and which were still without approved plans. Following the Local Government, Planning and Land Act 1980 it was no longer possible for structure plans, approved after the commencement of the Act, to call for such action area plans, but they still could be created if there was a need for that type of local plan.

The relationship between these three types of plan and the structure plan is further explained in Circular 22/84, especially with regard to the possibility of policies within different local

17 Ibid, para 3.15.

plans overlapping one another in a particular area. It was stressed that if each plan generally conformed with the policies within the structure plan, there should be no conflict. However, if conflict, or rather differences of policy, did occur in overlapping local plans, the most recently approved plan would prevail.

Content and scope As to the content of a typical local plan, it is true to say that no such beast exists, as each plan, if it was fulfilling its planning purpose, had to be specifically related to its own particular area and was therefore unique. It is possible, however, to consider the form that the content of these plans had to take, as that was clearly stated in the Town and Country Planning (Structure and Local Plans) Regulations 1982 and reiterated in Circular 22/84.

Local plans consisted of a written statement and a proposals map. The written statement clearly set out the local planning authority's proposals in such detail as might be appropriate, and which should be clearly distinguishable from the rest of the text. The remaining text contained a justification of the proposals, including their relationship to the structure plan, and included any such information or diagrams as were appropriate, providing that the latter did not confuse any information included on the proposals map. This map was based on an ordnance survey map showing the grid lines and numbers, so that it could easily be placed in its geographical context, and at an appropriate scale that was large enough to indicate individual properties if any were to be affected by the plan's proposals. There would only be one such map which would define the area of the plan and indicate all the proposals in the written statement insofar as they related to land use and development.

Finally, in the event of any conflict between the written statement and the proposals map, the written statement should prevail. Local plans were clearly intended to indicate the specific land use proposals that would form the basis of development control in all its local detail. For example, it should have been possible for a potential developer to refer to the local plan in order to ascertain what the specific land use proposals were for the site he intended to develop.

Returning to the content of such plans, it can be shown that, in practice, the range was very wide indeed. One contemporary analyst considered the content of seven local plans and gave examples of the policy statements that they contained.[18] For

18 Healey, ch 7.

example, the general employment policy from the Islington Development Plan stated:

> The Council will carefully consider the employment implications of all proposals for development and change of use and will treat these as being material considerations in the determination of planning applications. Subject to the specific land use and environmental policies set out elsewhere in the plan sympathetic treatment will normally be given to developments which bring employment benefits to the borough.[19]

Much more specific policy statements can also be found within the plans, such as the example quoted by another source from the Hucknall District Plan (Nottinghamshire):

> 18 hectares of land will be developed for industry and/or warehousing over and above that already with planning permission for such including
>
> (a) 5.3 hectares south of Watnall Road,
>
> (b) 0.6 hectares besides the Ambulance Station, Watnall Road, ...[etc].[20]

Many such examples could be quoted from any local plan, but all would be rather meaningless unless the reader was familiar with the specific area referred to within the proposals. This very point, however, serves to illustrate exactly what local plans were, and indeed still are – very local policy statements relating to the ways in which the land might be developed – all contained within documents that may run to over one hundred pages, or consisting of a single written page plus a map, that may be lavishly illustrated or contain no illustrations at all. 'One might say that the only common element about them is that they are on A4-sized paper',[1] and that they all consisted of a written statement and a proposals map.

DEVELOPMENT PLANS UNDER THE 1990 ACT

The development plans discussed to date – 'old style' development plans and 1971 Act local plans – have a limited life-span as they are gradually being replaced by the 1990 Act development plan system. The 1990 Act system calls for three types of plan – structure plans, local plans and unitary plans. Two of

19 Ibid, p 174.
20 Telling AE and Duxbury RMC *Planning Law and Procedure* (9th edn, 1993) p 63.
1 Healey, p 128.

these, structure and unitary plans, predate the 1990 Act and were retained, with revisions, in the present Act. Hence the decision to analyse their form and content in this section. In contrast 1990 Act local plans are of a very different nature from their predecessors. Since these three forms of plan now represent the current system it is essential to examine their nature and structure.

The survey The requirement to undertake a survey prior to preparing or revising a development plan has remained largely intact from its introduction in the 1971 Act. What is evident is that this process is now so familiar a part of plan making that little advice is needed. Consequently in the main policy document – PPG 12, Development Plans and Regional Planning Guidance – three brief paragraphs[2] are all that are offered to supplement the requirements set out in section 30 of the 1990 Act.

The need to undertake a survey does not distinguish between the local planning authorities who may be involved nor the type of plan to be produced. This is simply because the nature of the information collected – economic characteristics of the area, population distributions, transport networks – may be equally valid for any type of development plan. Indeed, PPG 12 suggests that local planning authorities should co-operate in sharing this information.[3]

The other point needing clarification is the requirement in the 1990 Act to survey all or part of the area. This is not an attempt to save money, but rather it recognises that survey work has been an integral part of the planning process for some time. For example, a local planning authority could have been involved in carrying out relevant survey work, since it was made a requirement in the Town and Country Planning Act 1968. Consequently, the need to conduct a survey for the purposes of any development plan preparation demands that only those areas as yet unsurveyed or in need of updating should be included in the new survey. Section 30 also requires that any matters included in the survey be kept constantly under review. A local planning authority can institute a fresh survey at any time if it is thought appropriate. Realistically, the possibility of an entire new survey being conducted in anticipation of the revision of any plan is extremely unlikely, due to the heavy cost, the amount of time needed, and the levels of expertise required.

2 Paras 4.1-4.3.
3 PPG 12, para 4.2.

Section 30 also requires that the local planning authority must 'institute' such a survey. This instruction is deliberate, and reflects a more realistic and modern approach to the creation of planning policy, in that local planning authorities are thereby empowered to seek the help of outside planning consultants in the preparation of the plans. Given the complexity of some of the issues that may have to be included in development plans, it would be unrealistic to assume that every planning authority would have the necessary planning experts 'in house'. Consequently, the use of outside experts where necessary has had the important effect of strengthening the development plan as a major policy document.

Finally, the local planning authority is under a duty to consider in the survey matters which might be expected to affect the development of the area. They are the principal physical and economic characteristics of the area, including the details of land use; the size, composition and distribution of the population; the whole of the communication infrastructure; and any other matters that are important to the full understanding of the area, or as may be prescribed by the Secretary of State. The most important requirement in planning terms, is that the survey must concentrate on the changes occurring or likely to occur in any of these matters. Where the subject matter demands it the survey must also take account of areas which lie outside the area of the local planning authority undertaking the survey.

The information accumulated from these surveys represents a unique set of data relating to each county and its districts. A synopsis of this information, moreover, is usually publicly available upon request and PPG 12 notes that this availability is underpinned by statute.[4] Such information thus provides a detailed social and economic data base that may be of use to both the private property development sector and academics.

Structure plans The notion, both official and academic, of exactly what structure plans are supposed to be and to do, has changed since they were first proposed in the Planning Advisory Group Report in 1965. What remains constant, however, is the insistence that these plans are to supply the rationale that underlies the policies of the local planning authority. At the same time they must avoid detailed land use proposals in relation to specific areas. They are, in effect, to outline and explain the strategic planning policies for the area in both its county and regional context, but quite what this entails, and

4 Local Government (Access to Information) Act 1985.

the manner in which it should be presented, has been redefined frequently since the 1965 Report.

Function The question of what exactly was the function of a structure plan was tackled directly in 1974 in Circular 98/74, The Functions of Structure Plans, and in the Town and Country Planning (Structure and Local Plans) Regulations 1974. These attempted to define the functions and content of structure plans in a manner that emphasised their general strategic role and the level of detail that should be included. The Circular listed three functions for the structure plan. First, structure plans should explain the local planning authority's policies and proposals for development, thereby giving guidance on issues of structural importance. Secondly, structure plans must demonstrate the integration and utilisation of national and regional policies within the area. Finally, they were to provide the basis for local plans by establishing the local planning framework. This precise description effectively laid the foundations for what were to become the established general functions of all structure plans and this has survived largely unchanged to the present day. Consequently, the modern concept of structure planning emerged in 1974 and has influenced the form, content and scope of the majority of plans approved after that date.

Structure plans were initially slow in appearing. No plans were, in fact, approved until 1975, when the first four appeared,[5] while only three more gained approval in 1976,[6] and in these cases it is unlikely that the modern concepts were included. Approvals gained in pace from 1977 onwards, however, and in these later plans it should be assumed that the 1974 concepts were fully integrated. Today, all parts of the country that need a structure plan have one in place but as PPG 12 notes, some are in need of revision and their scope and format should be amended in line with the advice provided within the policy note.[7]

Form PPG 12 confirms that the three functions of a structure plan remain unchanged in that the plans should:

- provide the strategic policy framework for planning and development control locally;

5 These were the Solihull County Borough Structure Plan, the Warwickshire Structure Plan, the Hereford and Worcestershire (Worcestershire) Structure Plan and the Coventry County Borough Structure Plan.

6 These were the Greater London Development Plan, the Hereford and Worcestershire (Herefordshire) Structure Plan and the Leicestershire (excluding Rutland) Structure Plan.

7 PPG 12, para 3.5.

- ensure that the provision for development is realistic and consistent with national and regional policy; and
- secure consistency between local plans for neighbouring areas.[8]

The structure plan itself consists of a written statement, and a key diagram, which takes the form of a generalised map of the area, and these documents must be accompanied by an explanatory memorandum.[9] The requirement for there to be an explanatory memorandum was introduced in the Local Government, Planning and Land Act 1980. Consequently, plans approved before 1980 will not have such a document, and the information normally to be found in the explanatory memorandum will be an integral part of the written statement.

As required by section 31 of the 1990 Act, the written statement must formulate the policy and proposals of the local planning authority. Such policies must cover conservation, the improvement of the physical environment and the management of traffic and also contain any other matters as directed by the Secretary of State. According to section 30(6) these policies and proposals must be formulated after regard has been had to any regional planning guidance, national policies and to the availability of resources needed to carry out the proposals for the area. Finally, section 30(5) requires that the whole statement must be illustrated by such diagrams as are needed to explain the plan more fully. This condition is amplified in the Regulations[10] where the need for a non-map-based key diagram is specified.

Prior to 1980, the written statement would also contain a full justification of each and every policy that the planning authority saw fit to place within the plan. Therefore, once the plan was approved by the Secretary of State, not only the policies within it, but also, by implication, the reasons supporting those policies, were given authority. Arguably, in considering policies in a pre-1980 structure plan, of which there are seventy-one, it is far more difficult to dispute the justification or appropriateness of any policy in that plan, since both the policy and the reasoning to support it have been formally approved.

After 1980, however, this 'justification' element has been transferred to the explanatory memorandum. The reason for this change is difficult to understand, as the level of reasoning that has to be included in the memorandum is no less de-

8 Ibid, para 3.4.
9 1990 Act, s 32(5).
10 Town and Country Planning (Development Plan) Regulations 1991, SI 1991/2794, reg 5.

manding than that which originally had to be included in the written statement. The memorandum, however, is not to be treated as forming part of the structure plan, despite being required as part of the formal submission. It may now be possible to dispute the justification for policies contained within post-1980 plans as they are not subject to approval. Current thought seems to suggest that the memorandum where relevant can be regarded as a material consideration.[11]

Content The content of the structure plan's written statement will vary depending on whether it is pre- or post-1980, but both forms of statement will indicate, in general terms, the county planning authority's policies and proposals for the development control of their area. Both PPG 12 and the Regulations[12] provide quite specific guidance on the subjects to be included in any revision or reworking of a structure plan but this advice will obviously only apply to future plan making activity and will not have been acted upon in existing plans. Before considering this advice in more detail, therefore, it is important to appreciate the form and the sources of the policies and proposals included in current structure plans in order to appreciate what constitutes an acceptable or unacceptable proposal.

The fundamental problem seems to lie in the structure of the plans themselves, where the policies expressed have to be broad enough to exclude specifically their interpretation as detailed development control policies. This, together with the fact that the topics that the plans could include were wide-ranging in the extreme, gave the local planning authorities a scope which they apparently found difficult to cope with. As various commentators have noted,[13] the content of structure plans has shown some marked changes since the first were approved in 1975. The early plans attempted a comprehensive approach, being much influenced by the strategies of regional planning.[14] Furthermore, due to the impossibility of analysing the enormous quantities of data that covered every aspect of what were often large county areas, the actual analysis often failed to go beyond even the most

11 *Encyclopedia of Planning Law and Practice*, Vol 2, p 31.05.

12 PPG 12; Town and Country Planning (Development Plan) Regulations 1991, SI 1991/2794.

13 For example: Drake M et al 'Aspects of Structure Planning' (1975) Centre for Environmental Studies Report 20; Barras R and Broadbent T A 'The Analysis in English Structure Plans' Urban Studies, 1979, p 1; Eke J F 'Structure Plans' Public Finance and Accountancy, 1977, p 149.

14 Davies C *Structure Plans: Theory and Practice* 1975, Midlands New Towns Society.

elementary levels[15] and the resulting policies were very broad and vague. For example, the following are two examples of policy statements taken from the City of Coventry Structure Plan, 1975:[16]

> *Transportation Policy*
> 5.5.1 The Council will pursue an integrated transport policy involving improvement and extension to the existing road network and public transport services and restraint on the use of the private car during the peak period by means of selective parking controls and traffic management.
>
> *Shopping*
> 5.7.4 Central Area
> The Council will encourage the quality, variety and extent of central area shopping provision by selective floorspace increase, concentrating upon the possible provision of a further department store and additional small shop units to improve trade mix, to ensure the maximum use of the resources of the City and enhance the commercial attractiveness of the City while having regard to the success of other policies which aim to absorb underutilised capacity of existing shops.

As can be seen, such statements are clearly capable of a wide interpretation, but it must be stressed that this does not negate in any way their standing as approved policy, providing that the structure plans from which they come are not in the process of being reviewed. Until such time, they remain a controlling force on the local planning authority, even if they no longer represent or indeed clearly state the policies of the authority.

Later plans, which were still in the process of preparation after the publication of the 1974 Circular,[17] all tended to concentrate on the advice which it contained, which was to isolate the key issues of the area rather than attempt the previous blanket approach. As a result, subsequent plans tended to be somewhat more specific in highlighting policies that were seen as fundamental to the effective planning of the area, and this trend continued until the last plan was approved in 1985. This concentration on specific policies, however, has not narrowed the range of subjects covered in the structure plan, as different counties concentrated on different issues, which naturally raises the important question of how certain issues were chosen and others excluded.

15 Barras and Broadbent.
16 These policies would now be integrated into the West Midlands Unitary Plan but remain effective examples of general strategy.
17 Circular 98/74, The Functions of Structure Plans.

The contents of some plans were clearly dictated by the geographical nature of the county, as in the case of the Cambridgeshire Structure Plan, which focused on the problems caused to the inhabitants by rural inaccessibility. However, as has been pointed out,[18] although the issues in the Cambridgeshire instance stemmed from the physical nature of the settlement pattern, the suggested policy solutions were of a distinctly social nature, effectively involving the redistribution of certain resources to disadvantaged groups. This raises the question of what constitutes acceptable policies within these plans, and the criterion seems to be that they must serve a genuine planning purpose. As to what exactly constitutes a planning purpose, this issue has been fully explored by the courts and will be considered in detail at the end of this chapter. At this stage it is sufficient to note that the House of Lords defined a planning purpose as that which related to the character of the use of the land.[19]

Little research has been undertaken on the question of how structure plan policies are produced.[20] What should be clearly understood is that structure plans are compromises in the truest sense, in that they reflect the intermediate course between conflicting opinions. The opinions include those of the planning officers in the local planning authority preparing the plan. There are also other groups whose opinions the plan-preparing authority has a statutory obligation to canvass. These include the district authorities within the county area, and local pressure groups, such as amenity societies, not to mention national pressure groups and central government itself. Added to this is the fact that local councillors will have ultimate control over the opinions that emerge as a result of the statutory consultation.

This may produce an interesting explanation as to the level of compromise included within the plans, as it has been suggested that: 'Policy choices spelt out too explicitly might generate opposition from councillors, from the districts, and from other powerful interests'.[1] This view has been supported by research.[2]

18 Bruce A 'Structure Plan Amendments Show Centralist Tendencies' Planning, 1980, 14 November, p 394.

19 *Westminster City Council v Great Portland Estates plc* [1985] AC 661, [1984] 3 All ER 744, HL.

20 Blowers A *The Limits of Power: The Politics of Local Planning Policy* (1980); Dare R 'Public Participation and State Power: the Case of South Yorkshire' Policy and Politics, 1979, p 337; 'The Dialectics of Policy-Making: Form and Content' in Healey P et al (Eds) *Planning Theory: Prospects for the 1980s* (1982).

1 Healey, p 58.

2 Blowers.

In terms of having their opinions incorporated as part of the plan, the most effective of these participating groups are probably the district councils and local pressure groups, followed by public agencies and central government departments who are motivated when policies touch on their specific interests. Least interested appears to be the private property sector, due possibly to the nature of these plans, containing, as they do, general rather than specific policies. These general policies tend to be non-site specific, insofar as, although they may be related to a particular part of the county area, such as a town centre, they do not, indeed must not, apply to any specific geographically definable parcels of land.

Consequently, it is only when such parcels of land are considered as suitable areas for housing development by the private sector, that concern would be shown regarding development policies within the structure plan. In taking this somewhat relaxed approach to structure plans, the private sector could be underestimating their significance within the planning system. Indeed, the requirement in section 54A that decisions should be made in accordance with the development plan unless material considerations dictate otherwise may provide the impetus for greater participation in the plan revising process. If development control decisions are to be plan-led, and PPG 1, General Policy and Principles, refers to a presumption in favour of development proposals which are in accordance with the development plan,[3] then private sector developers would do well to ensure that their views are made known when that document is in the process of revision.

Scope Having established that the policies and justifications contained, either within the written statement, or in the written statement and the explanatory memorandum, are compromises between the views of the various parties concerned, it is possible to consider the actual topics included. Ironically, clear guidance on what should be included only emerged in 1984[4] whilst the last structure plan was approved one year later. Obviously this advice was based partly upon what had actually been included in plans prior to that date and so provides an indication of the scope of such plans. More particularly, however, the guidance was undoubtedly observed in any modifications undertaken to structure plans between 1984 and 1991 when the advice underwent revision.

3 PPG 1, para 25.
4 Circular 22/84, Memorandum on Structure and Local Plans.

Circular 22/84 devoted a whole section to listing topics which should be considered within the plans. It emphasised that non-land use matters such as financial support, consultation arrangements and proposed methods of implementation should not be included as policies within the structure plan itself, but could be included in the explanatory memorandum if forming part of the reasoned justification. Further comments indicated that the plans should be precise but should not be over-detailed, particularly where they were quantified; that the policies should not be limited to any specific time duration; and that in relation to any revision of a plan, the current national or regional policies should be considered and included where appropriate. The importance of taking account of resources was then stressed, together with the importance of clearly stating the assumptions upon which various resource allocations were made.

The Circular then proceeded to cover the specific topics that should normally be included within structure plans. The first of these dealt with housing,the next covered industry and commerce, the third was shopping, the fourth transport facilities and the management of traffic. Comments then follow on agriculture and forestry, minerals, waste disposal, hazardous development, environment improvement and pollution control, environmental protection and conservation, green belts and recreation and tourism. Few significant points are raised, except to confirm the observation that policies within the plans may be reinforced by separate government policy or guidance.

Current guidance[5] on the topics to be included in structure plans, whilst it reproduces much of the earlier advice, now adopts a more prescriptive stance on what such plans should contain.

(i) Local planning authorities must have regard to regional and strategic planning guidance. This comes in the form of Regional Policy Guidance Notes.[6] The first guidance notes dealt with the metropolitan authorities who were then in the process of preparing unitary development plans. Guidance notes have now been published for the following regions: East Anglia, the Northern Region, the East Midlands Region, the South East and the South West. Strategic

5 PPG 12; SI 1991/2794.

6 The first three examples of regional planning guidance were in the form of Planning Policy Guidance Notes, but since 1989 all later examples have been issued as Regional Policy Guidance Notes.

planning guidance for Wales is also available.[7] Guidance notes are produced as a result of collaboration between the local authorities in the given region and the Department of the Environment. In this way structure plans within a given region will be able to relate to one another. This, in principle, removes the need for such plans to be approved by the Secretary of State.

(ii) Attention must be paid to national policy. This is not new but what has changed is that a list of such policy is now included as annex F to PPG 12. The list is comprehensive and is produced in the form of a matrix with eight broad policy areas identified, such as housing or the rural economy, and no less than eighty-three circulars, PPGs and related policy forming the rows. Indications are given in the cells of the matrix which policy statement should be consulted in relation to each general policy area.

(iii) Local planning authorities are to have regard to available resources and are urged, as they have been on previous occasions, to be as realistic as possible in forming policies.

(iv) Local planning authorities are to take into consideration any other matters that the Secretary of State may require. Whilst a list of these matters is provided for unitary plan authorities no such corresponding list exists for the producers of structure plans, which is in line with previous practice.

(v) Local planning authorities must consider social and economic issues, the latter being a new addition. Guidance as to exactly what should be included, such as levels of car ownership or rates of unemployment, is specified in PPG 12.[8]

(vi) Environmental issues must be considered. This is not new but there has undoubtedly been a change in emphasis as the government now places such issues high on its agenda. The significance of environmental issues is such that a substantial part of PPG 12 is dedicated to them. Local planning authorities are also urged to utilise the Department of the Environment's publication *Policy Appraisal and the Environment*.

7 PPG 12 (Wales), section 2.
8 PPG 12, paras 5.43 - 5.51.

(vii) Local planning authorities are required to have regard to the policies of urban development corporations. This is because such corporations do not have general strategic planning functions themselves and so their policies need to be brought into the context of strategic planning activity.

In the light of this and other guidance on the form, content and scope of structure plans, it seems surprising that the Secretary of State is no longer the individual charged with the decision of whether or not to adopt a revised or amended structure plan. This decision now rests with the relevant local planning authority. The Secretary of State possesses numerous supervisory powers including the power to direct a local planning authority to include or exclude policies from the plan[9] and to 'call in' the plan.[10] Resort to these powers is, however, not common. The Department of the Environment also monitors the revision of structure plans and can and does object to proposed policies. This still leaves unresolved the degree to which structure plans do observe central government guidance and policy. Given the enhanced legal status of these plans as a consequence of section 54A the degree to which they contradict central government policy could well become an important issue.

Approval Before a structure plan can be revised certain statutory procedures have to be observed. These are set out in the 1990 Act and the Town and Country Planning (Development Plan) Regulations 1991.[11] These documents go into considerable detail and it is sufficient here simply to note the most significant steps.

Prior to preparing its revisions the local planning authority must indicate the probable content of all relevant documents and consult with specified bodies.[12] After that consultation process is complete the plan is published and made available for public inspection for a six-week period. During this period interested parties can make representations to the local planning authority regarding its proposals. If there are objections to the proposals within the plan the local authority may attempt to reach agreement with the objectors and subsequently modify the proposed plan. Alternatively, and more usually, an Examination in Public (EIP) is held, either at the decision of the

9 1990 Act, s 17; *R v Secretary of State for the Environment, ex p London Borough of Islington* [1994] JPL B92.
10 1990 Act, s 18.
11 SI 1991/2794.
12 Ibid, reg 10.

planning authority or the direction of the Secretary of State, to consider the objections.

A code of practice has been agreed by the Secretary of State regarding the EIP.[13] Effectively, the procedure adopted is inquisitional, meaning that the inspectors, who are responsible for conducting the EIP, question the interested parties invited to attend in an attempt to clarify the points at issue. At the close of the EIP the inspector will produce a report for the local planning authority. On the basis of the report the authority can then either modify the plan, which results in another period of consultation and public participation or decline to do so. Ultimately, a point will be reached when the plan is considered satisfactory by the local planning authority, and the plan will be approved and published in the prescribed manner.

Local plans The underlying purpose of local plans has remained constant since their introduction in the early 1970s. It is to provide detailed policies in order to guide planning decisions.[14] Whilst under the previous legislation it was an option for local authorities to prepare local plans and also to decide what parts of the local authority area they would cover, it is now mandatory that various forms of local plan shall be prepared by planning authorities and that they shall cover the whole of the authority's area.[15]

Function The purpose of local plans is clearly if succinctly stated in the legislation:

> A local plan shall contain a written statement formulating the authority's detailed policies for the development and use of land in their area.[16]

This somewhat bald statement is further explained in PPG 12:

> In providing the detailed framework for the control of development and the use of land, local plans need, in general conformity with the structure plan:
> – to set out the authority's policies for the control of development; and
> – to make proposals for the development and the use of land and to allocate land for specific purposes.[17]

13 PPG 12, annex A.
14 Ibid, para 3.7.
15 1990 Act, s 36.
16 Ibid, s 36(2).
17 PPG 12, para 3.8.

In the light of what has been discussed earlier, it seems apparent that the function of local plans has remained constant but the form that they take has altered considerably.

Form Local plans now assume three distinct forms in non-metropolitan areas. First, there is the district-wide local plan normally prepared by the district planning authority. Secondly, there is the minerals local plan which typically covers the whole county and is prepared by the county planning authority. Thirdly, there is the waste local plan which is also county-wide and is prepared by the county planning authority. Clearly these new forms of local plan require some further explanation since they represent a departure from past practice.

District-wide local plans are always prepared by the district planning authority except in National Parks where different arrangements apply.[18] These plans contain the policies needed to control development within the area apart from policies concerning either minerals or waste, which are not within their remit.[19] In addition, these local plans may identify action areas, but these no longer require the preparation of a separate local plan.[20] Despite the fact that action areas no longer merit their own plan their purpose remains the same – areas selected for comprehensive development action by either the private or public sector which is to be completed within ten years.

Minerals local plans are to be produced by county planning authorities except within a National Park. Such plans shall:

> contain a written statement formulating the authority's detailed policies for their area in respect of development consisting of the winning and working of minerals or involving the depositing of mineral waste.[1]

The intention is to ensure that all areas possess sufficiently detailed policies relating to mineral development. Structure plans usually contain policies regarding such activities but of such generality that they are difficult to use in reaching a development control decision. Under earlier legislation, some but not all, authorities had produced subject plans covering these activities but the current legislation ensures that such

18 The Peak Park and the Lake District Park are planning authorities in their own right and prepare their own plans. In all other Parks joint boards are established whose members include the relevant county and district authorities. The latter are responsible for the preparation of the Park local plan.

19 1990 Act, s 36 (5)(a), (b).

20 Ibid, s 36 (8).

1 Ibid, s 37(2).

detailed mineral policies will be available throughout the whole of England and Wales.

Waste local plans are a little more complicated since not all local planning authorities will prepare them. The situation within National Parks is different since such policies will be found within the park's development plan. In England waste local plans will be prepared by county planning authorities but they are not obliged to have a separate plan but may include such policies in the minerals local plan.[2] In Wales, however, policies relating to waste are to be found in the district-wide local plans.[3]

Thus under the present system when all the new forms of local plan have been approved, there will always be a district-wide local plan and a county-wide minerals plan to supplement the county-wide structure plan. In addition a county-wide waste local plan may exist in England. Whilst these plans are in the process of preparation, questions of conformity and precedence are likely to rise, and detailed advice may be found to clarify what can be a complex situation.[4] Simply stated, all plans should conform to the relevant revised structure plan, whilst in the case of conflict between plans the general rule of thumb is that the most recent prevails.

Content and scope As with earlier versions of local plans it remains true that there is no such thing as a typical plan in relation to its content. On the other hand the form and content that such plans must follow is indicated, along with much else that has been considered above, in the appropriate regulations and guidance note.[5]

The requirements remain much the same as for plans formed under previous legislation. Plans must have titles and, in certain instances such as when minerals policy is contained within a local plan, sub-titles. Plans must contain clear statements relating to their objectives and reasoned justifications as to why these objectives are being proposed. Local plans must also contain proposal maps based on the appropriate scale of ordnance survey map.

As to the actual content of such plans, that depends upon the area included and the policies being proposed, and so it has little meaning for anyone not intimately involved with the actual

2 Ibid, s 38(2)(b).
3 PPG 12(Wales), para 1.9.
4 1990 Act, ss 46 and 54, PPG 12, paras 3.16 and 3.17 and 4.13-4.15.
5 Town and Country Planning (Development Plan) Regulations, 1991, SI 1991/2794, Pt 2; PPG 12, section 7.

physical location and its development. This fact thus serves to illustrate once again that local plans are intended to be just that – local policy statements designed to guide and control local development activity.

Approval The procedure for the formal adoption of local plans is laid down in the Regulations and PPG 12.[6] The process is very similar to that for structure plans. Any objections to a proposed plan may be considered at a local inquiry. Once considered, modifications may be put forward. The local planning authority possesses the power either to accept or reject such modifications and is responsible, subject to the supervisory powers of the Secretary of State, for the decision to adopt the plan.

The adoption of a local plan can be a lengthy process, particularly because of the increased interest that individuals and organisations are taking in their content. Other factors can also cause delay, such as the need to await a structure plan review since local plans cannot proceed when such a review is in progress. Because of the Department of the Environment's wish to have 1990 Act local plans in place by 1996, they have expressed concern at the time taken to produce a local plan. As a consequence a series of changes has been proposed, most of which are administrative in nature, such as a clearer lead from the inspector on the issues to be discussed at the local inquiry and the removal of excessive detail.[7]

Unitary development plans These plans are currently to be found only in the six metropolitan counties and Greater London. They were introduced in 1985 and their purpose, form and content has remained largely unchanged by later legislation. Simply stated, these plans combine the fea-tures to be found in structure and local plans and their purpose is identical. The only fundamental difference is procedural in that there is no county level authority within such metropolitan areas so that the preparation of the county-wide planning strategy is undertaken by the urban districts acting together as a joint planning body. With that exception, all procedures, form and content, are identical to that already discussed in relation to structure and local plans. Indeed, to emphasise this point PPG 12 states:

6 SI 1991/2794, Pt 4; PPG 12, section 4 and annex A.
7 Improving the Local Plan Process. Department of the Environment Consultation Paper, May, 1994.

> Unless the context otherwise requires, references in this PPG to structure plans include UDP Part Is and references to local plans include UDP Part IIs ...[8]

Unitary development plans are based on a survey, which is effectively the revised and updated survey inherited from the abolished Greater London Council and metropolitan county councils. Equipped with this information, the local planning authorities, in this case urban district councils, set about the preparation of the plan. The plan consists of two parts. Part I is a written statement, setting out the general planning policies and for all practical purposes is identical to a structure plan. Part II is a little more complicated in that it consists of a written statement setting out detailed proposals for specific areas or topics, accompanied by a map indicating these proposals geographically. In addition, this information is accompanied by a reasoned justification of the policies in Parts I and II, together with any explanatory diagrams that may be appropriate.

Consequently, it is only this combination in one document of what is in effect a structure plan and the local plans covering the same geographical area, that a unitary development plan differs from the development system to be found throughout the greater part of England and Wales.

Development plans and the law

The title to this section is somewhat misleading, as frequent references to legislative provisions have already been made elsewhere in this chapter. Development plans are a statutory concept whose creation and implementation is regulated by legislation. The purpose of this section is simply to describe the law's treatment of a development plan, once that plan has been approved. The contents of a development plan are subject to legal scrutiny in very specific circumstances, which occur only infrequently.

JUDICIAL REVIEW UNDER SECTION 287

The first of these occasions is when a development plan has been finalised and approved by the relevant authority. It is possible at this stage to challenge the validity of a development plan or a policy within the plan. This process is described as a review,

8 PPG 12, para 1.10.

since it is the task of the court to consider whether the content of a development plan and the procedures relevant to its making are in accordance with what is required by the law. If they are not, the court has the power to set aside the whole or a part of a development plan. It is not, however, the task of the court to consider the merits of the development control policies in a development plan. Section 287(1) of the 1990 Act is the current source of this power of review:

> If any person aggrieved by a unitary development plan or a local plan, minerals local plan, waste local plan, or by any alteration, or replacement of any such plan or structure plan, desires to question the validity of the plan or, as the case may be, the alteration, or replacement on the ground —
> (a) that it is not within the powers conferred by Part II, or
> (b) that any requirement of that Part or of any regulations made under it has not been complied with in relation to the approval or adoption of the plan, or, as the case may be, its alteration, or replacement,
>
> he may make an application to the High Court under this section.

What is plain from the wording of section 287 is that the judicial challenge contemplated has to be made within six weeks of the relevant date,[9] and on very specific grounds which do not permit the planning merits of any particular policy to be reconsidered. In addition, the challenge has to be made by 'a person aggrieved'. What that expression signifies is that only those individuals and organisations, for example, property companies and amenity societies, who have been involved in the preparation and approval of a development plan, can take advantage of the opportunity offered in section 287.[10] Given the very specific nature of the challenge, not to mention the costs involved in taking a case to the High Court, it is hardly surprising to discover that few development plans have been scrutinised by the courts in these circumstances. From the challenges which have occurred, however, certain points have emerged which deserve emphasis.

9 1990 Act, s 287(4), (5). The relevant date is defined simply as the date of the notice approving the plan.

10 The preparation and adoption of a development plan can take several years and may involve hundreds of individuals. According to Purchas LJ in *Buckinghamshire County Council v Hall Aggregates (Thames Valley) Ltd* [1985] JPL 634 at 638, only procedural irregularities related to the adoption of a plan can be challenged under s 244 (now s 287 of the 1990 Act), as opposed to all procedural irregularities. This, if correct, may limit those who can challenge the development plan.

On the issue of observing the requirements of the 1990 Act and its associated regulations, what cases there have been have focused on the adequacy of reasons given for accepting or rejecting the recommendations made at the conclusion of the public scrutiny of a development plan. For example, in *Westminster City Council v Great Portland Estates plc*,[11] it was alleged that the local planning authority had rejected, without pro-viding adequate reasons, the modifications to its local plan suggested by the inspector. In considering this point, the House of Lords indicated that, in the words of the test in *Re Poyser and Mills' Arbitration*,[12] adequate, proper and intelligible reasons must be given. In addition, the House of Lords approved the decision of the High Court in *E H Bradley & Sons Ltd v Secretary of State for the Environment*,[13] which was to the effect that adequate, proper and intelligible reasons might also be brief reasons. Applying these two tests to the situation in question, the House of Lords decided that they had been satisfied, particularly in view of the fact that the Council had indicated its justification for adopting particular policies in the development plan itself.

Yet, however briefly the courts may allow reasons to be expressed, they will insist that some reason is given. In *Barnham v Secretary of State for the Environment*[14] the Secretary of State had left untouched a policy in a structure plan which had been the focus of considerable argument at the Examination in Public. In so doing the Secretary of State appeared to contradict his own policy, as set out in a departmental circular.[15] Consequently, in removing that policy from the structure plan, the court stated that in failing to give a reason, however brief, for its retention, the Secretary of State had failed to comply with the provisions of the then current legislation.

When preparing a development plan a local planning authority must also be sure to include in the plan all relevant information relating to the operation of any particular policy. In *Westminster City Council v Great Portland Estates plc*, the Council had sought, as a development plan policy, to confine office developments to a central zone. Development outside the zone would not be permitted, save in exceptional circumstances. Guidelines would, however, be prepared, indicating what amounted to such circumstances. These guidelines would not

11 [1985] AC 661, [1984] 3 All ER 744.
12 [1964] 2 QB 467, [1963] 1 All ER 612.
13 (1983) 47 P & CR 374.
14 [1985] JPL 861.
15 Circular 15/84, Land for Housing (now superseded by PPG 3, Housing).

be included as part of the development plan, but would be published separately. Since the House of Lords believed that these guidelines embodied an important aspect of the Council's policy, their omission from the plan constituted a failure to comply with the relevant provisions of the legislation, and hence the Council's policy on office development was deleted from the plan.

Even if it can successfully be shown that the requirements of the 1990 Act have not been observed this is not an end to the matter. The court will agree to set aside a policy within the development plan which is affected, only if an additional factor can be proved. According to section 287(2)(b) of the 1990 Act, this requires the court to be satisfied that:

> the interests of the applicant have been substantially prejudiced by the failure to comply with any requirement of that Part or of any regulations made under it,...

The reasons for including this provision are easy to understand. Given the relative complexity of the procedure which has to be observed in the production and approval of a development plan, it may be all too easy for mistakes to occur. If the most trivial of errors led to portions of the development plan being set aside by the courts, this would be out of all proportion to their likely effects. This explains the requirement that the applicant's interests must have been substantially prejudiced. In *Westminster City Council v Great Portland Estates plc*, the omission of the office development guidelines from the development plan had substantially prejudiced the interests of Great Portland Estates, since it had deprived the company of the opportunity to question those guidelines at the public inquiry into the plan.

Apart from procedural errors, proof that the powers in the 1990 Act have been exceeded constitutes sufficient grounds for challenging the validity of a development plan. The 1990 Act envisages that development plans are specifically intended to contain policy on planning. Therefore, any attempt to insert policies in such a plan which do not have a clear planning purpose may well be adjudged to be beyond the powers of the 1990 Act or *ultra vires*. There is evidence to suggest, however, that the courts will be generous in their interpretation of what constitutes a planning purpose. In *Westminster City Council v Great Portland Estates plc*, objections were raised to Westminster City Council's industrial policy contained in the development plan, which was devised in order to retain certain well-established industrial activities in the area. As a result of this policy, the Council had indicated that it would be reluctant to grant planning permission for the redevelopment or rehabilitation of property where such industrial activities were being undertaken, if it caused the activities to cease. It was argued that the effect of this policy was to make it exceedingly difficult for landlords to refuse new tenancies to industrial tenants in these properties. Since policies in a development plan should relate only to the land and its development in a planning context, it was argued that this industrial policy had wider social implications which rendered it *ultra vires*. On this issue, the House of Lords contented itself with saying that a policy having no objective other than the protection of the individual, might be considered *ultra vires*. Here, however, the policy in question had a definite planning purpose, namely the protection of various industrial uses. The fact that the tenants of certain premises would benefit from this policy was irrelevant, since it was a consequence of, not the purpose of, that particular policy.

Apart from alleging that a particular policy has no planning purpose, it is also possible to argue that the policies in a development plan, even though they have a planning purpose, are totally unreasonable. If, for example, a development plan contained a policy restricting the construction of new houses to a particular field in a particular village, and nowhere else in the area covered by the plan, the policy could have a planning purpose but this might not be considered a reasonable one. According to the courts, when a policy reaches the stage of being so unreasonable that no reasonable local planning authority would have adopted it, then that is proof that the power to create that policy has been exceeded, and the courts will intervene. In *Buckinghamshire County Council v Hall Aggregates (Thames Valley) Ltd*,[16] the reasonableness of a minerals subject plan was the issue. The alleged unreasonableness related to the way in which certain areas were designated as 'preferred areas' for mineral extraction, and others were excluded. This designation was made, it was suggested, without sufficient information on whether economically workable reserves existed in the 'pre-ferred areas'. Here, the Court of Appeal made it clear that there must be overwhelming proof of unreasonableness, which was not apparent in this case. The suggestion that 'unreasonable' in this context be treated as the antonym of 'reasonable' was rejected. If it had not been, the courts might, in the future, have fallen into the error of substituting their view for that of the individuals or bodies charged with the duty of preparing the development plan.

16 [1985] JPL 634.

Certainly, in the past, the courts' decision to set aside a development plan policy on the basis of its being unreasonable has been criticised. The conclusion reached in *Fourth Investments Ltd v Bury Metropolitan Borough Council*[17] is an example. Here, the West Bury Local Plan had allocated some land to be included in the green belt rather than be used for residential development. Although at the public inquiry the inspector expressed the view that insufficient land was available to meet Department of the Environment advice on the supply of housing land, he went on to confirm this particular allocation of land to the green belt. In the view of McCullough J the inspector's failure to explain his reasoning was a serious omission, since the inspector had made no attempt to assess whether, in the light of this shortfall, the land in question might be required for housing. On this basis McCullough J concluded:

> on the inspector's findings (or his inability to make findings far enough into the future) about housing land requirements and upon his findings about the open land and green belt significance of the applicants' site, the chances that the applicants' site might be needed for housing before 1991 were sufficiently high for it to have been wrong to allocate a green belt notation to this site. This was not merely to say that he disagreed with the inspector's planning judgment. I believe that he had reached a conclusion which could not reasonably have been reached.[18]

Although the inspector's reasoning might have been at fault, this hardly seems a basis for concluding that his decision was one which no reasonable inspector could have reached.

The difficulty of challenging the validity of a development plan under the terms of section 287 should now be apparent. If an applicant is successful, however, the courts have considerable discretion in the action they take. Section 287(2)(b) provides that a court may:

> wholly or in part quash the plan or, as the case may be, the alteration, or replacement either generally or in so far as it affects any property of the applicant.

In *Westminster City Council v Great Portland Estates plc*, the House of Lords deleted that policy within the local plan which related to office location. In contrast, the offending policy in the West Bury Local Plan was deleted in *Fourth Investments v Bury Metropolitan Borough Council* only in so far as it affected the applicants' land. What the court cannot do, however, is to

17 [1985] JPL 185.
18 Ibid, at 187.

rewrite any part of a development plan. In *Buckinghamshire County Council v Hall Aggregates (Thames Valley) Ltd*, for example, the judge at first instance concluded that there were grounds for a successful challenge under the equivalent section of the 1971 Act. Instead of setting aside the minerals subject plan, he modified it in such a way that it was no longer acceptable to the local authority, a fact which was commented upon when his decision was set aside in the Court of Appeal.

DEVELOPMENT PLANS AND DECISION-MAKING

Once the six-week period for challenge provided for in section 287 has elapsed, a development plan, together with its policies, is incapable of direct review by the courts. Yet it can still be the object of judicial comment by virtue of the power given to the court in section 288 of the 1990 Act. Among other matters, this section allows the courts to set aside the Secretary of State's decision either to grant or refuse planning permission on appeal. This is done on the basis that his decision has been made in disregard of the relevant procedure, or in excess of his statutory powers. Section 70(2) of the 1990 Act sets out the factors that have to be taken into account when determining an application for planning permission.

> In dealing with such an application (for planning permission) the authority shall have regard to the provisions of the development plan, so far as material to the application, and to any other material considerations.

The courts have interpreted this as meaning that if the development plan is relevant to the decision being made it must be taken into account, but once that has been done, it is perfectly legitimate to use some other source of policy to resolve the development control issue.

This is understandable when the provisions of section 288 of the 1990 Act are recalled. All it allows the court to do is determine whether the correct procedure has been followed and the requirements of the 1990 Act observed. The same was true of the corresponding provisions under the 1971 Act. Under section 70(2) alone the courts cannot ensure that the policies of the development plan prevail. This point is illustrated in *Greater London Council v Secretary of State for the Environment*.[19] This case concerned the development of the Coin Street area of London. After various schemes had been proposed, outline

19 [1983] JPL 793.

planning permission was granted to Greycoat Estates by the Secretary of State.[20] During this period, political power changed hands on the Greater London Council and an administration which had previously backed the Greycoat scheme was ousted in favour of one which wanted to see the site developed differently. Once announced, the Secretary of State's decision was challenged in the courts by the new majority party on the Greater London Council, on the basis that he had exceeded his power by failing to take account of a change in council policy. This argument was rejected, since the court was convinced that the Secretary of State had taken into account all material considerations, including the change in council policy.

Throughout this dispute, little attention was paid to the relevant development plan and its policies on the redevelopment of Coin Street. These policies did not correspond with the opinions of either the Secretary of State or the Council. Arguably, there was little the court could do about this, since, once the development plan and every other material consideration had been taken into account, the Secretary of State was free to reach whatever conclusion he wished. In this fashion, the development plan, which was meant to play a major role in the development control process, had, so far as this particular area of London was concerned, become little more than a cipher.

Nor was that decision an isolated one. On numerous occasions the court has upheld the validity of a decision where some other material consideration has prevailed at the expense of the development plan.[1] Clearly the court was not to blame for this marginalising of the development plan since its views were based on what it saw as a proper interpretation of section 70(2). That interpretation said that the development plan was a consideration but not the only consideration in the decision-making process. Yet the practical effect of this was that even the most up-to-date development plan could be ignored.[2] This inevitably had consequences for the status of the development plan and undermined its standing as a key planning policy document.

As a consequence the political decision was taken to reassert the importance of the development plan. This took the form of an amendment to the 1990 Act. Section 70(2) must now be read

20 The application for planning permission had been called in by the Secretary of State.

1 *Ynys Môn Borough Council v Secretary of State for Wales* [1984] JPL 646, *Philglow Ltd v Secretary of State for the Environment* [1984] JPL 111.

2 *Waverley Borough Council v Secretary of State for the Environment* [1987] JPL 202.

in conjunction with section 54A[3] of the 1990 Act which states that:

> Where, in making any determination under the planning Acts, regard is to be had to the development plan, the determination shall be made in accordance with the plan unless material considerations indicate otherwise.

On the face of it section 54A seems to convey a clear message. If the policies in a development plan indicate that planning permission should or should not be granted then they are to be observed unless, as the section states, material considerations indicate otherwise. If, however, the development plan has nothing to say about the particular application then it will be determined on its merits in the light of all of the material circumstances.[4] This is undoubtedly an over-simplistic approach to section 54A. In the first place policies in development plans are normally general in nature. As one commentator has remarked '...it will be a very rare development proposal about which the standard development plan will not have a policy which is in some way "material" to that development proposal'.[5] Section 54A is, therefore, likely to be relevant to the majority of applications for planning permission.

Second, policies in a development plan will not necessarily be consistent with one another and will pull in different directions and hence give conflicting messages on how a particular application should be resolved. Nor, if the policies in a development plan are relevant, does section 54A say that they must be followed. There is undoubtedly a presumption to this effect but the strength of such a presumption is not immediately apparent. Development plans become 'stale' and may be overtaken by changes in central government policy. PPG 1 refers to the situation where:

> policies and proposals in the plan may have been superseded by more recent planning guidance issued by the Government, or developments since the plan became operative may have rendered certain policies or proposals in the plan incapable of implementation or out of date.[6]

In these circumstances the advice given is that factors such as these must be weighed against the development plan and the

3 As inserted by s 26 of the Planning and Compensation Act 1991.
4 PPG 1, General Policy and Principles.
5 Purdue M 'The Impact of section 54A' Journal of Planning and Environment Law, 1994, p 400.
6 PPG 1, para 27.

policies it contains. The implication is that this might well be an occasion when, rather than following the plan, 'material considerations indicate otherwise'. Quite clearly the meaning and weight to be attached to this phrase is crucial. PPG 1 also contemplates that even if a development plan is completely up to date there might still be circumstances when it will not be followed:

> Local planning authorities or the Secretaries of State may find it appropriate, on occasion, to permit a development proposal which departs from the development plan because the particular contribution of that proposal to some local or national need or objective is so significant that it outweighs what the plan has to say about it.[7]

Whilst the suggestion, when section 54A was first introduced, that it had the potential to transform the face of planning, is an over-exaggeration, it does undoubtedly mark a watershed. The era when the development plan was simply one factor amongst many to be taken into account has passed. Instead the plan now represents the starting point for determining planning applications and presumably departures from it must now be justified in some fashion. This raises the question of how the courts have interpreted the duty imposed on decision-makers by section 54A. This can be ascertained from a series of challenges mainly brought under section 288 where the courts have been asked to rule whether the demands of section 54A have been met. First the decision-maker has to have regard to the relevant policies in the development plan. What constitutes the development plan may not always be immediately apparent since the explanatory memorandum which accompanies the plan, for example, has not been regarded as part of the plan though it has been held to be a material consideration in determining whether or not to grant planning permission.[8] In contrast the Secretary of State's letter signifying approval of a plan does constitute part of the plan.[9]

Next the decision-maker has to apply those policies to the circumstances under consideration and in so doing may have to interpret them since the language used in development plans can be general in character. If those policies are misinterpreted

7 Ibid, para 30.

8 *Severn Trent Water Authority v Secretary of State for the Environment* [1989] JPL 21.

9 *South Western Regional Health Authority v Avon County Council* (1990) 62 P & CR 629, CA. For a contrary view see *Stratford-upon-Avon District Council v Sec-retary of State for the Environment* [1994] JPL 741 at 747.

this has been a ground in the past for the courts to intervene and set a decision aside,[10] though the warning has been voiced that 'the court should exercise great caution in taking into itself the task of interpreting the provisions of a development plan'.[11] Such matters are, it has been said, 'for those with experience and training in the subject'.[12] The increased emphasis placed on the development plan by section 54A may make it more likely that a decision-maker's interpretation of a policy will be challenged. This raises the question whether the courts should intervene only if there is an indisputable misapplication of the development plan. If the interpretation given by a decision-maker to a particular policy is a possible interpretation and plainly not wrong, then it should be allowed to stand. If this is not so the courts will begin to usurp the powers of the decision-maker via the process of review in section 288.[13]

If the development plan does contain relevant policies which suggest that an application for planning permission should or should not be granted, is that an end of the matter? In some cases it might be but this is not automatically so. In interpreting section 54A the courts have determined that it may create a presumption but one that can be rebutted where, in the view of the decision-maker, material considerations indicate otherwise.[14] What may be particularly relevant is whether the purposes of the development plan are harmed even though the letter of the plan may be ignored or, alternatively, whether any harm caused is outweighed by benefits occurring from the decision to depart from the plan.[15]

In the past the courts have had to deal with cases which arise when a development plan is in the course of preparation or revision. An application for planning permission may thus anticipate policy decisions to be made in a development plan. An application to build one hundred houses on a green field site, for example, may raise the issue of whether that land should be developed or allocated to the green belt. A local plan which

10 *Gransden & Co Ltd v Secretary of State for the Environment* [1986] JPL 519.

11 *Dibbon Construction Ltd v Secretary of State for the Environment* [1991] JPL 260 at 262. See also *H J M Caterers Ltd v Secretary of State for the Environment* [1993] JPL 337.

12 Ibid, at 262.

13 Purdue, pp 401-402.

14 *St Albans District Council v Secretary of State for the Environment* [1993] JPL 374, *Bylander Waddell Partnership v Secretary of State for the Environment* [1994] JPL 440.

15 *Bylander Waddell Partnership v Secretary of State for the Environment* (above) at 445.

is in preparation may be dealing with the identical issue. In contrast, an application for a change of use from house to nursing home may have little significance in relation to development plan policies. The courts appeared to take a pragmatic approach to the whole affair. If an application for planning permission was likely to have no repercussions upon a development plan in the course of preparation, then there was no reason for deferring a decision on the application. This was the opinion of the court in *J A Pye (Oxford) Estates Ltd v Secretary of State for the Environment*.[16] If, however, issues were raised by the application for planning permission which it appeared more appropriate to consider in the course of the public inquiry which accompanies the deliberations on a development plan, then an immediate decision on the application might be deferred. This was a matter for the exercise of judgment and not an automatic rule. As was said in *R v City of London Corpn, ex p Allan*:[17]

> But it is wrong to say...that a situation can come about where the holding of an inquiry into a proposed local plan creates a situation where it is wrong as a matter of principle for the planning authority to grant permission.[18]

These decisions have now to be seen in the light of section 54A. That section refers to a development plan, and by that means a development plan that has been approved rather than one in the course of production. This may mean, therefore, that an emerging development plan is no more than a material consideration to be taken into account with every other material consideration, although its 'weight' may be increased the closer it comes to approval. What will be crucial, as past authorities have stressed, is the effect the application for planning permission will have on the policies in that emerging plan.[19]

16 (1981) 261 Estates Gazette 368.
17 (1980) 79 LGR 223.
18 Ibid, at 227.
19 Graham T, 'Prematurity and Section 54A', Conveyancer, 1992, Vol 56, p 416.

Chapter 5

Local policy and special controls

The problem with this chapter is that two distinct, yet related, aspects of local planning control have to be considered. First, an examination must be undertaken of local policy, where it comes from, how it is used and the different forms that it can assume. Second, a detailed account will be given of those forms of local policy which manifest themselves as special controls. Essentially, special controls are part of the wider classification of local policy. In distinguishing between the two forms of policy the intention is to highlight the fact that some local policy has a statutory foundation, with the result that such policies, when implemented, are binding on those affected by them. The term special controls is, therefore, used to denote such local policy. In contrast, other local policy consists simply of informal planning documents whose status can vary in relation to the form in which it is presented. Finally, it should be made clear that, for the explanations contained in this chapter to be fully appreciated, it has to be read in conjunction with the previous chapter on development plans and the succeeding chapter concerning Department of the Environment policy. This is due to two important but distinct characteristics of the development control system.

First, it must be appreciated that although a development plan will contain policy which is local in its application and has a statutory basis, it is a unique document which is given special status in the development control process. The local policy which is discussed in this chapter is simply one of the 'material considerations' referred to in section 70 of the Town and Country Planning Act 1990. It is possible for such local policy to supplement a development plan or in the past substitute for one.[1]

1 The structure plan system now covers the whole of England and Wales. At present the local plan system is not totally comprehensive in its coverage but it is expected to be so in the near future since the preparation of local plans is now a mandatory requirement. Planning and Compensation Act 1991, Sch 4.

Second, the various means whereby the Department of the Environment exerts an influence on local policy must also be borne in mind. This is considered in some detail in the next chapter, particularly the influence of policy such as circulars and policy notes. These also constitute 'material considerations' in the context of section 70. The more general influence exerted by central government will be considered within this chapter.

The significance of local policy and its relationship with the development plan can best be illustrated by a simple example. A district planning authority is considering its conservation policy. This policy, which has as its objective the conservation of buildings and areas of particular architectural interest or especial character, can take several different forms. The county structure plan should contain general policy on the subject of conservation.[2] On the other hand, the district planning authority should include specific policies on conservation in its local plan. Such policy, since it is included in an approved local plan, has considerable influence in relation to any proposed developments within the area.

Depending on the level of control that a local planning authority wishes to achieve, other policy devices exist to conserve the historic environment. If its only concern is to protect specific buildings, or small groups of buildings, within its area from being developed in an unsophisticated way, then an approach can be made to the Secretary of State for National Heritage to list the buildings,[3] or as an interim measure, to place building preservation notices on those buildings.[4] Once the decision has been taken to list a building, no development can be undertaken without securing not only planning permission, but also listed building consent. This additional safeguard is prescribed in the Town and Country Planning (Listed Buildings and Conservation Areas) Act 1990 Act and, if ignored, can result in a criminal prosecution.[5] As a means of implementing local conservation policy, however, listing has the disadvantage that the

2 PPG 15, Planning and the Historic Environment.

3 By s 1 of the Planning (Listed Buildings and Conservation Areas) Act 1990, structures can be specially protected from alteration and demolition by being listed. This procedure and its consequences are fully considered later in the chapter.

4 By s 3 of the Planning (Listed Buildings and Conservation Areas) Act 1990, a structure can be protected for six months as if it were a listed building.

5 By s 9 of the Act, any unauthorised development of a listed building is an offence punishable by imprisonment and/or a fine. In theory the penalties are not inconsiderable, ranging from three to twelve months' imprisonment, while fines can be related to any benefit that has accrued to the developer as a result of the unauthorised development.

power to list buildings lies in the hands of the Secretary of State not the local planning authority. Consequently, it is at the discretion of the Secretary of State, based on advice from his officials, whether or not he chooses to list a building. That said, it is important to remember that, once listed, the ability to control what happens to that building is transferred back into the hands of the local planning authority.

In contrast, the power to designate an area a conservation area as defined in the Town and Country Planning (Listed Buildings and Conservation Areas) Act 1990 rests with the local planning authority.[6] When exercising its discretion to designate such an area, therefore, the local planning authority will base its decision on local planning policy. Various sources may have been tapped in formulating that policy. These include the planning officers themselves, especially if one of them is given particular responsibility for conservation, the councillors who comprise the planning committee, and the public who may work in, or, more probably, live in an area which has a character that may merit conservation. The end result will be a decision to designate a particular area within a specific boundary as a conservation area. The process of designation is simple, and there is no appeal, while the consequences are to activate special development control powers in the area. Therefore, by the creation of conservation areas, a local authority can achieve a great deal, since their inception has certain very positive legal and development control consequences.

Once established, it becomes necessary for the local planning authority to produce a policy document for the conservation area,[7] setting out the reasons why the area merits conservation and what special features need protecting. This document, once produced, will rank as an informal policy statement in the sense that, although its production is required by statute, how it is produced, and the degree to which the three policy sources of planning officers, councillors and the public should co-operate in its production, is not specified. Consequently, such an informal policy document is less important in the development control process than if it had gone through some formal procedures, such as those described in relation to development plans. Matters may be further complicated if the local planning authority chooses to increase the importance of such a document by instigating a form of approval procedure that mirrors, at least in part, the formal approval procedures that would accompany

6 Planning (Listed Buildings and Conservation Areas) Act 1990, s 69.
7 Ibid, s 71.

the production of a local plan. It may then be argued that the resulting document had been approved after due consultation, especially with the public, and this factor would be taken into account if the significance of such a document was being considered in a public inquiry.

Besides taking advantage of the procedures for listing buildings or designating conservation areas, there are other forms of special control that can be employed within a designated conservation area, or elsewhere within a local planning authority's district. For example, it is possible to protect trees.[8] This occurs automatically if an area is a conservation area, but any tree can be protected against felling or lopping, provided that the local planning authority decides it merits such protection. Another procedure often adopted in conservation areas of special merit is for a local planning authority to issue an article 4 direction.[9] This enables a specified area to be excluded from enjoying certain permitted development rights so that activities can be controlled which normally fall outside development control powers, such as the colour of external paintwork. In the case of an article 4 direction, however, a notice of the direction is required explaining its effect. Outdoor advertising is also carefully controlled in conservation areas under another set of special procedures.[10]

These examples show how a local planning authority can utilise special controls as part of its local planning policy in order to enhance the conservation of the built environment. Whilst this is a perfectly legitimate process there is a degree of uncertainty over the extent to which it is either desirable or feasible to integrate the use of such special controls into the development plan process. Government advice is that excessive detail should be avoided in development plans. PPG 15, Planning and the Historic Environment, indicates that development plans should set out authorities' broad criteria for the designation of new conservation areas but indicates that the actual process of designation 'should be pursued separately from the local plan process itself'. At a time when increasing emphasis is being placed upon development plans and commentators refer to 'plan-led decision-making' it is vital to appreciate the relationship between the plan and local policy including special controls that are not part of the plan.

8 1990 Act, s 198.

9 Town and Country Planning (General Permitted Development) Order 1995, SI 1995/418, art 4. See also chapter 3 for a discussion of permitted development.

10 1990 Act, s 221.

Local authority policy

Local planning policy can take many forms and be derived from several different sources. What follows is a description and analysis of the four main sources that can contribute to the creation of such policy. They are – central government, local planning officers, local councillors, and the public – the latter either in the form of individuals, including the developer, or organised groups.

CENTRAL GOVERNMENT

Central government influence on local planning policy takes many forms, apart from recognised channels, such as circulars and PPGs. The Department of the Environment obviously has the greatest impact, given its involvement with the planning process. Its Secretary of State can employ various means to exert an indirect or informal policy influence on local planning authorities. Changes of emphasis in policy can, and indeed often have been included in a speech, usually to the annual conference of some professional body, such as the Royal Town Planning Institute, or the Royal Institution of Chartered Surveyors. In his speeches, the Secretary of State often does little more than present some general comments on a current planning issue, but these are usually fully reported in the professional press, and thus may influence those who implement local planning policy.[11]

One such example concerns green belt policy. The majority of towns and cities prior to the passing of the Town and Country Planning Act 1971 did not possess a formally approved green belt. Green belt policy had been outlined in a circular and a policy note,[12] but green belts did not often figure as approved policy in development plans. The term 'green belt' was not infrequently utilised by local planning authorities as the natural argument when refusing planning permission for some proposed development that would have decreased the amount of open agricultural land around an urban area. In the mid 1970s, however, central government started to suggest that more land should be released for housing, especially in the South East,

11 See, for example, Independent, 9 March 1995 which reported the speech of the Secretary of State for National Heritage at the centenary dinner of the Architect's Journal. In this speech he announced various changes in policy in relation to listed buildings.

12 Circular 42/55, Green Belts; Development Control Policy Note No 4, Development in Rural Areas, 1969. The current policy statement on Green Belts is to be found in PPG 2 (1995).

where the London Metropolitan Green Belt had been established as a result of approved planning policy within the Greater London Plan. Pressure was applied by central government in various ways, but was particularly evident in informal requests to the Standing Conference on London and South East Regional Planning, asking them to indicate land within the green belt that they thought could be released for housing.

This government pressure, on what was a formally approved green belt, consequently left local planning authorities in other parts of the country in no doubt as to the direction of central government thinking on this particular planning policy. This gave local planning authorities only two options. They could comply, and release land for housing in those areas where they had previously utilised the green belt argument to reject applications for housing developments. Alternatively, they could formalise their green belt policy by creating local plans incorporating such policy. The result was that in some areas, local planning authorities set about the creation of formal green belts, normally by use of the subject plan. It may, therefore, be argued that these plans were, in a sense, a negative response to central government pressure which seemed to be seeking to undermine green belt policy.

Taking this idea of a negative response by local planning authorities to central government policy a stage further, it naturally introduces the question of the political differences that will, in some instances, undoubtedly exist between the two levels of government. Possibly one of the best known relatively recent examples of this is the situation that developed in 1985 between a socialist-led Liverpool City Council and the Conservative government.

The episode started with the victory of the local Labour Party in the Liverpool local government elections in 1983. At first, the results of the change in political power were slight, but direct confrontation between the local authority and the government became inevitable, when the local authority was accused of overspending by central government. Liverpool City Council had decided on a policy of urban regeneration,[13] an approach which, in general terms, was in line with Department of the Environment policy.[14] As part of its plans for regeneration, the Council

13 Liverpool City Council's Urban Regeneration Strategy became policy in December 1983. A synopsis of this policy and its progress was produced by Liverpool City Council in January 1986 entitled 'The Strategic Approach: Urban Programme 1986-1987'.

14 For example, the city was actually working in partnership with the Department of the Environment's Urban Renewal Unit.

concentrated on a much needed house building programme to provide accommodation for its tenants. The sites chosen for such development were all close to the inner city in areas that were unlikely to be of interest to the private developer.[15] This policy, however, soon produced confrontation with the government, not because the Council had embarked upon a major house building programme, but rather as a result of the financial demands that such a policy placed on the local authority. The regeneration programme thus caused the Council to 'overspend' in the eyes of central government which, as a result, attempted to impose financial restraints on the city. Liverpool City Council argued against such restraints on the basis that housing in the city was probably the worst in the country, a fact that had been recognised by many members of the government. Although it appeared that the Council had a strong case, confrontation with central government could not be avoided. This confrontation was ultimately resolved, but its effects on the planning and development of the area were far-reaching. The process of development control suffered for several reasons. These included the uncertainty of the Council's financial future, the disinterest expressed by the majority of the members of the then ruling party in any development, other than their own schemes for house building, and the arbitrary 'rules' that were applied to applications for planning permission involving housing, such as a totally inflexible height restriction.

Central government policy can thus affect local policy by indirect implication and direct confrontation, especially when political differences are involved. Confrontation of the type described above, however, is less common than the influence that other government departments regularly exercise over local authority planning policy, especially in relation to agriculture and transport.[16] In some instances such departments may be directly involved,[17] either in the procedures leading to the preparation of a formal development plan, or in a planning application, as has already been considered in previous chapters. What is more significant in the context of this chapter, however, is the effect that the general policies of other organi-

15 Nineteen priority areas were declared, fourteen of which were in the inner city and three on the outer estates.

16 The wide-ranging influence of other government departments has been referred to in chapter 2 and will also be mentioned later in this chapter.

17 For example, the Ministry of Agriculture, Fisheries and Food must be consulted over a planning application for non-agricultural development that involves loss of agricultural land; see Town and Country Planning (General Development Procedure) Order 1995, SI 1995/419, art 10(W).

sations can have on local planning policy. For example, the initial 'rationalisation' followed by the privatisation of both British Steel and the National Coal Board, involving the closure of steel works and pits throughout the country, has had an enormous impact on local planning policy in the areas affected. Yet, the closures were totally outside the control of the local planning authorities, who simply responded to such events as rapidly as possible, usually by producing some informal planning policy in an attempt to help alleviate the problems.

LOCAL PLANNING OFFICERS

Local planning officers receive an almost endless stream of policy advice in one form or another from central government. Such advice is supplemented by suggestions from other sources, notably local councillors and the general public. In this section the intention is specifically to consider the planning officers as sources of policy in their own right.

The majority of planning officers employed by local planning authorities are professionally trained in some aspect of the property system. Indeed, in the vast majority of instances, planning officers will have been educated to the equivalent of degree level in some aspect of town planning. During the course of their education they will have been presented with a variety of theories and possible explanations regarding the land use system and its development, including some suggested ideal solutions for the majority of planning problems. Although these ideas will have undoubtedly been tempered by the realities of practical, local authority town planning, many of them remain, providing a conceptual foundation for the local planning officer's ideas on planning control within his area.

To attempt to analyse these concepts in any sort of detail is beyond the scope of this book, but it is possible to illustrate, by way of an example, the effect they might have on the planning officer's policy suggestions. It is well established urban theory that certain general patterns of land use develop in any mature urban area.[18] In particular, certain land uses will attempt to repel each other, in the sense that they are not well suited as neighbours due to the incompatible nature of their particular functions.[19] The obvious example is, of course, housing and

18 For a discussion of such theories see Carter H *A Study of Urban Geography* (3rd edn, 1981) ch 8.

19 Harris C D and Ullman E L 'The Nature of Cities' Annals of the American Academy of Political Science, 1945, 242, p 7.

industry.[20] By way of contrast, however, other concepts suggest that the ability to travel to the place of work is an important factor,[1] since any attempt to isolate industry from housing may result in the 'working classes' being unable to bear the cost involved in transporting themselves to work. Immediately this introduces a new range of concepts, as the term 'working class' has to be defined,[2] while the importance of urban transport with all its related mathematical modelling must also be considered.[3] It should, therefore, be obvious that a large body of theory exists concerning the location of industry and its juxtaposition to areas of housing containing inhabitants of different classes.

Many of these urban planning concepts may already have been incorporated into policies contained in the formal development plan, but they may also generate informal policy proposals. For example, using these theories as a basis, the planning officers may advocate a policy that seeks to develop a 'social mix' within or between certain residential areas.[4] To control such a mix directly would be beyond the ability of any planning officer, except where he may be able to influence the local authority's housing department in its choice of tenants for the council's own housing estates, but indirect planning controls may be feasible. A development control policy concerning the density and type of housing in various housing areas could effectively introduce controls, albeit indirectly, on the social classes likely to inhabit the houses, as could a transport related policy on road layout within the housing area. In these circumstances, the planning officer would be attempting, quite validly, to use the planning system to create the ideal environment that his extensive background in planning theory has suggested. Naturally, the uniqueness of the locations of housing areas or industries would be of prime importance to any local planning policy decisions, but the general concepts would be drawn from such theories as those mentioned earlier.

20 As has been considered in chapter 3, the Use Classes Order 1987 distinguishes between Class B1 (Business) and Class B2 (General industrial). B1 includes industrial processes which can be carried out in a residential area without detriment to the amenity of the area.

1 Duncan O D 'The Measurement of Inner City Locational and Residential Patterns' Journal of Regional Science, 1960, 2, p 37.

2 There is no standard accepted definition of any of the so-called social classes. For example, see the discussion in Carter chs 9 and 10, or, for a classic study, Cole G D H *Studies in Class Structure* (1955).

3 For example: Blunden W R *The Land Use / Transport System* (1971); Lane R et al *Analytical Transport Planning* (1971).

4 For a discussion of this and other social concepts, see Bassett K and Short J *Housing and Residential Structure* (1980).

It should also be appreciated that the body of planning theory does not remain static, but changes in response to new ideas. A variety of sources, such as professional journals and conferences, offer the planning officer an opportunity to keep abreast of these changes. His views can also be influenced by exposure to a much wider range of information. This includes sources as diverse as official Department of the Environment guidance, to a chance conversation with a colleague from another local planning authority at a conference. In this fashion, the planning officer becomes a source of informed opinion, since he filters the information he receives and uses it to establish policy goals.

LOCAL COUNCILLORS

Councillors can effectively create policy in their own right, as well as direct and filter policy suggestions that may be received either from central government, or from their own planning officers. As was mentioned in chapter 2, councils have become increasingly political in their make-up over the last two decades, with the numbers of independent or ratepayer councillors declining and being steadily replaced by those who belong to one of the major political parties. In the context of planning control and the production of local planning policy, this process appears to have had an effect which varies depending upon the nature of the planning issues that the local authority has had to face. Clearly, there is little political capital in a local policy which aims to regulate advertisements in different locations, or control the design details for shop fronts in certain streets. Political stances are more likely to be taken over the supply of housing land, or the development of office blocks, and this can be reflected in local planning policy.

In order to illustrate this process, reference will again be made to Liverpool City Council's Urban Regeneration Strategy as published in 1984.[5] This policy must be viewed at several levels in order to appreciate its impact on development control within the city. First, the general policy of attempting to provide more housing can be justified on basic planning, as well as political grounds, as there was an undoubted need for such housing in the inner city residential areas. Second, the selection of housing areas where the city chose to concentrate its own housing developments was also acceptable as a planning policy. The main criterion used for selection was simply those areas of

5 The policy was never published as such, but documentation was produced by the City and made available to the general public. See n 13, p 187.

housing which were in local authority ownership, followed by an assessment of their condition. Thirdly, the designation of these areas had the effect of diverting into them most of the city's housing efforts. This tended to produce a negative planning policy in the rest of the city, by implication rather than intent, as the other areas of housing suffered from a relative lack of positive policy. Finally, the city's concern for housing development extended to specific development control policy regarding the design of the 'right type' of housing. This had the effect of producing a development control policy which seemingly resulted in planning permission being refused for any form of housing development over two storeys in height. The justification for such a policy can clearly be seen in the disastrous tower blocks that Liverpool has been forced to live with since the 1960s, but the two-storey policy was seemingly applied, not so much as a guide, but as a rule that could not be broken, often with what was apparently little regard for the actual merits of the proposed housing development.

Political motivation can, therefore, produce local planning policy, but so too can local circumstances. Examples may be found where planning authorities have attempted to introduce policies designed to check the proliferation of second homes.[6] Alternatively, much attention has recently been focused on planning permissions granted by North Cornwall District Council for development in open countryside, contrary to the structure plan and national planning policy, in an effort to help local inhabitants. Such policy is motivated by the perceived needs of the area, rather than by any specific political goals, and in this sense can be seen as the local councillors creating policy as local men and women rather than as a political group.

The acceptability of some of these policies, whether produced by political motivation, local need, or a combination of the two, is sometimes put to the test, more commonly in a public inquiry, but sometimes in the courts. The public inquiry will assess the legitimacy of such policies as planning policies, which have to be weighed against other planning policies. Therefore, a local policy designed to restrict the number of second homes, will have

6 The following condition was imposed by the Lake District Special Planning Board and appealed in 1985 (APP/5941/A/80/06966) 'The dwelling-house shall be occupied as a sole or main residence only by a person employed or to be employed or last employed locally and the dependants of such a person living with him or her and the widow or widower of such a person. "Locally" shall mean the area of the District Council of Allerdale. A "main residence" is a dwelling occupied for more than half of every year.' The condition was discharged.

to be viewed in the light of Department of the Environment policy, which is generally unsympathetic to any such attempts to regulate the housing market. In contrast, the courts are concerned with the legal validity of such policies and whether they can legitimately be taken into account when a development control decision is made.[7]

To conclude this consideration of councillor produced policy, it should be realised that a 'crusading' councillor who adopts a particular cause, could influence or even create policy if he had the personality to carry the majority of other councillors with him. Such councillors may often be motivated by what they perceive to be public opinion, and the policy which is likely to be produced from this source may be considered under that heading.

THE PUBLIC

In considering the public as a source of local planning policy it is appropriate to tackle the subject under two headings – the public at large, and the public as organised groups – both of whom can have a definite but distinct influence on local planning policy.

The public at large tends to have a sporadic and largely unregulated influence on local planning policy, much depending on the attitude of the local planning authority. As the local planning authority consists of both the local planning officers and the local councillors, the public can exert an influence on either or both groups. Any attempt to influence opinion is normally focused upon the local councillors. As politicians, these individuals are dependent on public opinion in order to be re-elected, and are, therefore, likely to be receptive to public opinion on various matters within their ward. This can affect planning policy indirectly. If a local councillor is aware that public opinion is against a particular policy, then he can make these views known to his fellow councillors as well as to the local planning officers, in the hope that the policy might be changed. Certain issues are almost always contentious, such as the building of new roads, or the demolition of the older, 'much loved' parts of town centres, and on these the local councillor will undoubtedly be made aware of public opinion. In these circumstances, however, it would be common practice for a local

7 See *Alderson v Secretary of State for the Environment* [1984] JPL 429 where a planning condition referring to persons employed 'locally' was held to be sufficiently certain to constitute a valid condition.

planning authority to canvass deliberately the views of the public, thus ensuring a degree of public participation which could have a direct influence on policy. Much depends on the attitude of a local planning authority, however, as only in certain circumstances is public participation mandatory, such as in the preparation of development plans.

Public participation exercises that are not mandatory can take various forms depending on the circumstances. Undoubtedly the most common type is the public inquiry, but despite its name, this is not quite as public an exercise as might be imagined. Public inquiries are most commonly held to consider a specific planning application for which planning permission has been refused by the local planning authority. As such, the procedural guidelines ensure that only interested parties are heard.[8] This normally includes the local planning authority representatives, the would-be developer and his representatives and any other directly affected parties. The developer can be considered as representing an aspect of public opinion, but public opinion in its true sense is better represented in these circumstances by those people who own or occupy adjacent property, whose interests might be affected if the proposed development goes ahead. In general, the opinion of the man in the street will only be heard at a public inquiry if the inspector asks for comments from the public gallery. Such a request is frequently made, and the response can vary greatly, though its ultimate effect on policy is unclear. The public inquiry has been called, not specifically to determine general local planning policy, but rather to assess its effect on a specific development proposal. The outcome of the inquiry often has implications for local planning policy, but the question of how much influence the public will have had on any decision is difficult to evaluate.

On the other hand, public participation exercises can be designed to elicit a more positive response and exert a more direct effect on planning policy. For example, such exercises may be held with the aim of producing supplementary policy that is intended to augment the general policy contained within the structure plan. Opinions can be canvassed on almost any planning topic from housing to leisure facilities. As has been indicated, the form of such public participation exercises can

8 Most significant are the Town and Country Planning (Inquiries Procedure) Rules 1992, SI 1992/2038, and the Town and Country Planning Appeals (Determination by Inspectors)(Inquiries Procedure) Rules 1992, SI 1992/2039. Other rules exist to govern other forms of special inquiry, for example, for enforcement.

vary, but public meetings and a standing exhibition are often arranged. The aim of the planning officers will be to present the public with an explanation of the alternative policies so as to elicit a response. In order to achieve this, public meetings will be arranged when possible policies can be discussed. This is often accompanied by attempts to illustrate, by means of models and artists' impressions, the impact a proposed policy of development may have on an area. Planning officers will also be at hand to answer any questions from the public while the public, in turn, may be asked to complete questionnaires as well as to make any comments on the proposals. After a specified period, the planning officers will attempt to gauge public opinion from all the information and comments received, the aim being to formulate possible future policies which take account of those views as far as possible. In this manner, the general public can have a direct effect on the policy process.

Arguably, however, it is public opinion, as represented by various organised public groups, that has the greatest influence on local planning policy. These groups are of various types, and include local sections of national organisations, such as the Georgian Group or the National Trust; groups that are specifically local and long-term, such as amenity societies or residents associations; groups that are local but short-term, which may have been formed in response to a specific problem within the community; and groups that may be a mixture, changing their form in response to local needs. Standing apart from these 'organised' groups is the developer, whose influence on planning policy will be considered at the end of this section.

Organised public groups can have an effect on local planning policy in the same way as the general public influences such ideas, namely, through public inquiries and public participation exercises. The impact of the organised group in these circumstances, however, is much greater than that of the public at large, mainly due to the fact that a group is often regarded by the local planning authority as having more 'standing', but this varies depending on the type of group. For example, local representative groups of national organisations, such as the Ramblers' Association, would possibly have more attention paid to its opinions by the local planning authority, than a purely local group concerned with public rights of way. This is for the simple reason that the weight of the national organisation, in terms of its influence and lobbying potential, could be brought to bear on a local issue. On the other hand, some purely local organisations, such as conservation area amenity societies, may gain extra influence, simply due to the fact that they are affiliated to the Civic Trust, a national organisation with considerable influence on conservation matters.

The final party that exerts an influence on local planning policy is the developer. It would be naïve to assume that developers only respond to local planning policy, rather than play a part in its creation. Their involvement in that process can take two forms, the one passive and the other active. The passive form is represented by the developer's willingness to undertake some form of development. Once the developer chooses to apply for planning permission, he then becomes the focus of whatever planning policy exists in order to control development. In these circumstances, his influence on local planning policy in general is not likely to be very great, although any development control decision taken in respect of his application for planning permission can, as has already been mentioned, have an indirect effect on planning policy. Another aspect of the developer's passive effect on planning policy is to be found in those instances where planning permission is not applied for, despite the fact that the planning officers have attempted to implement a policy that seeks to attract a particular form of development. For example, if the local planning authority has decided, as a matter of policy, to designate an area as a science park, and to offer various advantages to developers to build within the area, any failure to attract, or possibly divert, the attention of such developers from other areas of the region or city, may result in the policy being re-examined or dropped altogether.

The active effect that developers have on the planning policy of local planning authorities is not very different from that exercised by other groups, in that they have as much right to express a point of view as any other interested party. Such influence can be increased if a developer belongs to a national organisation, for example, the National Housebuilders Federation. The 'size' of the developer may also be significant. A small local house builder who makes representations regarding a local planning policy is likely to have less effect on that policy than if a representative of a national building firm were to make a similar comment.

The forms and functions of local planning authority policy

As discussed in the previous section, various individuals have a contribution to make in formulating local planning policy. The example may be considered of a local planning authority district in which residents and local councillors alike are perturbed by the number of mature trees being felled to make way for new developments. Pressure will mount, therefore, from both groups, for a local planning policy relating to trees. Such a policy will aim to ensure the preservation of mature trees and encourage the planting of new trees. Consequently, on being instructed to produce such a policy, the local planning officers are faced with the problem that it is simply not enough to have a policy, but some effort must also be made to ensure that the policy has the desired effect. Various means exist which can give 'teeth' to such a local planning policy, and these means and the powers they involve will be discussed in the remainder of this chapter. What should be borne in mind, however, is that the local planning authority is given the option of whether or not to take advantage of these powers, although, as will be apparent, specific guidance is available from the Department of the Environment on how these powers might most appropriately be used.

This leaves the question of how such powers relate to the development control process as a whole. In some instances it will be found that they allow a level of control in addition to the need to apply for planning permission. For example, the developer of a holiday caravan site must, in addition to securing planning permission, also obtain a site licence.[9] It is the licence in this case, that will be used by the local planning authority to control all the details of development on the site, such as the provision and siting of toilet facilities, or the creation of a suitable landscaped boundary to the site. In other instances, such powers also ensure that certain matters are given particular prominence as material considerations when a normal development control decision is being made. This is the case with any proposed development within a conservation area, when the special status of the area and its particular character will be a major factor in the development control issues under consideration.

Such powers thus play an important and fundamental role in the development control process in that they not only supply suitable vehicles for various policies, but also may be able to ensure that the policies can be effectively applied. In considering the forms and functions of these policy vehicles, however, the problem arises of how logically to group them for discussion. As has been suggested, their form and function is particularly varied, and can range from the protection of individual trees to

9 Caravan Sites and Control of Development Act 1960, s 3.

a general policy that attempts to ensure, through the use of planning conditions, that only local agricultural workers occupy new residential developments. As far as the operation of development control is concerned, probably the most significant question about such policy vehicles is whether or not they can be applied throughout the whole of the local planning authority area, or only be involved in the development control decision in certain specific instances. On this criterion, therefore, it has been decided to group these policy vehicles in relation to their specificity. The specificity of a policy simply refers to how widely it applies. For example, the policy regarding conservation areas is focused only within such areas and may not be applied elsewhere, while the policy decision to impose planning conditions can be applied to any part of a local planning authority's area. As a secondary consideration it has also been decided to note the form of 'authority' for any policy vehicle. This is accomplished simply by noting whether the policy vehicle is given its existence within a particular statute or is derived from other sources, always remembering that policy vehicles roiginating in a statute are not mandatory, but simply provide a specific form and function if the local planning authority chooses to utilise them.

There is, however, one important form of local planning authority policy that does not fit easily into either of these groups. This is what is normally termed informal local planning policy, which usually has two sources. The first may be some form of direction from another body. For example, a Department of the Environment circular or PPG may suggest that the local planning authority should prepare a policy document on housing supply. If the preparation of this document is not mandatory, then the local planning authority is free to ignore the suggestion. If, on the other hand, the document is prepared, then even if it is exactly on the lines suggested by the circular, it remains an informal policy document.

The second source is when the informal policy originates from within the local planning authority. If the planning authority decides that there is a pressing local issue, for example, acceptable designs for the modernisation of shop facades, which needs some form of policy direction, then if a document is produced, it becomes an informal policy document even though no circular has suggested its preparation. On some occasions, even when statute demands, as in the case of conservation areas, that local planning authorities should prepare policy documents in relation to these areas, such documents are also informal policy documents. This is mainly because their 'informality' stems from the lack of any set procedure involved in their preparation. Consequently, informal policy documents can be imbued with increasing levels of authority depending on the way in which they are produced, and, in particular, the degree of public participation involved. If the document is produced exclusively by the planning officers without public consultation and then approved by the planning committee, it is acceptable as a statement of policy. On the other hand, if the proposed policy was discussed with members of the public at an exhibition within the planning department, or at a series of public meetings, or was based on the results of questionnaires involving major public opinion surveys, then its 'standing' as policy would be greatly enhanced.

Informal policy plays an important role in the everyday life of many local planning authorities and is an essential source of reference on any number of development control issues. As it is always produced solely as a response to local planning issues, extensive examples of such policy would be pointless but its significance cannot be over-emphasised. Equally clearly, the Department of the Environment is the other major source of planning policy and its role in this aspect of the development control system will be considered in detail in the next chapter.

Taking into account, therefore, the existence of informal local policy within the development control system it is possible to return to consider those suggested headings under which the remaining forms of local policy will be examined. Once again, it is worth emphasising that the local policies about to be discussed should be distinguished from those policies considered in chapters 4 and 6. Undoubtedly connections exist between all these policy sources, which will be pointed out when appropriate, but the local policies discussed in this chapter should be considered as distinct, since they have an independent form and structure and produce a specific effect within the development control system.

Under the heading 'Specific policies supported by statute' will be discussed those policy vehicles which, should they be activated, apply only to a particular area or object and have a procedure, form and function allotted to them by specific sections of an Act. The heading 'Non-specific policies supported by various sources' will be used to accommodate those policy vehicles which may involve either a blanket coverage of the local planning authority's area, or rely on more indirect forms of support, such as statements made within the development plan or issues selected by the local planning authority.

SPECIFIC POLICIES SUPPORTED BY STATUTE

It is difficult to decide on the order in which to consider these policies and the different forms that they take, as the frequency of their use varies from one local planning authority to another. For want of a truly logical sequence, the intention is to consider first those policies and the special forms that they assume which relate to specific areas, such as conservation areas. This will then be followed by an investigation of those policies and their differing forms that can be applied to individual items, such as buildings, trees and advertisements. The sequence is not capable of remaining purely logical, however, as in the case of highways, the widening of a road may have a major effect on the transport system of the whole area, but at the same time raise quite specific planning issues in relation to the actual development operation.

In every instance, it is important to note, however, that policies relating to these issues may be included, often in some considerable detail, within the relevant development plan. The special forms that are about to be discussed, therefore, must not be seen as substituting for these development plan policies, but rather as applying an extra level of control. They can, of course, also be used to add to the policy of the local planning authority without the need to embark upon the lengthy procedure of amending the relevant development plan.

Conservation areas Areas designated conservation areas because of their particular environmental character or historic association should be indicated in the local plan and any policy related to the control of development in these areas should also be included.[10] Section 69 of the Planning (Listed Buildings and Conservation Areas) Act 1990 gives a local planning authority power to designate an area a conservation area. Indeed, the same section makes it a duty of the local planning authority to review its area from time to time to determine if any areas, not already designated as conservation areas, merit such treatment.[11] This task clearly requires that the local planning authority has some form of conservation policy. The initial task, therefore, must be to consider the derivation and nature of such a policy.

In this instance, some very specific policy guidance is to be found in PPG 15, Planning and the Historic Environment, and

10 PPG 12, para 7.14; PPG 15, section 2.
11 Planning (Listed Buildings and Conservation Areas) Act 1990, s 69(2).

in Department of the Environment Circular 8/87, Historic Buildings and Conservation Areas – Policy and Procedure. PPG 15 updates the advice within the Circular which is cancelled with the exception of certain directions which remain in force until new ones are produced. According to the advice offered in PPG 15 areas which, because of their special character, are worthy of designation as conservation areas, are to be found in almost every town and village.[12] Once a conservation area has been selected, a local planning authority then has to decide its attitude to proposed development within the area. In forming its views, the local planning authority is urged to take account of public opinion and in particular, to set up a conservation area advisory committee.[13] The membership of these committees should consist of local people, reflecting a cross-section of local opinion, together with, if possible, individuals with a professional background in planning or development. The purpose of the committee is to assist the local planning authority in:

> formulating policies for the conservation areas (or for several areas in a particular neighbourhood), and also as a continuing source of advice on planning and other applications which could affect an area.[14]

In addition, the local planning authority is expected to prepare proposals for the preservation and enhancement of conservation areas and submit them:

> for consideration to a 'public meeting' in the area, but wider consultation will almost always be desirable, both on the assessment of special interest and on proposals for the area.[15]

While the policy guidance on the creation and subsequent treatment of conservation areas is quite clear, no guidance is given as to what constitutes the unique local character that justifies the designation of a conservation area in the first instance. Such designation will clearly depend on a host of uniquely local features, and the interpretation and importance attached to these features by both the local planning authority and other interested parties, ranging from national and local conservation organisations, to the developer. In addition, the number and size of conservation areas, or potential conservation areas within the local planning authority district would have to be considered, as clearly the hardening of development control

12 PPG 15, section 4.
13 Ibid, para 4.13.
14 Ibid, para 4.13.
15 Ibid, para 4.10.

in these areas should be balanced by encouraging development in other areas. PPG 15 emphasises that conservation does not mean preservation but rather should focus on the control and management of change.[16]

Currently there are more than 8,000 conservation areas in England alone, demonstrating that this policy tool is widely used. The procedure for the designation of such an area is simple, once the area has been selected on whatever criteria the local planning authority thinks appropriate. The area becomes a conservation area by resolution of the local authority, and by formal notification to the Secretary of State, accompanied by publication of this information in the London Gazette, the local press, and an entry in the local land charge register.[17] The consequences of designation are complex, but can be appreciated by observing the effect they have on the local planning authority and the occupier of property in the area, particularly if the occupier intends to undertake any development.

Besides preparing policy proposals for the conservation area and setting up a conservation area advisory committee, the local planning authority has other decisions to make. There is the possibility of imposing even stricter controls on development within the area by using additional statutory powers. For example, an article 4 direction[18] can be issued which modifies permitted development rights, though the local planning authority is under no obligation to use this or any other power. When planning applications are received which are likely to affect the character or appearance of the area, the local planning authority is required to advertise them, both in the local press and near the application site, and in certain circumstances notice must also be given to the Historic Buildings and Monuments Commission.[19] Due regard must then be shown to any representations that are received, as is the case with any normal planning application.

The act of designating an area a conservation area also has certain important and automatic consequences for the occupiers of property in the area. For example, special permission in the form of conservation area consent must be obtained for the demolition of all or part of most buildings within the area even if the buildings are not specifically 'listed' in their own right.[20]

16 Ibid, para 4.16.
17 Planning (Listed Buildings and Conservation Areas) Act 1990, ss 69(4), 70(5), 70(7) and (8).
18 PPG 15, para 4.23.
19 Planning (Listed Buildings and Conservation Areas) Act, 1990, s 67.
20 Ibid, s 74.

Most trees within the area are protected in the same fashion as if they were the subject of a tree preservation order.[1] This means that anyone wishing to undertake work on a tree, including lopping or felling it, must give six weeks' notice to the local planning authority, which has that period to prevent such work. Once the six weeks have expired, consent is assumed. The permitted development rights are also automatically modified within a conservation area, the main difference being that the amount by which a dwelling-house, industrial building or warehouse can be extended is less in a conservation area than elsewhere.[2]

To conclude, it is worth mentioning that grants are sometimes available to finance developments and improvements within a conservation area. These grants are available from both local and national sources and consequently the local planning authority is not always involved in awarding such funding.[3] Therefore, although the availability of finance can have an important impact on conservation policy, a local planning authority cannot always employ grants as an incentive to ensure its conservation policy is observed.

Caravans It is no easy task for a local planning authority to devise a policy on caravans and the location and control of caravan sites. This is not from any lack of policy advice,[4] but rather because complications arise from the fact that caravan sites fall into a variety of categories – permanent sites for homes, sites for holidays containing static caravans, sites for holidays containing touring caravans and sites for gypsies, which form a special category. Clearly the planning implications for each category are different and may be subsumed, not only under the heading of planning policy but under some totally different policy. For example, policies relating to permanent sites for homes may quite justifiably be contained within the local authority's housing policies, while policies involving sites for holiday use may equally justifiably be found under tourism

1 1990 Act, ss 211-214; PPG 15, paras 4.38-4.40.

2 Town and Country Planning (General Permitted Development) Order 1995, SI 1995/418: conservation areas are designated as art 1(5) land and so more restrictive rules apply for example in Parts 1,8,17,24, 25,30,32.

3 PPG 15, para 4.10.

4 Circular 1/94, Gypsy Sites and Planning; Circular 22/91, Travelling Showpeople; Circular 14/89, Caravan Sites and Control of Development Act 1960 – Model Standards; Circular 23/83, Caravan Sites and Control of Development Act 1960; Circular 12/78, Report of the Mobile Homes Review; Development Control Policy Note 1969 No 8, Caravan Sites; Caravan Sites Act 1968; Caravan Sites and Control of Development Act 1960.

policy. On the other hand, it must also be admitted that all forms of caravan site pose common development control dilemmas, that range from the obvious ones, such as access and the provision of services, to the aesthetic issues of appearance and even noise.

General planning policy guidance is still to be gained from Development Control Policy Note 1969/8, Caravan Sites. In this, caravans are considered under three headings – caravans as homes, caravans for holidays and caravan sites for gypsies – and policy advice is offered for each group. Where caravans are used as homes, the all-important policy issue is one of location, preferably near existing housing areas as the service requirements are the same, but for location on the periphery rather than in the centre of the housing area. A location deep in the country or in the midst of the green belt is not considered appropriate, but it is noted that caravans can often be accommodated on sites unsuitable for houses, in the sense that they can occupy land that, due to its physical features, is unsuitable for permanent buildings. Where caravans are used as holiday homes, concern is shown for the fact that demand is concentrated in the most popular holiday areas. This creates particular problems, the most obvious of which is the unsightly nature of the caravan parks themselves, and the danger that too many caravans will swamp local facilities. In general, therefore, it is suggested that all holiday caravan sites should be strictly controlled, with the emphasis on sites located in inconspicuous positions in areas already established as caravan areas. Where caravans are occupied by gypsies, the sites are also often used by the gypsies to pursue their occupations, such as scrap dealing, and this fact should be taken into account when locating and planning the sites.

This general policy has been supplemented with advice from other circulars[5] so that the present situation is one of very strict and largely standardised control for all the different groups. Effectively, this control is based on the fact that not only must planning permission be obtained in the normal way, but also a licence under the Caravan Sites and Control of Development Act 1960 must be secured from the local authority in whose area the site is proposed, which will be the same authority from whom planning permission would have been sought. A licence must be granted once planning permission has been given, but this seemingly pointless exercise is given a very real purpose

5 Circulars 1/94, 22/91, 14/89, 23/83 and 12/78.

since the site licence will contain a whole list of conditions that would be difficult, if not impossible, to attach to a grant of planning permission. The conditions, which are part of the site licence, will be concerned with such matters as densities and how they should be measured, spacings, water and toilet supply arrangements, landscaping, and establishing specific boundary features to the site. Examples of model conditions appropriate to the various forms of caravan site are given in the circulars[6] and are generally adopted by local authorities. These controls are further complicated by a wide-ranging list of exclusions and exemptions relating to sites established before 1960 and to what are termed temporary sites.[7] In addition, local authorities possess a discretion whether to provide accommodation for gypsy caravans.[8]

The need for a local planning authority to have a policy on the development and control of caravan sites varies from one authority to another, depending on the level and the nature of caravan use within the area. In some areas, such as parts of the Welsh coast, the control of caravans will be an important aspect of planning policy, while in others, the only concern may be to provide gypsy caravan sites. What should be clear, however, from the preceding paragraphs, is that guidance exists to help a local planning authority formulate a policy on caravan sites, as well as control the development of those sites for which it is prepared to give planning permission.

Mineral workings A local authority which is a mineral planning authority is provided with considerable powers and much advice regarding its policy towards, and control of, all forms of mineral working and extraction.[9] This advice con-

6 Annex to Circulars 23/83 and 14/89.
7 Caravan Sites and Control of Development Act 1960, s 2, Sch 1.
8 The statutory duty to provide gypsy caravan sites was repealed by s 80 of the Criminal Justice and Public Order Act 1994. According to Circular 1/94, Gypsy Sites and Planning local planning authorities will be expected to take account of the accommodation needs of gypsies in their planning policy, including their development plans.
9 Circular 1/88, Planning Policy Guidance and Mineral Planning Guidance; Circular 28/87, Opencast Coal Mining; Mineral Workings Act 1985 ; Town and Country Planning (Compensation for restrictions on mineral working) Regulations 1985, SI 1985/698; Circular 25/85, Mineral Workings – Legal Aspects Relating to Restoration of Sites with a High Water Table; Circular 2/85, Planning Control over Oil and Gas Operations; Circular 58/78, Report of the Committee on Planning Control over Mineral Workings; Mineral Workings Act 1951. See also the Minerals Policy Guidance Notes, MPG 1 – MPG 12.

centrates upon the operations involved in the working and extraction of minerals but does not offer a definition of what constitutes a mineral in this context. Since the majority of mineral workings are undertaken in rural areas, with the possible exception of coal mining, it is normal for the mineral planning authority to be the county planning authority. In metropolitan areas and Greater London, however, either a metropolitan district authority or a London borough is the mineral planning authority.[10] Finally, where as a result of the present restructuring of local government in England and Wales, unitary local authorities are established, for example, in the whole of Wales, to replace the current two-tier system, the unitary authority will take on the role of mineral planning authority.

Local planning policy towards mineral working can normally be found in three possible sources. These are, first, the structure plan which may contain general policy on mineral extraction. Second, a minerals local plan which is expected to set out development control policy in relation to existing and future mineral working. The preparation of such plans which was once discretionary is now an obligation imposed on mineral planning authorities.[11] In metropolitan areas and Greater London, policy of this nature is to be found in Part I of the unitary plan. The remaining source of mineral working policy will emerge as a result of those periodical reviews that section 105 of the 1990 Act plus MPG 4[12] requires mineral planning authorities to conduct. Reviews are mandatory, in that they have to be undertaken periodically and five-yearly reviews have usually been thought to be the most appropriate. Their purpose is to monitor current mineral workings in order to determine whether their operation reflects contemporary development control policy. If this is not so mineral planning authorities possess the power to modify or revoke planning permission or prohibit the resumption of mineral working.

Since minerals are an important element of what is termed the national resource base, it is hardly surprising that there is a considerable amount of central government advice on the manner in which applications for planning permission to extract minerals should be considered. Such applications cannot be treated as raising solely local planning issues. Indeed, no fewer

10 1990 Act , s 1(4).

11 1990 Act, s 37. Inserted by the Planning and Compensation Act 1991, Sch 4, para 17.

12 MPG 4, The Review of Mineral Working Sites.

than three government departments – the Department of Energy, the Department of Trade and Industry and the Department of the Environment – consider minerals policy to be within their remit. Their main concern seems to be to ensure that industry gets the materials and power that it demands whilst ensuring that the countryside is protected as far as is practicable. This predisposition towards permitting mineral extraction has to be seen in the light of the advice offered in MPG 1, General Considerations and the Development Plan System.

MPG 1 urges that policies should be adopted by mineral planning authorities that attempt to maintain average levels of mineral production from within their areas as measured over the last few years. If such a policy involves opening up new areas of extraction, then a full examination of the development control consequences of the new mineral workings must ensue. This examination, which should allow for a considerable degree of public participation, must consider in detail the possible environmental and social impact of the new mineral workings, as well as taking into account the economic consequences these new workings might have on other mineral resources within the area. If the mineral planning authority has produced a minerals local plan, it may contain policies of constraint, indicating situations or locations where planning permission for mineral extraction is not likely to be given. Specific policies on particular minerals may also be adopted, as may policies on appropriate environmental safeguards for mineral working sites, but these policies should not be so inflexible as to render real discussion on particular applications for planning permission pointless.[13]

Assuming that planning permission is granted, current practice is for the mineral planning authority to impose a whole range of planning conditions. The aim of these conditions is to regulate the way in which the site is to be worked, and also to ensure that the site is appropriately landscaped once extraction is complete. Clearly, such conditions represent important policy controls over mineral working, but they have to be imposed with great care by the mineral planning authority since this activity has a long-term cumulative effect on the environment.[14]

In the past mining operations undertaken by the British Coal Corporation, as opposed to a private company, have been singled

13 See *Buckinghamshire County Council v Hall Aggregates (Thames Valley) Ltd* [1985] JPL 634.

14 For advice on the imposition of planning conditions in relation to mineral workings see MPG 2, Applications, Permissions and Conditions, paras 52-130.

out for special treatment largely due to historical circumstance. The British Coal Corporation could undertake new mining operations on land which was already being mined, or for which planning permission for mining had already been given.[15] Following the privatisation of the coal industry operators licensed by the Coal Authority enjoy certain permitted development rights [16] previously only available to the British Coal Corporation but subject to more stringent conditions regarding restoration of the site. In contrast, new coal mines, including opencast mines, require planning permission.

Obviously any planning application involving mineral extraction is likely to raise contentious issues, particularly environmental issues, and attract the attention of many important national and local pressure groups. This emphasises the need for a clear minerals policy at local planning level if there is to be effective development control in the area. Such a policy will not solve all the problems or cover all the issues, but it will at least provide the parameters within which the inevitable discussion will take place.

Special areas In the context of development control there are at present three forms of area that should be noted. The first form of special area is the enterprise zone. These were established by the Local Government, Planning and Land Act 1980[17] and are intended to aid the regeneration of a particular locality. Local authorities are invited by the Secretary of State to consider if an enterprise zone is needed in their area. If they conclude that such a zone is needed, then draft proposals are prepared and offered for public scrutiny in the manner required by the 1980 Act.[18] There are specified procedures for taking account of objections, and the draft proposals may be modified accordingly. Once these requirements have been observed, then the area may be designated an enterprise zone by the Secretary of State, normally for a period of ten years.[19]

The consequences of designation are mainly fiscal and bureaucratic, and so do not directly concern this work, but there is also a particular planning change that is relevant to

15 This was permitted under the Town and Country Planning General Development Order 1988,SI 1988/1813, Pt 20, now superseded.
16 Town and Country Planning (General Permitted Development) Order 1995, SI 1995/418, Pt 20.
17 Local Government Planning and Land Act 1980, s 179, Sch 32.
18 Ibid, Sch 32, Pt I.
19 Ibid; by implication the zones will last for ten years, which is the duration of the rate free period stipulated in Sch 32, para 27.

development control. Within the zones, planning control is mainly dependent on the development scheme that has been specified by the local planning authority for the zone. This means that if a proposed development within the zone complies with the requirements of the development scheme, planning permission is deemed to have been granted.[20] Alternatively, if the proposed development does not comply with the scheme, then planning permission must be sought in the normal manner. Such develop-ment schemes need take no account of any existing local planning policies, and indeed, the 1980 Act requires that existing development plans be reviewed, if necessary, to take account of the scheme.[1] The content of the schemes has varied considerably between the many enterprise zones that have been established, with some local planning authorities allowing a very broad range of development within the zones, while others have been much more specific.[2]

The effect of the zones has not been assessed specifically with regard to their impact on local planning and development control, but reports have raised issues which throw some light on this aspect.[3] Rather than create new development as was intended, the zones have undoubtedly caused the short distance movement of existing enterprises. This has had a detrimental effect on the areas adjacent to the zones, virtually negating any existing local planning policy on commercial development. As many local planning authorities have also allowed the development of large retail units within the zones, this can undoubtedly have an adverse effect on existing shopping centres some distance from the zone, with the resulting disruption of prevailing retail and transport planning policies. It is obvious, therefore, that although the zones themselves involve quite specific areas within the local planning authority's district, the effects produced by the zone on the planning of the district or even the county are very wide-ranging indeed.

The second form of special area was introduced by the Housing and Planning Act 1986, and provides for the setting up of simplified planning zones.[4] Simply stated, these are zones in

20 Ibid, Sch 32, para 17(1).
1 Ibid, Sch 32, para 23.
2 Grant M *Urban Planning Law* (1982, updated 1986) p 546.
3 Roger Tym and Partners *Monitoring Enterprise Zones*. Year Three Report 1984 (for the Department of the Environment); Report of the Comptroller and Auditor General Enterprise Zones, HC 209; 34th Report from the Committee of Public Accounts 1985-86 Enterprise Zones HC 293.
4 The relevant sections are now incorporated into the 1990 Act, ss 82-87, while policy advice is contained in PPG 5, Simplified Planning Zones (1992).

which modified development control regimes are employed on the lines of those found in enterprise zones. The local planning authority is required to consider which parts of its area may be suitable for a simplified planning zone. As might be expected, the establishment of such a zone is an involved procedure calling for public participation. The final decision on the designation of such zones lies with the local planning authority and will not involve the Secretary of State. On its designation, each zone will have documentation setting out the form and classes of development permitted without the need for planning permission, together with all their related conditions. As with enterprise zones, the simplified planning zones will remain in existence for ten years.

The effect of such simplified planning zones on the local planning policies and development control of an area, is open to speculation, as the zones are not very common.[5] Part of the explanation for this might be the time taken to secure the approval of a simplified planning zone scheme. It also seems that they lack the 'attraction' of enterprise zones, both to the local authority and the developer, as they offer no obvious financial advantage apart from the possible speeding up of the planning process. Hence although central government has promoted the simplified planning zone as offering a variety of benefits to potential developers such as certainty and savings in time, money and effort,[6] they have not proved popular.

The final form of special area is the designated area of either a new town development corporation or an urban development corporation. The creation of new towns has been a policy pursued by central government from the end of the 1939-45 war onwards. New town development corporations had the task of developing new towns and were given powers, such as the power to acquire and manage land, in order to do so. In the light of the present government's attachment to privatisation it is hardly surprising to discover that this particular initiative has been abandoned and the new town development corporations wound up. As for urban development corporations, these were a creation of the 1980s[7] and were a government device to regenerate run-down urban areas. Within their designated areas development corporations undertake all the normal duties of

5 J Cameron-Blackhall 'Simplified Planning Zones (SPZs) or Simply Political Zeal' Journal of Planning and Environment Law, 1994, p 117.
6 PPG 5, Simplified Planning Zones, para 2.
7 Local Government, Planning and Land Act 1980, ss 148-150, Sch 29.

local planning authorities. Besides removing an area from the control of the relevant local planning authority, the main effect that such areas may have on local planning policy relates to the fact that various forms of financial aid may be available for development within the designated area. Consequently, this may have repercussions for development in those local authority areas adjacent to the designated area, as development may be drawn into the designated area rather than establishing itself elsewhere. It is contemplated, however, that urban development corporations will have a limited existence and will be wound up once they have succeeded in their allotted task.[8]

Trees The contribution that trees make to both the urban and rural environment has long been acknowledged. Trees:

> enhance the quality of the countryside, provide a habitat for wildlife and soften and add character to built up areas.[9]

Consequently, local planning policy can quite legitimately be used to protect existing trees as well as to encourage the planting of new trees. Indeed, local planning authorities have the power to undertake their own tree planting schemes.[10] In addition, when they grant planning permission, local planning authorities can impose planning conditions which may require the planting of young trees, and should stress the importance of selecting the right trees for the right location. It is also worth contrasting the role played by local planning authorities with that played by the Forestry Commission. Whereas local planning authorities use trees to enhance the environment, the Forestry Commission encourages large-scale tree planting as a commercial proposition for the supply of timber.

If local planning policy requires the protection of existing trees, the local planning authority can resort to the use of tree preservation orders.[11] Individual trees or groups of trees are to be selected for protection '..in the interests of amenity'.[12] This apparently means that the trees in question, which should be visible from a public place, have to provide some positive degree of public benefit, either by:

8 This process is already under way. The Leeds Development Corporation, for example, was wound up in 1995.
9 Circular 36/78, Trees and Forestry, Preamble, para 2.
10 National Parks and Access to the Countryside Act 1949, s 89; Highways Act 1959, s 82.
11 1990 Act, ss 198-202.
12 Circular 36/78, para 40.

> their intrinsic beauty, or for their contribution to the landscape; or because they serve to screen an eyesore...[or] by their scarcity...[or] as a wildlife habitat.[13]

Usually several of these criteria have to be present in order to merit the imposition of a tree preservation order. It is also suggested that trees need not be imminently at risk to merit such an order and that '...the preservation of selected trees by precautionary orders may therefore be considered to be expedient'.[14]

The making of a tree preservation order by the local planning authority is not a difficult procedure, apart, that is, from the fact that the term 'tree' is not defined in the legislation. Consequently, the courts have been called upon from time to time to provide a definition.[15] The results of their deliberations have not always been especially clear. The term apparently does not extend to all forms of woodland growth, but neither does it relate simply to plants of a certain maturity or size. It can include an area of woodland and may also be applied even if that area is being coppiced.

A tree preservation order can be made using the form prescribed in the Town and Country Planning (Tree Preservation Order) Regulations 1969.[16] This requires that the trees to be protected be identified and indicated on a map at a scale large enough to show individual trees or woodland. Notice must be given to the owners and occupiers of the land containing the specified trees and they have 28 days within which to object. If no objections are received the local planning authority can confirm the order. In practice most tree preservation orders are made in such a way that they take effect immediately. In this way any attempts to fell the trees before the order is confirmed can be forestalled. The effect of a tree preservation order is that any person wishing to cut down, top, lop, or uproot a tree must apply to the local planning authority for permission to do so. Failure to apply may result in prosecution and the imposition of a fine. Powers do exist to enable dangerous trees to be felled

13 Ibid.

14 Ibid.

15 The definition provided by Lord Denning in *Kent County Council v Batchelor* (1976) 33 P & CR 185, that related to size, was rejected in *Bullock v Secretary of State for the Environment* (1980) 40 P & CR 246 where the word 'tree' was seen to bear its ordinary meaning.

16 SI 1969/17. The government proposes to revise these regulations in order to give local authorities greater powers and to simplify the administration of the TPO system. Primary legislation is needed to bring about these changes and is currently awaited.

without going through the whole of this procedure. The application to the local planning authority to carry out work on a tree is treated in the same way as an application for planning permission, and the same procedures apply.

Listed buildings The decision to list a building as being of special architectural or historic interest rests with the Secretary of State for National Heritage, not the local planning authority.[17] Although it cannot list buildings, the local planning authority can institute an interim measure, known as a building preservation notice.[18] This remains in force for six months, during which time it is intended that the building should be considered for listing by the Secretary of State. This power, however, must be used with discretion, as if the building is not listed the owner can apply for compensation for any loss or damage suffered as a consequence of the notice.[19] The process of listing is an ongoing one. Therefore, from time to time a nationwide review of the lists may be undertaken, county by county. In this way the lists are brought up to date with buildings being added and removed. Guidance is available on the qualities which make a building worth listing[20] and there is nothing to prevent a local planning authority drawing the attention of the Secretary of State to buildings which it considers worthy of listing. In their way, therefore, the criteria for listing are just as important to local planning authorities as they are to the Secretary of State, as those criteria form the basis for local planning policy on the issue.

The criteria effectively fall into two categories – the age of the building and other factors. In relation to age, the guidance is quite specific, suggesting that all pre-1700 buildings still surviving in anything like their original form, and most dating from 1700 to 1840 will, or should be, listed. Between 1840 and 1914, however, criteria other than age are relevant, and quality will play a role, although the importance of group value is also stressed. The same is true of buildings from the period 1914 onwards. Buildings which are less than 30 years old will be listed only in exceptional circumstances. Age, therefore, is an important criterion in selecting a building for listing, but even

17 Planning (Listed Buildings and Conservation Areas) Act 1990, s 1 empowers the Secretary of State for National Heritage acting on the advice of the Historic Buildings and Monuments Commission for England (English Heritage) to list buildings.

18 Planning (Listed Buildings and Conservation Areas) Act 1990, s 3.

19 Ibid, s 29.

20 PPG 15, Planning and the Historic Environment, section 6.

these apparently clear guidelines can, in reality, be blurred when a building has been altered and refurbished over several hundred years. In such circumstances the actual age of a building may be difficult to ascertain, and often its selection for listing will depend upon other criteria. Indeed, the real structural age of a building may not be known unless major works are undertaken.

Criteria apart from age are, therefore, of prime importance and PPG 15, Planning and the Historic Environment, highlights some important general issues. Particular attention should be paid to buildings which are of architectural merit because of their design, decoration or craftsmanship. Buildings employing certain techniques of construction or technological innovation may also be listed. The group value of buildings can be crucial particularly when they make up an important architectural feature such as a model village. Finally it is not simply the physical fabric of a building that should be considered, but also the building's historical associations, though this alone does not normally merit the listing of a building without some accompanying architectural merit. With regard to twentieth century buildings, all these factors are relevant, but the range of buildings to consider is greatly increased. English Heritage have therefore selected buildings as key examples of their type to form the basis of the selection from this period.

Once a building is listed, its grade of listing has to be determined. Grade I and II are to include buildings of outstanding architectural or historic interest, and there is usually a consensus among all concerned as to which buildings are to be included in this group. Grade II buildings, on the other hand, are to be buildings of special interest and 94% of all listed buildings fall into this category. The distinction between grades is important, as the grade of the listed building is a factor taken into account when development is proposed that will affect a listed building.

Once the selection has taken place, the listed buildings come under the planning control of the local planning authority. Before considering what that entails, it is worth mentioning some consequences of listing which may not immediately be apparent. Although reference has been made to the Secretary of State and the local planning authority, no mention has been made of the owner of a listed building. This is because the owner is not consulted, but merely informed that his property is to be listed; nor does he have a right of appeal. This is because it is argued that having a building listed does not materially affect the owner unless he wishes to undertake development. Research, however, has shown that listing a building, particularly a property used for commercial purposes, can reduce its market value because of the restrictions on its development potential.[1] In a recent speech, however, the Secretary of State for National Heritage announced his intention to give the owners of buildings that are candidates for listing a say before the final decision is taken.[2] The danger with such a proposal is that owners may be tempted to undertake alterations to their property once they discover that English Heritage is considering listing it. It is also possible that the presence of listed buildings, or listed buildings within in a conservation area may actively discourage development in the light of the planning controls involved.

Any works being undertaken by either the owners or the occupiers, or indeed any other party, that will affect the character of a listed building require a special form of permission known as listed building consent, which must be obtained from the local planning authority before the works commence. The criteria on which a building was listed are to be found in the lists held by the relevant local planning authority, and usually contain quite detailed information. For example, the following extract is taken from Liverpool City Planning Authority's lists for 10-12 Rumford Place, a Grade II listed building found within a conservation area in the commercial sector of the city.

> Office building c 1840. Stucco to ground floor and brick exposed above with stone dressings, slate roof. 3 storeys and 9 bays. All windows are tripartite sashes with glazing bars on ground and 2nd floors. Central rusticated cart entrance with pilasters and entablature. Parapet and cornice, sill bands between floors. 1st floor windows have marginal glazing bars only and central window with pediment, end windows with cornices on brackets. 2nd floor has 10 windows. Included for historical reasons as the headquarters of James Dunwoody Bulloch the Confederate Agent who commissioned Confederate Cruisers to be built in England, mainly on Merseyside, under cover of the Southern Cotton Commissioners. The most famous of these ships was the CSS Alabama. This building was in effect the Confederate Embassy in England.

Listed building consent and whether or not to grant it are entirely independent of the need for planning permission. Indeed, it may be required even if planning permission is not needed, if the works in question do not constitute development.

1 The Economics of Listed Buildings, Discussion Paper 43, Department of Land Economy, Cambridge University.
2 (1995) Independent, 9 March.

Clearly, therefore, a local planning authority's response to an application for listed building consent will have direct consequences, not only for its own policies regarding conservation and the built environment, but also its policies for encouraging development within its district. A range of possibly conflicting issues may thus be introduced. As PPG 15 notes, the real issue is one of stewardship of the historic environment since this represents a finite resource.[3]

> There should be a general presumption in favour of the preservation of listed buildings, except where a convincing case be made out, ..., for alteration or demolition.[4]

Applications for listed building consent will raise unique local issues as well as more general issues. It is on these general issues that advice is offered to the local planning authority.[5] Considerable stress is laid on the importance of considering thoroughly the possibility of a new use for a listed building, rather than permit its demolition, with the local planning policy being interpreted as flexibly as possible to allow the introduction of new uses if at all feasible. The importance of the setting of a listed building is also stressed, together with the need to interpret widely what the term 'setting' means. This is illustrated by reference to an example:

> where it [a listed building] forms an element in a group, park, garden or other townscape or landscape, or where it shares particular archi-tectural forms or details with other buildings nearby.[6]

The importance of the building and in particular those fea-tures which warrant its listing are also a relevant factor as are any potential benefits that will accrue from the proposed action. There can be little doubt, therefore, that the protection of listed buildings is considered to be an important aspect of planning policy from the point of view of the Department of National Heritage.

Before assessing how this advice is acted upon by the local planning authority, it is necessary to point out that, as may already be evident, the protection of a listed building is supp-orted by a considerable amount of legislative power which rests in the hands of the local planning authority. As the legislation relevant to listed buildings is quite complex and is more than adequately covered by other sources no attempt will be made

3 PPG 15, para 1.6.
4 Ibid, para 3.3.
5 Ibid, paras 3.5-3.19.
6 Ibid, para 3.5.

to examine it in any detail here.[7] To summarise, therefore, it should be noted that the owner of a non-listed building can apply for a certificate from the Secretary of State stating that the building will not be listed for five years;[8] that the local planning authority can undertake works to preserve an unoccupied listed building;[9] that loans and grants may be available from various sources, including the local authority, to help offset the costs involved in preserving the building; that it is an offence to undertake unauthorised works to a listed building;[10] that listed building consent can be granted with conditions if it is desired;[11] that certain buildings are exempt from listing; that listed building consent lasts for five years unless otherwise stated;[12] and that if listed building consent is refused and the building becomes incapable of reasonably beneficial use, a purchase notice may be served on the local authority.[13] Suffice it to say, therefore, that every possible action in relation to a listed building is regulated by statute.

From this brief summary of the legislation it is obvious that the local planning authority has both the power and the backing from the Department of National Heritage and the Department of the Environment to institute whatever policy it sees fit in relation to the listed buildings within its district. Local planning authorities are advised in PPG 15 to include in their development plans 'aspects of conservation policy that are relevant, directly or indirectly, to development control decisions'.[14] This might include policies on issues such as the change of use of listed buildings or development in the vicinity of listed buildings. Given the likely distribution of listed buildings throughout the whole of the local planning authority's area, however, a comprehensive policy for each and every building is almost impossible to produce. As a consequence, the treatment of listed buildings within a planning district is likely to be a matter of chance, and any application for listed building consent will usually be considered on its individual merits. How that application will be resolved depends upon a host of local circumstances that relate only in part to the reasons for the building

7 See, for example, Telling A E and Duxbury R M C *Planning Law and Procedure* (9th edn, 1993) pp 280-297.
8 Planning (Listed Buildings and Conservation Areas) Act 1990, s 6.
9 Ibid, s 54.
10 Ibid, s 7.
11 Ibid, s 17.
12 Ibid, s 18.
13 Ibid, ss 32 -37.
14 PPG 15, para 2.4.

being listed. For example, the local planning authority will have to consider how important the proposed development is in terms of new employment opportunities. This issue would then have to be weighed against the 'value' of the listed building in terms of its contribution to the history, character or architecture of the area. Such issues are, however, impossible to consider in the abstract, rendering further discussion unproductive.

Advertising The control of outdoor advertising is yet another area where a local planning authority is presented with comprehensive guidance.[15] The 1990 Act defines an advertisement as:

> any word, letter, model, sign, placard, board, notice, awning, blind, device or representation, whether illuminated or not, in the nature of, and employed wholly or partly for the purposes of, advertisement, announcement or direction, and (without prejudice to the previous provisions of this definition) includes any hoarding or similar structure used, or designed or adapted for use and anything else principally used, or designed or adapted principally for use, for the display of advertisements.[16]

The 1992 Advertisement Regulations distinguish between advertisements which are, and those which are not, subject to control. An advertisement is specifically not subject to control, if it is one which is:

(a) on or consisting of a balloon not more than 60 metres above ground level;
(b) displayed on enclosed land, and not readily visible from land outside that enclosure or from any part of any public right of way over such enclosure or from any land on such enclosure to which the public have a right of access;
(c) displayed on or in a vehicle;
(d) incorporated in the fabric of a building, other than a building used principally for the display of such advertisements or a hoarding or similar structure;
(e) displayed on an article for sale or on the container in, or from which, an article is sold;
(f) relating specifically to a pending Parliamentary, European Assembly or local government election;
(g) a notice required to be displayed by a Standing Order of Parliament;
(h) a traffic sign;

15 1990 Act, ss 220, 221, 223(1), 224(3) and 333(1); Town and Country Planning (Control of Advertisements) Regulations 1992, SI 1992/666; Circular 5/92, Town and Country Planning (Control of Advertisements) Regulations 1992; PPG 19, Outdoor Advertisement Control.

16 1990 Act, s 336(1).

(i) the national flag of any country;
(j) an advertisement displayed inside a building.[17]

All other outdoor advertisements are subject to the controls described in the 1992 Regulations and the accompanying Circular.[18] An attempt will be made, therefore, to assess the implications of these controls for the development control process.

Normally, it is the district planning authority that is responsible for advertisement control. Any individual wishing to display an advertisement must, therefore, apply to the local planning authority for permission to do so. Certain classes of advertisement, such as signs on business premises or those carried on flags, are however granted deemed consent in the 1992 Regulations subject to specified conditions.[19] What is quite clear is that in performing that function a local planning authority cannot exercise any form of censorship over the subject matter of the advertisement. Instead, consent is being sought from the local planning authority for the use of a site for advertising. Effectively, the situation can be summed up by saying that those advertisements liable to control may only be controlled in the interests of amenity or public safety. In this context, public safety involves the positioning of advertisements in such a manner that they do nothing to detract from the safe use of the highway. The main criterion, therefore, for the control of advertisements in all other instances, is their effect on the amenity of the area. Clearly, this may be a contentious issue since, as has been indicated in relation to other issues of development control, exactly what merits control in the interests of amenity is difficult to define. However, the drafter of the 1992 Regulations attempts to provide such a definition:

> A local planning authority shall exercise their powers...taking account of any material factors, and in particular –
> (a) in the case of amenity, the general characteristics of the locality, including the presence of any feature of historic, architectural, cultural or similar interest, disregarding, if they think fit, any advertisement being displayed there;[20]

It seems that this wide definition of what may be considered in the interests of amenity places a considerable amount of

17 Town and Country Planning (Control of Advertisements) Regulations 1992, SI 1992/666, Sch 2.
18 Circular 5/92.
19 Town and Country Planning (Control of Advertisements) Regulations 1992, SI 1992/666, reg 6, Sch 3.
20 Ibid, reg 4(1).

development control power in the hands of the local planning authority. That power, however, is not entirely unregulated. For example, once the local planning authority has made a decision to permit an advertisement to be displayed, certain standard conditions have to be attached to the consent. These provide that the advertisement must be kept in a clean, tidy, and safe condition.[1] In addition a local planning authority can impose any other conditions it sees fit, such as a requirement that the advertisement be removed at the end of a specified period.

The 1992 Regulations also deal with the display of advertisements in what are termed 'Areas of Special Control'.[2] These are rural and urban areas whose definition as special areas is dependent on the need for special protection. Outdoor advertising is more strictly controlled in these areas on the grounds of their important amenity value. The majority of open countryside has been so designated, but it is also possible to designate urban areas. PPG 19 does attempt to give some guidance on this point, by giving examples of what may be considered appropriate areas: '...a small enclave.. where there are important architectural, archaeological, historical or visual characteristics ...the precincts of a cathedral,..or an historic market-place'.[3] Indeed, PPG 19 makes clear that this special status is intended to cover a wide range of areas. Conservation areas need not automatically be designated as areas of special control. When considering an application for outdoor advertising in a conservation area or for display on a listed building local planning authorities are however expected to exercise particular care. The criteria for selecting these special areas for advertising control is totally in the hands of the local planning authority. If it can provide reasons which justify an area being designated, then the Secretary of State will approve the designation, as he has already done for over 45% of the area of England and Wales. The designation, which the local planning authority has to review every five years, effectively introduces even tighter controls over the classes of advertisements that can be displayed with or without express consent.[4]

In conclusion, it is interesting to note that despite all the regulations aimed at controlling advertisements, the interests of public amenity are often ignored, if not actually damaged, by advertising that is approved or allowed. A few examples will

1 Ibid, Sch I.
2 Ibid, Pt IV.
3 PPG 19, para 27.
4 SI 1992/666, reg 19.

illustrate this point. Traffic signs are excluded from control, assent being assumed for their display,[5] but they can have a visually detrimental effect, especially when they take the form of overhead gantries. Certain forms of 'fly posting' also carry deemed consent, for example, election notices, circus and fair posters. The problem here is that they are seldom removed after the event and thus are taken as a sign to the true 'fly poster' that the wall or hoarding is 'fair game'. Approved advertisements can also cause problems in certain sensitive areas, such as conservation areas. Local planning authorities often seem unable, or possibly unwilling, to suggest that a 'standard' advertisement, such as a shop fascia used by a national chain store, is inappropriate in the area, perhaps on the grounds that they will be faced with the argument that it has been accepted elsewhere. Even such a strictly regulated aspect of development control is, therefore, not capable of achieving in every instance the desired protection of amenity.

Highways The importance of the transport network, particularly in relation to development control where a major issue is often the traffic implications of a proposed development, is self-evident. Yet, the effective control, and indeed creation, of transport links is not simply a planning matter, since certain national responsibilities rest with the Secretary of State for Transport rather than the Secretary of State for the Environment. Furthermore, at a local level, some transport matters may be dealt with by the county planning authority and others by the district planning authority. An overall consideration of the planning issues that relate to road building and alteration is contained within PPG 13, Transport.

Trunk roads are major roads, including motorways, that are regarded as an essential part of the national highway system. Consequently, under the terms of the Highways Act 1980, the Secretary of State for Transport has the power to permit the construction of new trunk roads as well as the improvement, by widening or straightening, of existing trunk roads.[6] Clearly, such powers can have major implications for planning policy at both county and district level. As a result, when contemplating the construction of a new trunk road, particularly a motorway, the Secretary of State for Transport is obliged to consider the planning implications[7] and to adopt a special procedure. This involves publicising the proposals and, if there are objections,

5 Ibid, Sch 2, Class H.
6 Highways Act 1980, ss 1(1)(a), 18 and 24.

in normal circumstances holding a public inquiry. The inquiry procedure is outlined in 'Policy for Roads'[8] and represents the culmination of a process that may have taken up to ten years.

The construction of a new trunk road begins when a range of surveys is conducted which cover environmental and economic matters, as well as more specific traffic issues, such as traffic flows and destinations. Possible routes are then considered and the local planning authorities consulted, as are members of the public, as to their opinions on the likely effect of these routes. The information accumulated in this fashion is then considered by the Department of Transport which will, in time, announce a preferred route for the new road, or the form which any road improvements are to take. At this stage approximately three years will have elapsed from the initial surveys. The preferred route is then analysed in detail by the Department of Transport, and draft orders prepared, setting out precisely the possible effects that the road may have, so that these matters may be fully considered at a formal public inquiry. An inquiry can last for up to six months, if not longer, and the decision is often another year in preparation. At this stage, approximately seven years after its inception, the road proposal may be abandoned or approved. If it is approved, the process continues with the issuing of the relevant compulsory purchase orders. These orders enable the land needed for the building of the new road, or the improvement of the existing road, to be acquired by the Department of Transport even if the owners of the land do not wish to sell. The acquisition of land is followed by the final stage, the road's construction, which can take another two to three years.

This protracted procedure obviously has policy implications for local planning in any area through which the proposed road will pass. For example, the period of uncertainty over whether or not the road will actually be built, lasts for seven years on average, and can cause severe blighting problems with respect to the land values and uses that lie in its proposed path. That is to say, the land on the proposed route will be regarded by prospective owners or developers as not worth developing. As a consequence, the local planning policies for the area may, at best, be disrupted, or, at worst, simply swept aside, while the local planning authority remains helpless to do anything to remove the uncertainty that is the cause of the blight. When

7 Ibid, ss 10(2) and 16(8).
8 Cmnd 7132.

making development control decisions the problems are just as real since, until the route of the road is confirmed, it will be extremely difficult for the development control officers to judge accurately its traffic implications for current planning applications.

The proposed construction of trunk roads and motorways is an extremely contentious issue with the public at large and environmental groups in particular. In PPG 13, Transport, the government has committed itself to fewer motorised journeys and reduced reliance on the motor car. As a consequence of this greater sensitivity to environmental issues or more possibly because of a desire to cut government spending, fewer roads are likely to be built. What is far more likely to be a recurrent issue is the continued, and often very necessary, work that is being undertaken on highways in England and Wales which are not classed as trunk roads; work that is being undertaken by the local highway authority which can be either the county or district council or, in very specific circumstances, the parish council.[9]

Briefly, county authorities have the responsibility for all classified roads[10] within their boundary that are not trunk roads or motorways. District authorities exercise responsibility over non-classified urban roads, footpaths and bridleways. Effectively, therefore, a reference to a highway authority is, in most instances, a reference to the county authority. Consequently, a considerable amount of consultation will take place between the county highway authority and the district planning authority, since it is the district which will determine the great majority of planning applications, most of which will involve some highway or traffic issues.

Transport issues of a lesser nature, such as the making of a new access point, or the supply of parking on a development site, constantly recur as factors in the development control process. In relation to many of these, there are quite specific guidelines supplied by the Department of Transport which the highway authority may observe when appropriate. For example, the splay of sight lines in the design of an access point into a new development is recommended, with variations relating to the speed at which traffic is likely to be travelling along the road onto which access is proposed. There are also various standards

9 Local Government Act 1972, ss 124-127.

10 Town and Country Planning (General Permitted Development) Order 1995, SI 1995/418, art 1.

governing the width and materials used for the construction of roads within a development which are particularly significant if the developer wishes eventually to have the site roads adopted by the local authority.[11]

Overall, therefore, there are a whole range of transport factors that are directly related to the planning and development control issues of an area, but which are not under the control of the local planning authority. Some of these factors may be prescribed by the Secretary of State for Transport; others may be in the control of the county highway authority which has the power, in the event of its failing to reach a compromise on a transport issue with the district planning authority, to impose its decision. Even in relation to the specific development control powers held by district planning authorities, the highway issues may be largely prescribed by regulations and standards.

Waste land and waste disposal It appears somewhat anomalous to consider the disparate subjects of waste land and waste disposal in the same section. Yet there is method in this approach. Section 215 of the 1990 Act permits a local planning authority to take action over land which is deemed to be in such a condition that it adversely affects the amenity of its area. A notice can be served on the owner of the land requiring him to take steps to rectify the situation, or the local planning authority can carry out the necessary work at the owner's expense. This provision, therefore, effectively allows a local planning authority to ensure that its area remains clean and tidy. Such a power can be compared with other local authority powers, contained within the Civic Amenities Act 1967, that allow the disposal of waste or rubbish.[12] These permit a local planning authority to remove rubbish, in the shape of abandoned cars or beds, and designate areas where members of the public can dispose of such unwanted items, rather than dumping them on any open space. In this fashion local planning authorities can devise policies which will allow them to care for their area, rather than simply respond to others' actions.

While members of the public generally want to live in a pleasant area free of old mattresses and fish and chip wrappers, there is less agreement over where this accumulated rubbish should be dumped. It is hardly surprising, therefore, that the

11 Highways Act 1980, s 38.
12 Civic Amenities Act 1967, Pt III.

whole complex question of waste disposal is dealt with in a plethora of legislation, regulations and circulars.[13] Waste disposal is a county planning authority matter[14] and policies on this issue will be found in the structure plan and in the waste local plan.[15] Detailed advice on the content of waste local plans is given in PPG 23, Planning and Control. They should identify existing and future sites for the disposal, storage and treatment of waste and consider the potential for recycling and energy recovery. Other powers and duties in respect of waste disposal are to be found in the Environmental Protection Act 1990.[16] This requires county planning authorities to perform various functions including the preparation of waste disposal plans. These are meant to identify the kinds and quantities of household, industrial and comm-ercial waste that will need to be disposed of in its area and the methods of so doing. This is in contrast to the waste local plan which is concerned with the issue of where such waste will be treated and the implications of these processes. All forms of waste tipping, except, of course, those permitted by the General Permitted Development Order,[17] constitute a material change of use. The development control functions in this instance are exercised by the county planning authority,[18] which is logical as it has prepared both the structure plan and the waste local plan. It must, however, consult with the affected districts in the exercise of these development control functions, as well as with any water authorities which are similarly affected, and the Ministry of Agriculture, Fisheries and Food. This regulation and guidance applies to the disposal of any form of waste, but controls are even more specific in the case of what is euphemistically called 'special waste'.[19]

Little purpose will be served by examining in detail all the relevant legislation and guidance, as the development control

13 Depending on the form of waste involved, legislation ranges from the Planning (Hazardous Substances) Act 1990 to the Environmental Protection Act 1990, and also includes various sections within the Town and Country Planning Act 1990, for example, ss 215-219. Regulations proliferate, for example, SI 1982/935, SI 1982/1357, SI 1988/1207, SI 1992/656, as do Circulars 29/78, 21/87, 15/88, 11/92, 11/94 and PPG 23.

14 Town and Country Planning (Prescription of County Matters) Regulations 1980, SI 1980/2010.

15 1990 Act, s 38.

16 Environmental Protection Act 1990, Pt II.

17 Town and Country Planning (General Permitted Development) Order 1995, SI 1995/418, Sch 2, Pt 21.

18 Except in Wales where the functions are undertaken by the district authorities.

19 Environmental Protection Act 1990, s 62.

issues effectively remain the same in all instances. Fundamentally, the problem can be summed up as an example of what has been termed the 'NIMBY' response – waste dumps are admittedly needed but 'Not In My Back Yard' if I can help it. This response can come not only from individuals, but also from district planning authorities and even, in the case of nuclear waste, from the county planning authorities themselves. Depending upon the nature of the waste, the development control issues are likely to focus on the visual impact and size of the site, the duration of the proposed dumping, subsequent landscaping, screening the site, the safety of the site boundaries, traffic generated by the site and times when the site will be used, as well as pollution of all kinds, including noise and fumes. In all instances these issues will be solved only on a local needs and local factors basis that will take into account the unique effects of the proposed development on the local community and its area.

NON-SPECIFIC POLICIES SUPPORTED BY VARIOUS SOURCES

Apart from those aspects of planning policy which are site specific in that they are applied only to particular areas or objects, there are a whole range of other policies related to development control that a local authority can apply to a broad range of issues throughout the whole of its area. To cover all these issues and their related policies would constitute a book in itself, and would necessitate reference to a great deal of legal and regulatory detail which is not the focus of this work. The only possible solution is to make reference to a few examples and in this fashion to draw the reader's attention to the wide range of topics that may be covered.

Local authorities, for example, are responsible in part for the public health of the individuals within their authority boundaries.[20] Part of this duty includes a responsibility for controlling atmospheric pollution and noise. Both pollution and noise can be considered as planning issues, and can be directly controlled by the use of planning conditions in relation to new developments. Normally, however, alternative measures are relied upon to control noise and pollution, which are exercisable by some department within the local authority, other than the

20 For a synopsis of the local authorities' duties regarding public health see Webster C A R *Public Health Law* (1981).

planning department.[1] That is not to imply that these issues are not relevant planning issues. The pollution implications of any industrial development, for example, would obviously figure in any development control analysis. Rather, this indicates that pollution can be controlled by a whole variety of statutory provisions, of which the imposition of planning policy, in the shape of a planning condition, is simply one aspect.

By way of a contrast, local authorities are responsible for access to the countryside and the provision of country parks, both of which may feature in the planning policies relating to leisure facilities. As in the previous example, however, there are specific legislative provisions, which a local authority must observe, that are not to be found in the planning legislation but exist in their own right. The National Parks and Access to the Countryside Act 1949[2] and the Wildlife and Countryside Act 1981,[3] both provide local authorities with a range of duties and powers regarding the provision of access to the countryside. In addition, the Countryside Act 1968[4] confers on local authorities the power to set up and maintain country parks, which are areas provided for the public enjoyment of the countryside. These various statutory powers must be taken into account by the local planning authority when preparing its policy on leisure and recreational matters. Those powers will enable specific provision to be made for leisure facilities which might not otherwise have been the case if the local planning authority had simply relied on its ability to produce planning policy in respect of the issues.

Powers stemming directly from the Town and Country Planning Act 1990

While the local authority may use powers that are derived from a wide range of legislative sources to implement some particular aspect of its planning policy, it also possesses various general planning powers that can, in certain circumstances, serve the same purpose. Of these powers, the most significant are the ability of a local authority to acquire or appropriate land; to

1 For example, under the Health and Safety at Work etc Act 1974 the health and safety executive can effect various controls that are beyond the powers of a planning authority.
2 National Parks and Access to the Countryside Act 1949, Pt V.
3 Wildlife and Countryside Act 1981, ss 53-58.
4 Countryside Act 1968, ss 6-10.

develop land in its own right; to dispose of land; to impose planning conditions on any development; and to enter into an agreement with a developer.

COMPULSORY PURCHASE FOR PLANNING PURPOSES

This is a complex branch of planning law and administrative responsibility which is adequately covered in other works that concentrate specifically on the topic.[5] In essence, sections 226-231 of the 1990 Act give local authorities the right to acquire by compulsory purchase any land in their area for two primary purposes. They are that the land is needed to carry out (i) any form of development, redevelopment or improvement, or (ii) the proper planning of the area. Furthermore, once the land is acquired for a specific development, the local planning authority is free to undertake the development itself, or sell or lease it to a private developer to undertake the development, or work in partnership with the private developer to undertake the development. Naturally, all such actions are carefully prescribed by regulation and statute and all manner of safeguards to protect the individual are included.

In the context of this work, however, it is the implication that the ability to acquire land has for both the creation of local planning policy and development control, which needs to be considered. Realistically, that power is possibly not as significant as it may first appear, at least not in the past decade, as the desire, and indeed ability, of local authorities to participate in major development schemes either in their own right, or even in partnership with a private developer, is much reduced. In the 1960s and 1970s some local authorities became major developers of both housing, and, to a lesser extent, of retailing, often collaborating with a private developer to undertake major developments, such as the construction of large shopping centres. As far as the developer was concerned, the advantage of a partnership lay in the fact that a local authority could use its powers of compulsory purchase to assemble a development site relatively quickly. This was especially relevant in town centres where the fragmented nature of estate ownership made the job a nightmare for the independent developer. On the other hand, the advantage to the local authority was the dual one of sharing the risk, as well as gaining from the wider entrepreneurial expertise that a major developer could offer. In the

5 For a comprehensive account see Rowan-Robinson J and Brand C, *Compulsory Purchase and Compensation: A Practitioner's Guide* (1994).

housing field, however, local authorities tended to work alone, as the returns, if indeed there were any, were not attractive enough to interest the private developer, as much of the local authority housing built during these years was subsidised by central government grants. Besides being a prominent aspect of the development activity of those years, these schemes were part of the planning process, since the developments in question represented part of a declared planning policy usually contained within the development plan.

Today, however, although all the same options to purchase and develop land remain, the opportunity presents itself less and less frequently since neither the money nor the land is available. Local authorities have also become far more cautious due to some of the disasters, especially in the field of housing, that the flood of development produced, although even some commercial developments have failed to flourish as expected. In the majority of instances, therefore, development proposals found in newly produced local plans are unlikely to be implicitly supported by a local authority eager to use its compulsory purchase powers to enable a site to be assembled for development. On the other hand, this is not to suggest that local authorities are no longer prepared to enter into partnerships with developers for schemes they would like to see implemented.

DEVELOPMENT BY LOCAL AUTHORITIES

Section 235 of the 1990 Act authorises local authorities to become developers in their own right of land that they own, or, alternatively, to sell or lease it for private development. The connection between this power and the powers of compulsory purchase is obvious, but the important issue here is that the local authority gives itself planning permission. This is not to say that planning permission is simply given without any consideration of the normal development control issues. Indeed, this is far from the case, as the Secretary of State, as empowered by section 316 of the 1990 Act, has established procedures which must be observed in these circumstances.[6] Essentially, the procedures ensure that the local authority makes public its intentions and involvement regarding the proposed development. Any representations received by the local authority must then be given due consideration. The second stage of the procedure is when the local authority decides whether or not to give

6 Town and Country Planning General Regulations 1992, SI 1992/1492, regs 2-11.

either itself or the other party, who will be developing the site for the local authority, planning permission. It should not be assumed that this procedure in any way cuts short the normal development control debate undertaken by the planning committee in the process of reaching its decision. Provided those development control issues are properly considered, there is no way in which the local authority can be said to have prejudged the issue, as several cases have shown.[7] Whatever the safeguards, the procedure allows the local authority to give itself, or the developer, permission to undertake almost any form of development on land that it owns. As a last resort, members of the public alarmed by the power this places in the hands of a local authority can attempt to persuade the Secretary of State to call in the application for his personal consideration. However, this happens very infrequently.

As with compulsory purchase, this power must be seen in its true light where its use in relation to any major development is hardly a frequent occurrence. Notwithstanding this fact, however, it represents a significant weapon in the local planning authority's armoury of planning powers, as it clearly can be used to implement those developments that the local planning authority thinks are best for the area – a positive force amongst the negative regulatory powers that form the greater part of the day-to-day planning process.

PLANNING OBLIGATIONS AND PLANNING CONDITIONS

Beside it being possible for a local planning authority to give planning permission to itself to undertake development on land that it owns, it is also possible for the local planning authority to enter into a planning obligation with a developer by virtue of section 106 of the 1990 Act. A section 106 obligation may be mutually agreed by both parties or may be offered unilaterally by the developer and is for the purpose of:

> restricting the development or use of land in any specified way ...requiring specified operations or activities to be carried out in, on, under or over the land...requiring the land to be used in a specified way...or requiring a sum or sums to be paid to the authority.[8]

Section 106 obligations can be used as a means of obtaining from the developer what used to be known as planning gain.

7 *R v St Edmundsbury Borough Council, ex p Investors in Industry Commerial Properties* [1985] 3 All ER 234 and *R v Sevenoaks District Council, ex p Terry* [1985] 3 All ER 226.

8 1990 Act, s 106(1).

Planning gains may be seen as benefits for the community that the local planning authority seeks to extract from the developer (sometimes, but not always, by way of a section 106 obligation). In certain circumstances, such as those related to commercial developments in the Greater London area during the 1970's and early 1980's, an attempt to extract planning gain may seem justifiable, as it provided the only direct and immediate means whereby some community benefit would accrue from the enormous profits developers made from commercial schemes. Events, however, appeared to have got somewhat out of hand to the extent that a Circular was issued in 1983[9] which attempted, somewhat unsuccessfully, to clarify matters. This Circular was subsequently withdrawn when planning obligations were introduced into the 1990 Act but the whole issue of planning obligations and the possible resulting planning gain is examined in a more appropriate context in chapter 8.

The ability of a local planning authority to impose planning conditions when granting planning permission is yet another power which clearly can be used to ensure that the proposed development observes the local authority's planning policy. This power is provided for in section 72 of the 1990 Act and has been fully examined in Circular 1/85, The Use of Conditions in Planning Permissions. In essence, a local planning authority can grant planning permission subject to such conditions as it thinks fit, but these must have a planning purpose. This power gives the local planning authority a wide discretion in formulating conditions, and this will be used the better to implement planning policy. In every instance, however, as Circular 1/85 indicates, planning conditions must be shown to be relevant to the proposed development, enforceable, precise and reasonable, otherwise they may be the subject of an appeal by the developer to the Secretary of State, or of a challenge in the courts, as will be discussed in chapter 8.

Policy formulated by other bodies

As may have already been gathered, the local planning authority is not the only body either to produce policy relevant to town and country planning, or influence in other ways development control within a local planning authority area. Other bodies, of which there are a considerable number,[10] can

9 Circular 22/83, Planning Gain.
10 See chapter 2.

fulfil a similar policy generating role, but all exist on the fringes of what might be termed the 'normal' planning control of an area. That is to say, it is recognised that planning control generally rests in the hands of the local planning authority, but that in certain circumstances bodies, such as English Heritage, can have an effect on both local planning policy and development control. While reference may be made to such bodies in the planning legislation, their actual influence on the planning of an area is difficult to define. Given the number and range of these bodies, it would be impossible to consider each one in turn. Instead, by selecting what may be considered the most 'common', it is hoped to provide a series of examples of the possible effects that each can have on planning and development control.

The first of these examples concerns the Crown. Land belonging to the Crown, which includes land directly owned by any government department, is partially exempt from the need to apply for and obtain planning permission.[11] Instead, the Crown is expected to consult with the relevant local planning authority before undertaking development, the detailed arrangements being set out in Part XIII of the 1990 Act and Circular 18/84, Crown Land and Crown Development. Here it is made quite clear that the consultation is not simply a matter of form, and that any objections made by the local planning authority must be duly considered. If they are not, these objections may then be upheld by the Department of the Environment and a public inquiry may be held. However, this is only likely to occur when major developments are contemplated by the Crown. On the other hand, it is a matter of judgment for the Crown estate if a proposed development is covered by the General Permitted Development Order which is to be used 'as a general guide to the kinds of development they may carry out without consultation'.[12] This illustrates the anomaly of the Crown's position, since it is possible for a local planning authority to include proposals for Crown estate land in any of its development plans, just as it is possible for the Department of the Environment to list any buildings on Crown land, but it is impossible to ensure that any of these proposals are observed. Naturally, this can have an effect on local planning policy.

Another group of organisations that are likely to fall into the special case category, are statutory undertakers. These are defined in the 1990 Act by listing their various duties, which include:

11 In March 1994 the Secretary of State announced that legislation would be introduced to removethis Crown exemption. This legislation is currently awaited.

12 Circular 18/84, Pt IV, para 4.

railway, light railway, tramway, road transport, water transport, canal, inland navigation, dock, harbour, pier or lighthouse undertaking, or any undertaking for the supply of hydraulic power and a relevant airport operator.[13]

Statutory undertakers are not beyond the reach of planning control, as is the case with the Crown estate, rather they are on the fringe. This means that any development that a statutory undertaker carries out which is directly related to its duty as a statutory undertaker is permitted development.[14] Therefore, if a dock company decides that it needs to erect a new landing jetty within the limits of the dock, it can do so without planning permission. What is not included, however, are related developments that arguably are not directly attributable to the statutory undertaker's specified duty. In this instance, if planning permission were refused by the local planning authority, and an appeal was made to the Secretary of State, he must then consult with the relevant Minister, in this case possibly the Minister of Transport and they must jointly reach a compromise. The influence these events might have on a local planning authority's development control policy is obvious. They represent development that, besides being contentious, is effectively outside the local planning authority's control.

Central government Ministries can also affect local planning policy and development control. This has been discussed elsewhere, so a single example will suffice. The most obvious Ministry to mention is the Ministry of Agriculture, Fisheries and Food, which has a very wide remit covering agriculture as well as forestry, land reclamation, drainage, water supply and environmental pollution. In performing these tasks, the Ministry may well produce policy that is not specifically related to local planning policy, but the impact of that policy will be felt by most rural planning officers and their authorities. For example, the Ministry grades agricultural land according to its inherent food producing qualities.[15] Consequently, as high grade agricultural land has been effectively earmarked only for agricultural production, the ability of the local planning authority to produce proposals for alternative uses is severely restricted.

Many other bodies can be mentioned because they may have some effect on planning. These include the Countryside Commission, the Forestry Commission, the Nature Conservancy Councils, the United Kingdom Atomic Energy Authority, and

13 1990 Act, s 262(1).

14 Town and Country Planning (General Permitted Development) Order 1995, SI 1995/418, Sch 2, Pt 17.

15 PPG 7, The countryside and the rural economy, annex A.

English Heritage. All of these are connected in some fashion with the government, while other groups, such as the Civic Trust, the Ramblers' Association, the National Trust, and the Georgian Group have no direct links with government, simply a considerable amount of influence regarding certain issues.

It is beyond the scope of this book to consider each of these in turn, but a single example may serve to illustrate their possible impact on the planning process. English Heritage have a large number of 'townscape' schemes that allow works within designated conservation areas to apply for grant aid to English Heritage.[16] That body may then provide finance for the works jointly with the local planning authority. Clearly, the local planning authority is involved in the schemes, and, indeed, any local planning authority may approach English Heritage to consider including one of its conservation areas in the townscape scheme. The final decision remains in the hands of English Heritage, however, and when taken it will have an obvious effect on local conservation policy.

Finally, it should be noted that policy and with it the need for accompanying legislation can be introduced as a consequence of the United Kingdom's membership of the European Union. Possibly the best example is the need for planning authorities to assess the environmental effects of certain forms of development. The need to undertake such assessments was imposed as a result of European Community Directive 85/337 which was given the force of law in England and Wales in 1988.[17] The legislation was accompanied by a Circular[18] which set out the policy and explained the operation of the regulations. These effectively designate a range of developments, known as Schedule 1 and 2 developments, that require an environmental assessment to be made. As the Circular notes,[19] such assessments may well form an integral part of the planning application process, but nevertheless have to be supplied in the prescribed manner. With the consolidation of the planning legislation in the 1990 Act, the requirement for such assessments now forms part of the body of planning control.[20]

16 PPG 15, Planning and the Historic Environment, para 4.10.
17 Town and Country Planning (Assessment of Environmental Effects) Regulations 1988, SI 1988/1199.
18 Circular 15/88, Town and Country Planning (Assessment of Environmental Effects) Regulations 1988.
19 Ibid, para 6.
20 1990 Act, s 71A.

Chapter 6

Department of the Environment policy

In the opening chapter of this book it was acknowledged that land use planning is the '...art and science of ordering the use of land and the character and siting of buildings and communication routes so as to secure the maximum practicable degree of economy, convenience and beauty'.[1] The order of priority in which these objectives are arranged and the degree to which each is emphasised alters depending on planning policy. This policy varies from administration to administration and between central and local government, but in general terms represents the plan of action conceived in order to obtain the prioritised objectives. Within certain parameters, planning policy can have whatever content is thought most effective by the policy-making body to achieve a particular goal. If, for example, central government wishes to encourage new development, it can manipulate its land use planning policy in order to help achieve this goal. On the one hand, that policy may make more land available for housing, in the expectation that the opportunity to increase the number of housing starts will produce new development opportunities in the building industry. Alternatively, areas may be established where planning formalities are kept to a minimum, in the hope that new enterprises will be developed there and new jobs created. The land use policies are distinct yet their goal is the same. As for the parameters restricting such policy, basically, there are two. The need to observe the law and also to appreciate the basic constraints imposed by the theories of land use planning, such as those which attempt to explain the dynamics of urban structure.

This chapter is devoted to a study of central government policy, or, more accurately, to what is in the main Department of the Environ-ment policy, as it relates to development control. In analysing that policy, a critic might say that little indication

1 Keeble L *Principles and Practice of Town and Country Planning* (4th edn, 1961) p 1.

is given of what constitutes the content of that policy. Instead, this chapter concentrates on the form in which Department of the Environ-ment policy is expressed, for example, legislation, planning policy guidance notes and circulars. There is, however, a simple explanation for this. In a sense, the whole of this book is a testimony to years of Department of the Environment and central government policy. Chapter 4 on development plans is one such example. It was a central government policy decision that brought these plans into existence and, as that chapter explains, subsequent policy decisions have changed the nature of these documents and will undoubtedly continue to do so. The same can be said of the chapter on local authority policy, where a range of devices was considered which allow a local planning authority to initiate specific development control policies for its area. The origin of those devices is central government.

Yet, for all this power of central government to initiate policy, its relationship with the local planning authority is crucial, since it is the local planning authority which puts central government policy into practice, adapting that general policy to suit the specific needs of its area, and takes the bulk of the development control decisions. If it is correct to say that central government initiates and local government implements, what guarantees are there that this division of labour is observed? Briefly, they rely on the fact that central government policy is well publicised and, therefore, any attempt by a local planning authority to depart from that policy is likely to be apparent. In addition, there are, built into the development control system, opportunities for central government to oversee the activities of local government. Development plans, for example, are monitored, the creation of conservation areas is conditional upon approval, while a refusal of planning permission can always be the subject of an appeal. In this fashion central government can observe and, if need be, override a local planning authority which has been reluctant to implement central government policy.

Nor should it be imagined that only central and local government take an interest in Department of the Environment policy, as other individuals and organisations exist with an interest in development control to whom such policy is crucial. These range from property companies and the professional bodies, such as the Royal Institution of Chartered Surveyors, to members of the public. Central as well as local government policy will be used by them to estimate what type of planning application will be likely to succeed, or, alternatively, whether an appeal would be worthwhile.

The origins of policy

While no attempt will be made in this chapter to detail the content of Department of the Environment policy, it seems sensible to consider the origins of that policy before listing the forms in which it can be expressed. Obviously the policy pursued by the Department of the Environment at any particular time is influenced by the political beliefs of the party which is in government. This may, for example, cause shifts in emphasis between private and public sector development. If the government of the day is trying to encourage private sector development of housing and industry, it may contemplate policies that release more land for housing to private developers, create simplified planning zones for the establishment of industrial enterprises, and divert funds away from the public sector and, in particular, from local authorities. A government which wished to reverse such policies might behave in completely the opposite fashion, putting money into the public sector and controlling private sector development, perhaps by the imposition of a tax on profits. Therefore, a good deal of Department of the Environment policy is shaped by political motives.

Leaving aside the influence exerted by a government's political beliefs, there are other factors which shape the policies pursued by the Department of the Environment. They include the expert opinions volunteered by professional organisations, such as the Royal Town Planning Institute and the Royal Institution of Chartered Surveyors. Pressure groups, such as the Council for the Protection of Rural England or the Civic Trust, can also influence policy. This is because the Department of the Environment normally canvasses a wide range of opinion while legislation or circulars are being prepared. Even if their views are ignored within the Department of the Environment, some pressure groups, for example the National Farmers Union, have considerable influence in Parliament, which can be mobilised in order to try to secure amendment to legislation. Indeed, on rare occasions the content of a circular has proved so unpopular that pressure of opinion has forced its withdrawal.[2] Therefore, pressures shape policy. Since governments wish to be re-elected, it is the Department of the Environment's task to balance these often conflicting views in order to achieve a

2 A draft version of a circular on green belts proved so unpopular that it had to be withdrawn and rewritten. The rewritten version was Circular 14/84, Green Belts.

policy which is politically and electorally acceptable. Quite obviously, not every section of an Act of Parliament or paragraph of a circular is politically sensitive. Sometimes other considerations are uppermost, such as securing the most efficient way to administer a particular aspect of the development control process. Here policy takes a back seat. Attention will focus instead on the courts, and what they have to say on acceptable administrative behaviour. When Department of the Environment inspectors hear planning appeals, there are rules indicating how they must conduct such appeals in order to ensure procedural fairness.[3]

Making policy known

Once the content of a particular policy has been decided upon, the most appropriate way of implementing it has to be sought. The most obvious vehicle for putting policy into effect would seem to be legislation. It has the advantage of being publicly debated in Parliament, and will ultimately represent the law of the land which must be obeyed by all concerned. In the course of this book, Acts of Parliament have been considered which are statements of current Department of the Environment policy. They range from the Local Government, Planning and Land Act 1980 to the Town and Country Planning Act 1990. The overriding problem with using legislation to implement policy is that, once in place, legislation has either to be amended or repealed in order to take account of a change in policy. A space has to be found in the government's legislative programme and sufficient time allowed for the Bill to pass through all its stages. Nor is there any guarantee that the original Bill will remain intact and not fall prey to amendment. This apart, policy can be difficult to express in the precise language which legislation requires. It is not unknown for the courts to conclude that the meaning of a section in an Act of Parliament is either totally obscure, or the exact reverse of what was intended.[4] Nor is policy always capable of being expressed in absolute terms. Instead,

3 Town and Country Planning (Inquiries Procedure) Rules 1992, SI 1992/2038; Town and Country Planning (Determination by Inspectors) (Inquiries Procedure) Rules 1992, SI 1992/2039.

4 See, for example, *Windsor and Maidenhead Royal Borough Council v Brandrose Investments Ltd* [1983] 1 All ER 818, where the Court of Appeal commented on the obscurity of s 52(3) of the Town and Country Planning Act 1971.

it is subject to qualifications and exceptions which a parliamentary draftsman might be hard pressed to put into words. Legislation, therefore, is normally used to convey only the basic concepts of any development control policy.

In order to expand upon the role of legislation and to illustrate its relationship with other devices used to implement policy, it seems sensible to refer to an example, in this instance one which also illustrates the interdependence between distinct but closely allied government departments. Sections 1–6 of the Planning (Listed Buildings and Conservation Areas) Act 1990 are concerned with buildings of special architectural or historic interest. Provision is made for the establishment by the Secretary of State for National Heritage of lists of such buildings, which cannot then be demolished, altered or extended unless special permission has been secured from the local planning authority or the Secretary of State for the Environment. This is totally separate from the need to obtain planning permission. Failure to obtain consent can result in prosecution.[5] The policy behind these sections in the Act is the desire to preserve those buildings which are special, either because of their appearance or their history. Yet, apart from some very general comments in section 1(3), no detailed guidance is given in the Act on what constitutes a building of special architectural or historic interest. Further examination of these sections reveals that, while, according to section 8, listed building consent must be obtained before a listed building is demolished, altered or extended, there is only a passing reference to how to go about securing the same. This is to be found in section 10(2):

> Such an application shall be made in such form as the authority may require and shall contain –
> (a) sufficient particulars to identify the building to which it relates, including a plan;
> (b) such other plans and drawings as are necessary to describe the works which are the subject of the application; and
> (c) such other particulars as may be required by the authority.

Thus, although the section provides some indication of the procedure to be followed on such occasions, it is not comprehensive. On the question of the form an application for listed building consent is to observe, provision is simply made in section 10(3) for regulations to be produced.

Any individual, therefore, who wishes to know what makes a building worthy of listing or how to go about making an

5 Planning (Listed Buildings and Conservation Areas) Act 1990, s 9.

application for listed building consent must consult other sources apart from the Planning (Listed Buildings and Conservation Areas) Act 1990. PPG 15, Planning and the Historic Environment, supplies guidance for the selection of listed buildings. The Town and Country Planning (Listed Buildings and Buildings in Conservation Areas) Regulations 1990[6] describe the procedure to be followed when making an application for listed building consent. From this brief illustration, it should be apparent that what the 1990 legislation supplies is a framework for the policy which is supplemented with details from other sources. What those sources are, is not without significance. The Town and Country Planning (Listed Buildings and Buildings in Conservation Areas) Regulations 1990 represent delegated legislation. It will be recalled that section 10(3) of the Planning (Listed Buildings and Conservation Areas) Act 1990 refers to provision being made:

> by regulations under this Act with respect to –
> (a) the manner in which such applications are to be made;
> (b) the manner in which they are to be advertised; and
> (c) the time within which they are to be dealt with...

When an Act of Parliament authorises the making of rules, regulations or directions on a particular matter, those regulations have the same status as any provisions which appear in the original Act. Collectively such rules, regulations, directions or statutory instruments are known as delegated legislation.

It might occur to anyone reading this brief description of delegated legislation that regulations, such as the Town and Country Planning (Listed Buildings and Buildings in Conservation Areas) Regulations 1990, could just have easily been included in the Act. While this is no doubt correct, Ministers prefer to rely on delegated legislation because the procedure for introducing it, amending it or replacing it, is very straightforward indeed, and takes a fraction of the time required for amending an Act of Parliament.[7] The only limitations are that a power must exist in an Act of Parliament to make delegated legislation and it must be used correctly in accordance with the

6 SI 1990/1519.

7 Once the content of delegated legislation has been decided upon and interested parties have been asked for their comments, most delegated legislation is put before Parliament for 40 days. The intention is that during this period motions can be made for the annulment of the delegated legislation. That 40-day period should be contrasted with the months it takes most bills to pass through Parliament.

terms of the Act and certain general principles.[8] This apart, delegated legislation has the advantages of legislation without requiring a considerable period of parliamentary time to be devoted to its passage.

Given the convenience of delegated legislation, it might appear strange that the guidance for selecting listed buildings is not expressed in that form. The PPG which contains that guidance is not a piece of delegated legislation and, as will be demonstrated later, has no binding force whatsoever. The simple answer is that the Act gives no power to create regulations on this particular topic. While this is true, some further explanation is necessary for this apparent omission. According to PPG 15, age is a criterion for listing buildings. To quote from the PPG:

> Thus, all buildings built before 1700 which survive in anything like their original condition are listed; and most buildings of about 1700 to 1840 are listed, though some selection is necessary. After about 1840, because of the greatly increased number of buildings erected and the much larger numbers that have survived, greater selection is necessary to identify the best examples of particular building types, and only buildings of definite quality and character are listed. For the same reasons, only selected buildings from the period after 1914 are normally listed. Buildings which are less than 30 years old are normally listed only if they are of outstanding quality and under threat. Buildings which are less than ten years old are not listed.[9]

If an attempt had been made to express this passage in the form of binding regulations, then the result would have been less than helpful. This is because discretion is the essential factor in selecting buildings for listing. While, therefore, an indication can be given of what is important, for example, age, it is not possible to state categorically that every building built between 1840 and 1914 shall be listed. In contrast, certainty as opposed to discretion is the keynote of the Town and Country Planning (Listed Buildings and Buildings in Conservation Areas) Regulations 1990. An individual needs to be certain of whom to apply to for listed building consent, what details must be given, who must be informed and what publicity is necessary. The 1990 Regulations supply that information and more be-

8 The courts have a power to review delegated legislation in order to determine whether the correct procedure has been observed in its making. In addition, the courts can set aside delegated legislation where some unreasonable use has been made of the power to create it.

9 PPG 15, para 6.11.

sides. In this way they ensure that all concerned are treated fairly, and the fact that the Regulations are binding should guarantee this. To have used a PPG in this situation would not have ensured compliance. Yet, the mere fact that circulars and PPGs are advisory is not a reason for dismissing them without further comment. Theirs is a crucial role in disseminating Department of the Environment policy.

Department of the Environment planning policy: form and purpose

Department of the Environment planning policy is expressed in a variety of forms: circulars, planning policy guidance notes (PPGs), minerals planning guidance notes (MPGs) and regional planning guidance notes (RPGs). The breadth of subject matter covered by these policy documents can be illustrated by quoting a few examples at random. Circular 5/94, Planning Out Crime, offers guidance on designing developments to reduce crime as well as stressing the relevance of crime prevention as a factor in reaching development control decisions. PPG 5, Simplified Planning Zones, summarises the procedures for creating such zones and the benefits arising from their use by local planning authorities. Finally, MPG 4, The Review of Mineral Working Sites, explains the circumstances in which such reviews may be undertaken and the various steps a mineral planning authority may take at the conclusion of such a review. Currently there are over one hundred circulars, twenty-three PPGs, twelve MPGs and ten RPGs.[10] It is, therefore, impossible to consider the content of each in turn, Instead, an attempt will be made to indicate to the reader what planning policy guidance is, and how it is used in the development control process. By approaching the topic in this fashion, the hope is that when circulars, or other comparable forms of policy guidance mentioned in this book, are revised or superseded, as often happens, a basic understanding of the workings of planning policy will have been acquired.

10 Planning policy for the regions has been produced under a variety of titles and not simply that of RPGs. See, for example, PPG 9, Regional Guidance for the South East (1989). This has now been replaced by RPG 9, Regional Planning Guidance for the South East. Regional guidance for the former metropolitan counties, such as West Yorkshire, was issued under the original title of 'Strategic Planning Guidance'.

PPGs, circulars and comparable advisory documents are used to communicate shifts in policy.[11] In the 1980s, for example, the Department of the Environment made it abundantly clear in documents such as Circular 22/80, Development Control – Policy and Practice, and Circular 14/85, Development and Employment, that there was a presumption in favour of development in order to stimulate economic growth. As a result, development plans were disregarded and decisions by local planning authorities to refuse planning permission were overturned on appeal if they were out of step with this policy of economic expansion. Dissatisfaction was expressed with this policy, which was seen as undermining the status of development plans. Towards the end of the decade there was a re-evaluation of this approach. Planning policy guidance, such as PPG 12, Local Plans,[12] began to reassert the weight to be attached to up-to-date development plans when development control decisions were made. As this example shows, planning policy guidance documents were used to communicate substantial shifts in departmental policy and what they said was treated very seriously by those whose actions they affected. Consequently, the suspicion has been voiced that, on occasions, a circular or PPG may represent an attractive alternative to legislation, particularly if an issue is controversial. The dangers represented by such a practice need to be stressed, and should be kept in mind during the remainder of this examination of the role of government planning policy guidance.

Until comparatively recently circulars were, to all intents and purposes, the sole source of Department of the Environment planning policy.[13] Between six and fifteen were produced each year and in total they formed a considerable body of information. The problem with this system was that all manner of advice, ranging from the purely practical to authoritative policy statements, was communicated in this one format. Circular 1/85, The Use of Conditions in Planning Permissions, is a good example of an 'old style' circular. Much of the advice in the Circular is

11 In *Barnet Meeting Room Trust v Secretary of State for the Environment and Barnet London Borough Council* [1993] JPL 739 it was said by Auld J that a Minister might modify his policy in the course of giving his decision on a development control issue rather than issuing an amended circular or PPG.

12 PPG 12, originally issued in 1988 and now superseded by PPG 12, Development Plans and Regional Planning Guidance, issued in 1992.

13 Development control policy notes were issued from time to time but their infrequent appearance compared with the rate at which circulars were released implied that they were seen as incidental and carried no real policy 'weight'.

purely practical, dealing with legislative provisions relevant to the imposition of planning conditions, and tests laid down by the High Court to gauge the validity of conditions. In short, the Circular represents a compilation, derived from various sources, of information which a local planning authority should bear in mind when imposing planning conditions. Whether such a circular can be described as a policy statement is open to doubt, since policy normally refers to a plan of action adopted by central government, rather than the dissemination of advice from other sources.

The problem is that among this practical information can be found a number of important policy statements. For example, Circular 1/85 deals with domestic occupancy conditions, that is conditions imposed in order to restrict the occupancy of a new dwelling-house to a particular type of person. Arguably there may be good planning reasons why such a condition should be imposed, in order, for example, to prevent the proliferation of second homes. The Circular makes it plain, however, that in the opinion of the Secretary of State such conditions are not acceptable, save in exceptional circumstances.[14] In addition, the Circular acknowledges that there might well be a conflict between these views and policy statements made in development plans.

> The Secretaries of State recognise that some local authorities may have adopted development plan policies which may conflict with policies set out in this circular...Those authorities are invited to examine any such policies with a view to resolving any inconsistencies with the policy here stated.[15]

The overall effect of this policy statement is that even though as a matter of law the power exists to impose conditions of this nature, the Secretary of State will not normally allow a domestic occupancy condition to stand. If, therefore, a local planning authority imposes such a condition, it may expect to see it removed should there be an appeal. This may be so even though the relevant development plan contains policies to support its imposition, as the Secretary of State obviously intends either to override such polices or to ensure their removal from the plan if this is feasible.

The problem encountered with this mixture of practical information and policy statements is that the two can become confused. Yet they are intended to fulfil very different purposes.

14 Circular 1/85, paras 77, 80 and 81.
15 Ibid, para 88.

Any attempt in a circular to summarise the impact of legislation or the significance of a judicial decision is not authoritative. The courts are responsible for statutory interpretation and they will have no hesitation in saying that a statement made in a circular is wrong, should this be the case. Policy statements, on the other hand, are neither right nor wrong, though the content of one policy may be inconsistent with another. In applying a policy a decision-maker has the discretion to decide that the policy is not appropriate to the particular situation, or that some other policy takes precedence. There can be, and often is, disagreement between central and local government over the appropriateness of a particular policy. In these circumstances, while it is possible to give one party the final say, this is not equivalent to deciding that the other party is wrong. Yet the way in which both were presented in the same document led to confusion. It was in order to meet this criticism and make planning policy more accessible that PPGs and MPGs were introduced.

> PPGs and MPGs are intended to provide concise and practical guidance on planning polices in a clearer and more accessible form than in Departmental circulars...[16]

PPGs would deal with general and specific planning polices whilst MPGs would cover the control of minerals development. Circulars would continue to be produced but would now concentrate on giving advice on legislation and procedures. Given the variety of forms that national planning policy guidance can take, it seems sensible to consider each in turn in order to ascertain what role they perform in the development control process and whether they perform it well.

PPGs deal with the entire range of planning issues, minerals development apart and are, therefore, a prime source of Department of the Environment planning policy. Their key role is emphasised by the statement which prefaces PPG 15:

> Planning policy guidance notes set out Government policy on planning issues and provide guidance to local authorities and others on the operation of the planning system. They also explain the relationship between planning policies and other policies which have an important bearing on issues of development and land use. Local planning authorities must take their content into account in preparing their development plans. The guidance may also be material to decisions on individual planning applications and appeals.

16 Circular 1/88, Planning Policy Guidance and Minerals Planning Guidance, para 2.

PPGs offer advice on very broadly stated topics such as housing, town centres and retail developments, transport and green belts. Since their inception in 1988 twenty-three PPGs have been produced and some of the earlier ones, such as PPG 2, Green Belts, have already been revised.

Whether PPGs have achieved their objective of making planning policies clearer and more accessible is open to question. They have been criticised as 'confusing', 'complex' and 'vague in their terminology'.[17] In *Barnet Meeting Room Trust v Secretary of State for the Environment and Barnet London Borough Council*[18] much discussion centred around the phrase 'institutions standing in extensive grounds' which was used in PPG 2, Green Belts.[19] This was because the PPG advised that inside a green belt neither the construction of new buildings nor a change of use should be approved. There were, however, exceptions to this general rule and they included the construction of institutions standing in extensive grounds. The issue was whether a proposed meeting room for religious worship could come within this description. The judgment in that case criticises the use of such an imprecise expression without further explanation and sees it as defeating the purpose of planning policy guidance which is to give advice on policy issues:

> the vagueness of the expression and the lack of any indication or criteria as to its interpretation or application in the policy document in which it appeared were unsatisfactory. Developers and planning authorities both needed to know where they stood in relation to such a policy so that they could readily determine whether or not a particular proposal was likely to come within it and so that there might be reasonable consistency and fairness in its implementation nationally.[20]

Further evidence of the often imprecise guidance given in PPGs is not hard to find. PPG 3, Housing, for example, seems to be full of rather vague well-intentioned statements that few might argue with. For example, on the subject of housing in rural areas it puts forward the following views:

> Some villages may have reached the limit of their natural growth, while in others provision can be made for modest development without damage, either to the countryside or to the

17 Tewdwr-Jones M 'The Government's Planning Policy Guidance' Journal of Planning and Environment Law, 1994, p 106 at 113 quoting a report from the House of Commons Welsh Affairs Committee.

18 [1993] JPL 739.

19 Para 13. PPG 2 has subsequently been revised.

20 [1993] JPL 739 at 746.

settlement itself. Although the relationship between the size of a village and the level of service provision is not direct, new housing may help to maintain local shops, pubs, schools and other features of community life in rural areas. Where new housing is acceptable, the character of the particular settlement should always be respected, in terms of densities as well as scale and environmental quality. Villages vary widely in their character, and what might be appropriate in a village with a dense intricate pattern of development could be out of place in a sparser, more open settlement. The reverse may also be true.[1]

If these are intended to represent clear policies aimed at providing those involved in the development control process with such much needed direction, as opposed to vague expressions of opinion giving the obvious alternatives, then PPGs may have failed in their objectives.

An additional problem that has been encountered in relation to PPGs is that the policies which they contain are not always compatible. A good example of this occurred in *Pehrsson v Secretary of State for the Environment.*[2] Here the argument centred around a cricket pavilion situated in the green belt which its owner wished to convert into accommodation for staff employed in his home. Planning permission had been refused and this decision was the subject of a review by the Court of Appeal. In the course of delivering its judgment the court considered a bewildering range of circulars and PPGs. These included Circular 14/85 and PPG 1 with their presumptions in favour of granting planning permission as well as PPG 2 which deals with development in the green belt. From this mass of policy the Court of Appeal eventually produced a formula for evaluating proposed developments in the green belt.

The combined effect of planning policy guidance 1 and 2 was that an inspector must first determine whether a proposed development in the green belt was appropriate or not. If it was appropriate, the general presumption in favour of development applied and planning permission should be granted unless the planning authority could demonstrate that the development could cause demonstrable harm to interests of acknowledged importance. If the development was inappropriate, planning permission should not be granted unless the developer could show special circumstances which would outweigh harm to interests of acknowledged importance.[3]

1 PPG 3, para 19.
2 (1990) 61 P & CR 266.
3 Ibid, at 266.

As this example and others like it demonstrate once the courts have interpreted a particular policy the initiative has been taken away from the Secretary of State.[4] The policy may no longer be his policy but the courts' interpretation of his policy which is not necessarily the same thing.

As PPGs have become a major source of planning policy so circulars have been used more and more to give advice on legislative changes. This should not be allowed to obscure the fact that many circulars still exist, such as Circular 1/85, which still follow the old practice of combining practical guidance with policy. As a consequence it is often necessary to consult both PPGs and circulars in order to obtain a complete picture of national planning policy. Even recently published circulars still contain advice which appears indistinguishable from the policy advice given in PPGs. For example, Circular 1/94, Gypsy Sites and Planning, represents central government policy on planning control and the provision of gypsy sites. No attempt is made in this Circular to summarise judicial decisions or legislative provisions. Instead, it presents the views and opinions of central government. This is apparent from the tone of the statements in the Circular. To take a single example:

> Local plans and Part II of unitary development plans should wherever possible identify locations suitable for gypsy sites, whether local authority or private sites. Where this is not possible, they should set out clear realistic criteria for suitable locations , as a basis for site provision policies. They should also identify existing sites which have planning permission, whether occupied or not, and should make a quantitative assessment of the amount of accommodation required.[5]

The emphasis here and elsewhere in the Circular is on ensuring that sites are available for gipsies. Advice is offered on the appropriate way to treat applications for planning permission[6] as well as to enforce planning control if necessary.[7] The continued use of circulars as a policy vehicle may rest on the fact that PPGs concentrate on broad planning issues. It may not be thought appropriate, therefore, to employ them when more specific issues are under consideration.

4 In *Pehrsson* there was considerable discussion over the policies permitting change of use of redundant buildings and whether this policy was confined to redundant agricultural buildings. Once again the court appears to prefer its construction of that policy to that adopted by the Secretary of State. Ibid, at 274.

5 Circular 1/94, para 12.

6 Ibid, paras 20-25.

7 Ibid, paras 26-28.

MPGs are a very specialised form of national planning policy. There are currently twelve MPGs in existence covering very specific planning control issues which arise in relation to minerals working. They offer guidance on such topics as the provision of raw material for the cement industry (MPG 10 1991) and coal mining and colliery spoil disposal (MPG 3 1994). Others such as MPG 8, Planning and Compensation Act 1991: Interim Development Order Permissions (IDOS) – Statutory Provisions and Procedures, consist primarily of a commentary on a relevant piece of legislation.

The one remaining source of advice on planning policy is regional planning guidance (RPG). This is another comparatively recent creation in its present guise. Regional planning guidance takes the form of regional planning guidance notes for specific areas of England and Wales, such as the South East. Regional planning guidance is somewhat different in nature from other forms of planning policy, since it is directed at a particular region and comments on planning issues as they affect that region, though in a general fashion. The intention is to direct future development in the region, normally over a twenty-year period, and provide a policy framework for structure plan reviews. Among the issues that will be covered by such guidance are housing, transport, environment and agriculture.

> It (RPG) will normally identify the scale and distribution of provision for new housing to be made in development plans over a 15 year period, and may give an indication of provision for a further five years. It will cover priorities for the environment, transport, infrastructure, economic development, agriculture, minerals, waste treatment and disposal. Other topics covered will depend on the individual circumstances of each region and issues identified by PPGs as requiring coverage in regional guidance.[8]

RPG 9 for the South East, for example, follows this pattern by providing very specific advice on housing. It contains figures for the rate of provision of additional dwellings per year (57,000 per annum over the twenty-year period from 1991-2011) as well as information on the distribution of those new dwellings through-out London and the South East.[9] Beside this specific guidance RPG 9 also contains a number of very general statements such as the following comment on the urban environment.

8 PPG 12, Development Plans and Regional Planning Guidance, para 2.6.

9 RPG 9, Regional Planning Guidance for the South East, paras 5.7, 5.10, table 2.

> The Region contains a number of historic towns whose character needs to be protected from the effects of traffic and excessive urban development such as Brighton and Hove, Canterbury, Chichester, Colchester, Dover, Lewes, parts of London, Oxford, Rochester, St. Albans, Tunbridge Wells, Winchester and Windsor.[10]

The very general manner in which this view is expressed raises yet again the question whether advice of this character can accurately be described as planning policy, as opposed to a statement of what seems an unremarkable fact.[11]

Apart from their different functions the manner in which circulars, PPGs and MPGs are produced can be contrasted with the procedures employed in the preparation of RPGs. Circulars, PPGs and MPGs are the product of the relevant Ministry. On most development control issues this is usually the Department of the Environment in England and the Welsh Office in Wales. Normally the same circular is issued jointly by the two Ministries. Since the Department for National Heritage assumed responsibility for 'archaeology and the conservation of the built environment', it has produced the key policy statement on these issues in conjunction with the Department of the Environment.[12] The impetus for producing circulars, PPGs and MPGs varies. It can include the necessity to explain the impact that a particular piece of legislation will have on the development control process, to give guidance on an issue that is proving troublesome or to indicate a change of direction in policy. Once the decision to produce such a document has been taken, then the comments of interested individuals and organisations will be sought on its proposed contents. Should such comment be unfavourable, then the document may be modified or, on rare occasions, withdrawn. In contrast RPGs are produced after local authorities have been consulted for their views and regional conferences have been held in order to canvass the views of 'Government departments, business organisations, development interests, and bodies representing agricultural and conservation interests' as well as those of members of the public.[13] All these views are submitted to the Secretary of State who then produces draft regional

10 Ibid, para 4.12.

11 For a review of how well RPGs and other policy documents function as policy documents see Tewdwr-Jones M 'Policy Implications of the "Plan-Led" Planning System' Journal of Planning and Environment Law, 1994, p 584.

12 Circular 20/92, Responsibilities for Conservation Policy and Casework. PPG 15, Planning and the Historic Environment.

13 PPG 12, Development Plans and Regional Planning Guidance, paras 2.2, 2.3.

planning guidance, which, after a period for representations, is issued by the Department of the Environment. The purpose of this process of consultation within the region is to ensure that when the guidance is finally issued it enjoys a fair level of support.

> If regional guidance is based on advice which has the support of a wide range of authorities, it will be more effectively carried through into their plans.[14]

Department of the Environment planning policy: its legal significance

Neither circulars, PPGs, MPGs nor RPGs are binding in the sense that legislation binds those individuals affected by its provisions. On rare occasions circulars are used as a vehicle for the creation of delegated legislation. Circular 26/92, Planning Controls over Demolition, contained a direction from the Secretary of State to all local planning authorities indicating what buildings might be demolished without that activity constituting development.[15] With the exception of these rare examples, national planning policy is purely advisory in character yet this bald statement greatly misrepresents the actual legal significance of the Department of the Environment's policy statements.

There is no doubt that when a development control decision is taken, any relevant policy statement from the Department of the Environment should be taken into account. When, for example, a local planning authority is considering an application for planning permission, the 1990 Act directs that regard shall be had to the provisions of the development plan, where rele-vant, as well as to any other material considerations. Undoubtedly those material considerations can and do include any national policy guidance, such as a PPG, as well as other factors, such as the locality surrounding the development site. The fact that policy guidance must be taken into account does not mean that any advice which it contains has to be followed. It may well be that the advice is judged to be inappropriate or that it conflicts with another policy document that the local

14 Ibid, para 2.2.
15 Town and Country Planning (Demolition – Description of Buildings)(No 2) Direction 1992 has been replaced by the Town and Country Planning (Demolition – Description of Buildings) Direction 1995.

planning authority justifiably chooses to follow, such as the development plan. Alternatively, the guidance offered by a PPG or circular can be so vague that a local planning authority may be able to argue, with some justification, that it has observed any relevant advice. If a local planning authority chooses to ignore unequivocal advice from the Department of the Environment, such as the view offered in Circular 1/85 regarding the imposition of local user conditions, this is not evidence of bad faith on the part of the local planning authority provided it has taken the policy into consideration as demanded by the 1990 Act.

Yet a local planning authority which refuses planning permission in defiance of Department of the Environment planning policy or attaches an unacceptable condition runs the risk of having its decision appealed. On appeal the planning merits of the proposed development are considered afresh by a planning inspector. He too must have regard to all material considerations including the development plan and any relevant policy documents. Since the inspector is a Department of the Environment inspector there might seem to be a good chance that he would observe Department of the Environment policy when arriving at his decision. Indeed, research has confirmed that this is often the case.[16] So far as the courts are concerned they will not interfere with a decision provided they are satisfied that all material considerations have been taken into account and adequate reasons given by the decision-maker for following one line of policy as opposed to another.[17] The courts will also be keen to ascertain whether the decision-maker has interpreted the relevant policy correctly. As a consequence, the courts will take it upon themselves to construe policy documents in much the same way as they regard it as their task to interpret legislation. There are, however, a number of difficulties associated with this stance on the part of the court. Legislation is drafted in the knowledge that it may well be the subject of judicial scrutiny. In contrast, the policy produced by the Department of the Environment is meant to provide advice and guidance, and its language may reflect this fact. It is the language of conversation rather than legislation. To subject this to rigorous scrutiny is to invite problems. As was said in one judgment:

16 Tewdwr-Jones M 'The Government's Planning Policy Guidance' Journal of Planning and Environment Law, 1994, p 106 at 112.

17 *Surrey Heath Borough Council v Secretary of State for the Environment* [1987] JPL 199; *Stephenson v Secretary of State for the Environment* [1985] 1 EGLR 178, CA.

> These circulars were intended to provide local authorities with general guidance. Their paragraphs are to be read with common sense. Words are to be given their ordinary meaning and the sense and purpose of a paragraph as a whole, and indeed of a circular as a whole, is of greater importance than any individual phrase, or sentence contained in it.[18]

The courts should, therefore, intervene and set aside a decision reached by a planning inspector or the Secretary of State only if 'his interpretation was not within the ordinary and natural meaning of the words in their context'.[19] If, however, they disregard this warning and construe planning policy in a mechanistic, rather than a purposive fashion, the Department of the Environment may react by drafting its policy statements in a way that cannot be misconstrued. The result may be planning policy that is bland and uncontroversial. In addition, the more the courts intervene and 'interpret' policy, the more confusing the situation becomes for those who have to make everyday use of these documents.

The ability of the Department of the Environment policy to influence development control decisions and, in particular, the determination of applications for planning permission has been called into question with the implementation of section 54A of the 1990 Act. This section requires that:

> Where, in making any determination under the planning Acts, regard is to be had to the development plan, the determination shall be made in accordance with the plan unless material considerations indicate otherwise.

Since development control decisions now appear to be plan-led, does this mean that local planning authorities and Department of the Environment inspectors are bound to ignore central government policy guidance if it is in conflict with policies in the development plan? In answering this question it first of all needs to be appreciated that the policy guidance issued by the Department of the Environment can exert a powerful influence on the content of development plans. RPGs provide the strategic context for structure plans while PPGs, MPGs and, to a lesser extent, circulars contain specific policies on issues such as conservation and transport that could directly affect the content

18 *Mid-Bedfordshire District Council v Secretary of State for the Environment*. The decision is unreported, but a brief account of it is to be found at [1984] JPL 631.

19 *Northavon District Council v Secretary of State for the Environment and the Trustees of the Congregations of Jehovah's Witnesses* [1993] JPL 761 at 764.

of the plans. These policy sources also quite frequently offer guidance on what should be included in a development plan. PPG 15, Planning and the Historic Environment, for example, contains advice on what issues relevant to listed buildings and conservation areas should be dealt with in development plans. Conservation of the historic environment is regarded as one of the key topics to be dealt with in a structure plan. It is expected to provide the planning framework for the more detailed local plans.

> The structure plan should provide a broad planning framework, guiding the approach to be adopted in local plans to such issues as the capacity of historic towns to sustain development, the relief of pressure on historic central areas by the identification of opportunities for growth elsewhere, and the provision of transport infrastructure which respects the historic environment.[20]

The local plan is expected to translate these broad strategies into detailed policies for its area and hence provide the policy context in which day-to-day development control decisions can be taken.

> Local plans should set out clearly the planning authority's policies for the preservation and enhancement of the historic environment in their area, and the factors which will be taken into account in assessing different types of planning application – for example, proposals for the change of use of particular types of historic building or for new development which would affect their setting.[1]

Indeed, the Department of the Environment is apparently committed to monitoring development plans that are in the course of preparation in order to assess their compatibility with central government policy.

> Since the commencement of section 54A, the Secretaries of State have been examining development plans carefully to identify whether there appear to be conflicts with national or regional policy guidance. They will continue to do so and will normally draw the attention of local authorities to those conflicts which do not appear to be justified by local circumstances...if no such intervention is made, local authorities may take it that the Secretaries of State are content with the plan at the time of adoption and will attach commensurate weight to it in decisions they make on appeals or called-in applications.[2]

20 PPG 15, Planning and the Historic Environment, para 2.6.
1 Ibid, para 2.8.
2 PPG 1, General Policy and Principles, para 29.

If the Department of the Environment believes that insuff-icient regard has been had to its policy, it has a number of options open to it including making objections to the plan at public inquiry or issuing a direction to the local planning authority requiring it to include or exclude material from the plan.[3]

The content of many development plans will, therefore, be generally compatible with Department of the Environment policy. That said, examples can be found in the past of development plans that contained policies which were at odds with Departmental policy. In *Barnham v Secretary of State for the Environment*,[4] for example, the Secretary of State approved an amendment to a structure plan which apparently conflicted with Departmental policy in Circular 15/84.[5] Sometimes, of course, the inclusion of such a policy might be deliberate if local circumstances warrant an exception being made. On other occasions it may represent an oversight with hard-pressed Department of the Environment officials failing to notice potential conflicts. Indeed, such 'anomalies' might now become all the more common since neither structure nor local plans have to be directly approved by the Secretary of State.

Apart from policies in conflict with Department of the Environment policy slipping through undetected, there is another problem which has to be addressed. Central government policy is not static and is updated on a regular basis. A development plan which, when first adopted was perfectly consistent with central government policy, may cease to be if that policy changes. In these circumstances there might seem to be some justification for departing from the development plan. The Department of the Environment has made its views known on this issue in PPG 1, General Policy and Principles.[6] The implication is that although the development plan is the starting point in reaching development control decisions, if it is 'out-of-date' and that is a reference not to its age but its policies, then other material considerations may outweigh it. One way in which a plan's policies can become out-of-date which is specifically mentioned is where '...they have been superseded by more recent planning guidance issued by the Government'.[7] This

3 Read L and Wood M 'Policy, Law and Practice' in *Planning Icons: Myth and Practice*. Journal of Planning and Environment Law, 1994, p 6 at 9-10. This gives some examples of the Secretary of State intervening in the course of development plan preparations.
4 [1985] JPL 861.
5 Land for Housing, now withdrawn.
6 PPG 1, para 27.
7 Ibid.

seems to indicate that although a great deal of emphasis is now placed on the development plan and the policies that it contains, this emphasis can still be displaced by central government policy if the two are incompatible. What is less clear is whether a conflict which existed at the time the plan was adopted but escaped notice, can justify a departure from the development plan in favour of national planning policy. According to PPG 1, General Policy and Principles if the Secretary of State chooses not to intervene in the development plan process local planning authorities may assume that the Secretary of State is 'content with the plan at the time of adoption and will attach commensurate weight to it'.[8] There is comment to the effect that this may not stop the Secretary of State from reneging on his undertaking.

> This would probably not in law estop the Government from changing its mind and preferring its own policies to the plan but it would certainly be embarrassing.[9]

These views voiced by central government on how they will regard the relationship between the development plan and national planning policy are significant since they indicate how the Department of the Environment will deal with these problems when they arise. A note of caution should, however, be expressed regarding this interpretation of section 54A by the Department. It is quite common now and in the past for the Department of the Environment to offer guidance on how a particular piece of legislation should be interpreted. The courts have, however, in their turn, made it equally clear that statutory interpretation is a matter for them and not for government departments, although they have also acknowledged that such expressions of opinion by the Department of the Environment are exceedingly influential with local planning authorities and thus are likely to be followed by them.[10] As a consequence the Department of the Environment's views on section 54A will, as a matter of law, count for nothing if the court's interpretation of that section contradicts them. As has been discussed elsewhere,[11] the courts do seem inclined to accept that, although section 54A creates a presumption in favour of the development plan, it is one that can be overridden by other material consider-

8 PPG 1, General Policy and Principles, para 29.

9 Purdue M, The Impact of Section 54A, Journal of Planning and Environment Law, 1994, p 399 at 405.

10 *Coleshill and District Investment Co Ltd v Minister of Housing and Local Government* [1969] 2 All ER 525, HL; *R v Worthing Borough Council, ex p Burch* (1983) 50 P & CR 53.

11 See chapter 4 for a consideration of the legal interpretation of s 54A.

ations. Arguably these can and do include statements of national planning policy. In *Stratford-upon-Avon District Council v Secretary of State for the Environment*,[12] for example, the development plan was displaced in favour of national planning policy. Although this decision was reviewed and set aside it was not on the ground that the development plan had to be followed but because of a lack of adequate reasons for the Secretary of State's decision.

Other sources of policy

Apart from legislation, circulars and policy notes, one other Department of the Environment policy source needs to be mentioned and that is the Secretary of State for the Environment himself. The Secretary of State may use occasions, such as speeches to professional bodies, to indicate his views or policies on a particular matter. It might be assumed that such views will later be translated into legislation or circulars, and on most occasions this will be so. Yet, keynote speeches should not be neglected, since they may give an important indication of shifts in Ministerial policy. A valuable historic insight into the significance of such speeches is given by Richard Crossman in his book *The Diaries of a Cabinet Minister*. His entry for 21 September 1965 reads as follows:

> The day of my speech to the AMC annual conference at Torquay. I had to prepare the speech yesterday and go down last night because I was speaking first thing in the morning. I had previously agreed with the Department that I would speak on two topics: local government press relations; and the ethics of the councillor. However, yesterday I suddenly decided that I would add a third topic, the reform of local government; and I would announce that the situation was now getting unworkable and I was thinking of winding up the Local Government Boundary Commission. What should the next step after that be? I called in JD Jones, who was very good indeed, and with his advice I came to the conclusion that I should propose a committee of inquiry with very great authority and with terms of reference that instructed it to lay down the principles of local government reform. I rang up Harold to tip him off that I was going to do this and he liked the idea. There was a great rush to finish before I caught the train with John Delafons. We were met at the station at eleven o'clock by Francis Hill, the secretary of the AMC, and

12 [1994] JPL 741.

> taken back to the hotel for a drink. In the early morning I prepared the final draft fitting the new section in with the old sections, and I delivered it at eleven, answering questions for a full hour afterwards, and getting something like a standing ovation. I was quite sure that I had done well.

Ministerial statements may be used in order to signal policy changes, or to emphasise an aspect of Ministerial policy which is seen as particularly important. Obviously, however, the reliance which can be placed on such statements varies, according to whether or not they have been translated into legislation or a policy statement. There have, however, been occasions in the past where the courts have been invited to take account of them. In *Dimsdale Developments (South East) Ltd v Secretary of State for the Environment*[13] planning permission had been refused by the local authority for the erection of offices and residential accommodation in Brentford. On appeal, the refusal of planning permission was affirmed by the inspector, whose decision was then reviewed by the courts. In the course of the case, counsel for the developers drew the attention of the court to an after-dinner speech made by the then Secretary of State for the Environment, Patrick Jenkin. On the matter of whether such a speech was admissible, MacPherson J concluded that although he:

> wondered at first whether to receive it at all he had thought it best to take it into account, although he was bound to say that he doubted whether such manifestations should be used in argument.[14]

On analysing what the Secretary of State had to say, MacPherson J concluded that it did nothing to alter his opinion that there were no grounds on which to set aside the inspector's decision. It is a matter for speculation what the outcome would have been if the Secretary of State had announced some major shift in policy in his speech. Undoubtedly, if it was a change that required the introduction of new legislation, the court would have done nothing at that time except apply current legislation. As it was, the Secretary of State's speech registered his dislike of stale development plans, that is, ones long overdue for updating. In the case in question, the relevant development plan had been updated and, therefore, its policy to discourage office development of the type proposed, represented current policy. If this had not been so, the court might have taken the Secretary

13 [1986] JPL 276.
14 Ibid, at 277.

of State's speech into account, to the extent at least of considering whether the age of the policy made it less relevant. Quite clearly this decision now has to be seen in the light of section 54A and its emphasis on the development plan. Although the presumption in favour of the plan can be overridden it is perhaps questionable whether this can be achieved by an after-dinner speech unsupported by any other evidence of a shift in policy.

As well as after-dinner speeches, the Secretary of State will sometimes make statements in the House of Commons in order to clarify his policy. This was the case with a recent statement on his policy in relation to calling in planning applications. In it he made it clear that cases which raised significant architectural and urban design issues might be called in.[15] Undoubtedly, the significance to be attached to views expressed by the Secretary of State will vary. Factors, such as the occasion and the exact purpose of a statement, may well be relevant. Though the court may be uncertain exactly how to treat such statements, this does not mean that they can be discounted as a source of policy. Planners, inspectors and organisations concerned with the environment may well take their lead from what the Secretary of State has to say.

15 Hansard HC Debs, cols 314-315; 26 January 1995.

Chapter 7

The development site

This chapter will explore what is, in practice, one of the most important aspects of development control. This is the influence that the site, with its unique characteristics, and the surrounding area, exert on the planning application decision. Previous planning decisions involving the site also have to be taken into account, as they form part of its unique planning history. On every occasion the emphasis is on the word 'unique'. In this area of development control the local planning authority and developer are involved in a situation which necessitates the consideration of a particular set of development proposals for a specific site, in an equally specific location at a certain point in time. The problem is, therefore, of how adequately to analyse this important aspect of development control which is, in reality, comprised of a unique set of circumstances.

The site defined

It will be recalled that development can take two forms, either a material change of use, or a building, engineering, mining, or other operation.[1] In determining what constitutes 'the site', the type of development contemplated is crucial. If, for example, the proposed development involves the construction of new buildings, that is, a building operation, then the site is the equivalent of that piece of land within whose boundaries the building operation is to take place. The issue may be less clear when a change of use is contemplated. This is because, on any particular piece of land, there may be a number of separate uses. A piece of land, for example, may be being used with planning permission for the parking of lorries. Facilities may exist on the land for cleaning and repairing the lorries. Should the repair

1 Town and Country Planning Act 1990, s 55(1).

side of the business expand with motor cars being repaired in addition to lorries, then the planning officers may ask themselves whether there has been a change of use from storage, in the form of the lorry park, to vehicle repair. In such a situation what constitutes the site can be crucial, though in this context it is more usual to talk of planning units rather than sites. The explanation for this is straightforward. In the example, the terms planning unit and site are interchangeable, since allied to the main use of the land for parking lorries are the ancillary uses of cleaning and repairing them. The question facing the planning officers would be whether, having determined the extent of the planning unit, there had been a change of use within that unit, with an ancillary use becoming the prime use. In contrast, should a building on the lorry park have been rented to a manufacturer of pork pies, the terms 'planning unit' and 'site' would not be synonymous. The planning officers would then argue that there were two separate and unrelated uses on a single piece of land constituting two separate planning units. One planning unit would be the equivalent of the building used for the manufacture of pork pies and enforcement action against an unauthorised change of use might be contemplated. The other planning unit would be the lorry park on which no development had occurred.

Clearly, therefore, there is more to defining the site, or rather the planning unit, than is first apparent. The issue can be a complex one particularly when a single piece of land or a building is put to many individual uses. This explains why, in the past, the courts have found it necessary to pronounce on what constitutes the planning unit.[2] Their approach seems to be a commonsense one, reflecting the issues that would be pertinent to a planning officer when contemplating the problem. In *Burdle v Secretary of State for the Environment*,[3] three criteria were suggested to help determine the planning unit. In all instances it is the use that is the fundamental consideration. If there are distinct uses being carried out in discrete areas within a single unit of occupation for unrelated purposes, then each discrete area forms a planning unit. If there are distinct but related uses being carried on generally within the unit of occupation, then the whole unit forms the planning unit. If there is a single main use being supported by ancillary uses, then again, the whole unit is to be considered as the planning unit.

2 *East Barnet UDC v British Transport Commission* [1962] 2 QB 484.
3 [1972] 3 All ER 240.

The development plan and other material considerations

Once it is appreciated that the meaning to be attached to the term 'site' can vary with the particular situation, it remains to be seen how far those factors which have been considered in detail elsewhere, impinge on the site. Section 70(2) of the Town and Country Planning Act 1990 directs a local planning authority to have regard to the development plan, as well as other material considerations, when deciding whether or not to grant planning permission. The relationship of any site to the development plan is perhaps the more obvious, as it will be possible to locate the site, either generally or specifically, on the maps or diagrams which form part of the development plan. In many instances, therefore, the preferred land use for the area containing the site will be indicated, as well, possibly, as other factors relating to the density or height of any development.

According to section 54A of the 1990 Act the information contained within the development plan should be taken as the primary source of guidance when determining an application for planning permission. The plan is still seen as an advisory document rather than a zoning imposition, but its primacy in the decision-making process is clearly stated in section 54A. PPG 1 gives additional advice on how the development plan should affect decisions regarding planning applications.[4] This focuses on balancing the requirements of the two sections and refers to the extent to which the plan can be considered as directly material to the application. Obviously the relevance of policy within the plan, which is not simply a function of the age of the plan, is of prime importance and if this is judged to be relevant to the application then the decision will be formed in respect of these policies. However, when there are other material considerations which are also relevant, as is usually the case, then the plan should be taken as a starting point from which to consider the application.

On the matter of what will constitute material considerations, this varies in relation to the proposed form of each development. For example, the exact location and size of a proposed new entrance to the development site will always be considered a material consideration. The physical form of such an entrance, together with its width, and the sight lines that it affords for

4 PPG 1, General Policy and Principles, paras 25-28.

traffic using it, will also form material considerations, as indeed, would the amount and type of traffic that the site generates. Conversely, the costs of constructing such an entrance are unlikely to be considered material, as these will not be seen as planning issues.

Other more general factors directly related to the development and its site may also be considered as material considerations, particularly if they form part of local or even national planning policy. The question of whether the development is needed, both in relation to the needs of the area, and with regard to the appropriateness of the proposed use of the site itself, has often been accepted as a material consideration, especially in relation to proposed residential developments. These considerations concerning the need for the proposed development are not evaluated in isolation, however, as clearly they will often be related to other important issues. Consider an application for planning permission to develop a housing estate in a location that the local planning authority had decided was to be included in its green belt. The decision would be largely dependent on the developer proving that the need existed for such a development, not only in a general sense, in that more housing was needed in the area, but more particularly, in that such a development was needed on that site at that time. The local planning authority, on the other hand, would be considering the importance of maintaining its green belt policy. All of these factors are material considerations, and many will clearly be interrelated.

The planning history

Another important element that comes under the description of a material consideration is the planning history of the site. All the documented planning events from 1947 onwards that relate to either the whole or part of the site, constitute its planning history.[5] Since 1947, all activities constituting development, permitted development apart, should have been the subject of an application for planning permission or possibly a related permission, for example, listed building consent. Any

5 As the Town and Country Planning Act 1947 is seen as introducing the modern planning system, the planning history of a site is normally taken to start with this date.

such application will have been placed on record by the local planning authority and this information is available, together with any decisions reached, for examination by a member of the public.[6]

It appears possible to interpret these instances of past or existing planning permissions, or indeed refusals, in several ways. Consider, initially, the example of an existing planning permission for a one-acre site permitting the development of a four-storey block of sixteen flats, all with garages. This permission may not have been acted upon but is still current, the statutory five-year period having yet to elapse.[7] Arguably, this planning permission represents current planning policy for the site. If, therefore, a planning application is made to construct a workshop or small industrial development on the same site, the fact that planning permission has been granted for residential development is clearly not a material consideration and should be disregarded. In contrast, the fact that current planning policy favours residential, rather than industrial development on the site, is a material consideration, but reference should be made directly to the source of that policy, as well as to the planning permission that is based upon it. This necessity to refer, to both the policy as well as any previous planning applications, would be more imperative if a previous application for some form of non-residential development had been refused. Such a fact would be taken as an important material consideration, as the use relates closely to the use being proposed in the new application. In these circumstances, however, the reasons given for refusing the previous application would be most significant as they would probably contain reference, not only to the policy relating to the site, but also to the particular physical details of the development. Although the policy may still be current, it is likely that the physical details of the present application will be different, and it is this fact that should be emphasised. It is most important to remember that all planning applications must be considered on their own individual merits, and the physical features of the present proposed development may, therefore, be much more appropriate for the site than those presented in the application that was refused. It is factors such as these that will be

6 The planning register has to be maintained in the manner specified by the 1990 Act, s 69, and the Town and Country Planning (General Development Procedure) Order 1995, SI 1995/419, art 25.

7 1990 Act, s 91.

considered by the local planning authority as being particularly pertinent, while the planning history of the site should be viewed as providing a background to any current applications for planning permission.

The planning history of the site may also consist of various planning permissions that have been acted upon and, as such, these are normally considered to indicate the sequence of policy that has affected the site. Consider the example of a building that was originally a Georgian town house which has been used for several years as offices by a firm of solicitors. In the past a planning application may have been approved to extend the building to the rear to allow for an increased demand in office space. An adjacent building may then have been acquired by the firm of solicitors, and planning permission granted to join both buildings in order to increase still further the amount of office space. Each of these approvals would be considered as relevant aspects of the building's planning history if yet another extension were proposed, possibly upwards, by the addition of a new roof structure on both properties incorporating two new floors. When planning permission is sought, reference would be made to the fact that the local planning authority had, in the past, always allowed office expansion on this site. Although this would be relevant to the present application, it in no way constitutes a precedent that is binding on the local planning authority. It is, therefore, free to approve the present expansion proposals or to reject them, possibly on the grounds that the change in the roof line is unacceptable, or indeed that such an expansion could be taken as an undesirable precedent in an area where many similar applications might ensue as a result. This does not contradict the statement just made that planning permission does not constitute a precedent. As a matter of law this is true. In practice, however, it would be far more difficult for a local planning authority to justify a refusal for a similar development, as presumably whatever policy justified approval in the first example would still be applicable. It is, however, important to remember that this would apply only if the two buildings in question were virtually identical, since each application for planning permission must be considered on its own individual merits, and other details will be relevant, apart from the fact that planning permission has been granted for a similar proposal on a similar property. Many of these details will stem from the significant features of the site and the proposed development, so it is now appropriate to initiate an examination of these.

The significant features

To provide some logic to what follows these features have been divided into three. First, there are those features contained within the boundaries of the site that have an effect on the form of the development. Second, there are those features that are a direct consequence of the function of the development and the effect that they may have on the site. Finally, there are those features that derive from the general area in which the site is located. In all instances it is essential to remember that these three divisions are purely artificial and that, in reality, all these features would probably be considered as inextricably interrelated. The purpose of dividing them here is in order to simplify, by means of isolation, what amounts to a complex series of interrelationships. For example, it should be obvious that the size of a site will influence what can feasibly be developed upon it, and that the location of the site, perhaps in a residential area, or a city centre, will likewise affect the function of the proposed development. In addition, it should be clear that the different forms and functions of development will make different demands on any particular site in respect of transport or pollution or building height. The complex reality thus starts to emerge. By artificially isolating various factors, therefore, it is hoped that a better overall understanding will be achieved.

THE FORM OF THE DEVELOPMENT

Section 55 of the 1990 Act neatly encapsulates the basic form that any development must take, in that it must involve either a material change of use, an operation or both. The legal interpretation of this section has already been considered in chapter 3. At this stage, therefore, it is simply necessary to evaluate what implications this definition has for the range of developments that would normally occur on any site. A change of use is considered as significant by the local planning authority when the new use will have a markedly different effect on the site and the surrounding area from any existing use. It is important to realise that this would be a development control issue, even if the proposed use is unlikely to have a detrimental effect on the site or its locality. It is the effect of a use, rather than its possible positive or negative consequences, that is the real issue.

Another change of use which may, on occasion, be encountered, is an intensification of use. Here, an already established use experiences a change in emphasis of such proportions that planning permission is required. In this situation, both the site and its location assume particular importance as development control considerations, since the proposed intensification could impose pressures with which the site and the area are physically incapable of coping. A site may be used for the manufacture of concrete blocks, the production of which may have been limited by the size of the original business. If the business changes hands and is consequently greatly improved, the number of concrete blocks manufactured on the site could be quadrupled. Such an intensification of the original use would then be evaluated by the local planning authority. It would be judged in relation to the physical size of the site and its capacity for containing the production machinery, taking into account the ground contours of the site rather than its simple plan area. Also of importance would be the changed appearance of the site with the new machinery on it, as well as the frequency with which the concrete blocks were moved on and off the site. This latter factor would obviously have an immediate effect on both the traffic flows and the amenity of the surrounding area.

Use changes or intensifications are often, in reality, accompanied by some kind of building operation[8] most commonly in the form of a new building, an extension to an existing building, an extensive refurbishment of an existing building, or the construction of site infrastructure, such as roads, hard standing or walls. In every instance, the site and its location are once again of paramount importance in reaching the appropriate development control decision. In the case of new buildings, their position in relation to the size and shape of the site will be considered, taking into account not only the probable visual impact of the proposed structures given their size or density, but also their design and the materials to be used in their construction. Similar considerations would apply in the case of any proposed extensions or refurbishments, while accompanying features, such as roads and walls, would also be treated with the same degree of scrutiny.

Clearly the attention that will be paid to the physical details of any proposed development cannot be divorced from the use that is either being newly created, or intensified, as the two issues can often be realistically considered only as a single complex aspect of the proposed development. It should be

8 Or any other form of operation involving development, such as an engineering operation.

remembered that the policy for the site, or its more general location, will also form part of this complex equation. A proposal to erect new industrial units will be considered, first, in terms of the industrial policy of the local planning authority, then the policy that relates to the proposed development site, then the suitability of the site in respect of its size and shape, the existing or proposed connections to the surrounding road network, the location of other such units in the vicinity, the uses being made of the surrounding area, as well as the size of the proposed buildings, the materials to be used, the fencing of the area and the parking or unloading space.

THE FUNCTION OF THE DEVELOPMENT

From the examples used in the preceding section, it should be obvious that the actual use or function of the proposed development is particularly important in assessing the likely effects it could produce, both with regard to the site and the locality. Even to the layman the concept of a development that is incompatible with its surroundings is easy to comprehend, but the assessment of the impact of a proposed use is far more subtle than the obvious incompatibility of a tannery in the middle of a residential area. The range of possible uses or functions likely to be encountered in a lifetime considering planning applications in various environments is enormous, but the majority can be classified under surprisingly few heads, thus permitting the possible implications of each function for a site to be considered.

Retail The impact of this common land use function on the site clearly varies depending upon its scale and intensity but, as with all of the succeeding functions, the central issue is the suitability of the site for the proposed development. In the case of retailing this involves an assessment of the accessibility of the site, the need for which usually increases with the scale of the proposed development. The site would be viewed, not only from the point of view of the placing of the building within it, but also with regard to its ability to cater for accessibility-related demands, such as car parking. Clearly, these issues are further complicated when the enormous range of goods that might be offered for sale is considered, as the nature of the goods on sale is relevant to the number of people using a particular retail outlet. Retailing in all its many aspects has become a study in its own right and no attempt will be made here to cover even a fraction of the elements involved. Instead, a few examples will be considered to illustrate some of the important development control issues related to the site.

A national chain of jewellery shops wishes to open a shop in a city centre location, on a site that is in need of redevelopment. Given the site's central location, and therefore its high market value, the developer will probably wish to build on the entire site. The local planning authority would probably insist on this, particularly if existing buildings abut onto the site. This raises the question of the appearance of the new building, especially its ground floor window designs and any advertising incorporated into the proposed design of the shop front. The local planning authority is also likely to express concern over the appearance of the upper floors, if, for security reasons, small windows or even windowless walls are suggested by the developer. These design issues apart, however, what implications does the proposed retail use have for the site? Jewellery is what is known as a 'high order' good in retail jargon.[9] This means that the demand is infrequent, or put another way, only one person in one thousand is likely to be needing the services of such a shop at any particular time. As a direct consequence, the number of potential customers that the jewellery shop needs for it to run at a profit is comparatively large, so a city-centre location with a large customer flow is ideal. These facts, although known to the planning officers, are, in one sense, incidental, as they do not give rise to important development control issues. This follows from the fact that, since the goods on sale are small and of a relatively high value, there is unlikely to be a demand from the developer for customer car parking, nor indeed for special delivery arrangements to be made on the site. The planning officers' concerns in this instance are, therefore, limited, as the function produces no undue 'stress' on the physical nature of the site and its location.

At the opposite end of the retail spectrum, at least in a planning context, would be the out-of-town or suburban fringe retail location selling furniture or carpets. Here, the planning issues affecting the site are very different, caused, not so much by the 'middle order' goods,[10] but rather by the form of retailing that has been selected. In this instance the demands which the

9 Goods are ranked according to their cost and the frequency of demand for them. Those which are expensive and for which demand is infrequent, such as jewellery, are called high order goods.

10 Furniture and other similar goods, although expensive, are more of a necessity than the luxury high order goods and are thus ranked as middle order goods.

retail development will place on the site include extensive car parking facilities, good access to the surrounding major road network, as well as a large amount of retail or possibly storage space. The incorporation of these features of the proposed development onto the site will naturally concern the planning officers. Clearly, the impact that such a development would have on any site would be considerable, while the impact on the surrounding area is not confined to the traffic and aesthetic implications, but would also include the competition that such a retail development could exert on similar retail establishments in the more traditional town-centre locations. This last issue serves to illustrate the interface between planning policy and the detailed development of the site. The question of competition with other retail outlets, and indeed the location of such outlets, is effectively a policy issue that has to be judged in the context of both national planning policy on out-of-town retailing establishments, and the current local planning policy on retailing. These issues are, in turn, related to the nature of the development, particularly its size, whilst the immediate site issues are those concerned with its appearance and times of use. It will be a matter for the expertise and judgment of the planning officers considering the application as to which combination of these issues they will see as of paramount importance in making their recommendation to the planning committee.

Offices The main site-related issue regarding this function is one of scale. The impact an office development has on an area is normally restricted to its design and the number of employees it contains. The latter are significant for the impact they may have on the transport system in the area containing the office. As is common in many development control situations, these factors may be interrelated. Design may be affected by transport demands if these involve providing car parking on the site. Scale is, of course, the controlling factor, as the larger the office development, the more significant these issues are likely to be. Clearly, the use of a Georgian town house as a solicitors' office has very different development control implications as compared with the development of a two-acre inner-city site with 700,000 square feet of net lettable office space. The former would clearly have few design implications, unless the building was significant enough to be listed. Consequently, the main issue relating to the site would be the availability of parking for possibly a dozen cars, either to the rear of the site, or in the immediate vicinity. The nature of the surrounding uses, particularly if they were retail, would also be a relevant issue.

In the second development, the issues of design and transport are clearly of considerable importance. The design would be dictated by the shape and location of the site in the context of the surrounding buildings, with particular regard being paid to their height, materials and other design features. The transport issue must be resolved in the light of the local planning authority's transport policy. Such a policy would, in turn, depend upon the nature of the urban area containing the office development. If the area is not suffering from a high level of traffic congestion or, alternatively, if the public transport facilities are inadequate within the vicinity, a high level of parking provision on the site may be required by the local planning authority. This would obviously have implications for the design of the development as well as having an effect on the generation of traffic in the immediate area. If, on the other hand, the public transport facilities are good, or traffic congestion is a serious problem in the area, then the local planning authority would allow very few parking spaces within the development, with a consequent lessening of their impact on the design of the development.

Other policies, apart from transport policies, are also likely to affect the proposed office development, and these too could have significant implications for the site and the design of the development. There may well be height restrictions regulating the number of floors that the development can contain,[11] or plot ratio requirements that control the bulk of the building.[12] Policy issues such as these are, however, usually related to specific parts of a town or city and are considered in a later section.

Residential Once more the major site-related issue is scale. Here, planning applications will range from proposals to extend a single residential property, or to develop one unit on a site, to the reshaping of an undeveloped area with the construction of

11 Height standards may form part of local planning policy and are normally applied to certain forms of development in specific areas. They may suggest the maximum number of floors appropriate in certain areas, but this number is not in any way prescriptive and higher buildings may be allowed if there is seen to be sufficient justification.

12 A plot ratio is a form of density control usually applied to commercial developments in city centres. It is an aspect of local planning policy that attempts to control the bulk of a building by expressing the permitted floor space as a ratio of site area. For example, a plot ratio of 2:1 allows a two-storey building to be developed covering the whole site, or a four-storey building covering half the site, and so on. Plot ratios vary between cities and even within cities.

hundreds of units in a range of sizes. In general terms the site issues remain constant regardless of scale, focusing on access and appearance as well as the existing facilities within the area. With a small domestic extension, the question of appearance and the distance of the extension from the boundaries of the site are likely to be more important than the question of access. This is not so when a single new building is erected on a small, previously undeveloped site. Here, the matter of access is likely to be crucial, especially if there is no existing access or access has to be shared with another dwelling.

When a new access has to be constructed, the surrounding road network must be studied in deciding where that access should be, and an estimate made of the number of cars likely to use that access. The larger the development, the more vital these issues become, while other factors, including the impact of the proposed development on existing facilities, such as schools and shops, begin to feature. With all new developments, regardless of scale, the physical nature of the site and its existing boundaries must be examined in detail, since they play a large part in determining the visual impact the proposed development will make. With a small-scale development, planning permission is more likely to be given if building takes place behind existing walls and hedges, assuming them to be in a fair condition, than on an exposed site. Similarly, with a large-scale residential development, the contours of the site should be used to their best advantage, not only to provide views for the inhabitants but also to 'hide' to a certain degree the new development from the surrounding area, especially if that area is in a green belt.

Industrial Here, questions of scale and the nature of the industrial use will be vital in assessing the suitability of the site for the proposed development. As has already been mentioned in previous chapters, there are regulatory provisions governing certain types of industrial use,[13] and these too must be taken into account in assessing the site. The amount and type of traffic generated by an industrial development is also crucial. For example, an industrial use that produces heavy goods traffic, even on an occasional basis, can be distinguished from the industrial use that relies upon small goods vehicles. The environmental impact of each type of transport on the area surrounding the site is likely to be very different. Indeed, this

13 The various industrial groups are defined in the Town and Country Planning (Use Classes) Order 1987, SI 1987/764, Pt B.

example can be taken a stage further to emphasise the uniqueness of each site. On a site in a flat area the level of noise produced by heavy goods traffic is likely to be less than in a hilly area, where the constant use of low gears would produce considerable engine noise. On the other hand, it may be argued that in a flat area heavy goods traffic might be tempted to travel at greater speeds and thus increase the problem of road safety.

While the importance of these issues increases in proportion to the scale of the proposed operation, it should not be imagined that only large-scale industrial development produces planning problems. Indeed, given that large-scale industrial development is often located within existing industrial areas, or alternatively, within new purpose-built industrial parks, the planning issues are normally reduced. In the case of small-scale industrial development in inner-city or residential areas, the problems are often much greater, a major one being intensification. In these circumstances, an industrial use develops on an existing site in such a way that its presence becomes more and more intrusive. This is as a result of increased traffic, more noise, longer hours of work, or even the building of a new extension. These factors, depending on the location and size of the site, may obviously become a planning issue if the various forms of intensification begin to have a noticeable environmental effect. On the other hand, this growth of the industrial concern has then to be set against the fact that it is providing more employment in the surrounding area. Department of the Environment policy emphasises the importance of encouraging the growth of small industrial enterprises.[14] Against this local planning authorities will have to assess the environmental damage that may be caused by the intensification of the enterprise in that particular location.

Design issues may also be important when considering industrial development, especially if the scale of that development is such that it can be seen over considerable distances. The physical nature of the site is all-important. If it is on low ground, the development may be screened by suitable landscaping and trees. Should the site be such that landscaping will not offer an effective screen, the appearance of the industrial buildings will be an important consideration, especially if the site is located in a mixed or non-industrial area. The visual impact of related activities, for example, the storage of raw materials and the equipment used to handle them, will also be taken into account, though the chances are that such

14 See PPG 4, Industrial and Commercial Development and Small Firms.

large-scale industrial developments are likely to be within established industrial areas where the impact of these elements is considered to be less significant.

Storage This function raises those issues discussed in relation to industrial uses. Normally the main difference stems from the fact that processing does not take place on the site so eliminating problems with noise or fumes, although this very much depends upon what is being stored. There is considerable variety within this category, as storage includes the warehousing on an inner-city site of goods intended for retail sale in the commercial core of the city, the storage of cars for export on a dockland site, as well as the storage of oil and grain in purpose-built structures or immense stockpiles of minerals covering acres. Clearly, the impact of each form of storage on the site and surrounding area will vary enormously, especially on the matter of its visual impact and the form and frequency of transport which it generates.

The visual impact of an oil storage depot, or a pile of one million tons of coal is too obvious to mention, but what may be less obvious is the difference in the frequency of use which can occur between such sites. An oil storage depot, although visually intrusive and practically impossible to hide, may at least have the advantage of generating very little traffic, as what is stored may be pumped in and out by underground pipeline. Alternatively, the site could be used as a supply depot for oil tankers, which would then distribute petrol to garages in the area, thus creating very different planning problems from those in the first instance. The same is true of the coal dump. It could be that all movement in and out may be by rail, but, on the other hand, heavy lorries might be used to transport the coal which would raise a major planning issue.

Transport This category includes all aspects of transport from private taxi-cab bases, bus, coach and train stations, to airports and seaports. The site-related issues are clearly dominated by the level and type of traffic generated, which, in turn, is dictated by the scale of the operation. Design issues, although related to the scale of the transport operation, can depend on the location of the operation, and become more significant in environmentally sensitive areas.

As with some of the functions already discussed, planning problems related to the site do not necessarily increase in proportion to increases in scale. The use of a site in a residential area as a private taxi-cab base may cause many local planning problems regarding on-street parking, late night use and traffic noise. In contrast, the use of an inner-city site as a bus station may be far less contentious in the matter of its impact on its immediate locality.

Undeniably, the main issue in every instance is the level of traffic generated, and the effect this has on the surrounding area, rather than the site itself. This is due to the fact that the site will usually be physically suitable for the particular transport use. In the case of road transport, this means the site should be flat, large and with the necessary connections to the road network. The traffic generated by the use of the site is fundamentally important, bearing in mind that a single use may generate a wide range of different types of traffic. For example, the traffic at a bus station does not consist simply of buses, but includes private cars and taxi-cabs, not to mention pedestrians. The environmental impact will naturally vary; an airport is likely to be more environmentally damaging than a railway station, but this should be reflected in its location. In other words, an international airport will have been planned and its location considered to a far greater extent than the building of a new suburban bus station. The whole question of the traffic generated by these different transport functions is an issue so complex that normally it is dealt with by specialist transport planners and traffic engineers,[15] and their findings can often be the determining factor in whether or not such developments should be permitted.

Leisure Once again the range of possible leisure pursuits is so wide and their effect so diverse that it is almost impossible to generalise. The obvious initial categorisation is into outdoor and indoor leisure pursuits. As outdoor leisure pursuits associated with urban areas normally demand sites that are large and grassed, such uses may often by regarded by the local planning authority as contributing positive environmental benefits to the surrounding area. If this is so, any development control issues will tend to focus on the level and frequency of use. Obviously not all outdoor leisure facilities result in large grassed areas, but those which do not are in the minority, and arguably even hard surfaced tennis courts may exert a positive environmental influence by virtue of the open space they provide in what otherwise may be a densely built up area.

15 In most local authorities there is a specialist transport department that handles all issues concerned with transport.

As mentioned, the main site-related development control issues focus on the level and frequency with which the site is used, as well as its physical size. For example, a golf course may cover many acres of pleasantly landscaped country but the planning issues go far beyond this positive environmental benefit. The very size of the site may be an issue as it may be taking up land that could be used more appropriately. This alternative use question is somewhat more complex than simply considering an alternative use for the land, since market forces normally ensure that the most economic use is the one favoured. Rather, the issues concern the overall supply of land within the planning district, and the impact that the loss of a large site for a golf course would have on the remaining undeveloped sites within the area. Such wider issues clearly require reference to be made to the local policy of the development plan, or even Department of the Environment policy, and again such policy will obviously be taken into account in arriving at the eventual development control decision.

Using the example of the golf course, it should be obvious that the intensity and frequency of its use will vary considerably daily, weekly and even seasonally. The focus of that use is likely to be the clubhouse and its related facilities, so the fact that the site covers many acres is not reflected in the manner in which it attracts traffic to a single spot. The traffic issues are similar to those that arise when any form of suburban development is contemplated, with much importance attached to the location of the golf course in relation to the road network.

With indoor leisure pursuits the issues are slightly different, but tend to focus mainly on traffic and the location of the site. The design of the facility may also be relevant, as sports centres can demand a relatively large building with few external features and many blank windowless walls. Obviously in this respect the location of such a facility and its site is crucial, as design problems may be overcome simply by appropriate landscaping, if this is possible. The same factors are important when assessing traffic generation and on-site parking. In a city-centre location the relationship with public transport facilities is crucial if on-site parking is limited. In the suburbs, attention may be paid to the amount of traffic likely to be generated if the site is located in a residential area.

The heading 'leisure' encompasses not only sporting facilities, but also a wide range of other activities, such as amusement arcades, cinemas, restaurants and public houses. It is clearly very difficult, and arguably of little benefit, to consider the possible implications that each of these proposed uses would have for the site, nor can any general comments be made. All that can be done is to draw attention, once again, to the all-important issue of the likely effects that the proposed use will have, and the ways in which these effects may be moderated or intensified by the site and its location.

Institutional The range of functions under this heading is extremely diverse. It includes educational facilities from nursery school to higher education institutions, health facilities from the local general practice surgery to regional hospitals, as well as the facilities for central and local government, statutory undertakers and the armed forces. In many instances it is a public body or quasi-public body[16] undertaking the development, but this does not automatically guarantee that the implications which the development has for its site and the surrounding area will be handled sympathetically. Indeed, in the case of some institutional developments, such as hospitals, no planning permission is required as the land in question forms part of the Crown estate. Should this be the case, it is likely that the advice of the local planning authority will be sought and largely heeded, so control over institutional developments will, in reality, be much the same as with any other development. Of the site issues, the most important are scale, design and traffic generation. In the majority of instances there are likely to be clear policy statements from a variety of sources on the development of the various uses.[17] These need not necessarily be policies produced by the local planning authority. In relation to schools, for example, there should be a clear policy on education produced by the local education authority.[18] Such a policy obviously has development control implications, in terms of the number of schools needed and their locations, and will thus form part of the development control debate.

Agricultural Agricultural uses can cover anything from horticulture and horse breeding to forestry. When a proposed agricultural development is being considered, the situation is complicated by the fact that policy generated from sources other

16 A British university, for example, may be considered as a quasi-public body in this context, as it will be financed largely by central government but not otherwise directly controlled by central government.

17 For example, regional health authorities will have a clear policy on the development of health centres; the National Rivers Authority will have policies on water storage.

18 Legislation demands that local education authorities produce a wide range of education policies.

than the local planning authority and the Department of the Environment, notably the Ministry of Agriculture, Fisheries and Food, has to be taken into account. Added to this is the image that the majority of people have of the countryside and its use, which is often far removed from the realities of the situation. The basic problem is summed up in the dichotomy between the countryside seen as part of our landscape heritage which should be protected at all costs, and the countryside seen as a vital food-producing industry that should be as efficient as possible. Indeed, early in 1987, these issues came to the fore when Ministerial statements suggested that due to the success of the agricultural policy of the European Community, food production should be cut back and surplus farm land be put to other uses, such as housing and industry.[19] This statement was badly received by groups such as the Council for the Protection of Rural England, who saw it as heralding a development free-for-all that would effectively destroy our rural heritage. The issue is still current and has been most recently considered in PPG 7, The Countryside and the Rural Economy.

With this dichotomy in mind, the main issue that is likely to arise in relation to an agricultural planning application can be summarised as follows – how does the planning officer ensure that the correct balance is maintained between the efficient use of rural resources and the conservation of the rural environment? The problem is exacerbated by the fact that a considerable amount of development that is directly related to agriculture is permitted development, over which the planning officer has no control.[20] Where controls do exist, therefore, over development not associated with agricultural production and especially change of use, such as the building of a farmhouse extension for the purpose of taking in bed and breakfast guests, the planning officer may be tempted to be over-cautious to compensate for the lack of control over agricultural developments. The correct path is a narrow one, but if the normal development control considerations that would apply to the development of any site are analysed, the most appropriate decision can usually be reached.

In arriving at an appropriate decision, the site and its location become crucial. Consider, for example, a planning application by a farmer to establish a permanent camp site in one of his fields. As was mentioned in chapter 5, if caravans are to use

19 Circular 16/87, Development Involving Agricultural Land.
20 Town and Country Planning (General Permitted Development) Order 1995, SI 1995/418, Pt 6.

the site, then a whole host of regulations have to be observed, but this is incidental to the real development control issues related to the site and its location. The visual impact of the proposed development has to be assessed, and not only when the site is full, as the presence of even one or two bright orange tents may be considered unacceptable in certain sensitive locations. That visual impact must be examined from different viewpoints. It may be appropriate that the site is visible from the main road, as this will ensure that camping traffic will head immediately for the correct location. On the other hand, it may be inappropriate that the site can be clearly seen from a viewing point at the other end of the valley. On this issue, therefore, the physical features of the site and its immediate surroundings are crucial, as they may dictate whether or not the camp site can be effectively screened.

Using the same example, the likely frequency and intensity of use must also be assessed, not so much for their impact on the actual area of the site, but rather for their effect on the surrounding environment and the transport system. As the use is likely to be seasonal, the maximum capacity of the roads should be calculated, as well as the traffic implications of any new means of access that may, in the summer months, lead onto what is then a busy road. In addition, the need for the camp site has to be carefully assessed, taking into account any existing sites and the impact any additional site is likely to have on local services.

Mixed and other uses In respect of these, little, if anything, can be added to what has already been said. Obviously, when dealing with a mixed use the implications for the site of each aspect of each use should be considered, the fundamental question being whether the site is capable of sustaining not only the individual uses, but, more particularly, the proposed mix. The basic issue is the likely effect that such uses would have on the site and its location, an issue that can be decided in relation to a particular site in a particular location with a specific set of proposed uses.

THE LOCATION OF THE DEVELOPMENT

The significance that the location of the site can have for the development control issues raised by the use or function, has been constantly referred to in the previous section. This is as a result of the fact that the issues related to the development of any site, regardless of function, have also to be considered in the context of that part of the urban area in which the site is located.[1] Consequently, it is perhaps useful to consider the implications that the location of the site produces under some general location headings, starting with the commercial core of the inner city and moving outwards into the rural hinterland.

The commercial core or central business district This area is readily defined within any major urban area as consisting of the shop and office quarters, although in many smaller urban centres the shopping function may be dominant.[2] Whatever the size of the town or city, however, this area has certain characteristics, and an understanding of these is crucial for the way in which they may affect the use of any development site. First, the commercial core is always relatively small in relation to the area of the whole town or city, so that vacant sites are likely to be small[3] and all forms of development opportunity scarce. Consequently, when development opportunities occur, the pressures for an intensive use of the site are likely to be great. Second, the area is always the focus, or possibly, as a result of pedestrianisation, the near focus, of the road transport network.[4] The uses of the area are, therefore, geared to gain the maximum benefit from this concentration of people. Any development site in the commercial core thus has the potential to exploit this central position, either by providing on-site parking provision, or by fully developing any frontage onto a pedestrianised precinct. Third, the area is likely to contain one of the highest concentrations of historic buildings within the town or city[5] which may impose certain conservation and design restraints on any new development.

The combined effect of these factors will make itself felt on the development proposals for any site within the commercial core, particularly on its design, as the proposed uses are

1 It has long been observed that all urban areas larger than a village tend to sub-divide into areas of distinct uses.

2 In smaller urban areas the development of the commercial core may not be so advanced that the office functions have separated themselves from the shopping functions. Consequently, many of the office functions tend to locate on the upper floors, leaving the ground floors to be dominated by retail uses.

3 Vacant sites are usually formed by the demolition of a single building, which, if it dates back to the nineteenth century, is unlikely to cover a large area, besides having a restricted frontage.

4 Urban areas almost always developed around a convergence of routes and this feature will have intensified as the urban areas grew.

5 The centre of any urban area is normally the oldest part as most urban areas tend to 'grow' outwards, with the new buildings always being furthest away from the centre.

invariably restricted to shops and offices. On the matter of design, the planning officer will often move from the general issues of plot ratio and building height, to particular issues of detail and materials. Particular attention will be paid to the specific location and size of the plot, as well as to the design of the surrounding buildings, unless the site is so large as to be considered independent of its surroundings.[6] In most instances, however, the proposed design will fall into one of three categories: the pastiche, possibly the most acceptable publicly; the well-designed modern, which will always have its supporters and detractors; and the 'non-designed' modern, which appears to have occupied little, if any, of an architect's time and yet is frequently to be seen in the centre of many towns and cities. Department of the Environment policy suggests that the planner should not attempt to exercise undue control over the aesthetic aspects of a development.[7] In the case of city-centre development, however, it is almost impossible for the local planning authority to follow that advice on all occasions. This is due to the fact that any new developments in this location will invariably be seen by the majority of the people using the city centre and so will, in effect, act as a form of advertisement for the development control efforts of the local planning authority. The more prominent and public the site, therefore, and the larger the development, the more crucial the decision becomes.

The inner-city fringe or transition zone This location may have all the problems associated with the commercial core plus some characteristic ones of its own, because within the urban area it contains the greatest mix of functions.[8] In smaller towns, this area may be indistinguishable from the commercial core, but, in larger urban areas, it assumes a particular importance, since it can be the focus of major planning problems. As the zone surrounds, or partially surrounds, the commercial core, it obviously covers a much greater area. The transition zone, therefore, has the theoretical advantage of containing extensive

6 A large site, such as an area surrounded by roads on all sides, is isolated, to a certain extent, from the nearby buildings.

7 PPG 1, General Policy and Principles, annex A.

8 The transition zone, as its name suggests, is that part of the urban area that is continually changing as the uses of the commercial core expand into it, or conversely, move out of it. Consequently, it contains a very large mixture of uses, to which may be added some residential uses, as a result not only of immediate post-war redevelopment by local authorities, but also as remnants of nineteenth century residential areas.

potential development sites. The road network is often almost as dense as that in the commercial core, but the greater mix of functions in the transition zone generates a much wider range of traffic, including heavy industrial traffic. The area can contain a high proportion of historic buildings, though the likelihood is that any conservation issues will be aggravated by the fact that many of these buildings may be in a poor condition. Empty sites in this part of the city may remain undeveloped for long periods of time, and the threat of obsolescence and dereliction is a constant worry for the local planning authority.

The net effect of these factors on the development of any particular site can be many and varied. Depending on the location of the site in relation to the main traffic routes through the area, the generation of additional traffic may pose problems, usually concerning access and congestion. As compared with the commercial core, however, design, in terms of compatibility with fine buildings, is less crucial. If, however, the site is to be developed for residential use, as may occur within the transition zone, design factors can be important if the development is to be successfully shielded from the usually incompatible mix of uses that may surround the site. The main planning issue affecting any site in this part of the urban area is the question of the market demand for a particular form of development in a specific location. Due to the variable nature of the area, which creates zones of potential growth and decline,[9] market demand is likely to reflect these variations by being either inconsistent, weak or strong, depending on the exact location of the development site. This process of flux will consequently tend to favour certain locations and ignore others, mainly as a reflection of development opportunities that are being experienced within the commercial core. In a favoured location, therefore, demand for development is likely to be strong, and a proposed development should be judged on the same criteria as those used within the commercial core. On the other hand, in a location which is more remote from such changes, the major issue concerning any planning application is likely to be the potential dereliction or obsolescence of the site should the application fail. In such circumstances, it is quite likely that some of the normal site constraints may be given less emphasis, in the hope that the proposed development will be successful and contribute to revitalising the area.

9 See Preston R E and Griffin D W 'A Restatement of the Transition Zone Concept' Annals of the Association of American Geographers, 1966, 66, p 339.

The residential suburbs These cover the largest area in any urban complex but are unlikely to contain the widest range of sites, either in terms of size or use. Sites are usually limited in size except, possibly, in inner-city residential areas where large-scale redevelopment may be undertaken by a public or quasi-public body. Although the great majority of development is likely to be residential in character, other functions are to be found, including schools, shops, libraries and other service functions. The main planning objective is to maintain the residential nature of the area, and this will be considered paramount when non-residential uses or different residential uses, such as sheltered accommodation, are being considered.[10] Site issues are normally related to access and design, both of which tend to increase in importance with the scale of the development. Access can be crucial, and may affect the development of a site large enough to accommodate only a single dwelling almost as much as a site that can hold fifty. Attention must be paid to the road network surrounding the site, as well as to the levels of traffic flow and the times that peaks occur. The positioning of an access point from the site onto the road is crucial, and its inadequacy can be sufficient reason for refusing planning permission.

In many residential areas design seems a secondary issue, presumably on the basis that the public have a very traditional image of a house and providing this is observed, then a proposed development is likely to be acceptable. Obviously in the case of large-scale developments, especially those involving the construction of multi-storey flats,[11] the design and the location of the site become far more significant. The question of how well visually the scheme fits within the immediate environment will be important, as will the retention of existing features, especially mature trees. If the site is located within one of the many conservation areas that are often to be found within the older suburbs, the design compatibility of the proposed development with existing buildings will be assessed, but even in these circumstances the access issue is, more often than not, the one that determines whether the application will be approved.

10 Town and Country Planning (Use Classes) Order 1987, SI 1987/764, gives some indication of the limitations regarding non-residential uses in residential areas. See Class B1, Business.

11 Multi-storey flats tend to be typified by the residential tower blocks built during the 1960s and early 1970s, ranging from six to thirty storeys in height.

The urban rural fringe This is the area which is second only to the commercial core in the development pressures it experiences. Sites in this location may vary considerably in size, but they tend to be large, often comprising several hundred acres of previously farmed land. The functions to be found in this area may be varied, with a proportion of industry and some farming or horticulture, but the major pressure for development is almost exclusively residential. In this location, therefore, the central issue is the need for additional housing rather than any specific site factors, apart, that is, from the capacity of the chosen site to hold a specific density of housing. If the need for such housing is proved, therefore, and its provision is in accordance with both local and national planning policy,[12] the proposed development will then be considered in the light of other important factors, such as access and scale. Design in this location may also be significant if the development is large, and attempts may be made to ensure that the visual amenity of the area is protected by landscaping.

If the proposed use for a site in this area is an industrial use, other criteria related to the site apply. Access and the traffic generated remain important factors, with design a significant feature. As with a large-scale residential development, increasing emphasis may be placed on the landscaping of the site as the scale of the development increases.

Rural locations To date these have been the most carefully protected areas, with local planning authorities generally unwilling to consider development that does not consist of the in-filling of certain sites in specifically designated villages.[13] As has been mentioned, this attitude may be in the process of changing,[14] but the site-related issues are likely to remain constant. The questions of scale and access are of prime importance and are obviously related to the use, while the likely pressures that the development might exert on local resources will also be a significant consideration. The emphasis placed on design will vary depending on the location of the site. In certain areas, such as the National Parks,[15] design will be considered fundamental, while in other areas it will be given much less weight.

12 PPG 3, Housing.

13 Normal policy, especially in green belts (see PPG 2, Green Belts) is for the local planning authority to designate in some way certain villages in which growth will be allowed in preference to other village sites.

14 PPG 7, The Countryside and the Rural Economy.

15 PPG 1, annex A, para A4.

Some common issues

What follows is a summary of those common issues that affect the development of various types of site, many of which have already been referred to in the previous discussion. These issues may be broadly categorised into those that create a visual impact and those that create a local impact. In this context local impact refers to those issues that have an effect on the local environment as a result of factors not related to the appearance of the development.

VISUAL ISSUES

Foremost amongst visual issues must be questions related to the scale, size and site coverage of the proposed development. Clearly site size will be the fundamental factor, but the problem of an appropriate development scale is not simply a function of site area. Arguably scale, in the sense of the bulk and height of the proposed development, should also be related to any existing developments in the immediate vicinity, regardless of the maximum capacity of the site. Scale is very much an issue when an existing building is extended, and should be considered regardless of whether the existing building has any intrinsic architectural merit, as an inappropriate extension is unlikely to improve matters. Site coverage, or the amount of the ground area of the site that is to be built upon, is also important, as too few buildings as well as too many can produce an inappropriate development, regardless of the intrinsic quality of design. Clearly, in the commercial areas of town centres, total site coverage will usually be the norm, while the scale of the development in terms of its bulk will have to be carefully considered in relation to the surrounding townscape.[16] Buildings which provide a contrast with, as opposed to matching, existing buildings, can sometimes prove more acceptable, and a local planning authority may require a tall building in order to contrast with the surrounding townscape.

The size of a proposed building, together with related issues, is obviously an important aspect of the overall design, and it is in this area that local planning authorities are forced, willingly or unwillingly, into considering architectural aesthetics. In the

16 Townscape is the term often applied to urban landscape. See Johns E *British Townscapes* (1969).

annex to PPG 1,[17] the Department of the Environment draws attention to the fact that design issues are fundamental to the planning application process and that good design should be the aim of all those involved. The suggestion is made, therefore, that control over design should be exercised only when there is a justifiable reason for so doing and that authorities should not impose their aesthetic taste on applicants. Apart, however, from acknowledging that some areas, National Parks, for example, are likely to need sensitive treatment in this respect, no guidance is offered on what constitutes a justifiable reason for attempting to control the design of a development. The design of the development and the environment of the site upon which it is to be built should be indivisible, but, in reality, this is not always the case as standard designs, especially for residential developments, are continually being used on a wide range of sites.

As should now be obvious, the location of the site is crucial, in that the design criteria and scope for the development of a city centre site are very different from those employed in the development of a residential site in the suburbs, or an industrial site on the urban fringe. The main difference is that the site in the town centre is likely to be small, probably confined between other buildings, and demands to be fully developed in order that the developer stands a chance of recouping costs, all of which allow little, if any, scope to arrange any development on the site in such a way that its effect can be enhanced with landscaping. The whole design impact relies on the building in terms of its bulk, the materials employed and the detail of its features. The range of possible materials and details, such as fenestration, is so enormous that little would be served by singling out any particular aspect. Perhaps all that can be said is that people seem to know what they like, but clearly everyone does not like the same thing in the same place. The planning officer's personal taste may be moderated by the way in which the planning committee chooses to act on his advice, but what remains certain is that it is more often than not the design of a building that most excites the general public, particularly those buildings that they see every day and associate with a particular part of the townscape. There appears little point, therefore, to the warnings in the annex to PPG 1, as planning officers seem doomed to satisfy neither the Department of the Environment nor the general public.

On non-central sites, the scope for design control may be enhanced simply because of the size of the site and the

17 PPG 1, General Policy and Principles.

possibility this offers for suitable landscaping. The insistence of a local planning authority on the landscaping of a proposed development is less controversial than a direct attack on the design, and indeed landscaping requirements are often imposed quite routinely as a planning condition. In this way the nondescript designs of a considerable amount of both residential, industrial and out-of-town retail developments may be hidden from the sensitive eye, providing that the site is capable of being suitably landscaped.

The significance of the visual impact of any development on its site cannot be over-emphasised. It is likely to be the one issue that is considered potentially contentious by the general public, more so even than an inappropriate use, as the use may be only intermittently obvious, while the building remains visible all the time. The details of the design of a building, despite the advice given in PPG 1, are likely to be just as contentious as its bulk or position. Materials often seem to generate strong feelings, with concrete being at the top of the public's hate list, closely followed by almost any form of ceramic tiling. Experience suggests that the public's aesthetic appreciation extends to the finer details of texture and colour, so that it is not enough simply to have brick walls and a tile roof, but rather to have the correct colour and texture of bricks and tiles. The visual impact of the developed site, therefore, may be as major a consideration in the development control process as is any issue of policy or other planning guideline.

LOCAL IMPACT

As important as the visual impact are those wider issues related to the potential local impact of a proposed development. Usually these include its transport implications as well as other factors associated with the proposed use, such as need, local competition and environmental issues, including noise and smells. Obviously these matters are inextricably interrelated, as the transport implications of a development cannot, in reality, be considered without reference to the proposed use which clearly affects the level and type of traffic generated. While acknowledging these relationships, however, it is easier to consider the implications of each issue if they are examined separately.

The transport implications of the proposed development are likely to raise some major development control issues.[18] First,

18 PPG 13, Transport.

the specifically site-related issues of access and parking can be considered. The question of access has to be considered in conjunction with estimates of the amount of traffic likely to be generated by the proposed development. It should be emphasised that access for a single car can, in certain circumstances, be just as crucial as access for one hundred 40-ton lorries daily. The important factor is the exact location of access onto the site in relation to, not only the proposed development, but also the surrounding configuration of the road network. At issue will be questions of road safety, especially visibility, and the likely disruption to existing traffic flows. The visibility or sight lines for traffic leaving the site can be improved by controlling the width of the access point and the level of any surrounding structures. If, however, the access point is at the top of a steep rise on the site, the problem may be an intractable one. The matter is further complicated if the road onto which the access is made is a busy one, or if the access itself is near to a junction.

Parking provision on the site is obviously related to the amount of traffic likely to be using the site, as well as the positioning of buildings. Indeed, demand for on-site parking may restrict the amount of development that the site can accommodate. Rules, or more accurately rules of thumb, tend to exist in different local planning authorities indicating the number of parking spaces that will normally be required given the nature of the development, its location and the size of site. The development control issues centre around the level of demand for parking spaces that the site will generate, and the way in which this demand will fluctuate. This obviously varies greatly from one form of development to another, but a typical example may serve to illustrate the general issues. Consider the parking demands that may be generated by a tennis club in a residential suburb. In calculating what might be considered adequate car parking provision, importance will be attached by the local planning authority to the number of courts, and the existence of a clubhouse, as well as the use made of them. Sufficient car parking spaces will be required to cope, not only with the average daily maximum number of cars, but also with any additional demand that might be produced if the clubhouse is frequently used for dances. Of course the number of spaces required will inevitably be a compromise between the maximum demand foreseeable, and the constraints of the site. It would be considered unreasonable to demand a car park large enough to provide parking spaces for all the cars likely to be generated by the occasional dance.

The need for the use must be assessed by taking account of other similar uses in the immediate area, or, conversely, the lack of them. Consider, for example, the range of uses in a small village centre. One greengrocer's shop may not serve local needs adequately, so another shop may be permitted, but if planning permission were sought for a third shop, the question of the need for this additional facility and its effect on existing businesses could not be ignored. These questions are comparatively easy to determine in relation to retailing activities, but with other uses the difficulties may increase. For example, how many large houses within an established residential area is it appropriate to convert into old persons' residential homes? Once planning permission has been granted for one, this will be used as an argument in support of attempts to gain planning permission for others. A stage will be reached, however, when the local planning authority will have to decide whether its area has a sufficient number of residential homes. The grounds on which this decision is made are often vague. Obviously, if every other property in the area was converted it would be inappropriate, but to what level such a use should be permitted before it can be considered to have a detrimental effect on the area – 5% of the properties; 10% of the properties – can be judged only in relation to the specific sites in a particular area.

The environmental effects of a use, for example, noise, fumes or other forms of pollution, are also significant and can be treated separately from those of scale and design. They occur, not only in the more obvious industrial context, but in relation to other uses. The use of a property as a hotel in a residential area may raise the issue of noise if the hotel has drinking and dining facilities that are open to non-residents. In these circumstances noise might emanate from the building as well as from any adjoining car park, and at times which were regarded as particularly unacceptable. Once again, the nature of the site and its location is crucial, insofar as these problems may be virtually eliminated by landscaping or other design features, depending on the actual physical features of the site.

Fumes and other forms of pollution are, on the other hand, normally related to industrial uses, but arguably the fumes from a small brewery in a village centre may be just as inappropriate as the chemical emissions from a tannery. The site itself can have little effect on such emissions unless it is particularly large or isolated, as clearly it is not possible to diminish the impact of smell by any form of physical landscaping. Consequently, such uses are normally seen as inappropriate for any site that is not specifically allocated for industrial use. As with almost every aspect of development control, however, there are exceptions, the most obvious being the location of crematoria. These can hardly be located in industrial areas and tend to occupy sites adjacent to existing cemeteries which are inevitably close to residential areas, or new green field sites on the urban fringe.

This brief examination of some of the commoner site-related issues of development should have illustrated the significance that the site holds in the development control process. Despite the importance of policy in development control decisions, it is always a question of applying that policy in relation to a particular application for a particular site, and since each site is unique, any decisions must be considered with that in mind. It is specifically for this reason that the concept of precedent does not exist in relation to planning permission. Planning decisions arrived at regarding development on one site cannot be directly related to the decisions on the development of the adjacent site, even if it is for the same use and at the same scale. Naturally such decisions are not ignored for the purpose of comparison, but they should never be considered precedents.

Chapter 8

Planning permission – the decision

According to section 70(1) of the Town and Country Planning Act 1990, a local planning authority can, after considering an application for planning permission, either grant planning permission conditionally or unconditionally, or refuse it. A local planning authority may also decline to determine an application for planning permission if, within two years of a called-in application for planning permission being refused permission by the Secretary of State or an unsuccessful appeal against a local planning authority's refusal of planning permission, a similar application is received.[1] Eight weeks is the period allowed for a local planning authority to reach its decision once a planning application has been received, though that period can be extended by agreement with the applicant.[2] Should a decision not be made in the requisite period, then that counts as a refusal of planning permission.[3] The purpose of this chapter is to consider the implications of these various alternatives. In order, therefore, to place the discussion which follows in context, a few basic facts and figures should prove helpful. In a typical three-month period district planning authorities in England will receive well in excess of 100,000 applications for planning permission and related consents. The bulk of such applications, over 80%, will be for planning permission. The rest will consist of applications for listed building consent, conservation area consent and advertising consent. In contrast, county planning authorities receive between four and five hundred applications

1 1990 Act, s 70A. For advice on the use of this discretionary power see Circular 14/91, Planning and Compensation Act 1991, annex 2, paras 4-9.
2 Town and Country Planning (General Development Procedure) Order 1995, SI 1995/419, art 20.
3 1990 Act, s 78.

for planning permission in a typical three-month period. Overall between 80% and 90% of all applications for planning permission are successful.[4]

This high success rate appears far from surprising. A glance at the current applications for planning permission advertised in a local newspaper will show that the developments in question are fairly low-key. Permission for a new house, or a kitchen or bathroom extension, is the norm, not large-scale commercial or residential developments. Yet this can be misleading, since the decision to build a new house in an established residential neighbourhood with the possible subsequent loss of trees and walls, and disruption to the architectural homogeneity of the area, may be just as damaging in its small way as the building of a sixty-house estate on a green field site. The problem is that local planning authorities are urged by central government to take a positive attitude towards development. This is best summed up in PPG 1, General Policy and Principles:

> The planning system should be efficient, effective and simple in conception and operation. It fails in its function whenever it prevents, inhibits or delays development which should reasonably have been permitted. It should operate on the basis that applications for development should be allowed, having regard to the development plan and all material considerations, unless the proposed development would cause demonstrable harm to interests of acknowledged importance.[5]

Although elsewhere PPG 1 asserts the government's commitment to conservation, environmental assessments, and protecting the countryside from encroachment by the city, the emphasis is undeniably on a local planning authority granting, rather than refusing, planning permission. This policy commitment to granting planning permission has, however, to be read in the light of section 54A of the 1990 Act. Section 54A emphasises the need to reach decisions on whether or not to grant planning permission in accordance with the policies set out in the development plan, unless material considerations indicate otherwise. There is no evidence that the courts are interpreting section 54A in such a manner that any proposed development which is contrary to the development plan will be

4 Planning statistics are published on a regular basis in the Journal of Planning and Environment Law. Applications for planning permission tend to fluctuate from year to year with applications rising during periods of economic growth and falling during periods of recession.

5 PPG 1, para 5.

regarded as automatically causing, in the words of PPG 1, '...demonstrable harm to interests of acknowledged importance'. Instead this is an issue to be assessed by reference to the circumstances surrounding each specific application for planning permission.[6]

In addition, what these statistics for planning applications cannot take into account is development that takes place without planning permission. The way in which such unauthorised development is treated is considered in a later chapter, but what needs to be understood here, is that development can and does occur without a local planning authority having the opportunity to scrutinise it, and, as a consequence, in some instances refuse planning permission. Nor should it be imagined that such unauthorised development is always insignificant. A business may completely change its character over the years. What was a depot for parking lorries may become a workshop for repairing them. What was an arable field may be utilised as a gypsy caravan site. When this happens a local planning authority has lost its initial development control opportunity to weigh up the pros and cons of a proposed development. Instead, it is in the unenviable position of having to decide what approach to take to a development which is already in being, a situation which can involve considerations that are very different from those under discussion in this chapter.[7]

To return to the theme of this chapter, namely the various ways in which a local planning authority can determine an application for permission, it is, perhaps, sensible to begin the discussion by indicating why this chapter occupies the position it does in this book. It might appear logical that a chapter entitled 'Planning permission – the decision' should immediately follow the chapter 'Planning permission – the application'. The fact that it does not is deliberate. It is to emphasise that when a local planning authority is faced with an application for planning permission, it may refer to some or all of those factors discussed in the intervening chapters before reaching a conclusion. At the end of this process of examination the likelihood is that a planning application will fall into one of three categories. These are:

6 Purdue M, 'The Impact of Section 54A' Journal of Planning and Environment Law, 1994, p 399.

7 The local planning authority can invite the developer to apply retrospectively for planning permission – 1990 Act, s 73A. Alternatively, it can start enforcement proceedings against the developer, a process that is considered in chapter 9.

(i) applications for planning permission which, in the opinion of the local planning authority, are totally unacceptable because they are incompatible with some particular aspect of development control;

(ii) applications for planning permission to which, in the opinion of the local planning authority, there are no development control objections;

(iii) applications for planning permission to which there are, in the opinion of the local planning authority, development control objections but those objections are not so fundamental as to warrant immediate rejection.

In commenting on each of these categories in turn, a start will be made with those planning applications which are unacceptable on development control grounds. Various factors can conspire to make a proposed development unacceptable. A policy in a development plan, a statement in a Department of the Environment PPG, the contents of an informal local policy document, the physical configuration of the site, or a combination of all these factors can persuade a local planning authority to refuse planning permission. Even if the proposed development has some points in its favour, these might, in the local planning authority's opinion, be outweighed by its negative aspects. In the event, should a local planning authority refuse planning permission, the applicant has a number of courses of action open to him. The first of these is to appeal to the Secretary of State.[8] Planning appeals are discussed in the following chapter so at this stage it is sufficient to mention that the purpose of a planning appeal is to consider afresh the issue of whether or not to grant planning permission. The very development control issues that persuaded the local planning authority to refuse planning permission will be reassessed. An appeal to the Secretary of State, therefore, should be contemplated only if an applicant believes that his proposed development has some points in its favour.

If this is not the case, or if an applicant is simply unwilling to risk time and money on an appeal to the Secretary of State, he has the alternative of entering into discussion with the local planning authority. When it refuses planning permission a local planning authority is under an obligation to give its reasons for doing so.[9] By studying those reasons and discussing them with the planning officers, an applicant may be able to make

8 1990 Act, ss 78,79.

9 Town and Country Planning (General Development Procedure) Order 1995, SI 1995/419, art 22.

modifications to his proposed development. In the light of those modifications, such as reducing the density of housing, a fresh application for planning permission may then be successful. Obviously, it makes greater sense to consult the relevant planning officers before any planning application is submitted. Should this not be the case, an applicant can always seek their advice at this stage. It should be made clear, of course, that even if any advice given by the planning officers is followed to the letter, it cannot guarantee the success of a planning application, as this decision normally rests with the planning committee.

Planning conditions

As for the two remaining categories of planning applications, those to which there are no, and those to which there are some, development control objections, the intention is to combine the discussion of the two. This is because both raise the issue of planning conditions. According to the terms of section 70 of the 1990 Act, when a local planning authority decides to grant planning permission it can impose whatever conditions it sees fit. This ability of a local planning authority to impose planning conditions is important, and raises a number of issues. The first of these is the role of conditions in the development control process. In order to begin to appreciate that role, an example may be helpful. A builder applies for planning permission to build five bungalows in what was formerly the orchard of a large Victorian villa. In one sense the application is unobjectionable, since the proposed development is situated in a residential area, and from the plans it appears that the development has been well designed. Vehicular and pedestrian access do not seem to pose any problems, nor does the site appear to be too small for the number of dwellings proposed. There would seem to be every reason, therefore, to decide to grant planning permission.

If such a decision was taken the development, when complete, could have a far from favourable impact on the amenity of the area. For example, the sandstone wall enclosing the site could have been demolished and replaced with a white painted fence. Mature trees might have been felled. The bungalows might have been constructed using yellow London brick with tiled roofs whereas the commonly used building materials in the area are red Ruabon brick with slate roofs. There may have been no attempt to landscape the site when building had finished. As for the vehicular and pedestrian access, concrete and tarmac may have been employed in their construction in harsh contrast to the York stone paving commonly used in the area. The end result, therefore, could be a thoroughly unsympathetic development.

In order to prevent this happening, the solution is to impose planning conditions when granting planning permission. In the example just given, the following set of conditions would not be unusual.

(i) Samples of all materials to be used externally to be approved prior to building commencing.
(ii) All boundary walls to site shall be retained at their present height and repointed in a suitably coloured mortar.
(iii) All existing trees to be protected during work. Any tree damaged or which dies within two years to be replaced with agreed trees in first available season.
(iv) Details of all hard ground surfaces to be approved (wholesale tarmacking or concreting will not be acceptable).

In this fashion it should be possible to ensure that the proposed development is as compatible as possible with the existing environment. Indeed, the justification, in planning terms, for the imposition of these conditions will be to enhance the visual amenity of the area.

In the light of this example, it is now possible to consider the role of conditions in the development control process. Do planning conditions represent an avenue whereby a local planning authority can implement its development control policy? In a broad sense this is undoubtedly true. A local planning authority, particularly a rural one, may have a policy that new factories can be built in its area only if they are to be occupied by local firms. It is possible to attach a condition to a planning permission which seeks to guarantee that this policy is observed. That condition could state, for example, that 'the factories in question may be occupied only by local firms'. It should be obvious, however, that this is a far from satisfactory planning condition, since it gives the applicant for planning permission no guidance on what constitutes a 'local firm'. To refer, therefore, to planning conditions as a device for implementing development control policy is not totally accurate. This is because policies often have to be broad rather than specific, whereas conditions, in order to have a role to play, must indicate clearly what is required.

If planning conditions do not provide a means for a local planning authority to implement directly its development control policy, what is their role? A clue is to be found in Circular 1/85, The Use of Conditions in Planning Permissions, which states:

> The power to impose conditions when granting planning permission is very wide, and can enable many development proposals to proceed where it would otherwise have been necessary to refuse planning permission.[10]

The value of planning conditions, therefore, seems to depend on the scope they give a local planning authority to regulate the details of a proposed development. As was mentioned, an application for planning permission to construct bungalows in an established residential area may be perfectly acceptable in principle. What may be unacceptable is the loss of trees and walls, and the unsympathetic construction of the new buildings. This is where planning conditions come into their own. They can be used to ensure the retention of trees, of walls, of building lines and the use of materials which are compatible with existing buildings. To this extent, planning conditions are being used to implement development control policy, for example, the policy of enhancing the amenity of a pleasant residential area. The same is true of all conditions. Most local planning authorities will have development control policies on noise, on the opening hours of businesses, on the provision of car parking spaces and on roads. Planning conditions allow the generality of such policies to be applied to the specific circumstances of a particular development. In that sense they are a means of implementing policy, not directly, but at one remove.

Having explored the relationship between development control policy and planning conditions, the next step is to discuss in greater detail the content of conditions. Circular 1/85 regards conditions as falling into two general categories, those concerned with regulating the development, and those which are applicable after the development has occurred. In the first category are conditions which impose time limits on the commencement of development, which ensure the provision of the necessary infrastructure, such as sewage disposal, access roads and parking spaces, and which provide for the landscaping of the development site. In this fashion, a local planning authority is attempting to guarantee that planning permissions are not acted upon, and that buildings are not occupied before the necessary services have been supplied. Conditions which are

10 Circular 1/85, para 1. This Circular has been updated as Circular 1/95 but not substantially changed.

applicable after the development has occurred are more contentious. As Circular 1/85 points out, such conditions:

> will remain in force after the development has been carried out...They can place onerous and permanent restrictions on what can be done with the premises affected, and they should therefore not be imposed without scrupulous weighing of the balance of advantage.[11]

In this category are conditions which attempt to restrict who can occupy houses, industrial or commercial property, which allow temporary or seasonal development to occur, which attempt to control noise or which are aimed at restricting rights under the General Permitted Development Order.[12]

Obviously this question of the content of conditions is related to the circumstances in which conditions are imposed. It will be recalled that this discussion of planning conditions began with a reference to the fact that some applications for planning permission will raise development control issues, and others will not. Planning conditions are a way of dealing with those development control issues while, at the same time, letting a proposed development proceed. The logic of this is that planning applications raising no development control issues will be granted planning permission unconditionally, a possibility which section 70 acknowledges. There is, however, a slight flaw in this logic, besides the obvious flaw of whether all planning applications are bound to raise development control issues. Section 91 of the 1990 Act provides that, with some exceptions:

> (1)...every planning permission granted or deemed to be granted shall be granted or, as the case may be, be deemed to be granted, subject to the condition that the development to which it relates must be begun not later than the expiration of -
> (a) five years beginning with the date on which the permission is granted or, as the case may be, deemed to be granted; or
> (b) such other period (whether longer or shorter) beginning with that date as the authority concerned with the terms of planning permission may direct.

11 Ibid, para 65.

12 The Town and Country (General Permitted Development) Order 1995, SI 1995/418, Sch 2, sets out certain classes of activity which rank as permitted development, that is, those activities that can proceed without the need to secure planning permission. It is possible to impose a planning condition restricting such rights. Circular 1/85 gives some examples, while, at the same time, discouraging the use of such conditions unless there are valid planning reasons for their imposition. A planning condition may also be used to restrict rights under the Use Classes Order. On this point see *Dunoon Developments v Secretary of State for the Environment* [1992] JPL 936, CA.

(2) The period mentioned in subsection (1)(b) shall be a period which the authority considers appropriate having regard to the provisions of the development plan and to any other material considerations.

It would seem, therefore, that all planning permissions will be accompanied by at least one condition. This is to the effect that development must begin within a specified period, normally five years.[13] Such a condition might be described as a standard condition, in that it is inevitably used, whatever the circumstances.

One other planning condition can also be described as standard. This is the condition, attached to a grant of outline planning permission, reserving certain matters for subsequent approval by a local planning authority. It will be recalled that where the proposed development consists of the erection of a building, outline planning permission may be requested. The local planning authority will be given certain basic details concerning the proposed building and, on that basis, will decide whether or not to approve the development in principle. If the authority does, it will grant outline planning permission subject to whatever conditions it thinks necessary. One of these conditions will invariably require local planning authority approval of certain details, usually termed 'reserved matters'. These can include the siting of the proposed building, its design and external appearance, access to it and the landscaping of the site on which it is to be erected.

Apart from these two standard planning conditions, Circular 1/85 states quite categorically that '...as a matter of policy, a condition ought not to be imposed unless there is a definite need for it'.[14] This would seem to suggest that the practice of imposing conditions automatically whenever an application for planning permission is approved, is to be avoided. Failure to do so results in the development control system being brought into disrepute. There must, therefore, be a planning justification for every planning condition imposed. This is not to say, of course, that planning conditions do not exist whose use is exceedingly common. It may be seen as sensible development control

13 In the case of a grant of outline planning permission, approval for reserved matters should normally be sought within three years, with development beginning two years from that date, or five years from the original grant of outline planning permission, whichever is later. The local planning authority has the power to vary any of these periods if it so wishes: 1990 Act, s 92.

14 Circular 1/85, para 12.

practice to specify the hours when machinery can be used when planning permission is granted for a factory, or to make provision for landscaping whenever a major building operation takes place. A local planning authority, besides being aware of the need to use common planning conditions intelligently, should also appreciate that the power to impose planning conditions is a wide-ranging power. It can be used to frame very specific conditions to deal with a particular problem.

In considering what limits there are on local planning authorities' powers to impose planning conditions, reference needs to be made initially to section 70 of the 1990 Act. This suggests that local planning authorities can impose 'such conditions as they think fit', indicating, perhaps, that the authorities have a totally free hand in the matter. In reality, both the Secretary of State for the Environment and the courts have formulated rules which broadly restrict the content of planning conditions. It is only logical that the Secretary of State should have devised such rules, since it is to him that an individual will appeal when the content of a planning condition is considered unacceptable. The tests applied by the Secretary of State are set out in Circular 1/85. They demand that a condition should be:

(i) necessary,
(ii) relevant to planning,
(iii) relevant to the development to be permitted,
(iv) enforceable,
(v) precise, and
(vi) reasonable in all other respects.

Before considering the significance of each test in turn, a word should be said about their sources. Some of these tests have been formulated by the courts and relate to the legal validity of a planning condition. These will be apparent from the reference to decided cases. In contrast, the Secretary of State has formulated tests to assess the development control merits of a condition. The distinction is an important one and will be referred to elsewhere in this chapter. A local planning authority should observe all the tests.

The first test is that a planning condition must be necessary. Circular 1/85 states, by way of explanation, that the:

> argument that a condition will do no harm is no justification for its imposition: as a matter of policy, a condition ought not to be imposed unless there is a definite need for it.[15]

15 Ibid.

When employing planning conditions, therefore, a local planning authority should tailor the condition to meet the specific problems of a particular development. Used in this fashion, planning conditions can permit development to go ahead, while keeping to a minimum any unfavourable impact it may have on a neighbourhood. That, of course, is the theory. Little direct evidence is available on whether local planning authorities use conditions intelligently, or simply attach the same standard planning conditions to each and every planning permission. Nor is there a great deal in the way of indirect evidence. If a planning condition is breached and a local planning authority commences enforcement proceedings, that is good evidence of how necessary that planning condition was.[16] Unfortunately, there are no figures for the reverse situation, that is, of a planning condition being breached and no enforcement proceedings being taken.

Perhaps the greatest guarantee that a planning condition is necessary rests with the fact that a local planning authority has, under the terms of the General Development Procedure Order, to give reasons to the applicant for its imposition of planning conditions.[17] Circular 1/85 warns against giving vague reasons, such as to protect the amenity of the neighbourhood.[18] Instead, local planning authorities are advised that if:

> the reasons for the imposition of conditions are clearly explained, developers will be better able to understand the need for them and to comply with them in spirit as well as in letter.[19]

This should in turn, it suggested, reduce the number of appeals to the Secretary of State.

The second requirement is that planning conditions should be relevant to planning. This is a test devised by the courts and its significance can best be appreciated by referring to the case of *R v Hillingdon London Borough Council, ex p Royco Homes Ltd.*[20] Here, the council attached conditions to the planning permission granted to Royco Homes, one of which was that the

16 1990 Act, s 187A gives local planning authorities the power to serve a breach of condition notice. This is an alternative to more traditional enforcement procedures. See Hainsworth D, 'Breach of Condition Notices – Theory and Practice' Journal of Planning and EnvironmentLaw, 1993, p 903.

17 Town and Country Planning (General Development Procedure) Order 1995, SI 1995/419, art 22.

18 Circular 1/85, para 8.

19 Ibid.

20 [1974] QB 720, [1974] 2 All ER 643.

occupants of the residential development which the company were proposing to build should, for ten years, be drawn from the Council's housing waiting-list. The court found that such a condition was invalid. Basically, the reasoning which accompanies this decision is simple. Section 70 of the 1990 Act[1] allows a local planning authority to impose whatever conditions it thinks fit. This would seem to suggest that a condition, such as the one under discussion, would be perfectly legitimate. This, however, is not the case. Since the power to impose conditions appears in the 1990 Act, then any conditions must further the purpose of that Act within the statutory framework it establishes. In other words, they must have a planning purpose. In the *Royco Homes* case, the court held that the condition in question had no such purpose. Instead, it appeared to be an attempt by the local authority to force Royco Homes to carry the financial burden of the local authority's duties as a housing authority.

Other decisions have confirmed this approach by the courts towards conditions which have no planning purpose.[2] Faced with such a condition, therefore, an applicant has several courses of action open to him. He can, if he wishes, accept the burden and act upon it, though this in no way alters the fact that a condition of this nature is invalid. Alternatively, the applicant can appeal to the Secretary of State, giving as his reason the content of that particular condition. In these circumstances, the Secretary of State may remove the offending condition, since the Secretary of State should, and indeed does, observe the tests for validity laid down by the courts and in his own policy.[3] By taking this course of action, the applicant runs the risk that, once the offending condition is removed, the Secretary of State may no longer feel able to grant planning permission. Finally, if all else fails, the applicant can refer the offending condition to the courts since they have the power to strike it out.[4]

In addition to having a planning purpose, the courts have also made it clear that, in order to be valid, a condition must be

1 At the time of the decision the relevant section was s 29 of the Town and Country Planning Act 1971.

2 See, for example, *Hall & Co Ltd v Shoreham by Sea UDC* [1964] 1 All ER 1, CA; *M J Shanley Ltd v Secretary of State for the Environment* [1982] JPL 380.

3 The Secretary of State will, therefore, be judging a condition both on its development control merits and its legal validity. See also s 73 and s 73A of the 1990 Act

4 1990 Act, s 288. If, however, the court determines that the condition is invalid but, because it deals with some important issue, is not severable, then the entire planning permission will be lost.

relevant to the development to be permitted. The significance of this test can be illustrated by referring to *Newbury District Council v Secretary of State for the Environment.*[5] Here, a company had applied for planning permission in 1962 to use two hangars on a disused airfield as warehouses for storing synthetic rubber. Planning permission was granted subject to conditions, one of which was that the hangars should be removed by 31 December 1972. When the company did not remove the hangars by that date, enforcement proceedings were begun. On appeal by the company, the Secretary of State set aside the enforcement notice. He agreed with his inspector's recommendation that the condition requiring the hangars' removal was void on the grounds that it did not relate to the purpose for which the original planning permission was sought. When subsequently this decision was reviewed by the court, this reasoning was vindicated, the court agreeing that the condition was not relevant to the proposed use.[6] Other examples of conditions which are unacceptable on these grounds are given in Circular 1/85.

> For example if planning permission is being granted for the alteration of a factory building, it would be wrong to impose conditions requiring additional parking facilities to be provided for an existing factory simply to meet a need that already exists, and similarly wrong to require the improvement of the appearance or lay-out of an adjoining site simply because it is untidy or congested; despite the desirability of these objectives in planning terms, the need for the action would not be created by the new development.[7]

While the logic of this caveat on the content of planning conditions seems to be reasonably clear, its relationship with section 72(1) of the 1990 Act needs scrutinising. That subsection provides:

> Without prejudice to the generality of section 70(1), conditions may be imposed on the grant of planning permission under that section –
> (a) for regulating the development or use of any land under the control of the applicant (whether or not it is land in respect of which the application was made) or requiring the carrying out

5 [1981] AC 578, [1980] 1 All ER 731, HL.

6 Neither was the condition valid under the terms of s 30(1)(b) of the Town and Country Planning Act 1971 (now repealed) which permitted planning permission to be granted for a specified period, at the end of which buildings must be removed.

7 Circular 1/85, para 21.

of works on any such land, so far as appears to the local planning authority to be expedient for the purposes of or in connection with the development authorised by the permission.

It might appear on first reading that this section provides the justification for such conditions. In reality this is not so. The words '...so far as appears to the local planning authority to be expedient for the purposes of or in connection with the development authorised by the permission', mean that a condition made under the terms of this subsection must be as relevant to the development to be permitted as any condition made under section 70.

The next requirement is that a condition must be enforceable. In order to clarify what this entails, this test is best considered in conjunction with the fifth test that a planning condition must be precise. This is because if a condition is imprecise the chances are that it will not be capable of being enforced. In the case of *M J Shanley Ltd v Secretary of State for the Environment*,[8] for example, the debate was over a residential development in the green belt. The contentious condition demanded that the first opportunity to purchase the houses in the proposed development should be given to local people. The imprecision of this condition is obvious, and relates to what constitutes both a 'first opportunity' and 'local people'. In these circumstances the court had no hesitation in setting the condition aside, since its imprecision rendered it unenforceable.

Views on what is or is not precise, depend on the particular facts of a case. In *Alderson v Secretary of State for the Environment*,[9] the argument centred again on the use of the word 'local' in a condition restricting the occupation of premises to persons 'employed locally in agriculture'. The Court of Appeal held that in this context the word had a perfectly intelligible meaning, so that the condition was sufficiently precise. This was fortunate, since the condition was in common use among local planning authorities who had relied on Department of Environment advice that it was acceptable.[10]

One damaging consequence of imprecision is that it brings the process of development control, and planning conditions in particular, into disrepute, although it is worth mentioning that, even if a planning condition is imprecise and thus invalid, it may still have a perfectly legitimate development control purpose.

8 [1982] JPL 380.

9 (1984) 49 P & CR 307.

10 It was set out in Circular 5/68 which, at that time, was the current circular on planning conditions.

Faced with a vague condition a developer will be uncertain what is required of him. If that developer then chooses to do nothing, the local planning authority may find itself in an equal predicament, since it will be impossible to take action to enforce the condition. This is not to suggest that every planning condition which is unenforceable is imprecise. There are examples of planning conditions which are perfectly clear in what they require but are still unenforceable. Circular 1/85 gives the example of a condition, imposed for traffic reasons, restricting the number of residents at any one time in a block of flats.[11] What makes the condition unenforceable in these circumstances is the impossibility of monitoring whether or not it is being observed. For all the good it is doing, therefore, the condition may as well not be there.

The final test for a valid condition is that of reasonableness. This is by far the most difficult proposition to explain. It is possible to give examples of what might constitute an unreasonable planning condition and Circular 1/85 does precisely that.[12] To allow a factory for canning vegetables to be built and then restrict its hours of operation from 11 am to 3 pm represents an unreasonable condition, since it defeats the purpose of granting planning permission. Another instance would be a condition that demands something of a developer which is beyond his control, for example, requiring him to carry out work on land that he does not own. Yet, examples, particularly extreme examples, do not adequately convey the essentials of unreasonableness. This is perhaps because, in the context of development control, the concept varies according to whether it is the Secretary of State or the court which is employing it. The Secretary of State may consider a planning condition unreasonable on development control grounds, meaning that what is demanded is not conducive to good planning. The objection to local user conditions may fall under this heading. To grant planning permission for factories or houses, then restrict who occupies the property to local firms or residents is not something which the Department of the Environment encourages at present.[13] Basically, this is because, in the eyes of central government, there are no good planning reasons for the practice except on very rare occasions.

In contrast, the court's use of the expression 'unreasonable' is somewhat different, as the court is neither equipped, nor does

11 Circular 1/85, appendix B.
12 Ibid, para 30.
13 Ibid, paras 74-80.

it have the authority, to make development control judgments. Its task is to ensure that the law is observed. Therefore, in a case such as the *Royco Homes* case, the decision to impose a condition which had no planning purpose was described as unreasonable by the court, indicating that it is unreasonable for a local authority to behave in a way for which there is no legal justification. Sometimes, however, the expression 'unreasonable' will denote activity on the part of a local authority which no reasonable local authority would engage in. A planning condition described in this fashion could have a planning purpose, and be precise in its wording, but could be so crass in its demands as to be totally unreasonable. A local user condition, for example, would not fall into this category unless it restricted the occupants of a proposed residential development to individuals who had been living in a particular village for thirty years. Unreasonable in this context should mean an unlawful use of power, though it has to be said that some decisions may demonstrate a failure on the part of the courts to appreciate this fact. Examples can be discovered of the courts performing the Secretary of State's role rather than the one specifically allotted to them.[14]

If a planning condition is a valid planning condition, judged by the six tests in Circular 1/85, then it is binding on the individual who receives the planning permission. Failure to observe the condition may result in enforcement proceedings. However, there would be no logic to the whole concept if a planning condition were binding on the developer who made the application for planning permission but no one else. That developer might sell the land or property in question before any work started. In order to overcome this particular problem, conditions are regarded as part of the whole package of granting planning permission. Anyone, therefore, who decides to act on that grant of planning permission must observe the planning conditions. This rather obvious point, however, conceals a more important truth about the nature of planning conditions. This point relates to their duration. As Circular 1/85 indicates, planning conditions fall into one of two categories. There are planning conditions which regulate the development, and those which remain in force after the development has been carried out. In the former group are conditions specifying time limits for the commencement and completion of the development and the provision of certain basic services, such as sewers. Once the

14 See on this point *Fourth Investments Ltd v Bury Metropolitan Borough Council* [1985] JPL 185.

development has been completed, these conditions have been discharged.

On the other hand, conditions which are intended to remain in force after the development has been completed, may have no limit on their duration. In this category are conditions which restrict the hours of operation of an industrial development, or the level of noise it is permitted to generate. Here, the aim of the planning condition is to reduce for all time the impact a proposed development might have on the amenity of an area. Yet this is not all. The more contentious of these conditions have about them the air of social engineering, or seemingly infringe an individual's right to dispose of and use his property as he wishes.

As remarked upon in Circular 1/85, conditions which remain in force after the development has been carried out 'can place onerous and permanent restrictions on what can be done with the premises affected'.[15] It seems hardly surprising to find, therefore, procedures in the 1990 Act which allow a condition to be varied or removed. Section 73A is specifically designed to deal with conditions that have been breached when a planning permission has been acted upon. The local planning authority can grant planning permission with retrospective effect which omits the need to comply with the conditions which have not been observed. In contrast, section 73 deals with the situation where the planning permission has not been acted upon and allows the individual with planning permission to apply to the local planning authority for permission to proceed without complying with the conditions attached to the grant of planning permission. This procedure ensures that only the planning conditions are considered. Thus the local planning authority can grant planning permission subject to different conditions or unconditionally or can refuse the application, which leaves the original planning permission intact, together with its original conditions. The use of this procedure avoids the dangers associated with an appeal to the Secretary of State or a challenge in the courts – namely, that a successful review of a condition may result in the whole planning permission being lost.

In bringing to a close this examination of planning conditions, it will be recalled that the discussion arose out of an analysis of the various ways in which a local planning authority can resolve an application for planning permission. Yet, even planning conditions have their limitations, and with this in mind, local

15 Circular 1/85, para 65.

planning authorities often make use of planning agreements as a valuable adjunct to planning conditions in controlling development within their area. Since planning agreements and planning obligations are normally negotiated at the same time as an application is being made for planning permission, it seems appropriate to consider them in this chapter. The aim is to assess their advantages and disadvantages as compared with planning conditions.

Planning agreements and planning obligations

The power to conclude binding agreements between local authorities and developers has a long history. A variety of statutes authorises the practice and they include section 111 of the Local Government Act 1972, section 278 of the Highways Act 1980, local private Acts of Parliament and past as well as present Town and Country Planning Acts. The nature of these transactions varies according to the statutory authority on which it is based. Section 278 of the Highways Act 1980,[16] for example, allows highways authorities to enter into agreements with developers whereby the latter will meet either the whole or part of the costs of works to the highway. The development control significance of such an arrangement is that it allows a local authority to secure a contribution from a developer towards works to the highway which may be necessary in order to allow development to proceed. Hence the term 'planning agreement' is used throughout this chapter to describe such an arrangement although its development control implications are not immediately apparent.

One of the most familiar powers to enter into a planning agreement was that in section 52 of the Town and Country Planning Act 1971. Section 52 (which subsequently became section 106 of the 1990 Act and has now been repealed) provided that:

> A local planning authority may enter into an agreement with any person interested in land in their area for the purpose of restricting or regulating the development or use of the land, either permanently or during such period as may be prescribed by the agreement; and any such agreement may contain such incidental and consequential provisions (including provisions of

16 Section 23 of the New Roads and Street Works Act 1991 inserted a new s 278 into the Highways Act to replace the original version.

a financial character) as appear to the local planning authority to be necessary or expedient for the purpose of the agreement.

The manner in which this power was used by local planning authorities varied. On some occasions it was used to achieve very specific development control objectives as the following extract from a section 52 agreement demonstrates:

> Now therefore it is agreed as follows: 1. For the purposes of this deed it is agreed between the parties hereto that the line marked 'XYZ' on the said plan is the boundary between the respective developments of the corporation and the developer. 2. The corporation and the developer hereby covenant in respect of the following rights and restrictions and by reference to the said plan and plan no 2 attached hereto as follows: (a) the corporation hereby covenants and agrees with the developer that the developer may build up to the said line XYZ and along its length at levels B, D and E on the said plan no 2. (b) the developer hereby covenants and agrees with the corporation that the corporation may build up to the said line XYZ and along its whole length at levels B and D... (c) The corporation hereby further covenants and agrees with the developer that above level E the developer may build as follows: (i) Between points X and to a level of 5.3 metres above level E or higher if the point is contained within an angle of 50 degrees measured from a point 5.3 metres above level E along the line XY as shown on section AA of the said plan no 2. (ii) Between points Y and Z to a height contained within an angle of 50 degrees measured from a point 3 metres from the boundary YZ and at a height of 8 metres above level E as shown in section BB on the said plan no 2. 3. The developer hereby further covenants and agrees with the corporation that the developer will not build on its land edged purple on plan no. 1 to a height exceeding 16 metres above the present ground level at point X shown on the said plan no 1.[17]

What is immediately apparent is that a planning agreement of this nature was fulfilling a purpose which was remarkably similar to the purpose served by planning conditions. While this is true, some explanation is needed of why this should be so. There was apparently a two-fold reason:

> Although local planning authorities sometimes use an agreement in order to achieve a measure of development control which would otherwise be clearly impossible...by reference to the legal limits of planning conditions, it seems to be more frequently the case that an agreement is resorted to either in order to avoid the uncertainties of planning law or in order to reinforce

17 *Windsor and Maidenhead Royal Borough Council v Brandrose Investments Ltd* [1981] 3 All ER 38 at 42.

> development control,...there seems to be a feeling in practice that there is a greater likelihood that a developer will comply with an element of development control which is incorporated in a formal, legal agreement.[18]

The notion that section 52 agreements could be used in circumstances where a planning condition might not be valid, needs to be qualified. In the first place, such agreements drew their force from the fact that some accord had been reached between a local planning authority and a developer. In this respect, they were distinct from planning conditions, which are imposed whether or not a developer is agreeable. If, therefore, a local planning authority was unable to impose a valid planning condition, it could not, as an alternative, force a developer to enter into a section 52 agreement. Devices to force a developer's hand, for example, a planning condition to the effect that no start could be made on a proposed development until a section 52 agreement had been concluded, were of doubtful validity.[19]

Apart from the necessity of securing a developer's compliance if a planning agreement was to be used, doubts were raised over the proposition that what could not validly be embodied in a planning condition could form the subject matter of a section 52 agreement. In *Bradford City Metropolitan Council v Secretary of State for the Environment*,[20] Lloyd LJ expressed this view:

> If the condition was manifestly unreasonable, and so beyond the powers of the Planning Authority to impose it, whether or not the developers consented, it had to follow that it was also beyond the powers of the Planning Authority to include the condition as 'an incidental or consequential provision' of an agreement restricting or regulating the development or use of the land under section 52.[1]

The appropriate test for determining the validity of a section 52 agreement was not an issue in this case since none had been concluded. In later cases, however, this question was to prove particularly problematic. This was because apart from using section 52 agreements to secure development control objectives evidence began to emerge of their use for another more contentious purpose, namely to procure planning gain.

In the past planning gain has been defined in the following manner:

18 Hawke J N 'Planning Agreements in Practice' (Pt II), Journal of Planning and Environment Law 1981, p 96.

19 [1980] JPL 841 (Ministerial planning appeal decision).

20 [1986] JPL 598.

1 Ibid, at 600-601.

> a term which has come to be applied whenever, in connection with a grant of planning permission, a local planning authority seeks to impose on a developer an obligation to carry out works not included in the development for which permission has been sought or to make some payment or confer some extraneous right or benefit in return for permitting development to take place.[2]

The issue of planning gain normally arises when major developments are under consideration. It might mean that a developer who is applying for planning permission to construct offices, shops and flats on a two-acre site in the centre of a major city, will offer, with or without prompting from the local planning authority, to construct for them a community centre or a tourist information centre as part of the development. The offer and indeed acceptance of planning gain can be viewed in a variety of ways. It represents either a local planning authority's attempt to levy a 'tax' on development, or a developer's attempt to 'buy' planning permission or the community's attempt to recover some of the hidden costs of development which are normally paid for from the public purse. Obviously, if a developer is prepared to accommodate any demands that are made of him or freely to offer planning gain, it can be argued that there are no grounds for concern unless, of course, this convinces a local planning authority to turn a blind eye to his scheme's shortcomings. Alternatively, if a developer refuses to provide planning gain then this does not stop him from applying for planning permission when his proposed development will be considered on its merits. This latter proposition may appear a shade ingenuous if the local planning authority considering the application is one which specifically refers to planning gain in its development plan.[3] In such circumstances, planning gain is perhaps seen as the community's share of the profits to be made from a development. The flaw in this reasoning, though some might not acknowledge it as such, is the power it puts in the hands of local authorities to decide upon an appropriate 'levy' without parliamentary sanction for the practice.[4] In addition there are discrepancies in England and Wales over the availability of planning gain. While a developer in the south of England might be willing to concede a gain, the same may not be true in the north of England

2 Circular 22/83, Planning Gain, para 2 (now cancelled).

3 *Westminster Renslade Ltd v Secretary of State for the Environment* [1983] JPL 454.

4 It is a basic rule of constitutional law that taxes can be levied only with parliamentary approval. This has been upheld by the courts in cases such as *AG v Wilts United Dairies Ltd* (1922) 38 TLR 781, HL.

where it is the local authorities who have to offer inducements to prospective developers.[5]

Planning gain is an issue on which it is difficult to be categorical. Major development proposals do place burdens on the community at large, whether in the shape of increased traffic levels or strains on the public transport system or on local schools, whose costs have to be met by the community as a whole. Planning conditions cannot be used to deal with this problem since there are legal limits on what they can require of a developer. Planning agreements, however, can go some way to ensuring that the hidden costs of development are met by the developer rather than the community. The problem is to devise a formula whereby what is demanded of the developer is proportionate to the demands placed on the infrastructure by his development rather than a tax on that development or an attempt to 'buy' planning permission for an unsatisfactory scheme.

Section 52 agreements were a key element in this debate since they were the legal vehicle selected to secure planning gain. On occasion, doubts were expressed by the courts over the legitimacy of the contents of such agreements. The suggestion was made in the *Bradford* case[6] that for a section 52 agreement to be valid it had to comply with the tests that the courts had imposed to determine the validity of a planning condition. In other words the agreement had to be for a planning purpose, had fairly and reasonably to relate to the permitted development and must not be manifestly unreasonable.[7] Later cases, however, such as *Good v Epping Forest District Council*[8] rejected this approach. According to the judgment of Ralph Gibson LJ in that case, section 52 had to be interpreted on the basis of its wording and the context in which those words were used. This meant that any agreement had to be 'for the purpose of restricting or regulating the development or use of the land' and must not be unreasonable. The extent of the powers possessed by the planning authority to impose planning conditions were

5 Due to the concentration of private commercial development in the South East, the local authorities in other parts of England and Wales have little opportunity to extract planning gain from the relatively few developments that take place in their areas. Instead, developers may have to be offered inducements to undertake work, such as those to be found within enterprise zones, as discussed in chapter 5.

6 [1986] JPL 598, CA.

7 *Newbury District Council v Secretary of State for the Environment* [1981] AC 578 at 618, [1980] 1 All ER 731 at 754, HL.

8 [1994] 2 All ER 156.

immaterial, since the 'two statutory powers are distinct and the exercise of either of these distinct powers has separate consequences and is subject to different procedures'.[9] Indeed Ralph Gibson LJ made the very logical point that if this were not the case then there would seem little point in enacting section 52 '...if s 52 agreements were confined to those matters which could be dealt with by way of conditions'.[10]

Whilst the argument over the correct test to determine the validity of a section 52 agreement might seem an exercise in 'hair-splitting', and lack relevance in view of the fact that section 52 has now been repealed, it is significant. It demonstrates the uncertainty that existed over whether the 'gain' demanded in a planning agreement had fairly and reasonably to relate to the permitted development in order to be valid. In other words, was it a legal requirement that whenever a planning agreement called for planning gain, any such benefit had to be linked in some fashion to the proposed development or did no such constraint exist? Clearly this point is fundamental and in the cases where the issue arose the courts were equivocal in their response to the question. An added complication was the policy guidance given by the Department of the Environment in Circular 22/83 Planning Gain (now cancelled) which stated quite categorically that planning gain was legitimate only if it reasonably related to the development for which planning permission was sought.[11]

In 1991 the decision was taken to recast section 106 (which had succeeded section 52 when the planning legislation was consolidated in 1990) and to replace the planning agreement with the planning obligation.[12] It was said the reasons for taking this step were practical, such as the need to speed up planning appeals by expanding the notion of a planning agreement to include unilateral undertakings.[13] Another factor was undoubtedly the growing feeling that the private sector could and indeed should provide finance for:

9 Ibid, at p 167.

10 Ibid.

11 Circular 22/83, paras 5-7.

12 A new s 106 was inserted into the 1990 Act by s 12 of the Planning and Compensation Act 1991.

13 Special provision was made to ensure that s 52 agreements remained enforceable. When, however, the new s 106 was inserted by s 12 of the Planning and Compensation Act 1991 it appears no similar provision was made to preserve 'old style' s 106 agreements. See *Encyclopedia of Planning Law and Practice*, Vol 2, p 106.06.

off-site infrastructure costs, often going beyond traditional areas such as highways and sewers to include schools, colleges, creches, and community centres.[14]

Section 106 represents, therefore, the latest attempt to augment planning conditions by authorising binding commitments from developers over the steps they will take to diminish any adverse effects of their proposed development.

TOWN AND COUNTRY PLANNING ACT 1990, SECTION 106

According to this section:

> (1) Any person interested in land in the area of a local planning authority may, by agreement or otherwise, enter into an obligation ...
> (a) restricting the development or use of the land in any specified way;
> (b) requiring specified operations or activities to be carried out in, on, under or over the land;
> (c) requiring the land to be used in any specified way; or
> (d) requiring a sum or sums to be paid to the authority on a specified date or dates or periodically.

As can be appreciated a section 106 planning obligation can be distinguished from an 'old style' section 52 agreement in a number of ways. In the first place it embraces unilateral as well as bilateral undertakings. If, therefore, a developer and the local planning authority cannot agree terms the developer has the option of offering a unilateral obligation. If his application for planning permission is refused this offer can be taken into account on appeal as a material consideration and may persuade an inspector to decide in his favour. This of course raises the question whether all planning obligations will automatically be regarded as material considerations however remote their connection is with the proposed development.

Secondly, what may form the subject matter of a section 106 planning obligation is addressed in far greater detail than was previously the case. As well as restricting the use or development of land, a planning obligation can require positive actions on the part of the developer. This power is used to permit developers to undertake operations, such as the construction of facilities both on and off the development site.[15] In addition,

14 Ibid, p 106.08.

15 See the example of the planning obligations entered into in *R v Plymouth City Council, ex p Plymouth and South Devon Co-operative Society* [1993] JPL 538. The major supermarket chains involved in this case had agreed

section 106 authorises agreements whereby a developer provides the local planning authority with money though the section does not specify that this has to be for a particular purpose. Since, however, the power to make payments is in the Town and Country Planning Act, it may be assumed, that any payment in order to be legitimate has to have a planning purpose.[16] One activity that is not specifically referred to in section 106 is the transfer of land and there has been speculation whether such a transfer can form the subject matter of a planning obligation. In *Wimpey Homes Holdings Ltd v Secretary of State for the Environment*[17] a developer unilaterally undertook to transfer land to meet a planning objection to a proposed development. The court held in that case that since this undertaking did not restrict the use or development of land, as required by section 106, it was not validly entered into under the terms of the section. Later cases have adopted a different approach to this issue. In *R v South Northamptonshire District Council, ex p Crest Homes plc*[18] a bilateral agreement was entered into under section 106 whereby the developer agreed to transfer land to the local authority for planning purposes. This was held to fall within the scope of section 106 since the obligation could be expressed in a negative fashion and hence constitute a restriction on the use or development of the land.[19] Perhaps it is only in the case of a unilateral obligation that section 106 will not permit a transfer of land, although even in these circumstances it could be expressed in a negative manner.[20]

Finally, section 106 is seen by some as an attempt to place planning gain on a more secure statutory footing and hence achieve a much greater degree of regulation over what may or may not legitimately be claimed. The accuracy of this evaluation

to construct items such as a tourist information centre and a bird watching hide on the development site even though they were not related to their application for planning permission. This decision was subsequently upheld on appeal [1993] JPL B81, CA.

16 See *R v Plymouth City Council* above, where the developers agreed to make substantial financial contributions toward a creche and industrial development.

17 [1993] JPL 919.

18 [1995] JPL 200, CA.

19 In this particular case development was not to commence under the terms of the s 106 agreements 'without taking all necessary steps including entering into any necessary additional legal agreements and bonding arrangements to bring all the terms of this Agreement into effect'. These additional steps could include the transfer of land.

20 There is, however, the additional problem that a local authority cannot be forced to accept a transfer of land.

is supported by the content of Circular 16/91[1] which sets out Department of the Environment policy regarding the use of planning obligations. In the first place the Circular makes the point that the term planning gain is 'imprecise and misleading' since it extends beyond what can legitimately be required of a developer. As a consequence, instead of explaining when planning gain may legitimately be required, the Circular advises when planning obligations may legitimately be used. Local planning authorities are instructed that planning applications should be considered on their merits. If there is some objection to a proposed development then thought should be given to the imposition of a planning condition. If this is not feasible then a planning obligation may be appropriate. The Circular then goes on to state the circumstances in which it will be reasonable to seek a planning obligation.[2] The first criteria for assessing a planning obligation's reasonableness is whether what it requires is needed to allow the development to take place, such as the provision of adequate car-parking space. Alternatively, if the developer is to make a financial contribution, will it meet the costs of whatever is needed. A planning obligation will also be acceptable if what is required by way of the obligation is so intimately related to the development and its subsequent use that permission should be withheld if it is not provided. Here, the provision of adequate open space or of community facilities that relate directly to the development are cited as examples. If what is required is designed to secure an appropriate balance of uses in a mixed development or to implement local plan policies, such as the inclusion of lower cost 'starter' homes in a large residential development, this too will be reasonable. Finally, a planning obligation can be employed to offset the loss to amenity produced as a consequence of the development. A developer may, for example, create a nature reserve if his development has led to the loss of wildlife habitats.

The Circular comments that section 106 obligations can affect property that is not the subject of the planning application, but if this is the case there does need to be some connection between the two. For example, if a development adversely affected a wildlife habitat, it would be acceptable for an obligation to offer to develop another suitable site in the ownership of the developer as an alternative wildlife habitat, providing that it was within a reasonable distance of the site to be developed. Finally, the question has to be asked whether what is being

1 Planning and Compensation Act 1991, Planning Obligations.
2 Circular 16/91, paras B8-B10.

required by a planning obligation '...is fairly and reasonably related in scale and kind to the proposed development'.[3] In other words, what this Circular is making plain is that planning gain, though it rejects the use of the expression, should be sought only where it is '...necessary to the granting of planning permission, relevant to planning, and relevant to the development to be permitted'.[4] The Circular makes it plain that this is the policy which Department of the Environment inspectors will pursue. It also warns that local planning authorities which ignore this advice may be susceptible to challenge in the courts.

In the light of these warnings it seems hardly surprising to discover that section 106 planning obligations have been the focus of a steady stream of litigation. Three general points have been raised:

(i) the criteria for determining whether a section 106 planning obligation is valid;

(ii) the appropriate test for concluding whether a section 106 planning obligation is a material consideration when resolving an application for planning permission;

(iii) the significance of Department of the Environment Circular 16/91.

The manner in which these issues have been resolved can be summarised in the following fashion. The House of Lords in *Tesco Stores Ltd v Secretary of State for the Environment*[5] has stated quite categorically that the validity of a planning obligation 'depends entirely on the terms of section 106'.[6] Provided these terms are observed and the obligation in question serves a planning purpose and is not totally unreasonable, then that planning obligation cannot be challenged on the grounds that it does not relate to any development for which planning permission is sought. In this respect the House of Lords has followed the reasoning in *Good v Epping Forest District Council*[7] even though the latter case was dealing with a section 52 agreement.

The *Tesco* case also has some relevant points to make on the question of whether a planning obligation is a material consideration when resolving an application for planning permission. In the *Tesco* case a number of supermarket chains had applied for planning permission to build superstores in the vicinity of Witney. One such application was not determined by

3 Ibid, para B9.
4 Ibid, para B7.
5 [1995] 2 All ER 636.
6 Ibid, at 656.
7 [1994] 2 All ER 156, CA.

the local planning authority within the required period and was the subject of an appeal. At the same time the Secretary of State called in Tesco's application so that both applications could be considered together. One of the issues that arose at the planning inquiry was the severe traffic congestion experienced in Witney town centre. A new road needed to be constructed but the relevant highway authority lacked the funds – £6.6 million – to embark on the project. Tesco offered to provide funding for the road but were still unsuccessful in securing planning permission which was granted to their rival. The Secretary of State, rejecting his inspector's recommendation, referred to his policy on planning obligations and in particular the requirements that any obligation should directly relate to the planning permission, should be necessary to the granting of planning permission and relevant to the development. In this case there was no evidence that the construction of a superstore would do anything other than marginally increase city centre traffic. Hence the planning obligation offered by Tesco did not measure up to Department of the Environment policy. Tesco then challenged this decision to refuse them planning permission. They did so on the grounds that the Secretary of State had failed to have regard to a material consideration, namely their offer of a planning obligation.

In its judgment the House of Lords made the point that it was a matter of law whether a consideration was a material consideration. In the context of an application for planning permission a material consideration meant a relevant consideration. The relevancy of a planning obligation would be established if it was for a planning purpose, fairly related to the proposed development and was not totally unreasonable. The court rejected the argument that to be material a planning obligation must also be necessary, that is, capable of making acceptable what was otherwise an unacceptable planning application. The point was made in the House of Lords and has been repeated in other cases that a planning obligation that has nothing whatsoever to do with the proposed development is not a material consideration.[8]

The House of Lords' judgment in the *Tesco* case then went on to say that if, using the criteria just outlined, a planning obligation was a material consideration, then quite clearly the

8 See *R v South Northamptonshire District Council, ex p Crest Homes plc* [1995] JPL 200, CA. In the course of his judgment (at 205) Henry LJ suggests that a 'benefit disproportionate to the adverse planning impact of the development to which it was linked would not fairly and reasonably relate to that development'.

Secretary of State must take it into account as he had done in this case. At this stage, however, it became a matter for his discretion how much weight he chose to give to the obligation. In determining this he could be guided by his own policy as set out in Circular 16/91.

> If it [the planning obligation] has some connection with the proposed development which is not de minimis, then regard must be had to it. But the extent, if any, to which it should affect the decision is a matter entirely within the discretion of the decision-maker and in exercising that discretion he is entitled to have regard to his established policy.[9]

Hence the *Tesco* case indicates the circumstances in which Circular 16/91 is relevant. It should, however, be recalled that that case involved a decision by the Secretary of State. In the *Plymouth* case[10] the local planning authority granted planning permission to two supermarket chains which had offered substantial benefits in the shape of planning obligations. On this occasion the decision to grant planning permission was unsuccessfully challenged. Here the planning obligation was a material consideration but the party deciding what weight to give it was the local planning authority. It would appear that in circumstances such as these the planning authority can totally disregard Circular 16/91 if it thinks fit. Since planning permission has been granted there will be no appeal and hence no occasion for the Secretary of State to reinstate his policy. The justification for this might be that some local planning authorities specifically refer to planning obligations in their development plan.[11] Since according to section 54A planning applications are now to be determined in accordance with the development plan unless material considerations indicate otherwise, the local planning authority is perfectly entitled to pursue its policy in relation to planning obligations.

Once concluded, various consequences accrue from the existence of a section 106 obligation, one of which is that the agreement is binding on any subsequent purchaser of the land.[12] Section 106A of the 1990 Act does, however, allow a planning obligation to be discharged or modified either by agreement or on the application of the person against whom the obligation is

9 *Tesco Stores Ltd v Secretary of State for the Environment* [1995] 2 All ER 636, at 647.

10 *R v Plymouth City Council* [1993] JPL B81, CA.

11 An example of this can be found in *R v South Northamptonshire District Council, ex p Crest Homes plc* [1995] JPL 200 at 203, CA.

12 1990 Act, s 106(3).

enforceable. Any unilateral request is considered initially by the local planning authority. Under section 106B, if the local authority does not agree to that request, an appeal can be made to the Secretary of State. Five years must elapse before the person against whom a planning obligation is enforceable can apply to have it varied or discharged. This corresponds to the period which is allowed for the implementation of a planning permission. The logic is that during that period a developer will be bound to act on his planning permission and hence undertake some of the commitments made in the planning obligation. The legislation also makes it plain that the local planning authority should agree to the modification or discharge of an obligation only if it is demonstrated that the obligation no longer serves a useful purpose, or that, if it does, the purpose may be equally well served by modifying the obligation.[13]

The mere fact that the machinery exists for discharging or modifying section 106 obligations emphasises the burden placed on the developer by these agreements. It is open to argument whether corresponding burdens are placed on a local planning authority. Questions have been raised over the ability of a local planning authority, which is a party to a section 106 obligation or to a planning agreement concluded under earlier planning legislation, to exercise other statutory powers and so negate the effect of that obligation or agreement. If, for example, a section 106 obligation is in place between a local planning authority and a developer, which is aimed at regulating the comprehensive development of a city centre, can that same local planning authority exercise its powers under section 69 of the Planning (Listed Buildings and Conservation Areas) Act 1990, and designate the area of redevelopment a conservation area? The effect of this would be to require the developer to obtain conservation area consent before demolishing buildings. It has always been regarded as a cardinal principle of English law that a public body cannot become involved in any activity that may hinder or fetter, in any way, the discharge of its statutory duties.[14] Any attempt, even if totally innocent, will be considered unlawful by the courts, and hence, of no effect. This is, of course, crucial to the lawful operation of a section 106 obligation, and it raises questions over the extent to which the local authority is legally bound.

Although planning obligations are freely negotiated agreements the situation may arise when a developer refuses

13 Ibid, s 106A(6).

14 See, for example, *British Oxygen Co Ltd v Minister of Technology* [1971] AC 610, HL.

to honour his undertakings in such an agreement. Faced by this prospect a local planning authority is entitled to pursue any remedies available to it under the law of contract, since a section 106 planning obligation is a legally binding agreement. This approach is illustrated in *Avon County Council v Millard*.[15] In this instance a section 52 agreement had been concluded to regulate the working of a quarry. Certain provisions in the agreement, requiring the construction of an access road and a fresh application for planning permission, were not observed. The issue here was whether the local authority must rely on enforcement proceedings in order to rectify the breach. While enforcement proceedings remain the appropriate remedy for rectifying a breach of planning control, a section 52 agreement represented a contract between the parties. In these circumstances, the Court of Appeal was prepared to affirm that the local authority might rely on ordinary civil remedies, including an injunction, to restrain the breach of the agreement. Civil remedies apart, a local planning authority which is a party to a planning obligation can also enforce it by carrying out any works required under the agreement which the developer refuses to perform and then recovering the costs of so doing from him.[16]

OTHER POWERS TO CONCLUDE AN AGREEMENT

Apart from section 106 planning obligations other statutes give local authorities the power to conclude agreements with developers. Some of these powers are very general in nature and do not specifically mention planning. A good example is section 111 of the Local Government Act 1972. It provides:

> Without prejudice to any powers exercisable apart from this section but subject to the provisions of this Act and any other enactment passed before or after this Act, a local authority shall have power to do anything (whether or not involving the expenditure, borrowing or lending of money or the acquisition or disposal of any property or rights) which is calculated to facilitate, or is conducive or incidental to, the discharge of any of their functions.

From its terms, it should be clear that the purpose of the section is to validate actions on the part of a local authority

15 [1986] JPL 211.
16 1990 Act, s 106(6).

which are not specifically mentioned elsewhere, but are crucial to the discharge of its functions. The kind of transactions, therefore, which will have a bearing on the development control process, and will fall within the scope of section 111 are likely to be business transactions. This section may be seen as authorising a lease of land to a developer, or a business arrangement between a local authority and a developer to undertake some large-scale project, such as the construction of a leisure park.[17] An anticipatory agreement of this nature, anticipatory in the sense that the whole transaction may depend on whether planning permission is granted or refused, can give a local authority a say in the development control process which it may not normally enjoy. An example will help to demonstrate the truth of this statement. A local authority owns a plot of land. It enters into an agreement with a company to build the English equivalent of Disneyland on the site. Some of the development will be undertaken directly by the local authority. The remainder will be financed from capital raised by the company. Obviously, as a business partner, the local authority will have a considerable say on how that project is undertaken and the final form it takes.

Yet business agreements with developers can be a source of considerable difficulty. The fact that such an agreement exists may mean that the developer finds himself applying for planning permission to that very local authority with whom he is in partnership. This can lead local residents to believe that, in granting planning permission, the local planning authority has not displayed that impartiality which is expected of it. In a series of decisions,[18] the courts have expressed the opinion that a local planning authority which behaves in this fashion is doing no more than it is permitted to do by law. The only exception would appear to be where an undertaking is given by a local planning authority to obtain planning permission for the proposed joint venture. In these circumstances a local planning

17 For examples of such agreements see *R v St Edmundsbury Borough Council* [1985] 3 All ER 234, *Steeples v Derbyshire County Council* [1984] 3 All ER 468.

18 *Steeples v Derbyshire County Council* [1984] 3 All ER 468, *R v Amber Valley District Council, ex p Jackson* [1984] 3 All ER 501, *R v Sevenoaks District Council, ex p Terry* [1985] 3 All ER 226, *R v St Edmundsbury Borough Council* [1985] 3 All ER 234, *R v Carlisle City Council, ex p CumbrianCo-operative Society Ltd* (1985) 276 Estates Gazette 1161, *R v Merton Borough Council and Speyhawk Land and Estates Ltd, ex p Burnett* [1990] JPL 354. See also the Town and Country Planning General Regulations 1992, SI 1992/1492.

authority will be regarded as rendering itself incapable of exercising its discretion to grant or refuse planning permission.[19]

In contrast to this very general power some statutes authorise a very specific type of agreement. Section 278 of the Highways Act 1980,[20] for example, permits a highway authority, which is often the local planning authority, to enter into an agreement whereby, in return for the authority undertaking highway works, an individual will meet either the whole or part of the costs of those works and may also contribute toward their maintenance once complete. When concluding an agreement of this nature the highway authority has to be satisfied that it will be of benefit to the public. If this is so the authority can exercise its powers of compulsory purchase to acquire land for the scheme and can incorporate special features at the request of the other party to the agreement. In the spirit of privatisation section 278 makes it clear that the costs the highway authority can recover can include much more than the construction costs alone.[1] In addition should an individual renege on his promise to meet these costs the highway authority can impose a variety of sanctions including denying access to the works in question.[2] What section 278 makes clear is that, as a matter of policy, central government now expects developers to meet the costs of remedying certain development control objections to their projects.

The relationship between agreements of this kind and other planning agreements, as well as planning conditions, needs to be considered. It will be recalled that a planning condition is unlikely to be valid if it requires a developer to undertake work on land which is not his, and over which he has no control. If, therefore, a developer proposes to build a block of flats, a local planning authority may feel that a grant of planning permission is in order, provided the road which runs alongside the flats is widened to cope with the extra traffic entering and leaving the building. A condition requiring the developer to undertake this

19 *Steeples v Derbyshire County Council* [1984] 3 All ER 468. Here the local authority had promised to use its best endeavours in order to obtain planning permission. Although the judgment refers to the decision of the planning committee as being biased, the better explanation would appear to be that the terms of the agreement were regarded as fettering the discretion of the planning committee to grant or refuse planning permission.

20 Section 23 of the New Roads and Street Works Act 1991 inserted a new s 278 into the Highways Act 1980 to replace the original version.

1 Highways Act 1980, s 278(2).

2 Ibid, s 278(5).

work will not be valid for the reasons given above,[3] though a condition which forbids a start being made on the development until the road works are complete might be acceptable.[4] As for section 106 of the 1990 Act, this sanctions agreements only if the developer has an interest in the land affected, which would not be the case in the situation under consideration. Section 278, therefore, offers a solution to this particular dilemma, since the work is carried out by the responsible body but not without a financial contribution from the developer who is deriving particular benefit from it.

It should be appreciated that section 278 agreements will be very specific in their contents. As such, they do not represent a direct implementation of development control policy. If, on the other hand, a local planning authority makes it a general policy requirement that any new development should not overload the existing road system, section 278 offers the opportunity to ensure that, in specific instances, general policy is observed. In that sense, this particular planning agreement offers a means to an end.

Finally if none of these powers is appropriate a local authority can sponsor a local Act of Parliament whose purpose is to give that local authority specific powers which it can exercise in its administrative area. The procedure for securing the passage of such an Act is distinct from that observed in the case of an Act of Parliament, which affects the population at large. These Acts are mentioned because they can offer an alternative to public general Acts. One example is to be found in the Oxfordshire Act 1985.

> 4(1) In order to achieve such provision as in the opinion of the local planning authority is appropriate having regard to the nature of any proposed development of land within the county, the local planning authority may, at the request of any person interested in the land, enter into agreement with such persons as they consider appropriate to secure the provision of all or any of the following matters or any related or consequential matter, including matters of a financial character:
>
> (a) the construction of new roads and road improvements required for or in connection with the development; and
>
> (b) the provision, maintenance or use of facilities for the parking of vehicles for or in connection with the development.

3 That is that it requires work to be undertaken on land not under the control of the developer. See *Bradford City Metropolitan Council v Secretary of State for the Environment* [1986] JPL 598, CA.

4 See, for example, *Grampian Regional Council v City of Aberdeen District Council* [1984] JPL 590, HL.

The extent of any powers may vary from Act to Act. What needs emphasising, however, is the existence of yet another opportunity to enter into an agreement with a developer. On the face of it, there may appear little to distinguish these powers from those already discussed. While undoubtedly the underlying purpose is the same, the wording in a local Act of Parliament may be tailored to that authority's needs, thus giving local Acts of Parliament the edge over public general Acts such as the Highways Act 1980.

Chapter 9

The last resort – appeals and enforcement

In entitling this chapter 'The last resort' the intention is to emphasise that beyond the local planning authority there is a second level of decision-making, capable of passing judgment on and reversing, either totally or in part, a local planning authority's development control decisions. This second level of decision-making is undoubtedly the last resort, since from it there is no appeal on the development control merits of a decision. Challenge in the courts is reserved for determining whether or not the law has been observed. There are two occasions when the development control decisions of a local planning authority will be re-evaluated. The first of these will be when an individual, having observed the development control system, is unhappy with the decision he has received. His challenge to that decision will take the form of a planning appeal. The purpose of a planning appeal is to re-examine the very issues which were relevant when the original development control decision was made.

In contrast, enforcement is appropriate only when the development control process has been disregarded. This book has proceeded on the basis that the development control system is observed by every individual and organisation wishing to undertake development. On this basis, any development that occurs is as the result of a reasoned development control decision taken in full knowledge of the circumstances, by a local planning authority. Unfortunately, this is far from being the true picture. Development can and does occur without an application being made for planning permission. Alternatively, the terms on which planning permission is granted may be deliberately ignored. When breakdowns occur in the development control system a local planning authority is faced with the decision whether or not to take enforcement proceedings. Little space is devoted in this book to the mechanics of enforcement. This is because enforcement is a formal and legalistic process whose complexities would take chapters to describe. Instead, the sole objective in considering enforcement is to see what light it sheds on the development control process. An attempt will be made to do this in two ways. First, by considering why individuals choose to ignore the development control system, and what convinces a local planning authority to take enforcement action. This can usefully be compared with a local planning authority's decision whether or not to grant planning permission. Secondly, a comparison can be made between planning appeals and enforcement appeals in order to determine what factors are relevant when challenging a local planning authority's decision to take enforcement proceedings. It remains to be seen whether they are the same factors that are relevant in the course of a planning appeal.

Planning appeals

There are several types of planning appeal. The commonest is the appeal which occurs when an individual is either refused planning permission, including a deemed refusal when a local planning authority fails to deal with an application for planning permission within the prescribed eight weeks, or is granted planning permission but subject to unacceptable conditions.[1] Since this is the most common, reference will be made to this type of planning appeal in order to illustrate the argument.[2] Unless specifically stated otherwise, it can be assumed that exactly the same considerations apply to all other forms of planning appeal.

WHY APPEAL?

There is a dual purpose to the question – why appeal? Initially, it raises the issue of why a right of appeal exists. If a local planning authority, which is fully aware of national planning policy, the development control policies of its own area and the planning needs of the community, either refuses or grants

1 Town and Country Planning Act 1990, ss 78 and 79.
2 Other forms of planning appeal include appeals to the Secretary of State against refusal of listed building consent – Planning (Listed Buildings and Conservation Areas) Act 1990, ss 20, 21 and appeals against refusal of permission for the display of advertisements – Town and Country Planning (Control of Advertisements) Regulations 1992, SI 1992/666, reg 15.

planning permission subject to conditions, then it seems logical that that should be an end to the matter. In an ideal world that might be so, but in practice, the local councillors who make up the planning committee may, in reaching their decision, have neglected national planning policy, or placed undue emphasis on a single factor, such as the strength of local protest, while failing to take account of other material considerations. Furthermore, since development control and planning permission are inextricably linked to the ability of the individual to use his property as he thinks fit, then the appeal can be seen as a form of quality control.[3] In this context it allows an official, who normally has no connection with the locality and the personalities involved, to make a fresh determination of the issues, applying relevant development control policies. The official can either confirm a local planning authority's decision to refuse planning permission, or reverse it. In the case of an appeal against the content of a planning condition, the appellant might find that even more onerous conditions are imposed in addition to the one he originally found objectionable, while the conclusion that a condition is unacceptable could result in planning permission being refused outright. All this is a consequence of the fact that a decision on appeal is a fresh development control decision. It should not be imagined from this that a local planning authority is incapable of being objective or impartial. Instead, the appeal allows an applicant for planning permission to pursue the matter if the applicant feels that this is warranted on the merits of the application.

The right of appeal, if acted upon, can place a considerable strain on the resources of a local planning authority. Obviously, the longer the period which elapses between a decision and an appeal, the greater that strain can become. Circumstances can change, not to mention personnel, as well as fresh proposals being received for the building or land in question. In the light of these facts, the relevant legislation limits the time for making a planning appeal to six months from the date the decision was notified to the individual, or the expiry of any relevant period.[4] The only exception is an appeal to the Secretary of State against

3 As has been said elsewhere a planning appeal can also serve as a means of ensuring that government development control policies are observed. For a more detailed discussion of the purposes served by planning appeals, see Purdue M *Planning Appeals: A Critique* (1991) pp 2-5.

4 Town and Country Planning (General Development Procedure) Order 1995, SI 1995/419, art 23. The relevant period referred to is the eight-week period mentioned in art 20 within which a local planning authority should reach a decision on a planning application.

the decision of a local planning authority refusing consent for, or restricting the display of, an advertisement. Here, the relevant period is two months, the shorter period being justified by the very specific issues such an appeal will raise.[5]

The emphasis on the use of the appeal as a means of re-evaluating the merits of a planning application raises a second issue. The Planning Inspectorate Annual Report for the year ended 31 March 1994[6] showed that 14,979 planning appeals were received. This compares with 17,959 in the previous year. It demonstrates that those who choose to appeal represent a minority of those who are refused planning permission. Numerous explanations can be offered for this. The applicant may be convinced that his application is so at odds with local or national planning policy that it will stand no chance of success. Alternatively, it may be clear after consultation with the local planning authority, that if the scheme were modified in some way then planning permission would be granted, or an onerous condition removed. In such circumstances a fresh application for planning permission may be made instead of an appeal. In addition, the right of appeal may not be utilised because an applicant does not possess the resources, particularly the financial resources, to proceed. Appeals take time and cost money.[7]

Whatever the reasons for either choosing or declining to take advantage of the appeals process, the decision is one for the applicant to reach. It is, however, in the interests of both central and local government to have as few appeals as possible. This is because appeals stretch the resources of the local planning authority, since officials within its planning department will have to prepare a full justification of the development control decision. The Department of the Environment has also to provide adjudicators to listen to and resolve such appeals as speedily as possible. Circular 18/86, Planning Appeals Decided by Written Representations, makes the point that appeals should be exceptional rather than routine:

5 Town and Country Planning (Control of Advertisements) Regulations 1992, SI 1992/666, Sch 4, Pt III.

6 Journal of Planning and Environment Law, 1994, p 978.

7 In planning appeals the parties normally meet their own costs. Circular 8/93, Award of Costs Incurred in Planning and Other (Including Compulsory Purchase Order) Proceedings, gives advice on the circumstances when the Secretary of State may award costs against one of the parties in a planning appeal. An appellant may recover costs if, for example, a local planning authority gives a fresh reason for refusal of planning permission at a late stage in the proceedings (annex 2, para 4).

> before a disappointed applicant for planning permission lodges an appeal there should be consultation and negotiation. Difficulties can be more quickly and cheaply resolved by discussions of this kind than if an appeal is made to the Secretary of State. An appeal is intended to be, and should remain, a last resort.[8]

Potential appellants are advised to:

> assess the merits of their case and the prospects of success and balance these against the costs and time involved in an appeal. In particular, careful study of the policy background – in development plans, Department circulars, advice notes and elsewhere – is essential. Clearly stated policies which have been endorsed through the structure and local plan system and which remain relevant to present day circumstances are unlikely to be set aside lightly.[9]

The Department of the Environment's view of planning appeals is a correct one in some respects. Obviously, if an appeal can be avoided this will save time and money. Yet the exhortation to look to policy may, on occasions, have a hollow ring. It may be precisely because an applicant has looked to all the appropriate policy documents that he is persuaded, in the first place to apply for planning permission, and then, to appeal. The structure plan may be vague, no district-wide local plan may exist and Department of the Environment circulars and planning policy guidance notes may appear to contradict what little local policy there is. Planning appeals may be symptomatic, not of the obstinacy of applicants, but of the shortcomings of the development control system, particularly with regard to policy.

APPEAL TO WHOM?

If an applicant does decide to appeal, then the next matter to be settled is who will determine that appeal. Normally, appeals are made to the Secretary of State. The sheer number of planning appeals means, however, that some machinery has to exist for others to hear appeals on the Secretary of State's behalf. The individuals with responsibility for doing just that are planning inspectors. It is their task to assess the development control arguments put forward in the course of a planning appeal and it is not their function mechanistically to apply

8 Circular 18/86, para 7.
9 Ibid, para 8.

Department of the Environment policy.[10] Planning inspectors are well qualified to perform this task. Some may hold formal planning qualifications, others may be professionally qualified in other fields, such as law or surveying.

The role of the planning inspector in resolving planning appeals has changed over the years. In the past, he would hear an appeal and then prepare a report containing his recommendations. These recommendations would then be submitted to the relevant Minister for him to take the final decision. If, therefore, the Secretary of State did not intend to adopt an inspector's recommendation, he had to explain why. As long as the ultimate responsibility for determining planning appeals lay with the Secretary of State, the inspector's role could be seen as one involving the gathering of evidence, the summarisation of argument and the preparation of recommendations. The Secretary of State was then free to reach a different determination on those facts and arguments.

In terms of time and resources, such a method of proceeding can hardly be described as efficient. Therefore, the Secretary of State, using powers he possesses has sought to rectify the situation.[11] Regulations have been issued, specifying classes of appeal which may be determined not by the Secretary of State, but by a person appointed by him, that is, a planning inspector. The current regulations are the Town and Country Planning (Determination of Appeals by Appointed Persons) (Prescribed Classes) Regulations 1981.[12] Appeals covered by these regulations include all appeals against the refusal of planning permission, or the content of conditions attached to planning permissions, appeals against enforcement notices and appeals against the refusal of listed building consent, or consent to demolish buildings in a conservation area.

Even though the purpose of the 1981 Regulations is to allow others to determine planning appeals on his behalf, the Secretary of State can, if he chooses, direct that an appeal shall be determined by him. At present, the Secretary of State is still

10 Planning inspectors are no longer part of the workforce of the Department of the Environment. The Planning Inspectorate became an executive agency on 1 April 1992. Executive agencies have been created to improve efficiency. They are managed independently and are expected to observe certain performance targets. They function within the policy framework set by the relevant government department, in this case that of the Department of the Environment.

11 1990 Act, Sch 6, Determination of Certain Appeals by Persons Appointed by the Secretary of State.

12 SI 1981/804.

responsible for considering certain appeals which involve Grade I or Grade II listed buildings, as well as appeals in relation to buildings for which grants have been made under the Historic Buildings and Ancient Monuments Act 1953.[13] In addition, appeals which concern development by statutory undertakers will normally be determined by the Secretary of State.[14] Apart from any indication given in the 1981 Regulations, it is a matter of judgment for the Secretary of State whether he considers an appeal so important as to merit scrutiny by his Department. The factors which are relevant in persuading him of this fact have been identified as follows:[15]

(a) residential development of 150 or more houses;
(b) proposals for development of major importance and having more than local significance;
(c) proposals giving rise to significant public controversy;
(d) proposals which raise important or novel issues of development control;
(e) retail development over 100,000 square feet;
(f) proposals for significant development in the green belt;
(g) major proposals involving the winning and working of minerals;
(h) proposals which raise significant legal difficulties;
(i) proposals against which another government department has raised major objections;
(j) cases which can only be decided in conjunction with a case over which inspectors have no jurisdiction.

From this it is apparent that planning appeals will be singled out for determination by the Secretary of State which, because of their size, complexity or sensitive nature, raise important development control issues. Some of the criteria in this list are, however, far from specific. At what level opposition to a proposed development becomes 'significant public controversy' is a matter for conjecture. Nor is the list intended to provide more than a guide, the Secretary of State may always act and 'call-in' an appeal if he feels that the circumstances warrant it.[16]

The consequence of transferring jurisdiction to determine planning appeals to inspectors, is that the majority of appeals will be dealt with in this fashion. Exceptions, apart from those

13 Planning (Listed Buildings and Conservation Areas) Act 1990, ss 20, 39.
14 SI 1981/804, reg 4.
15 Planning Appeals, Call-in and Major Public Inquiries (1986) Cmnd 43, para 36.
16 On average 2% of planning appeals are recovered for determination by the Secretary of State each year. That amounts to between 400 and 500 appeals.

already mentioned, include appeals against a local planning authority's refusal or failure to issue either a certificate of lawfulness of proposed use or development or a certificate of lawfulness of existing use or development.[17] The explanation for their referral to the Secretary of State lies in the fact that they call for a narrow determination of whether or not the decision was 'well founded', rather than an interpretation of development control policy. Appeals against the refusal or restriction of permission to display an advertisement also go direct to the Secretary of State.[18]

In principle, allowing inspectors to determine planning appeals on behalf of the Secretary of State seems unobjectionable. The inspector will, in all probability, have viewed the site and heard the arguments. There seems to be no good reason, therefore, why he should not finally determine the matter in the majority of cases. This makes even greater sense when it is recalled that in the days when inspectors were restricted to submitting their recommendations, those recommendations were, in the main, adopted. If objections are to be raised to this practice they must surely relate to uncertainty over the exact role of the inspector when he determines appeals on behalf of the Secretary of State. In addition, this raises the related problem of consistency. According to Schedule 6 to the 1990 Act:

> An appointed person shall have the same powers and duties–
> (a) in relation to an appeal under section 78, as the Secretary of State has under ... section 79.[19]

What this fails to explain, however, is the way in which the inspector is to make use of planning policy. For example, a builder refused planning permission to build fifty houses may appeal. The inspector conducting the appeal will listen to the arguments for and against granting planning permission. On behalf of the builder, reference may be made to PPG 3, Housing, and the following statement:

> Marginal shortfalls in the supply of housing land are not in themselves an overriding reason for granting planning permission. However, where an up-to-date land availability study shows a substantial short fall in land supply, the need to

17 The power does exist for jurisdiction to be transferred to planning inspectors – 1990 Act, s 195(6) – but it has not been acted on.

18 Town and Country Planning (Control of Advertisements) Regulations 1992, SI 1992/666, reg 15.

19 Sch 6, para 2(1).

increase supply should be given considerable weight in dealing with planning applications, particularly where development can be permitted which would in other respects be in accordance with the policies in the plan.[20]

This may be supported by the allegation that there is no adequate supply of housing land. In its turn, the local planning authority may attempt to refute this argument, as well as advancing clear planning objections to the residential development of the land in question. Any such objections may be reinforced by reference to policies in the development plan. In these circumstances, it is the task of the inspector to interpret the application of these policies to the land in question.

Since, however, the Secretary of State is an initiator of development control policy, it is always possible for him, when determining an appeal, to decline to follow his own policy guidelines. Alternatively, he might use the occasion to create new policy rather than rely on policy already set out in the usual sources. This may be exceptional, but it is perfectly feasible as long as the Secretary of State justifies his decision with adequate reasons.[1] The ability of an inspector similarly to create new policy, is more questionable. In considering his role in conducting an appeal the courts have had occasion to make the following observations. In their view, the inspector should not be treated as a policy-maker.[2] Such an assertion seems incontrovertible if it merely points out that an inspector cannot totally disregard existing policy and attempt instead to produce his own policy on the day.

The situation can, however, arise where an inspector is faced with a circular, PPG or development plan whose wording is vague and needs clarification. In the course of determining an appeal he may seek to clarify or interpret that policy. In a sense, this could be regarded as policy-making. The difficulty is that if several inspectors are faced with the same problem they may not agree. In *Chelmsford Borough Council v Secretary of State for the Environment*,[3] the following view was expressed on the status of inspectors' decisions:

He [the inspector] was not, and should not be regarded as having any authority on behalf of the Secretary of State to lay down any general policy, or as giving a decision which should be treated

20 PPG 3, para 53.
1 *Gransden & Co Ltd v Secretary of State for the Environment* [1986] JPL 519 at 521. Decision affirmed on other grounds in [1987] JPL 365, CA.
2 *Sears Blok v Secretary of State for the Environment* [1980] JPL 523.
3 [1985] JPL 316.

> as a precedent for other planning applications or other planning appeals in the area, save to a limited extent.[4]

That limited extent would seem to entitle an appellant to bring to an inspector's attention as a material consideration other inspectors' decisions, including their interpretation of a particular policy. This does not mean that those decisions have to be followed, though presumably reasons should be given for distinguishing between them.[5] In the event, this view of the role of inspectors could give rise to inconsistency in the way a particular policy is applied.

While making it clear that inspectors are not policy-makers, the courts have been prepared to acknowledge that they may, by virtue of their background, possess considerable professional expertise. This may be used in evaluating expert evidence, and the arguments produced in the course of an appeal. In *Mason v Secretary of State for the Environment*,[6] an inspector was said to have misconstrued expert evidence on noise. In rejecting this contention, it was said:

> an inspector was not bound to follow expert evidence even if it was unchallenged. He had to bring to bear on the issues in the appeal his experience, his own expertise and his common sense. This might be particularly important where noise was concerned for it was common knowledge that the effect of noise on human beings was very variable. The measurement of noise emission by instruments was simply the best that science could do in a very subjective field.[7]

THE CONDUCT OF APPEALS

Planning appeals can be conducted in two ways, either by written representations,[8] or by local public inquiry.[9] Written representations necessitate the appellant and the local planning

4 Ibid, at 333.

5 *Rockhold Ltd v Secretary of State for the Environment* [1986] JPL 130 at 131, *Barnet London Borough Council v Secretary of State for the Environment* [1992] JPL 540.

6 [1984] JPL 332.

7 Ibid, at 333.

8 For the procedure to be observed when a planning appeal is conducted by written representations, see the Town and Country Planning Appeals (Written Representations Procedure) Regulations 1987, SI 1987/701.

9 For the procedure to be observed when a planning appeal is conducted by public inquiry, see the Town and Country Planning (Inquiries Procedure) Rules 1992, SI 1992/2038, and the Town and Country Planning Appeals (Determination by Inspectors) (Inquiries Procedure) Rules 1992, SI 1992/2039.

authority fully setting out their arguments in writing. Other interested parties can also submit their views in writing. The appeal is then determined, without the parties meeting, on the strength of that written evidence, though the individual determining the appeal can make a site visit beforehand.

In contrast, a public inquiry allows a personal confrontation between the parties. It resembles, in certain respects, a judicial hearing. Each party, who may or may not be legally represented, puts their case and can call expert evidence to support it. The inspector, who conducts the inquiry, takes note of the arguments produced and can seek any further clarification that he thinks necessary. Once the public hearing comes to an end, there is a site visit. After considering all the evidence, the inspector will determine whether, on the development control issues, to allow or reject the appeal. The decision is normally communicated to the parties by letter several weeks after the conclusion of the public inquiry.

There are advantages and disadvantages to these alternative methods of hearing an appeal. The advantages of written representations are that they allow an appeal to be dealt with more speedily and at less cost. When a public inquiry is to be held, a date for that inquiry has to be specified some time in advance in order to allow those concerned to prepare their case and to take account of the availability of an inspector to hold the inquiry. In contrast, where written representations are used the parties can work to a strict timetable.[10] That said, the advantage of a public inquiry is that it allows a direct exchange of views. Members of the public can attend and, if they are permitted to, can comment on the proposed development. In such circumstances what appear to be insignificant points can assume a new importance. The written representations method obviously lacks immediacy, and it is not accessible to the public at large.

In the opinion of the Department of the Environment, however, the advantages of the written representations method, in terms of cost and speed, outweigh its disadvantages. This view is apparently shared by those involved in planning appeals since the majority are conducted by written representations.[11]

10 That timetable is to be found in Circular 11/87, Town and Country Planning (Appeals) (Written Representations Procedures) Regulations 1987, annex A.

11 According to the Planning Inspectorate Annual Report for the year ending 31 March 1993, 82% of appeals were dealt with by the written representations procedure.

Although this procedure has points in its favour there are drawbacks associated with it. The parties involved do not always observe the strict timetable. In such circumstances a decision can be made on whatever material has been received, although this is a discretionary power that the decision-maker may be reluctant to exercise.[12] There has also been debate over the exact purpose of the site visit and whether, as a matter of course, the parties to the appeal should be allowed to attend.

Whilst written representations may be satisfactory in the majority of planning appeals, circumstances may exist where this will not be so. Obviously, the more complex a development appeal, the more issues involved and the greater the level of public interest, the more justification there may be for holding a public inquiry. As matters stand at present, the choice of procedure is determined by the parties. Hence, it is possible for either the local planning authority or the applicant to insist on a public inquiry however straightforward the appeal. Alternatively, the parties could agree to use the written representations method in circumstances where the complexity of the issues involved would suggest otherwise. When such situations arise, the Department of the Environment appears to have some discretion in the matter and may suggest an informal hearing as an alternative.[13] The informal hearing represents a halfway house. Both parties set out their case in writing and then a hearing is held which they attend together with any interested third parties. The purpose of the hearing is to allow the discussion of issues and it is the job of the inspector to determine how any debate will be structured. There is no legislation regulating the conduct of such informal hearings, simply a code of practice.

As to the correct procedure to be followed on appeal, that depends on how the appeal is to be conducted. If it is to be determined by the written representations method then a timetable is set by the Department of the Environment which indicates what information should be sent, to whom and when. A diagrammatic representation of that timetable is set out in Circular 11/87. The aim is to ensure that before a decision is reached:

12 Town and Country Planning (Appeals) (Written Representations Procedure) Regulations 1987, SI 1987/701, reg 9(1). See *Geha v Secretary of State for the Environment* (1993) 68 P & CR 139, CA.

13 The number of appeals conducted by informal hearing has grown steadily. 1,862 informal hearings were held in the year ending 31 March 1993. See Stubbs M 'Planning Appeals by Informal Hearing' Journal of Planning and Environment Law, 1994, p 710.

(i) the appellant has notified the local planning authority of his reasons for appealing;
(ii) the local planning authority has informed the appellant of its reasons for arriving at the decision to which he objects;
(iii) each party has had the chance to comment on their opponent's case;
(iv) the views of interested third parties have been taken into account and commented upon when necessary;
(v) any exchange of views is as succinct as possible, though a local planning authority is given an opportunity to expand its argument beyond the reasons it may initially have given when determining the application.

By observing the timetable and these simple rules, it should be possible to guarantee that an appeal has been handled fairly and cannot, therefore, be the subject of a challenge in the courts on the grounds of some procedural impropriety.[14]

Where an appeal is conducted, not by the written representations method but by means of public inquiry, the procedure to be followed is set out in the Town and Country Planning (Inquiries Procedure) Rules 1992[15] and the Town and Country Planning Appeals (Determination by Inspectors) (Inquiries Procedure) Rules 1992.[16] Additionally Circular 24/92 which has been prepared to cover both sets of Rules contains a 'Good Practice at Planning Inquiries' guide as an annex. The set of Rules to be followed depends on whether the Secretary of State or an inspector will finally determine that appeal. Each set of Rules gives a description of what has to be done prior to the holding of an inquiry, the procedures to be observed in the course of the inquiry, and post-inquiry conduct. Broadly, the requirements of the two sets of Rules are similar. The aim is to ensure, once again, that when a decision is reached, there are no grounds for challenging it in the courts on the basis that it was not fairly made.

Clearly, where an appeal is conducted by public inquiry the rules must anticipate such eventualities as a request for postponement, which will not arise when an appeal is determined by the written representations method. Consequently, the detail to be found in the Inquiries Procedure Rules is much greater than that to be observed in the timetable for written

14 1990 Act, s 288.
15 SI 1992/2038.
16 SI 1992/2039.

representations. It is also a truism, but one which deserves repeating, that the greater the detail, the greater the opportunity for errors to be made. A failure to observe the correct procedure can be a ground for challenging a decision in the courts, but only if it causes substantial prejudice to the person concerned.[17]

While no detailed account will be given of the Inquiries Procedure Rules, certain general points need to be made concerning their operation. Attention needs to be drawn to the fact that the procedure to be observed during the duration of the inquiry is to a degree, according to the Inquiries Procedure Rules, a matter for the inspector's discretion.[18] For example, an inspector has discretion in the matter of who may appear at a public inquiry, apart, that is, from those parties who have a right to appear.[19] Where the Rules do indicate what should occur, on the issue of cross-examination,[20] for example, parallels are immediately suggested between a public inquiry and a judicial hearing. Whether such a comparison is appropriate depends, perhaps, on what a public inquiry seeks to achieve. A judicial hearing is an adversarial process with one party trying to prove, and the other disprove, a particular contention. In contrast, the purpose of the public inquiry is to allow the correct development control decision to be taken.

The use of judicial techniques, such as cross-examination, at a public inquiry has its critics, but the fact that these procedures are employed may be a reflection of the desire to treat each party fairly. This has not prevented calls being made for inspectors to adopt a more inquisitorial approach to the public inquiry procedure.[1] An inspector, it is argued, should actively seek information from the parties, rather than simply listen to argument. If, however, an inspector is minded to do just this, he should avoid doing so in circumstances that cause others to believe either that he has prejudged the issue, or that he is not

17 1990 Act, s 288(5)(b).

18 Town and Country Planning (Inquiries Procedure) Rules 1992, SI 1992/2038, r 14(1); Town and Country Planning Appeals (Determination by Appointed Persons)(Inquiries Procedure) Rules 1992, SI 1992/2039, r 15(1).

19 Town and Country Planning (Inquiries Procedure) Rules 1992, SI 1992/2038, r 11; Town and Country Planning Appeals (Determination by Appointed Persons) (Inquiries Procedure) Rules 1992, SI 1992/2039, r 11.

20 Town and Country Planning (Inquiries Procedure) Rules 1992, SI 1992/2038, r 14(3), (4), (5); Town and Country Planning Appeals (Determination by Appointed Persons) (Inquiries Procedure) Rules 1992, SI 1992/2039, r 15(3), (4), (5).

1 Keeble L *Fighting Planning Appeals* (1985) pp 30-31.

giving the other party a chance to rebut what 'his opponent' has said.[2] This is again a reflection of the need to be fair.

The same need to be fair also accounts for the quite detailed rules on the procedures to be observed once a public inquiry has ended. Should new evidence be offered by one of the parties and be taken into account, or a new issue of fact be raised, then both parties must be given an adequate opportunity to comment, including the option of asking for the public inquiry to be reopened.[3] The one positive point in favour of this apparent obsession with fairness, is that any judicial challenge is unlikely to succeed if the rules are observed. Whether, on the other hand, it leads to important development control issues being neglected or obscured is another question.

THE DECISION

If a planning appeal is determined using the written representations method or a public inquiry, and whether the responsibility for the decision rests with an inspector or the Secretary of State, the culmination of every appeal is a decision letter. The decision letter is exceedingly important, since it contains a summary of the arguments raised during the course of the appeal, as well as the reasons justifying the particular decision reached. Its contents have a twofold importance. They indicate to the appellant and the local planning authority what factors, including development control policy, were crucial in reaching that particular decision. In addition, that letter can provide the basis for a challenge to the courts. Although that process is discussed in the next chapter, it should be appreciated at this stage that it is from the decision letter that evidence will be sought to support such a challenge.

This puts the writer of the decision letter in a dilemma. However carefully such a letter is drafted, there may be the occasional ambiguity or omission. If this occurs, and if it is made the subject of a judicial challenge, the courts have to assess whether its presence warrants the setting aside of that particular development control decision. In evaluating the decision letter the courts can either subject it to a detailed analysis, or regard it as unsuitable for such treatment, since the letter is intended to be read as a whole and against the

2 See, for example, *Halifax Building Society v Secretary of State for the Environment* [1983] JPL 816.

3 Town and Country Planning (Inquiries Procedure) Rules 1992, SI 1992/2038, r 16; Town and Country Planning Appeals (Determination by Appointed Persons) (Inquiries Procedure) Rules 1992, SI 1992/2039, r 17.

background of the earlier proceedings. Evidence can be produced from the cases to illustrate each approach.[4] If one approach is to be preferred, however, it is to consider the decision letter as a whole. Not only does this appear the more sensible approach, but it seems to be the one favoured by the courts. Indeed, the courts appear to have gone even further by suggesting that the decision letter which determines an appeal by written representations can be briefer and more to the point than the decision letter which determines a public inquiry.[5] The distinction is justified on the basis that written representations appeals will be straightforward with no disputes over facts.

Enforcement

WHY DO BREACHES OCCUR?

Research seems to suggest that there are a variety of reasons why an individual may fail to observe the development control system. Ignorance is certainly a factor. It can range from total ignorance of the existence of the development control system, to partial ignorance. An individual may not appreciate the significance of the term 'development', believing that the planned activity either does not constitute development, or is permitted development. Obviously, advice can be sought from the local planning authority, but this fact may not be appreciated.[6] There is, of course, the additional burden of planning fees which are levied each time an application is made for planning permission. Given these circumstances, therefore, an individual may prefer to trust his own understanding of the planning system. Ignorance apart, the instances where an individual deliberately decides to flout the development control system may be comparatively rare.[7] Much will depend on the

4 Some judges examine a decision letter line by line, others take a more generous approach. See, for example, *Dimsdale Developments (South East) Ltd v Secretary of State for the Environment* [1986] JPL 276; *Chelmsford Borough Council v Secretary of State for the Environment* [1986] JPL 112.

5 *Sir George Grenfell-Baines v Secretary of State for the Environment* [1985] JPL 256 at 257.

6 Individuals and organisations are encouraged to seek advice from local planning authorities. See, for example, PPG 4, Industrial and Commercial Development and Small Firms, para 13. No charge can be made for pre-application advice. *McCarthy & Stone (Developments) Ltd v London Borough of Richmond Upon Thames* [1992] 2 AC 48, [1991] 4 All ER 897, HL.

7 These are more likely to be associated with a situation where the individual has been warned of restrictions on his ability to act. For example, where a tree preservation order is in existence.

particular circumstances of the case. The temptation to ignore some aspect of the development control system may be strong if it will, for example, result in an immediate financial gain.[8] Other deliberate breaches of development control may simply be incidents in a wider set of events. The decision to establish a caravan site without planning permission may be seen by the instigator as a protest against the failure of a local authority to provide gypsy caravan sites.

Apart from dealing with failures to apply for planning permission or other consents,[9] enforcement proceedings may occur when conditions attached to a grant of planning permission are deliberately flouted. Here, there is no question of ignorance. As has already been mentioned, an individual who believes a condition is uncalled for can challenge it in a variety of ways.[10] The decision not to do so but simply to ignore it, is definitely premeditated.

HOW ARE BREACHES DISCOVERED?

A breach of the development control system will not automatically come to the attention of a local planning authority. Breaches become apparent in various ways – the most usual is a complaint by a neighbour. An individual may become self-employed, selling rustic bird tables from his home. As the business becomes more successful neighbours may become aware of lorries delivering materials to the house, noise from equipment, and individuals arriving to purchase bird tables. Once traffic and noise reach a certain level, neighbours may complain and it is at that stage that a local planning authority may be alerted to a possible breach of the development control system.

8 This factor is taken into account when setting the penalties for flouting the development control system. Section 179 of the 1990 Act, for example, deals with prosecutions for non-compliance with an enforcement notice. If the offence is tried in a magistrates' court a fine of up to £20,000 may be imposed. If tried on indictment there is no limit on the fine. In both cases the court is required to have regard to any financial benefit which may have accrued in setting the level of the fine (s 179(9)).

9 These include listed building consent or consents needed in relation to a tree preservation order for the felling of trees.

10 These methods include an appeal to the Secretary of State under s 78 of the 1990 Act and an application to the local planning authority under s 73 of the 1990 Act for permission to proceed with the development of land without complying with the conditions attached to a grant of planning permission. If a planning permission has been acted upon without a relevant condition being observed s 73A of the 1990 Act permits an individual to apply for retrospective planning permission to act in this fashion.

There is evidence that local planning authorities rely to a considerable extent on members of the public alerting them to breaches of development control.[11] The alternative is for local planning authorities themselves to have some systematic scheme for monitoring development in their area. In terms of manpower and resources, this is not feasible although the development control system does offer some opportunities for planning authorities to be proactive in their pursuit of breaches.[12] Once alerted to a possible breach the local planning authority has a number of powers which allow it to investigate the allegation in order to discover whether it is well-founded. These include powers to enter property[13] as well as to issue a planning contravention notice.[14] The latter requires certain information to be provided to the local planning authority in the expectation that this will enable the authority to determine what is happening, whether it is authorised and what steps should be taken.

THE ENFORCEMENT PROCESS

Having described the circumstances in which breaches of the development control system can be detected, it now becomes necessary to comment on the process of enforcement. In the past the system was criticised for its excessive technicality and delay. As a consequence a thorough overhaul of enforcement procedures occurred[15] and Part VII of the 1990 Act is the result.[16] Substantial guidance on both the operational and the policy aspects of enforcement are provided in Circular 21/91 and PPG 18.[17] The power to initiate enforcement action is given to a local planning authority in section 172(1) of the 1990 Act:

> The local planning authority may issue a notice ... where it appears to them –
>
> (a) that there has been a breach of planning control; and

11 See Millichap D *The Effective Enforcement of Planning Controls* (1991) ch 2.

12 When conducting mineral workings reviews for example. Ibid, ch 2.

13 1990 Act, ss 196A, 196B and 196C.

14 Ibid, ss 171C-171D.

15 Carnwath R, Enforcing Planning Control (1989). The recommendations in this report were implemented by the Planning and Compensation Act 1991 which amended Pt VII of the 1990 Act.

16 Separate enforcement procedures exist for listed buildings – Planning (Listed Buildings and Conservation Areas) Act 1990, ss 38-46.

17 Circular 21/91, Planning and Compensation Act 1991: Implementation of the Main Enforcement Provisions; PPG 18, Enforcing Planning Control.

(b) that it is expedient to issue the notice having regard to the provisions of the development plan and to any other material considerations.

The first point to note about this power is that it is discretionary. A local planning authority may act but it is under no duty to do so.[18] Second, in exercising its judgment the authority must have regard to those very factors which are relevant when the local planning authority is determining whether or not to grant planning permission. Therefore, despite receiving numerous complaints about a breach of planning control, a local planning authority can choose on planning grounds not to act. In practice, it appears that enforcement is regarded as a last resort. A local planning authority may try to resolve a problem by negotiation, or by accepting a retrospective application for planning permission. Indeed, minor breaches may be totally ignored if they appear to be causing no inconvenience.[19] Far from denigrating this approach, it has the support of the Department of the Environment in PPG 18.[20]

When the alleged breach consists of a failure to observe a planning condition the local planning authority has the option of issuing a breach of condition notice.[1] As Circular 1/85 stresses, planning conditions should be used only if they are necessary to permit a particular development to proceed.[2] If those very conditions are then flouted, every effort should be made to rectify the situation. A breach of condition notice provides an apparently simple and focused procedure for achieving this which avoids some of the complexities associated with conventional enforcement action, such as an appeal to the Secretary of State. In practice, however, misgivings have been expressed over the wisdom of using a breach of condition notice in all but the clearest of cases. The simplicity of the process is said to hide a 'maze of complexities'[3] which raise very difficult points of law.

18 Its decision not to take action could, however, be the subject of judicial review. *R v Sevenoaks District Council, ex p Palley* [1994] EGCS 148. For a discussion of judicial review see chapter 10.

19 This appears logical since the main reason for taking enforcement action should be to prevent damage to the amenity of an area.

20 PPG 18, para 5.

1 1990 Act, s 187A.

2 Circular 1/85, The Use of Conditions in Planning Permissions, para 12.

3 *Encyclopedia of Planning Law and Practice*, Vol 2, p 187A.05. See also Bourne F *Enforcement of Planning Control* (2nd, edn 1992), chapter 9 and Hainsworth D 'Breach of Condition Notices – Theory and Practice', Journal of Planning and Environment Law, 1993, p 903.

If a local planning authority does decide to use its powers under section 172 to issue an enforcement notice, the object of that notice is to rectify the breach of planning control. Therefore, besides specifying the breach, the notice will also indicate the steps which must be taken to achieve this. According to section 173:

> (3) An enforcement notice shall specify the steps which the authority require to be taken, or the activities which the authority require to cease, in order to achieve, wholly or partly, any of the following purposes.
> (4) Those purposes are –
> (a) remedying the breach by making any development comply with the terms (including conditions and limitations) of any planning permission which has been granted in respect of the land, by discontinuing any use of the land or by restoring the land to its condition before the breach took place; or
> (b) remedying any injury to amenity which has been caused by the breach.
> (5) An enforcement notice may, for example, require –
> (a) the alteration or removal of any buildings or works;
> (b) the carrying out of any building or other operations;
> (c) any activity on the land not to be carried on except to the extent specified in the notice; or
> (d) the contour of a deposit of refuse or waste materials on land to be modified by altering the gradient or gradients of its sides.

The notice should also indicate the period within which such steps should be taken.

It is very plain that the object of an enforcement notice is remedial as opposed to penal. No punishment is to be inflicted on the individual who breaches planning control. This is in direct contrast with the position of an individual who fells a tree protected by a tree preservation order,[4] or who demolishes or alters a listed building without authorisation.[5] In these situations a criminal sanction, in the form of a fine, is immediately imposed, presumably on the basis that such actions may be much harder, if not impossible, to rectify.

While the principle underlying an enforcement notice seems comparatively clear, its contents have long been a source of potential legal challenges. Cases abounded on whether an enforcement notice specified with sufficient clarity the steps which had to be taken to remedy a breach, or the relevant key

4 1990 Act, s 210.
5 Planning (Listed Buildings and Conservation Areas) Act 1990, s 9.

dates, such as the date for compliance.[6] This emphasis on precision in enforcement notices may seem unduly legalistic. Its justification lies in the fact that any individual, who is the object of an enforcement notice, may have to undertake activities which involve a considerable financial burden. Arguably, it is only fair that he knows exactly what the breach is, and how and when it is supposed to be remedied. A vaguely worded notice may cause work to be undertaken which is not necessary, or indeed, which is not intended. Nor should it be forgotten that failure to comply with an enforcement notice is a criminal offence. The concept of fairness is seen as crucial, requiring exacting standards of behaviour from a local planning authority. Section 173 as it is currently worded represents an effort to clarify what an enforcement notice should contain and if mistakes occur there are opportunities to correct them most particularly on appeal to the Secretary of State.[7] Undoubtedly care is still required in preparing an enforcement notice since the presence of some errors can still result in the notice being declared a nullity or invalid.

Apart from requiring precision in the content of an enforcement notice, the legislation also places important restrictions on the initiation of enforcement proceedings. The first of these restrictions are the time limits set out in section 171B:

> (1) Where there has been a breach of planning control consisting in the carrying out without planning permission of building, engineering, mining or other operations in, on, over or under land, no enforcement action may be taken after the end of the period of four years beginning with the date on which the operations were substantially completed.
> (2) Where there has been a breach of planning control consisting in the change of use of any building to use as a single dwelling-house, no enforcement action may be taken after the end of the period of four years beginning with the date of the breach.
> (3) In the case of any other breach of planning control, no enforcement action may be taken after the end of the period of ten years beginning with the date of the breach.

From this it is apparent that the aim is to ensure that enforcement proceedings must be taken within four years in respect of operational development and within ten years in

6 See, for example, *Metallic Protectives Ltd v Secretary of State for the Environment* [1976] JPL 166, *Rhymney Valley District Council v Secretary of State for Wales* [1985] JPL 27, *King and King v Secretary of State for the Environment* [1981] JPL 813.

7 1990 Act, s 176.

relation to changes of use (with the exception of a change of use to a single dwelling-house) and anything else. The logic is that if no action is taken during these two periods, then those particular breaches of planning control can hardly represent a threat to the amenity of the neighbourhood. Yet the point was made earlier in this chapter that a breach of planning control may not always be particularly apparent. Material changes of use can happen gradually over a period of years. The same is not true of building, mining, engineering or other operations. It seems sensible, therefore, to treat the two in a different fashion.

It should be plain at this stage that the decision to issue an enforcement notice is not one to be taken lightly. It requires many factors to be taken into account. Once an enforcement notice has been issued, however, then the individual receiving the notice can either comply or appeal to the Secretary of State. Section 174(2) sets out the grounds for appeal. They are:

(a) that, in respect of any breach of planning control which may be constituted by the matters stated in the notice, planning permission ought to be granted or, as the case may be, the condition or limitation concerned ought to be discharged;
(b) that those matters have not occurred;
(c) that those matters (if they occurred) do not constitute a breach of planning control;
(d) that, at the date when the notice was issued, no enforcement action could be taken in respect of any breach of planning control which may be constituted by th0se matters;
(e) that copies of the enforcement notice were not served as required by section 172;
(f) that the steps required by the notice to be taken, or the activities required by the notice to cease, exceed what is necessary to remedy any breach of planning control which may be constituted by those matters or, as the case may be, to remedy any injury to amenity which has been caused by any such breach;
(g) that any period specified in the notice in accordance with section 173(9) falls short of what should reasonably be allowed.

There are two aspects to enforcement appeals. Those aspects are the grounds on which such appeals can be made and the form which such appeals take. Both of these will be discussed, starting with the grounds for appeal which were outlined in the previous paragraph. An initial reading of those grounds for appeal will reveal that some require little explanation. Grounds (b) and (c) involve factual issues such as whether particular events have occurred and, if they did, whether they constitute a breach of planning control. Ground (d) is concerned with the observation of section 171B time limits for taking enforcement action. In contrast ground (e) raises the more complex issue of who should be served with an enforcement notice. Section 172(2) of the 1990 Act gives guidance on this issue:

> (2) A copy of an enforcement notice shall be served –
> (a) on the owner and on the occupier of the land to which it relates; and
> (b) on any other person having an interest in the land, being an interest which, in the opinion of the authority, is materially affected by the notice.

The term 'owner' is defined in the interpretation section, section 336, of the 1990 Act. The other categories of individual who may require notice range from those with some definite legal interest in the land, such as a licensee, lessee or mortgagor, to trespassers who are in illegal occupation of the property. Although a local planning authority may try its utmost to serve everyone affected with an enforcement notice, someone with the necessary interest in the land may still be forgotten. If this is so then grounds for appeal exist and can be raised by any person with the right to appeal whether or not an enforcement notice has been served on them.[8]

Even if a breach of section 172 is proved, this does not necessarily have an effect on the validity of the enforcement notice. Section 176(5) of the 1990 Act provides:

> Where it would otherwise be a ground for determining an appeal under section 174 in favour of the appellant that a person required to be served with a copy of the enforcement notice was not served, the Secretary of State may disregard that fact if neither the appellant nor that person has been substantially prejudiced by the failure to serve him.

Failure to serve an individual with a copy of an enforcement notice may result in his not being alerted to his right of appeal, as well as rendering him liable to a criminal prosecution. This could be regarded as substantial prejudice. Where an individual appeals without receiving a copy of the enforcement notice, this can be regarded as proof that no substantial prejudice has been suffered. Therefore, the usefulness of paragraph (e) as a basis for appeal may depend on who exactly is making an appeal.

8 It should be noted, however, that the range of individuals entitled to be served with an enforcement notice is wider than the list of individuals entitled to appeal. Trespassers, for example, should receive notice but cannot appeal against it.

Grounds (f) and (g) are an attempt to question, not the validity of an enforcement notice, but rather, to allege that too much is demanded by the local planning authority. Too much, that is, either in the nature of the steps required to remedy the breach, or the time allowed in which to do it. Should the Secretary of State agree, then he is able to vary the terms of the enforcement notice under the powers given to him by section 176(1) of the 1990 Act.

Finally, it is necessary to consider the grounds for appeal set out in paragraph (a), namely, that planning permission ought to be granted or a condition discharged. On first reading this appears a most unusual ground for appeal. Enforcement proceedings are normally taken only when a local planning authority is convinced that the unauthorised development poses an unacceptable threat to the amenity of its area. If the local planning authority had been willing to grant planning permission then presumably it would have asked for a retrospective application or, in other circumstances, the local planning authority would not have attached the condition which is being ignored. Perhaps the explanation for this particular ground for appeal lies in the fact that the local planning authority's decision to take enforcement action is regarded as being equivalent to the refusal of planning permission.[9] Therefore, this ground for appeal is the equivalent of the appeal to the Secretary of State when planning permission is refused.

Should an individual wish to appeal on the basis that planning permission should be granted, or a condition be discharged, then argument will centre on development control issues. It is interesting to compare an appeal on this basis with appeals which do not dispute the validity of the enforcement notice, but simply ask for more time, or for the remedial work to be modified in some way. In these circumstances, the most that can be expected is that the Secretary of State will vary the enforcement notice. This can in turn be contrasted with an appeal which disputes the truth of what is alleged in the enforcement notice. Success here will lead to the enforcement notice being discharged. Improprieties associated with the

9 In determining whether or not to take enforcement action a local planning authority has regard to such matters as the development plan and other material considerations. These are exactly the same factors which are relevant in determining a planning application. If, therefore, a local planning authority believes that the unauthorised development could remain, it would invite an application for planning permission. Its decision to take enforcement proceedings is, therefore, tantamount to refusing planning permission.

service of an enforcement notice may or may not result in its being discharged, depending on the degree of prejudice suffered.

It would appear, therefore, that an individual served with an enforcement notice has a host of alternatives open to him on appeal, not all of which will result in the enforcement notice being discharged. One ground for appeal appears, however, to be missing, that is, an opportunity to assert that the contents of the enforcement notice are defective since, for example, they do not give in sufficient detail the steps which have to be taken in order to remedy the particular breach of planning control. When this occurs, the relevant course of action is not an appeal to the Secretary of State. Since the enforcement notice is not drawn up in accordance with section 173 of the 1990 Act, it is a nullity, that is, of no effect. An appeal cannot correct something which, in the eyes of the law, does not exist. Consequently, action must be taken in the courts to have the enforcement notice set aside.[10]

Apart from the grounds for appeal, reference was also made to the procedure adopted on appeal. Briefly, the procedure is, in most respects, similar to that already described when discussing planning appeals. It is set out in sections 174 and 175 of the 1990 Act and the Town and Country Planning (Enforcement Notices and Appeals) Regulations 1991[11] and the Town and Country Planning (Enforcement) (Inquiries Procedure) Rules 1992.[12] The idea is that once an individual has given notice of appeal, there should be an exchange between the parties, that is, between the appellant and the local planning authority, of the arguments on which they intend to rely. The intention is that the exchange should take place as speedily as possible. The parties then have the choice between the appeal being heard at a public inquiry, by means of an informal hearing or decided by written representations.[13] Finally, the majority of enforcement appeals are determined, not by the Secretary of State, but by an inspector[14] the one exception being enforcement appeals involving statutory undertakers.

10 The appropriate remedy to achieve this is an application for judicial review. See *Rhymney Valley District Council v Secretary of State for Wales* [1985] JPL 27.

11 SI 1991/2804.

12 SI 1992/1903.

13 Written representations are said not to be an appropriate method of appeal when grounds (b), (c), (d) or (e) are involved. Bourne, p 133.

14 Town and Country Planning (Determination of Appeals by Appointed Persons) (Prescribed Classes) Regulations 1981, SI 1981/804.

Once an enforcement appeal has been determined, this is not an end to the matter. It is possible to pursue it a stage further by applying to the High Court. According to section 289 of the 1990 Act, either the appellant or the local planning authority, or indeed any other person with an interest in the land to which the notice relates, can appeal on a point of law to the High Court provided they secure the leave of the court to do so.[15] The powers of the court in dealing with such cases are limited. It is not possible for the court to quash an enforcement notice should an error have been made. Instead, if there is an error of law, the matter is referred back to the Secretary of State, who is expected to rectify the matter himself, by rehearing the appeal for example. In certain circumstances it may also be possible to question the validity of a decision made on an enforcement appeal under the terms of section 288 of the 1990 Act.[16]

What should be apparent at this stage is the opportunity for delay between the issue of an enforcement notice and its final confirmation. Modifications made to the enforcement system have tried to minimise such delays[17] though, by its very nature, there are limits to how greatly the process can be expedited. Throughout the whole of this period the unauthorised development remains, possibly causing considerable disruption to the neighbourhood. Once, however, an enforcement notice has been confirmed, the owner of the land, or any person who is in control of it or has an interest in it can be guilty of an offence, punishable by fine, if they fail to comply with the order. Even at this stage, when the individual is the subject of a criminal prosecution, it is still possible to raise a variety of defences, including the argument that the enforcement notice is a nullity.[18] It is, however, not possible at this late stage to raise any of the arguments which are set out as grounds for appeal under section 174 of the 1990 Act.

15 The need to secure the leave of the court is designed to filter out undeserving cases.

16 S 288 allows a decision to be challenged because the person making it has exceeded his powers, or not observed a relevant procedure. This contrasts with the right of appeal in s 289. According to s 288 read in conjunction with s 284, only the Secretary of State's decision either to grant planning permission or discharge a condition in the course of an enforcement appeal can be reviewed in this fashion.

17 Acting on the recommendations made in the Carnwath Report. For example, if an individual appeals on a point of law under s 289 of the 1990 Act the court may order (s 289(4A)) that any enforcement notice shall take effect either in full or in part pending the outcome of proceedings before the court.

18 If it can be shown to be a nullity then quite obviously it cannot have been contravened.

In the past, the enforcement process has been condemned as long and complex, although steps have now been taken to refine the procedure. Indeed, it is tempting to allow the complexities of the procedure to obscure the significance of enforcement for the development control system. That significance is a negative and indirect one. Development control concerns itself with restricting the right of the individual to use his property as he wishes. The justification for this is the good of the community as a whole. Rarely does the development control system go beyond this regulatory function and demand that an individual use his property in a particular way.[19] Enforcement ensures that an individual, who decides to ignore the system and do what he likes with his property, is brought back into line. What is important, if the integrity of the development control system is to be maintained, is why the individual decides to step out of line and the way he is then forced to comply.

Stop notices

As an addendum to this section on enforcement two additional methods of securing compliance with the development control system need to be briefly discussed: stop notices and injunctions. One of the difficulties associated with an enforcement notice is that a breach of planning control can continue while an appeal is made against the enforcement notice. In order to prevent this occurring, section 183 of the 1990 Act allows the service of a stop notice. Section 183(1) describes the circumstances in which this can occur.

> Where the local planning authority consider it expedient that any relevant activity should cease before the expiry of the period for compliance with an enforcement notice, they may, when they serve the copy of the enforcement notice or afterwards, serve a notice (in this Act referred to as a "stop notice") prohibiting the carrying out of that activity on the land to which the enforcement notice relates, or any part of that land specified in the stop notice.

From this it is plain that a stop notice can be used only in conjunction with an enforcement notice, in order to prevent allegedly unauthorised activities from continuing. Under the terms of section 183 there are certain activities which cannot be restrained by a stop notice. They include the use of any

19 His property can be acquired from him using powers of compulsory purchase, so that some other individual can use it in a particular way.

building as a dwelling-house or changes of use – but not operational development – which commenced more than four years before the decision to serve a stop notice.

A stop notice can take effect almost immediately after it is served, namely within three days.[20] A stop notice ceases when the enforcement notice is withdrawn, or an individual complies with the enforcement notice. It is, according to section 187 of the 1990 Act, a criminal offence punishable by a fine to fail to comply with a stop notice. An individual charged with such an offence can, however, question the validity of the stop notice in the course of those proceedings. It may be alleged, for example, that the activity in the stop notice falls within that list of activities which cannot be restrained by a stop notice.

From this description, a stop notice would seem the ideal device to employ if a local planning authority wishes to restrain behaviour which is seen as damaging to the amenity of the area. In practice a degree of caution is needed in using it. If a stop notice is issued and the enforcement notice which it is designed to supplement is, for example, quashed or varied on appeal, relying on one of the grounds mentioned in section 174(2)(b)-(g) then compensation becomes payable. Under the terms of section 186(2) of the 1990 Act, the payment is to compensate for any loss or damage directly attributable to the prohibition contained in the notice. It is certainly possible to imagine situations where a stop notice could cause considerable loss. Circular 21/91, for example, cites the following examples:

> The costs to a firm may vary from having to modify a production process, at little or no additional cost (at one extreme), to the complete cessation of a business (at the other), with consequent loss of jobs, failure to complete contracts, or bankruptcy.[1]

With these dire warnings ringing in its ears, and the prospect of having to pay considerable sums by way of compensation if a mistake is made, it may be a brave local planning authority which chooses to issue stop notices freely.

Injunctions

There is one remaining way whereby a local authority may attempt to deal with unauthorised development swiftly. This is by use of an injunction. Section 187B of the 1990 Act permits

20 1990 Act, s 184(3).
1 Circular 21/91, annex 3, para 21.

a local planning authority, provided it considers it expedient, to apply to the court for an injunction to restrain an actual or apprehended breach of planning control. Failure to comply with an injunction is a contempt of court and can result in imprisonment. Although this seems to place considerable power in the hands of the local planning authority, it is the court which ultimately determines whether or not to award an injunction. At present the courts seem prepared to construe this power liberally.[2] Perhaps this is in recognition of the fact that section 187B refers to actual as well as apprehended breaches of planning control and makes it plain that there is no necessity for other enforcement measures to have been initiated before requesting an injunction. This is in stark contrast to the manner in which the courts have interpreted section 222 of the Local Government Act 1972. Section 222 also permits a local authority to apply to the court for an injunction and indeed is not limited to breaches of planning control. In a series of cases the courts have made it clear that they will grant a section 222 injunction only when an individual has deliberately flouted the law and seems likely to continue to do so, with all the consequent damage to the environment that this may cause, unless restrained by an injunction.[3]

2 *Runnymede Borough Council v Harwood* [1994] 1 PLR 22, CA, *Croydon London Borough Council v Gladden* [1994] 1 PLR 30, CA.

3 *Runnymede Borough Council v Ball* [1986] 1 All ER 629, CA; *Runnymede Borough Council v Smith* [1986] JPL 592, *Waverley Borough Council v Hilden* [1988] JPL 175.

Chapter 10

The courts: their role in the process of development control

The aim of this final chapter is an ambitious one. It is to analyse the role played by the courts in the development control process. Reference has regularly been made throughout this book to statutes and judicial decisions. The danger is that these frequent citations of the law in examining the development control process can cause its importance to be over-exaggerated and the role of the courts misunderstood. This book is an attempt to redress the balance. Policy, formulated from a mixture of political dogma, economic forces, planning theory and design principle, is revealed as the driving force of the development control process. Legislation, such as the Town and Country Planning Act 1990, is merely an engine to put that policy into practice or, alternatively, a barrier to be negotiated before a policy goal may be achieved.

If the content of planning legislation were to be analysed, much of it would be seen as concerned with procedural matters. Great importance is attached to having a procedural framework which specifies who must be consulted, when they must be consulted, and to what end. Although the value of certain procedural requirements, such as the need to consult, has been questioned from time to time, there is strength in the argument that, by its very nature, a procedural framework does much to ensure the making of reasoned decisions.[1] Instead of being applied in an arbitrary fashion, therefore, planning policy is forced to take account of the individual circumstances of each case, since the procedural framework operates with this end in view. Yet these procedural requirements are not responsible for creating the policy, but merely create a channel to prevent that policy overwhelming other relevant factors.

1 Although in the case of enforcement proceedings, the procedural requirements may represent a disincentive. See chapter 9.

Other issues dealt with in planning legislation include the creation of powers which may be exercised at the discretion of a local planning authority. The power to designate conservation areas is one such example.[2] It is a matter for the local planning authority which specific areas will benefit from the exercise of such a power. Key terms, such as 'development', are also defined in planning legislation.[3] Yet, for all the thousands of words devoted to the analysis of such terms, they are merely a means to an end. Should a proposed scheme not fall within the legal definition of the term 'development', then this means that its quality will not be assessed in the light of a local planning authority's policy on development. Policy is rarely mentioned in planning legislation. Rather, reference to policy is implied, as in section 70(2) of the 1990 Act, which mentions 'any other material considerations'. However, a lack of any specific mention of the term should not obscure the fact that essentially planning legislation is designed to secure the application of development control policy.

The function of the courts

Before moving on to questions of detail, certain general points need to be made about the tasks performed by the courts. Essentially, the courts function as watchdogs. On the one hand, individual citizens may flout the development control system and development may go ahead without planning permission. In such circumstances, the courts are a last resort, with powers to punish the offender by fine or imprisonment.

On the other hand, those who administer the development control system can just as easily flout the system they are meant to observe. Statutory procedures may be ignored, or matters may be taken into account which have no relevance to the decision to grant or refuse planning permission. In such circumstances, while it is desirable that the courts intervene, punishment, in the shape of a fine, is not seen as appropriate. Instead, the courts will remedy the damage done by setting aside any decision which has been affected by an administrative body's oversight. What should be clear from this brief description of the courts' powers, is that it is not their task either to approve, or to disapprove of a decision on its merits. Rather,

2 Planning (Listed Buildings and Conservation Areas) Act 1990, s 69.
3 Town and Country Planning Act 1990, s 55.

the courts are there to ensure that the law is observed by everyone, from the Secretary of State downwards, who is involved in the development control process. In performing that function the courts are said to act as a review body, that is, they review the legality of decisions. This should be contrasted with the courts' ability to function as an appeal body. When hearing appeals, the courts can substitute their decisions for those of another body. The power to review limits the courts to inquiring whether a decision has been legitimately made.[4] What follows is a more detailed analysis of what exactly that function entails.

REVIEWING THE ADMINISTRATION

The 1990 Act sets out the circumstances in which the courts can review the activities of those who administer the planning system. Section 288, for example, provides:

> (1) If any person –
> (a) is aggrieved by any order to which this section applies and wishes to question the validity of that order, on the grounds –
> (i) that the order is not within the powers of this Act, or
> (ii) that any of the relevant requirements have not been complied with in relation to that order; or
> (b) is aggrieved by any action on the part of the Secretary of State to which this section applies and wishes to question the validity of that action, on the grounds –
> (i) that the action is not within the powers of this Act, or
> (ii) that any of the relevant requirements have not been complied with in relation to that action,
>
> he may make an application to the High Court under this section.

Section 287 of the 1990 Act, which is concerned with questioning the validity of structure, unitary and local plans, is drafted in a similar fashion. From the wording adopted in these sections, it would appear that their common salient features are: the meaning to be attributed to 'any person aggrieved'; the fact that any challenge must be made within six weeks; the grounds for such a challenge; and the orders and actions affected by such powers. If these matters, such as who, what, why and when, are analysed, the hope is that the role of the courts will become clearer and the contribution which they make to the development control process will be better understood.

4 Whether the courts observe this distinction between review and appeal is another question.

'Any person aggrieved' The fact that this phrase is used, as opposed to 'any person', indicates that only certain individuals, rather than members of the public in general, can take advantage of these legislative provisions. Over the years the courts have agonised over, and changed their opinions on, the question of who will constitute a person aggrieved. The rigid approach, that only those who had some legal right jeopardised by the development control decision in question could be considered persons aggrieved, has now been abandoned.[5] Fortunately for prospective litigants, the court revised its views in *Turner v Secretary of State for the Environment*.[6] It did so in the light of the interpretation given to the term 'person aggrieved' when it occurred in other legislative provisions. In addition, the content of the Town and Country Planning (Inquiries Procedure) Rules 1969,[7] with their provisions allowing individuals to appear at an inquiry at the inspector's discretion, was significant. It persuaded the court that it was only fair that those same individuals should be able to challenge before the courts the validity of the very procedure in which they had participated. Indeed, the judgment in *Turner v Secretary of State for the Environment* suggests that the classification of persons aggrieved can extend beyond those who participated in a public inquiry:

> On the other hand I see good reason, so long as the grounds of appeal are so restricted [by time], for ensuring that any person who, in the ordinary sense of the word, is aggrieved by the decision, and certainly any person who has attended and made representations at the inquiry, should have the right to establish in the courts that the decision is bad in law because it is ultra vires or for some other good reason.[8]

This implies, and there is later authority to support this view, that the term 'person aggrieved' can include not only individuals and organisations, such as companies and amenity societies, who have participated in a planning appeal but also anyone who is adversely affected by the decision in question even though

5 It was typified by the decision in *Buxton v Minister of Housing and Local Government* [1961] 1 QB 278, [1960] 3 All ER 408, a decision which has been overtaken by events, particularly the rules on who may appear at public inquiries.

6 (1973) 28 P & CR 123.

7 These rules have been revoked and their place taken by the Town and Country Planning (Determination by Inspectors) (Inquiries Procedure) Rules 1992, SI 1992/2039 and the Town and Country Planning (Inquiries Procedure) Rules 1992, SI 1992/2038.

8 (1973) 28 P & CR 123 at 139, per Ackner J.

they have not been a party to any appeal.[9] In addition, the term includes a local authority.[10] If, for example, a local planning authority grants an individual planning permission, subject to certain conditions, the Secretary of State may modify or remove those conditions on appeal. It may be clear from the decision letter that the Secretary of State has failed to give adequate reasons for his decision. In these circumstances, the local planning authority can challenge his decision as a person aggrieved. Should, however, the Secretary of State have affirmed the conditions, then however greatly the local planning authority may take exception to something said in the decision letter, the local planning authority cannot be regarded as a person aggrieved.

This very situation arose in *Greater London Council v Secretary of State for the Environment*,[11] where, on appeal, an inspector refused planning permission for a proposed development. Although the Greater London Council was in agreement with this decision and had directed the local planning authority, Harrow London Borough Council, to refuse the original application for planning permission,[12] there were remarks in the inspector's decision letter to which the Greater London Council took exception. These related to the feasibility of concluding a planning agreement[13] to overcome objections to the proposed development, as well as the correct approach to

9 See, for example, *Westminster City Council v Great Portland Estates plc* [1985] AC 661, [1984] 3 All ER 744, HL; *Bizony v Secretary of State for the Environment* [1976] JPL 306, *Wilson v Secretary of State for the Environment* [1988] JPL 540, *Times Investment Ltd v Secretary of State for the Environment* [1991] JPL 67, CA. The majority of planning appeals are conducted by means of written representations rather than public inquiry. Although third parties may participate in the written representation process this may not be usual. Hence the notion that a 'person aggrieved' is exclusively someone who participated in the process is, in this context, unnecessarily limiting.

10 *Cook v Southend Borough Council* [1990] 2 QB 1, CA. This decision was not concerned with s 288 of the 1990 Act. It does, however, make the point that a local authority can be a person aggrieved if it has 'an adverse decision made against it in an area where it is required to perform public duties' (p 75).

11 [1985] JPL 868.

12 The Greater London Council possessed the power to act in this fashion by virtue of the Town and Country Planning (Local Planning Authorities in Greater London) Regulations 1974. With the abolition of the Greater London Council these regulations have been revoked.

13 Under the terms of what was then s 52 of the 1971 Act. This gave local planning authorities the power to enter into an agreement with the owner of land to restrict or regulate the development or use of that land. The ability to enter into planning agreements, or more accurately planning obligations, is now regulated by s 106 of the 1990 Act.

be taken to the over-supply of offices. In this case, the court held that the Greater London Council was not a person aggrieved in relation to the inspector's decision. Rather the Greater London Council was aggrieved by the inspector's reasoning which it feared would have an adverse effect on future development control decisions. In the court's view this was an entirely different matter and to allow those in whose favour the decision had been made to take advantage of section 288[14] was not compatible with the wording of that section. Instead, an individual or organisation aggrieved by an inspector's reasoning should make an application for judicial review. Sections 287 and 288 of the 1990 Act are, therefore, reserved for those adversely affected by a decision.

'Within six weeks' Any challenge must, according to the relevant sections, be made within six weeks. This immediately raises a number of questions. The two most obvious are why have a time limit, and within six weeks of what. The justification for the time limit is seen essentially as a practical matter. The period is short, certain in length and allows no exceptions. On occasions, the courts have interpreted legislative provisions designed totally to prevent access to the courts in such a way as to remove completely any such restriction.[15] However, in *R v Secretary of State for the Environment, ex p Ostler*,[16] the possibility of treating a provision of this nature in a similar manner was considered and rejected. This was on the basis that a distinction can be made between provisions which totally prevent access to the courts, and those which merely restrict the right. Six weeks, therefore, means exactly that. If the period were longer or not of any specific duration, then developers might have to delay the start of a scheme, or else face the prospect of having the legality of a development challenged when buildings had been demolished or foundations laid. It is also important to note that the six-week period does not run

14 In this particular case it was s 245 of the 1971 Act which has been replaced by s 288 of the 1990 Act. The wording of the two sections is, however, practically identical.

15 See, for example, *Anisminic Ltd v Foreign Compensation Commission* [1969] 2 AC 147, [1969] 1 All ER 208. Here a legislative provision purporting to prevent any decision reached by the Foreign Compensation Commission from being considered by the courts was said to be of no effect by the House of Lords. This was on the basis that the Commission's decision was void and hence not a decision.

16 [1977] QB 122, [1976] 3 All ER 90, CA.

from the date when any decision letter is received. In *Griffiths v Secretary of State for the Environment*,[17] the House of Lords was of the opinion that the six-week period runs from the time when a relevant decision is made. In this case, the decision under consideration was the Secretary of State's determination of a planning appeal. Once the letter recording that determination has been typed, signed and date-stamped, then, according to the House of Lords, the decision is complete and the six weeks begin to run. This means that, in reality, allowing for the vagaries of the post, an individual will have less than six weeks to challenge a decision.

'The grounds for challenge' According to sections 287 and 288 of the 1990 Act, a person resorting to the courts must demonstrate either that the activity in question is not within the powers of the 1990 Act, or that relevant requirements related to that activity have not been followed. Each of these grounds for challenge needs further consideration. As will be seen, sections 287 and 288 cover a variety of activities and decisions. Two examples, however, should serve to make clear the purpose of these sections. An application for planning permission is refused. An appeal is made to the Secretary of State, who confirms the refusal of planning permission. That decision taken by the Secretary of State can be challenged under the terms of section 288. Alternatively, a local plan is drawn up and after being scrutinised at a public inquiry, is adopted by a local planning authority. The validity of that local plan can be challenged under the terms of section 287.

If the intention is to show that the powers of the 1990 Act have been exceeded, in either case the argument is the same. It is that either the contents of the decision letter, or the contents of the local plan, demonstrate one of a number of situations which are examined below.

(a) A relevant factor has not been taken into account What is relevant varies with the circumstances and may on occasion be specified in the legislation. When an application for planning permission is determined, for example, the decision-maker must, according to section 70 of the 1990 Act, have regard to the development plan and to any other material considerations. Whilst clearly the development plan is relevant it is for the court to settle what may constitute other material considerations and

17 [1983] 2 AC 51, [1983] 1 All ER 439.

hence what else may be taken into account in reaching a decision.[18] If a decision letter fails to deal with a relevant factor, or the contents of a local plan fail to take account of a relevant policy, this may be evidence that the powers of the 1990 Act have been exceeded. In *Penwith District Council v Secretary of State for the Environment*,[19] an inspector's apparent failure to take into account a development control policy note[20] on amusement centres resulted in his decision being set aside since it was a relevant consideration. If he had taken it into account, and that was not clear, he should have given reasons for declining to follow the advice it offered.

(b) An irrelevant factor has been taken into account In this context an issue will be considered irrelevant, either because it is not a development control issue or, if it is, because it is one which is irrelevant as far as the matter in hand is concerned. In *Westminster City Council v Great Portland Estates*,[1] for example, it was argued that some of the policies in a local plan did not have a planning purpose but were designed to benefit certain individuals. If this had been so, these policies would have been removed from the local plan, since the local planning authority would have exceeded its powers by taking account of an irrelevancy when compiling its local plan. In the event this was found not to be the case.

(c) A decision is so unreasonable that no reasonable individual could have arrived at it As compared with other methods of challenging the validity of a decision, this is by far the most difficult to prove. It does not mean that a decision is unreasonable in the sense that the court, faced with the same set of circumstances, might have come to a different decision. Instead, to be considered unreasonable the decision should be such that it is totally arbitrary and illogical. In the event very few decisions are capable of being described in this way. This cannot, however, obscure the fact that the courts have been known, on occasions, to use this reasoning as a way of substituting their development control decision for that of the

18 *Bolton Metropolitan Borough Council v Secretary of State for the Environment* [1991] JPL 241, CA. In this case which deals generally with the topic of statutory review the whole process of taking relevant factors into account was analysed in detail.

19 [1986] JPL 432.

20 The forerunner of planning policy guidance notes.

1 [1985] AC 661, [1984] 3 All ER 744, HL.

relevant body or individual. Judicial decisions exist which have been criticised on those very grounds.[2] Undoubtedly, the practice, if it occurs, is to be deplored. The Court of Appeal made this very point in *Buckinghamshire County Council v Hall Aggregates (Thames Valley) Ltd*.[3] Here, the decision of the judge at first instance that portions of a minerals plan were so unreasonable that they should be set aside, left a development plan which was acceptable to neither the local planning authority nor the gravel mining company.[4] In setting aside his decision, the Court of Appeal reaffirmed the specific meaning to be attached to the term 'unreasonable', namely an illogical, perverse or arbitrary decision.

(d) A decision is contrary to the rules of natural justice There are two rules of natural justice. Their aim is to ensure that a decision-maker is impartial and arrives at a decision only when the parties involved have had a chance to state their case. In short, the rules of natural justice are designed to ensure procedural fairness. Obviously, there is a connection between the rules of natural justice and the procedures set out in legislation such as the Town and Country Planning (Inquiries Procedure) Rules 1992.[5] Normally, these procedures are drawn up with the rules of natural justice in mind, and in particular, the requirement that both parties should have an opportunity to state their case and respond to the argument against them. The rule that the Secretary of State, should he take account of fresh evidence after the close of a public inquiry, must allow the parties to comment on it or reopen the inquiry, is just such an attempt.[6] Therefore, compliance with the relevant procedures will normally guarantee compliance with the rules of natural justice. It is always possible, of course, that no procedure will have been specified. In these circumstances, the courts will still insist on compliance with the rules of natural justice. The question will be asked whether or not that particular decision

2 See, for example, *Fourth Investments v Bury Metropolitan Borough Council* [1985] JPL 185.

3 [1985] JPL 634 at 643, 644, per Purchas LJ.

4 Ibid, at 641-642.

5 SI 1992/2038. These rules govern the procedure to be followed at a planning inquiry where the final decision will be taken by the Secretary of State for the Environment. Where the final decision is to be taken by an inspector the relevant procedure is to be found in the Town and Country Planning Appeals (Determination by Inspectors) (Inquiries Procedure) Rules 1992, SI 1992/2039.

6 Town and Country Planning (Inquiries Procedure) Rules 1992, SI 1992/2038, r 16.

has, in the circumstances of the case, been arrived at fairly.

While it can be comparatively easy to ensure, with or without a specified procedure, that each individual is given an opportunity to state his case, the rule against bias can present more, if less obvious, opportunities for its breach. The rule against bias is designed to ensure that a decision-maker is impartial. This does not mean that an individual, seeking to show that this rule of natural justice has been breached, must prove actual bias.[7] It is sufficient simply to prove one of two things. If it can be shown that a decision-maker has a financial interest in the matter before him – owning shares, for example, in the company making a planning appeal – that will be sufficient to persuade the court that any decision is biased.[8] Alternatively, if the behaviour of the decision-maker is such as to convince the court that there is a real danger of bias on their part this too can lead to a decision being set aside.[9] The aim of this second objective test is to ensure that only those decisions are set aside where sufficient evidence exists to render them suspect.[10]

Financial interests apart, bias can take many forms. In the context of sections 287 and 288 of the 1990 Act, it normally involves allegations concerning either the inspector, or conceivably the Secretary of State. If, for example, it can be shown that an inspector is related in some way to one of the parties participating in a planning appeal, that may constitute a breach of the rule against bias.[11] Also included is behaviour on the part of an inspector which indicates that he has prejudged the issue before him.[12] Even indulging in a conversation with an individual who is opposed to a particular development, has been sufficient to cause a decision to be set aside on the grounds of bias.[13] What is unclear, however, is whether bias can occur in a situation where a decision-maker, by his actions,

7 It would undoubtedly be exceedingly hard to prove that a decision was affected by bias. What the rule against bias seeks to avoid is the suspicion of bias, though in reality a decision may have been fairly made.

8 *Grand Junction Canal Co Proprietors v Dimes* (1852) 3 HL Cas 759.

9 *R v Gough* [1993] 2 WLR 883.

10 If this were not so, then decisions might be set aside on the slightest pretext with considerable disruption to the administrative process.

11 *R v London Rent Assessment Panel Commitee, ex p Metropolitan Properties (FGC) Ltd* [1969] 1 QB 577. The case concerned not a planning inspector but the chairman of a rent tribunal.

12 *Halifax Building Society v Secretary of State for the Environment* [1983] JPL 816.

13 *Simmons v Secretary of State for the Environment* [1985] JPL 253. Compare this with the decision in *Cotterell v Secretary of State for the Environment* [1991] JPL 1155.

appears to have given himself no choice in the decision he will reach.

To explain this situation more fully, reference can be made to the House of Lords' decision in *Franklin v Minister of Town and Country Planning*.[14] Here, the Minister had designated Stevenage the first New Town. Local residents objected, a public inquiry was held and the Minister confirmed that Stevenage would be the first New Town. When this decision was challenged on the grounds that the Minister who made it was biased, the House of Lords disagreed. While the Minister had made plain his determination that Stevenage should be the first New Town, he had held a public inquiry and taken account of the conclusions which it had reached. The Minister's decision to affirm his original opinion could not, therefore, in the circumstances, be described as biased. In reaching this conclusion, particular emphasis was placed on the administrative nature of the task being performed by the Minister.[15] While labels such as 'administrative' can, on occasion, do more harm than good, the description serves to stress that the Minister's role was one where he might be expected to have a policy, rather than maintain judicial impartiality.

From this and other related decisions,[16] it would appear that a Secretary of State who adheres to a particular development control policy, and employs it in resolving planning appeals, cannot be described as biased. This is provided that an opportunity is given to those who oppose that policy to state their case, and to try to dissuade the Secretary of State from applying it. It is only if a particular policy renders the Secretary of State incapable of properly exercising those powers which he possesses that it can be challenged in the courts. A policy which, for example, requires all planning appeals involving agricultural land to be referred to the Minister of Agriculture for comment, may cease to be legitimate if the Secretary of State automatically defers to those comments.[17] This is on the basis, not that the Secretary of State is biased, but that he is no longer capable of exercising the discretion given to him by statute.

14 [1948] AC 87, [1947] 2 All ER 289.

15 [1948] AC 87, at 102, per Lord Thankerton.

16 *R v St Edmundsbury Borough Council* [1985] 3 All ER 234, *R v Sevenoaks District Council* [1985] 3 All ER 226.

17 It is very difficult on occasions to distinguish between the legitimate application of a policy and the complete surrender of a discretion. An important factor appears to be the willingness of the discretion holder to listen to argument.

(e) The decision must represent an effective exercise of any discretion given by the statute As already indicated, an individual can exceed his powers by failing effectively to exercise a discretion entrusted to him. What the courts require is proof of some factor – an agreement, not necessarily a contract, or an unauthorised delegation – which convinces them that the discretion has not been properly exercised.[18] For example, a Minister of Housing and Local Government's decision to defer to the view of the Minister for Agriculture on planning appeals involving the loss of agricultural land fell into this category.[19] While, as has already been stated, the courts acknowledge the major role played by policy in the development control process, even policy can be so rigidly applied as to stifle the proper exercise of discretion. The court's task, therefore, is no easy one. It is to pinpoint those instances, rare though they are, when the freedom of choice which is implicit in the term discretion, has been surrendered.

(f) A mistake of fact may cause a decision to be set aside The principle that a mistake of fact can vitiate a decision has been repeated on several occasions, but rarely acted upon. The problem is that in order to warrant a decision being set aside, the mistake must be one which, in all probability, has caused the individual making it to arrive at a decision which is different from the one he would have arrived at, had the mistake not been made. In *Mason v Secretary of State for the Environment*,[20] for example, an error was made over the distance of a house from premises which it was proposed to use as a vehicle repair shop. The distance was said to be 250 feet when, in reality, it was 125 feet. The following explanation was given for refusing to set aside the inspector's decision:

> But to vitiate a decision the mistake of fact had to be material, that was, there must be grounds for thinking that the decision might have been different if the mistake had not been made.[1]

18 The mere fact that a contract exists will not automatically prevent the exercise of a discretion. On this point note the ability of a local planning authority to enter into s 106 planning obligations and yet still exercise its development control powers. See *Windsor and Maidenhead Royal Borough Council v Brandrose Investments Ltd* [1983] 1 All ER 818, CA.

19 *H Lavender & Son Ltd v Minister of Housing and Local Government* [1970] 1 WLR 1231. Compare this with the court's decision in *Stringer v Minister of Housing and Local Government* [1971] 1 All ER 65. Here an understanding whereby development in close proximity to Jodrell Bank radio telescope would be discouraged was acceptable providing it did not prevent each case being considered on its individual merits.

20 [1984] JPL 332. See also *Jagendorf and Trott v Secretary of State for the Environment* [1987] JPL 771.

1 [1984] JPL 332 at 333.

Since the inspector in question had viewed the site and had seen how far apart the buildings were, the mistake was not regarded as material.

(g) The terms of any relevant legislation must be observed It may be apparent from the terms of a particular piece of legislation that the powers which it confers on the Secretary of State are to be exercised only in certain circumstances. Any attempt to exercise those powers when such circumstances do not exist, can be challenged.[2] The power of the Secretary of State to grant or refuse planning permission on appeal depends on development being undertaken. If the courts were to find that there was no development, then the Secretary of State is exceeding his powers by refusing or granting planning permission. Though it is the court's responsibility to interpret statutes, the Secretary of State's determination that a particular activity constitutes development will not readily be disturbed unless there is ample evidence that it is untenable. In *Coleshill and District Investment Co Ltd v Minister of Housing and Local Government*,[3] the House of Lords was not prepared to disturb the Minister's decision that demolition of a structure could amount to development.

Apart from the list of situations whose existence may cause a decision to be set aside on the grounds that the powers of the 1990 Act have been exceeded, one more item remains to be discussed. This is the separate ground for challenge, mentioned in sections 287 and 288, that a relevant requirement has not been observed. Relevant requirements are procedural requirements which must be followed when action is taken, or a decision arrived at, under the terms of the 1990 Act. Such requirements are to be found in the 1990 Act as well as in the Tribunals and Inquiries Act 1992 and regulations made under that Act.[4] It is a provision of both sections 287 and 288 that, in order for such a challenge to succeed, the applicant must show that his interests have been substantially prejudiced by the

2 *Re Ripon (Highfield) Housing Confirmation Order 1938, White and Collins v Minister for Health* [1939] 2 KB 838, CA. Here land which was part of a park could not be the subject of a compulsory purchase order. Therefore an order made in respect of parkland was quashed by the courts.

3 [1969] 2 All ER 525.

4 The provisions of the Tribunals and Inquiries Act 1992 are applicable to planning inquiries, and s 10 of that Act, for example, provides that reasons must be given for a decision, but only if requested. See also the Town and Country Planning (Inquiries Procedure) Rules 1992, SI 1992/2038 and the Town and Country Planning (Determination by Inspectors) (Inquiries Procedure) Rules 1992, SI 1992/2039.

failure to observe the relevant requirements.[5] This necessity to show substantial prejudice is a practical matter, designed to ensure that projects which may be a matter of urgency are not delayed and financial loss is not caused merely because a trivial procedural error has occurred.

As for the contents of these relevant requirements, they reflect the necessity to take any action or to arrive at any decision fairly. Parties are given an opportunity to state their case and refute their opponents' arguments. A conclusion, once reached, must be justified by reasons. Nor are the courts content merely to see the letter of the law being observed. Reasons, for example, will not be considered sufficient if they are unintelligible. Over the years, in a series of decisions, the courts have insisted that such reasons must be clear and intelligible,[6] as well as dealing with the major points raised in the course of the arguments.[7]

In concluding this discussion of the grounds for challenge, it is worth stating that even though sections 287 and 288 mention two separate grounds for challenge, the courts have not maintained a rigid distinction between the two.[8] As has already been mentioned, there is common ground between the rules of natural justice and the procedural requirements of the 1990 Act. Therefore, the courts have, on the whole, been at pains to use sections 287 and 288 flexibly, in order to set aside decisions which are flawed, not by minor omissions, but by what amounts to serious neglect of the terms of relevant legislation.

'The orders and actions capable of being reviewed in this fashion' It must be clearly understood that the power of the court to review decisions under sections 287 and 288 is a limited power, in the sense that it affects only certain decisions and actions. Section 287 is concerned primarily with development plans – that is structure, local and unitary plans – and the

5 1990 Act, s 287(2)(b) and s 288(5)(b). On the issue of whether substantial prejudice has been caused see *Save Britain's Heritage v Secretary of State for the Environment* [1991] 2 All ER 10 at 22, HL.

6 See, for example, *French Kier Developments Ltd v Secretary of State for the Environment* [1977] 1 All ER 296, *Thanet District Council v Secretary of State for the Environment* [1978] JPL 250, *Save Britain's Heritage v Secretary of State for the Environment* [1991] 2 All ER 10, HL.

7 *Camden London Borough Council v Secretary of State for the Environment* [1980] JPL 31, *Save Britain's Heritage v Secretary of State for the Environment* [1991] 2 All ER 10, HL.

8 *Reading Borough Council v Secretary of State for the Environment* [1986] JPL 115.

actions necessary to bring such plans into existence, as well as amend them. Subsection 287(3), however, extends the operation of the section to other activities. These include the Secretary of State's order to stop up or divert a highway to allow development to take place, as well as to extinguish the right of vehicles to use a highway or a public right of way over land. The 1990 Act sets out the circumstances in which such orders can be made,[9] and provides in section 287 a means of challenging their validity. As well as the Secretary of State's orders, a local authority's orders to authorise the stopping up or diversion of a footpath or bridleway, or to extinguish a public right of way over land, can also be challenged in this fashion. Finally, the direction of the appropriate Minister discharging a statutory undertaker from obligations imposed on it, but which are impractical to carry out,[10] is subject to review under section 287.

Section 288 is concerned with the activities of local planning authorities, mineral planning authorities and the Secretary of State. The impact of the section is selective and renders liable to review, not every action, but only certain actions of the bodies or individuals mentioned.[11] Orders made by local planning authorities requiring the discontinuance of a use, or the alteration or removal of buildings or works are subject to challenge, as are tree preservation orders. The decision of mineral planning authorities to make an order prohibiting the resumption of the winning and working of minerals is equally susceptible. A whole range of activities on the part of the Secretary of State is capable of challenge under section 288. They include the Secretary of State's decision on an appeal against a planning decision, as well as his grant of planning permission on appeal against an enforcement notice.[12]

The significance of this list of activities is twofold. What is included is subject to challenge in the manner already described. A question remains, however, regarding those activities which are excluded, by reason of the fact that they are not mentioned. One such example is the decision of a local planning authority to grant planning permission. If someone wishes to question the validity of that decision, on the grounds that there has been a breach of the rules of natural justice, the 1990 Act does not appear to provide a way of doing so. An appeal to the Secretary of State can only be made by the party applying for planning

9 1990 Act, Pt X.
10 Ibid, s 277.
11 Ibid, s 284(2).
12 Ibid, s 284(3).

permission, not by a third party. Sections 287 and 288 are not applicable to the original decision of a local planning authority to grant planning permission. In these circumstances, the course of action open to an individual is to make an application for judicial review.

APPLICATION FOR JUDICIAL REVIEW

The application for judicial review is a remedy designed to control the public activities of public authorities. In contrast with the powers of review detailed in sections 287 and 288 of the 1990 Act, the application for judicial review is not confined to assessing the legitimacy of specific activities of particular individuals. Instead, it is a general remedy and a complex one.[13] The description of judicial review which follows, therefore, is intended only to highlight those points that the courts consider essential when determining whether or not to award a remedy.

The procedure which must be followed in order to make an application for judicial review is set out in Order 53 of the Rules of the Supreme Court and the Supreme Court Act 1981.[14] It consists of a preliminary application, made by the individual seeking judicial review.[15] The purpose of the preliminary application is to secure the court's leave to proceed with the action. In this way, the court can weed out frivolous and unarguable applications.[16] Apart from this, the applicant then has to convince the court to award him a remedy. It is perhaps worth mentioning that the application for judicial review amalgamates, under a single head, what were previously six separate remedies.[17] The applicant must, therefore, specify what combination of remedies he wishes the court to award him. In

13 For a comprehensive discussion of judicial review see Craig P *Administrative Law* (3rd edn) (1994) Pts 2 and 3.

14 1981 Act, s 31.

15 Rules of the Supreme Court, Ord 53, r 3.

16 For the way in which the court should treat applications for leave see *R v Secretary of State for the Home Department, ex p Doorga* [1990] COD 109. Research has shown that approximately one-third of leave applications are rejected. See Le Sueur and Sunkin 'Applications for Judicial Review: The Requirement for Leave' Public Law 1992 102.

17 Those remedies are *certiorari*, prohibition, *mandamus*, injunction, declaration and damages. Briefly the purpose of the remedies is to quash an invalid decision (*certiorari*); to prevent or restrain an invalid decision or action being taken (prohibition, injunction); to force the carrying out of a duty (*mandamus*) and to secure a statement from the court that an activity is unlawful (declaration).

order to obtain them successfully, the applicant must show the court that:

(i) he has sufficient interest in the matter in hand;
(ii) there has been no delay in bringing the issue before the court;
(iii) there are grounds for awarding a remedy;
(iv) the court should use its discretion to award a remedy.

Does the applicant have sufficient interest in the matter in hand? At first sight this question may make little sense. Its immediate origins may be found in the wording of Order 53, which indicates that only an applicant with sufficient interest in the proceedings may be awarded a remedy.[18] In *IRC v National Federation of Self-Employed and Small Businesses Ltd*,[19] the House of Lords indicated that what constituted sufficient interest depended on a number of factors. These included the terms of the legislation under the authority of which the public body has purported to act, the nature of any alleged illegality, as well as, in the opinion of some of their Lordships, the merits of the particular claim.[20] In short, there are many factors influencing the court's decision on whether or not an applicant is perceived as possessing sufficient interest. That said, certain members of the House of Lords in the *Inland Revenue Commissioners* case made it very plain that a public body should not be able to escape the consequences of its unlawful activities merely on the technical point of lack of sufficient interest. As a result of this decision it can be difficult to predict whether an individual or an organisation will possess sufficient interest. In cases involving planning issues the parties participating in a proposed development,[1] a neighbouring landowner,[2] members of an amenity society[3] and a rival developer[4] have all been held to have sufficient interest. In *R v Secretary of State for the Environment, ex p Rose Theatre Trust Co*,[5] however, the Trust, which consisted of a group of concerned individuals who wished to challenge the Secretary of State's decision not to schedule a site as a monument of national

18 Rules of the Supreme Court, Ord 53, r 3(5).
19 [1982] AC 617, [1981] 2 All ER 93.
20 [1982] AC 617, at 647, per Lord Diplock.
1 *R v Camden London Borough Council, ex p Comyn Ching & Co (London) Ltd* (1983) 47 P & CR 417.
2 *R v North Hertfordshire District Council, ex p Sullivan* [1981] JPL 752.
3 *Covent Garden Community Association Ltd v Greater London Council* [1981] JPL 183.
4 *R v Canterbury City Council, ex p Springimage Ltd* [1994] JPL 427.
5 [1990] 1 QB 504.

importance, was held not to possess sufficient interest. This was apparently on the basis that the legislation in question[6] gave no indication that the public could question such a decision.

There has been no delay Since the application for judicial review is concerned with the public activities of public authorities, any challenge to the lawfulness of those activities needs to be made promptly. If this were not so, a local planning authority might face the prospect of having a decision which was made several years earlier, and indeed acted upon, challenged in the courts. As has already been observed, under the terms of sections 287 and 288 of the 1990 Act, six weeks is allowed for challenge. Under the terms of Order 53, any challenge must be made promptly, meaning, in normal circumstances, within three months.[7] The courts have a discretion to extend this period, provided that their decision will not imperil the rights of the parties or good administration.[8] The three-month period begins to run from the date when any irregularity became apparent.[9] Since, however, the emphasis is on any challenge being made promptly, it is possible for a challenge made within the three-month period to be dismissed, on the basis that it was not made promptly enough.[10]

Grounds for awarding a remedy Basically, the grounds on which the lawfulness of a public authority's decision may be challenged, are the same as those already considered in the context of the 1990 Act. An applicant must show that the public authority has exceeded the powers given to it, either in an Act of Parliament, or from some other source.[11] There are various

6 Ancient Monuments and Archaeological Areas Act 1979.

7 Rules of the Supreme Court, Ord 53, r 4. The Supreme Court Act 1981, s 31(6) mentions no specific period.

8 The court has to balance the interests of the applicant against the possible administrative disruption which could be caused if a decision which has been acted upon has its validity called into question. On this point see *R v Stratford on Avon District Council, ex p Jackson* (1985) 51 P & CR 76, CA.

9 This need not necessarily be the date when any decision was taken. For example, circumstances constituting bias may not become apparent until some time after a decision is taken.

10 *R v Greenwich London Borough Council, ex p Cedar Transport Group* [1983] RA 173.

11 For example, powers derived from the royal prerogative. It was thought that such powers were unreviewable but in *Council of Civil Service Unions v Minister for the Civil Service* [1985] AC 374, the House of Lords indicated that this was not so. Prerogative powers are normally concerned with such matters as the administration of justice and national security rather than development control.

ways in which this can be proved. It may be that the procedure, which has to be observed in making a decision, has been ignored. Alternatively, a public authority may have misinterpreted the legislation which gives it its powers, and arrived at a conclusion which it has no power to make. If the legislation in question gives the public authority a discretion, such as the power to attach to the grant of planning permission such conditions as it sees fit, the courts will insist that the discretion is exercised in a reasonable fashion. This means taking account of relevant factors, ignoring irrelevant ones, and not using the power to achieve an improper purpose such as acquiring land by compulsory purchase in order to make a gain rather than out of necessity. Nor must the exercise of a discretion be so illogical that no reasonable public authority could have arrived at such a conclusion. Finally, a public authority must not do anything, such as enter into an agreement, which prevents that authority from exercising its discretion. Nor must it, in reaching a decision, breach the rules of natural justice.

In short, the courts possess a whole range of powers, designed to ensure that any decision arrived at by a public authority is a lawful decision. The ever-present problem is, however, that the distinction between the courts ensuring that a decision is lawfully made, and simply substituting their decision for that of the public authority, is a narrow one. At what stage does a decision become so unreasonable that no reasonable public authority would have arrived at it? Is it when the decision is not one which the court itself would have made if it had been in the position of the public authority? Although this concept runs counter to the way in which the courts should use their powers of review, examples of this occurring in practice can be found.[12]

The courts' discretion to grant or refuse a remedy It is as true of the application for judicial review, as it was of the power to review in sections 287 and 288 of the 1990 Act, that the courts have a discretion whether to grant or refuse a remedy.[13] The fact that little damage may have been caused, even though a public body has exceeded its powers, could persuade the court to refuse the remedy sought. A more difficult

12 For this narrow line between review and appeal in the context of Ord 53, see *Bromley London Borough Council v Greater London Council* [1983] 1 AC 768, HL.

13 All the remedies which constitute the application for judicial review are discretionary. Even though it can be shown that a public body has behaved unlawfully, the court may feel that the applicant's conduct is so reprehensible as not to deserve a remedy.

issue altogether is, however, presented by the following situation. A local planning authority refuses planning permission for works which, in its opinion, constitute development. If the developer believes that the work in question does not constitute development, he faces a dilemma. Should he appeal to the Secretary of State as provided for in the 1990 Act? Alternatively, should he make an application for judicial review in the manner just described? If he does request the court to review the lawfulness of the local planning authority's decision, will the court, in the exercise of its discretion, refuse him a remedy on the ground that an alternative remedy exists, namely an appeal to the Secretary of State?

The circumstances when the courts will refuse a remedy on this basis have been considered by the courts.[14] The effectiveness of the alternative remedy as compared with judicial review and whether any challenge raises questions of law or fact are relevant issues. Consequently, much will depend on the circumstances of the case when determining whether an individual should be forced to pursue an alternative remedy. In the few development control cases where the existence of an alternative remedy has been discussed, emphasis has often been placed on the need for speed.[15] Several months might pass before the Secretary of State, for example, would arrive at a decision which may or may not provide a remedy. In such circumstances, the courts will normally be prepared to hear an application for judicial review in order to expedite the matter. Hence, the application for judicial review, beside supplementing the remedies specifically provided in the 1990 Act, can also be an alternative to those remedies.

As a postscript to this analysis of the application for judicial review, as well as the remedies provided by the 1990 Act, one important point remains to be made. Each of these remedies allows the court to assess whether a public authority has acted within its powers. If this is found not to be the case, then normally all that the court can do is to set the decision aside. A court cannot substitute its decision for the one found to be at fault, since this would constitute an appeal and not a review. In the case of section 287, this will mean that the offending

14 See *R v Chief Constable of Merseyside Police, ex p Calveley* [1986] 1 All ER 257, CA.

15 See, for example, *Runnymede Borough Council v Ball* [1986] 1 All ER 629, CA; *R v Hillingdon London Borough Council, ex p Royco Homes Ltd* [1974] QB 720, [1974] 2 All ER 643.

policies will be struck out of the relevant development plan.[16] Should a decision or action be found to be invalid under the terms of section 288, then the court will set it aside and remit the matter to the individual responsible for a fresh decision.[17] Therefore, if the Secretary of State exceeds his powers when deciding a planning appeal, the court will remit the matter to him after setting his original decision aside. The Secretary of State will then arrive at a fresh decision, which must take account of any guidance given by the court. He is, of course, free to reach exactly the same decision as before, provided he can do so by acting within his powers.

It is only the application for judicial review which can offer a wider range of remedies. It has been pointed out that six individual remedies were combined to create the application for judicial review. Consequently, an individual taking advantage of this remedy can ask the court to do more than simply set a decision aside, though it has to be said that on most occasions this is precisely what the applicant will want. The application for judicial review can be used to restrain an anticipated breach of its powers by a public body, as well as to force an official to carry out his duties. Damages can also be recovered when appropriate by using this remedy.

Although a considerable amount of space has been devoted to review by the courts, it also needs to be stressed that of the countless development control decisions made during the course of a year, a very small proportion indeed are the subject of review by the courts. Consequently, it may be useful at this stage to mention an alternative to the courts, which is cheaper by far, namely the ombudsman.

Ombudsmen

If an individual is dissatisfied with either the behaviour of a local authority, or the Secretary of State for the Environment, it might be possible to refer the matter to the ombudsman. The ombudsman charged with the task of overseeing the activities of central government is the Parliamentary Commissioner for Administration. His local authority

16 1990 Act, s 287(2)(b). The policies may cease to have effect either generally or as they affect the applicant's property. On this latter point, see for example, *Fourth Investments Ltd v Bury Metropolitan Borough Council* [1985] JPL 185.

17 1990 Act, s 288(5)(b).

counterpart is the Local Commission for Administration. There is an English Commission with three commissioners and a separate Welsh Commission with one commissioner.

The task of the central and local government ombudsmen is broadly similar. It is to consider whether a central government Ministry, such as the Department of the Environment, or a local authority, is guilty of maladministration thereby causing injustice to a complainant. There is no definition of the term 'maladministration' in the relevant legislation. Instead, a definition has been built up over the years.[18] Maladministration concerns itself more with the activities which lead up to the making of a decision than the quality of the decision itself. Therefore, the losing of a file, undue delay, failure to observe some undertaking have all, in the past, been accounted maladministration. The fact that a decision is judged illogical or perverse can also constitute maladministration,[19] even though the relevant legislation makes it clear that the merits of a decision are not a subject for consideration by the ombudsman.[20] In reality, however, little reliance would appear to be placed on this particular aspect of maladministration aimed, as it appears to be, at the totally unreasonable decision.[1] That said, the term 'maladministration' is undoubtedly sufficiently broad and vague to include some of those activities which can be the subject of judicial review. Since it is a matter for the discretion of an ombudsman whether or not he investigates a complaint, much will depend on the way the original complaint is phrased. Vague allegations of unfairness will not be sufficient. An act or omission must be identified which has prejudiced the making of a fair decision.

In assessing their ability to offer an alternative to the courts, the term 'maladministration' is a source of strength and weakness to the ombudsmen. It is perhaps unfortunate that other aspects of the legislation which regulate their

18 A working definition can be found in the Annual Reports of the Parliamentary Commissioner and the Local Commissions. See also *R v Local Comr for Administration, ex p Bradford Metropolitan City Council* [1979] QB 287 at 311, 314, 319.

19 Annual Report of the Parliamentary Commissioner for Administration (1970) p 96. Here a decision not to award costs to a company which had appealed against an enforcement notice and won was made by the Minister of Housing and Local Government. There was nothing wrong with the way the decision was made, it was simply illogical.

20 Parliamentary Commissioner Act 1967, s 12(3); Local Government Act 1974, s 34(3).

1 Probably because of the inherent difficulty in concluding that a decision is perverse or illogical.

investigations are much clearer. The cumulative effect of these may be said to be to reduce the effectiveness of the ombudsman as an alternative remedy. Into this category comes the provision which prevents a complaint being made directly to the Parliamentary Commissioner, requiring it instead to be referred to him by a Member of Parliament.[2] If the Parliamentary Commissioner does receive direct what appears to be a complaint worthy of investigation, he must return it to the complainant. It is, however, his practice to indicate to the complainant's Member of Parliament his willingness to investigate, should the complaint be referred to him in the proper manner. The need for an intermediary is seen as having a twofold purpose. On the one hand, it prevents the Parliamentary Commissioner from being overwhelmed by complaints. On the other hand, it preserves the role of Members of Parliament as individuals charged with resolving their constituents' complaints. No similar restriction exists in relation to the Local Commission who may receive complaints either direct from members of the public or via local councillors.

Other restrictions exist which curb the freedom of an ombudsman to investigate. They include a time limit of one year which runs from the date when the circumstances giving rise to the complaint first became known.[3] A complainant is also under an obligation to exhaust alternative remedies, such as legal proceedings, before approaching the ombudsman.[4] Each of these restrictions can, however, be waived at the discretion of the ombudsman.[5] In contrast, only bodies designated in the relevant legislation are capable of investigation.[6] Here, the ombudsman has no choice in the matter. The Parliamentary Commissioner would, therefore, be forced to decline to investigate a complaint against the Post Office, since its activities are not subject to his scrutiny.

Even though an ombudsman is restricted in what he may investigate, the same is not true of the manner of his investigation. Individuals can be questioned and documents inspected with a freedom that is the equivalent of that enjoyed

2 Parliamentary Commissioner Act 1967, s 5(1)(a).

3 Parliamentary Commissioner Act 1967, s 6(3); Local Government Act 1974, s 26(4).

4 Parliamentary Commissioner Act 1967, s 5(2); Local Government Act 1974, s 26(6).

5 Parliamentary Commissioner Act 1967, ss 5(2) and 6(3); Local Government Act 1974, s 26(4)(b).

6 Parliamentary and Health Service Commissioners Act 1987, s 1(1), Sch 2; Local Government Act 1974, s 25(1).

by the court.[7] Indeed, in some respects the freedom is greater, since the ombudsman can ask to inspect any relevant files. In contrast, a litigant has to specify to the court the exact documents he wants produced, which is no easy task when he has little idea of what documents exist and whether they are relevant.[8]

On the other hand, when it comes to reaching a decision on a complaint, the courts have the advantage over the ombudsman. The courts expect their judgments to be obeyed and are rarely disappointed. The ombudsman has no power to enforce his judgments. Instead, he must rely on the willingness of central and local government to co-operate. In reality, there are few instances where the Parliamentary Commissioner has had a finding of maladministration rejected out of hand.[9] When this occurs, a special report is presented to Parliament, and this may result in a Minister being questioned in the House over his refusal to accept the recommendations of the Parliamentary Commissioner.[10]

Local authorities are, on the whole, more likely to reject an ombudsman's finding. Even so, in only a small proportion of those cases where a complaint is found to be justified, will an amicable conclusion not be reached.[11] A local commissioner can issue a second report to try to force recalcitrant local authorities into action.[12] If this fails the local commissioner can then require a notice to be published in a local newspaper stating what action the commissioner recommended and the local authority's reasons for not complying.[13] Beyond this the Local Commission is powerless to act.

Even if an ombudsman's findings are accepted, however, he lacks the courts' power to set aside a decision. A central government Ministry or local authority may agree to revise its procedures to prevent a similar incident happening in the

7 Parliamentary Commissioner Act 1967, s 8; Local Government Act 1974, s 29.

8 The process which is known as discovery is very strictly regulated by the courts in order to avoid the production of sensitive information as well as 'fishing expeditions'.

9 There was an adverse reaction by the government to the Parliamentary Commissioner's report on the Court Line Affair, 498 HC Debates (5th series) Vol 897, col 566, 6 August 1975.

10 Parliamentary Commissioner Act 1967, s 10(3).

11 In the Commission for Local Administration in England, Annual Report 1993-94, it is noted that 21 further reports were issued, meaning that in 21 instances a satisfactory remedy for maladministration had not been provided. There were in total 330 findings of maladministration causing injustice in the same period.

12 Local Government Act 1974, s 31(2).

13 Nine such statements were published in the year ending 31 March 1994.

future. An ex gratia payment may be made to the complainant, or the case may be reopened if this is still possible. Sometimes an apology has to suffice. The appropriate remedy varies and much will depend on the particular circumstances of the case. The ombudsman can and does offer guidance on what he considers appropriate. The problem is that the complainant may wish to have the situation return to the way it was before the offending decision was taken. In many instances this is simply not possible, because the decision has been acted upon in a way which makes it incapable of reversal.

For all the restrictions on the type of complaint that can be investigated, the ombudsman can offer a very satisfactory alternative to the courts, besides providing a remedy on occasions when the courts would be unable to intervene, where a file has been lost, for example.[14] An analysis of the subject matter of the complaints investigated, shows that planning is high on the list of complaints received by the local commissioners. For the year 1993-94, the English Local Commission recorded that planning was the second most complained about subject, only housing drawing more complaints. Typical of the kind of complaints received by the English Local Commission and judged to amount to maladministration were the following: wrongly advising an individual that planning permission was not required for a dormer extension and the taking of enforcement action against him; failing to check the accuracy of plans for a proposed development even when advised that they were inaccurate and then attaching an unenforceable condition to the planning permission; relaxing a planning condition regarding the height of a building even though the official doing so had no authority to act in this fashion.[15] As for the impact such investigations will have on the development control process, this is a matter for conjecture. It is argued that, besides providing a remedy for the individual, the ombudsman raises the general standard of administration. This ensures that decisions are taken and individuals dealt with in the fairest way possible. There is, however, the possibility that the presence of the ombudsman discourages innovation. Local government officials, in particular, may abandon new procedures designed to ensure greater public involvement, returning instead to established

14 The aid of the courts can only be sought where it is possible to make a claim the basis of an action for negligence or breach of contract.

15 Commission for Local Administration in England, Annual Report 1993-94, pp 42-43.

routine.[16] In this fashion complaints to the ombudsman may be avoided but at a price.

Other functions of the courts

Until this stage discussion has centred on the role of the court as a review body. Under the terms of the 1990 Act the court has other functions to perform. In the previous chapter, for example, reference was made to enforcement proceedings and, in that context, the court has an appeal function as well as a policing role to play, punishing individuals who ignore enforcement notices. There are other occasions when the court is required to act as an appeal body. It has to be said, however, that it is rare for the court to be called upon to play this role in the context of development control. The explanation is simple. Since most development control appeals involve issues of planning policy, the court is not an appropriate body to resolve them.

In concluding this discussion of the role of the courts in the development control process, various points have emerged. First, the main role of the court is as a review body but this is not an exclusive role. Other tasks are assigned to the courts by the 1990 Act, not to mention those general powers possessed by the court to award damages for the negligent performance of development control functions.[17] From this assessment of what exactly the courts do, emerges a second point. It appears that the courts have a peripheral, as opposed to a central, role in the development control process. Development control policy, its formulation and application in individual cases, is not their business. The courts can indicate whether the formulation or application of policy is lawful by determining whether a policy maker has the power to do whatever is proposed. The courts can punish those who fail to comply with development control policy. The appropriateness of that policy in planning terms is, however, not an issue which the courts can legitimately consider.

16 On the basis that it is better to be safe than become the object of an investigation by a local commissioner.

17 See for example, *Davy v Spelthorne Borough Council* [1983] 3 All ER 278, HL.

Index